GW00976302

The Curate and the General

Roger Bowen was born in Swansea and has lived and worked in London and then East Devon for most of his life. He worked in industry in Exeter before retiring to Budleigh Salterton. During his career he was successively a member of the Engineering Industry Training Board, chairman of the Chamber of Commerce in Exeter, chairman of the EEF in the southwest, a governor of three schools, a member of the Employment Tribunals and for eight years he was the founder and organiser of the Budleigh Salterton Music Festival. He is engaged in charity work and has been a member of the local council. During his time as chairman of the Devon Historic Buildings Trust some 14 of Devon's buildings at risk have been restored to their former pristine condition.

Amongst the buildings brought back from a ruinous prospect is the Haldon Belvedere, once part of the magnificent estate established by Robert Palk. It is the history of the Belvedere that inspires this book. Many people have become involved in the restoration project and of these a surprising number have been attracted to the history surrounding its creation as a tribute in stone from one friend to another.

The Curate and the General

ISBN-13: 978-1492778851
ISBN-10: 1492778850

BISAC: Biography & Autobiography / General

published 2014

www.rtbrbowen.org.uk

ROGER BOWEN

The Curate and the General

A Lifelong Friendship

Books by Roger Bowen:

Anthology of Children's Poetry (Ed) published 2007
Lunacy to Croquet published 2013

Contents

Illustrations

Preface

The incentive for preparing this book about the lives of two eighteenth century adventurers came out of a project to restore, in 1994, the Devon Historic Buildings Trust's "Haldon Belvedere" or "Lawrence Castle". The building is a remnant of an estate that bubbled with activity during the second half of the eighteenth century following the return to England from India of Major General Stringer Lawrence and Sir Robert Palk. The building is open to the public and visitors often ask about its history and the reason for its existence. They always wish to know more than is available from current easily-accessible literature.

An excellent guide to the history of the Palk family is available from its author Iain Fraser entitled *Haldon House & Torquay* and there is a short monograph produced by the Rev'd Christopher Pidsley - *The Tower on the Hill.* Interesting though architectural and genealogical descriptions are it seemed to me that there is so much more to the story of the General and the Curate that should be made available in a more accessible form.

Having said that there is a large bibliography, dealing with separate parts of the story, dating to 1820 and earlier, that is detailed and fascinating because the events took place during a period of history that has attracted the attention of many authors. Any study of the two gentlemen and their life and times must draw heavily on such sources and in this case two authors are preminent: Col. J. Biddulph in his books *Stringer Lawrence, The Father Of The Indian Army, 1901; The Pirates Of Malabar; An Englishwoman In India,1907; Duplieix, 1910;* important, too, is the work that Col. Dove was commissioned to write, in 1922, reviewing the Palk correspondence preserved by Robert Palk during the years after he returned from India to Devon before 1786. This archive consists of over 600 letters and documents collected by Mrs Bannatyne giving an unique insight into the growth of the British Empire in India during its most critical period.

Many other authors have written about the struggle for trade supremecy between the Dutch, the French and the English. François Pierre Guillaume Guizot 1787–1874) was one of these. Prime Minister of France, historian, orator, and statesman he was a dominant figure in French politics prior to the Revolution of 1848, who produced *Mémoires pour servir à l'histoire de mon temps* (8 vols., 1858–1861). This work has an interesting section about Dupleix and his colleagues with lithographs some of which are reproduced in this book. Guizot provides a French perspective on the times when it could well have been France and not England who built an empire in the subcontinent.

There are many other accounts that have been consulted hopefully to give a fair and detailed picture of the times and of the relationship between two men, the soldier and the administrator, that lasted from 1750 until Stringer Lawrence died in 1775.

Acknowledgements

This book was written at home close to the Exe estuary and the Haldon Hills where much of the action took place 250 years ago. Sadly, Roger Brien, librarian in Exeter, who was so helpful, passed away before this book could be published. He kindly provided assistance from the excellent Devon & Exeter Institution library as it relates to the life of Robert Palk and in the journals of the time. Thanks, also, to the staff of the Devon Heritage Centre for assistance with references to Robert Palk's extended family.
I am grateful to the Devon Historic Buildings Trust's secretary Debbie Parnall who was most helpful in both proof reading suggestions for improvement and to DHBT for supplying extracts from the Haldon Belvedere archive.

Other members of the Trust have been encouraging and in this respect I am particularly grateful to William Burkinshaw, who led the reconstruction of the Belvedere and made many helpful suggestions after reading the draft of this book.

Finally it is to Brenda, my lifelong partner, that I owe the most in this as in so much else.

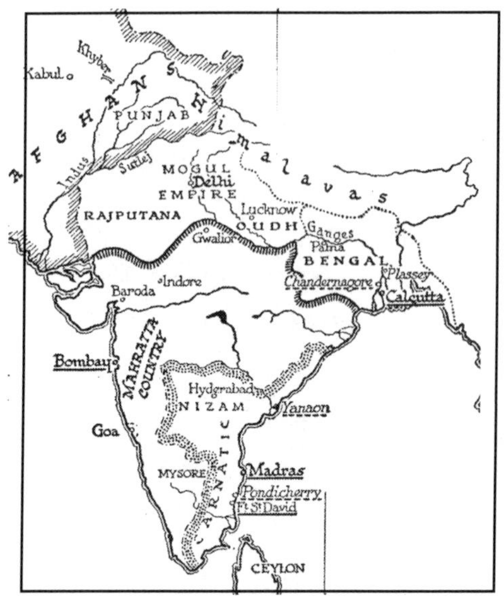

The India of Stringer Lawrence

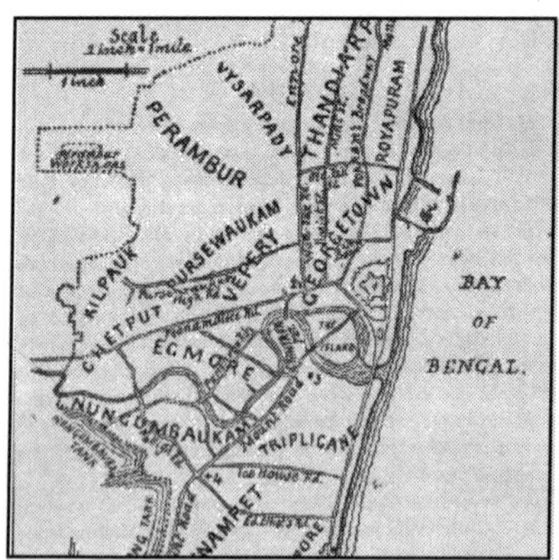

Madras

India in 1760

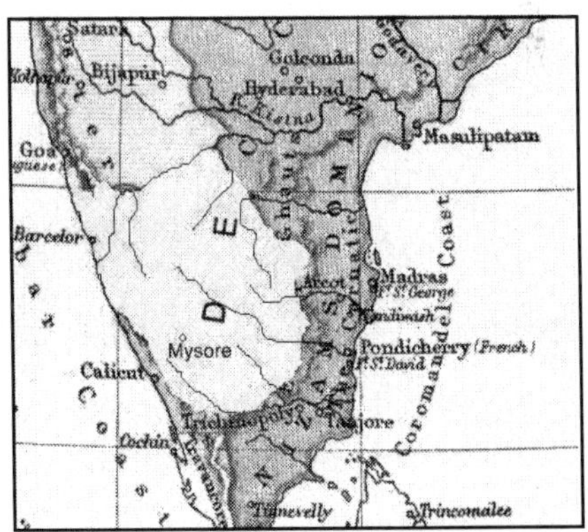

The Coromandel Coast

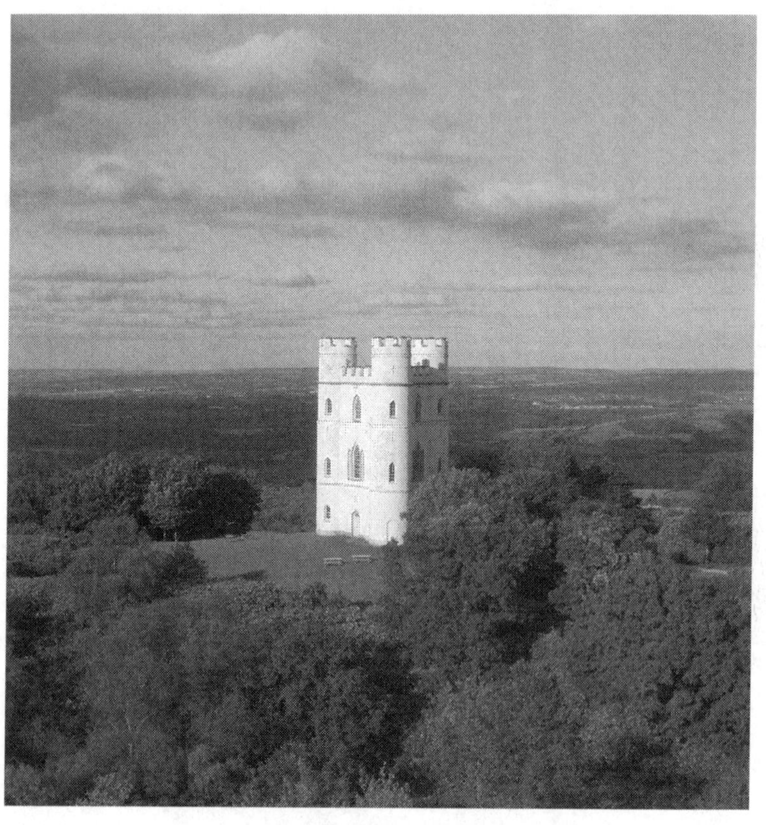

Lawrence Castle and the Haldon Hills

Small miseries, like small debts, hit us in so many places, and meet us at so many turns and corners, that what they want in weight, they make up in number, and render it less hazardous to stand the fire of one cannon ball, than a volley composed of such a shower of bullets.

Rudyard Kipling

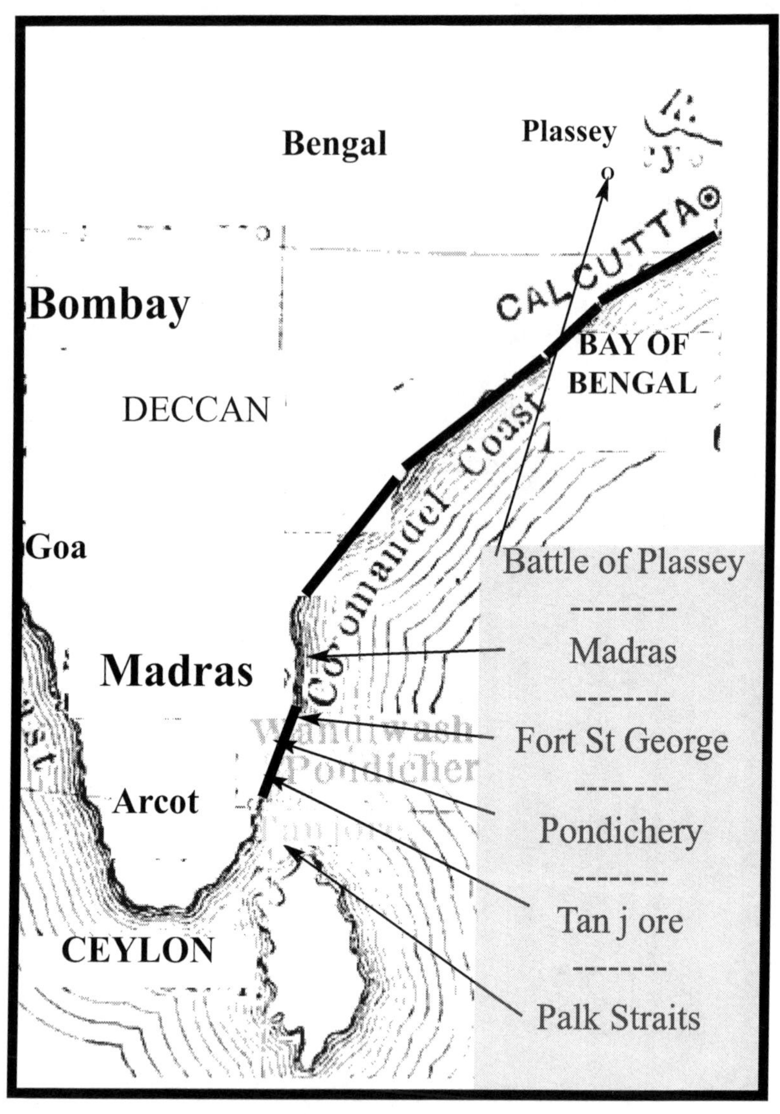

Orientation map showing the areas of India that were contested by the English and the French in 1749-79

Part One
Introduction

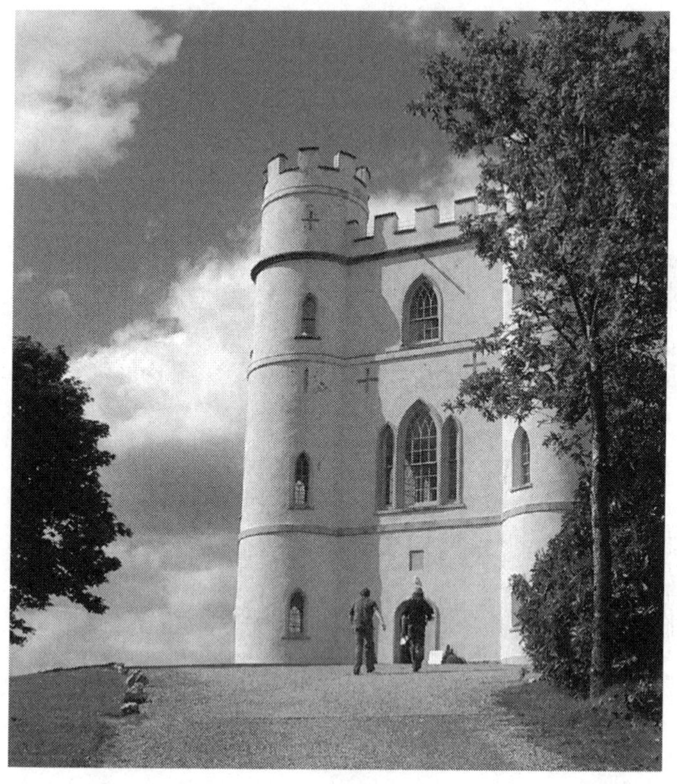

Haldon Belvedere

I
A Friendship Formed, 1750

Perched above Exeter, high on the Haldon Hills, lies a magnificent memorial to Major General Stringer Lawrence who was generously described by Sir Robert Clive as the 'Father of the Indian Army'. It is as prominent an architectural statement as is the mausoleum for the Aga Khan overlooking Aswan, in Egypt, across the Nile.

It is visible from three counties in good weather: from the East when travelling the road beside Gold Cap in Dorset, to the far West from Cornwall and again to the North from Exmoor. Known variously as the Lawrence Castle or more usually as the Haldon Belvedere this is a stone-built edifice constructed on a triangular plan with towers at each corner and a roof that affords magnificent views across the moors of North Devon and to Bodmin, the Exe estuary and far beyond.

As a monument it is an unforgettable sight and is as touching a tribute to an old friend as can be imagined.

The surface finish of lime render is painted in cream as if to ensure that those travelling the Exe valley from Exeter down to Exmouth will look up and wonder at its height and aspect. Once the tower formed part of an impressive country house standing in spacious grounds. Now it stands almost alone in a clearing of the Haldon Forest with its only surviving companions being the remains of the servant quarters and stables of the once grand Haldon House Estate. Sadly, the mansion itself was abandoned over a period of years leaving only a few remnant buildings to mark where it once stood.

The Curate and the General

Haldon House was the home of the Rev'd Robert Palk, bought with the booty he acquired when returning home from his service in India in 1767. Later, as Sir Robert Palk, he became a Member of Parliament and respected advisor and confidant to many of the officials he left behind in the Indian Carnatic.

Robert Palk had very good reason to build in the grounds of his Haldon estate. His career in India was marked by a friendship that grew from an unpromising start of his time there and blossomed until he retired, a wealthy man. He wished to celebrate his long friendship with a soldier who, by his deeds and acumen, made possible the huge riches that were acquired by the East India Company and, individually, by its servants. General Stringer Lawrence was that friend. Together they went to India and both returned home with rich rewards to live out their days in London and Devon. Robert Palk eventually became Governor of Madras.

The Haldon Belvedere, or Lawrence Castle as it has been called, was designed as a place to enjoy a *fete champetre*, far enough away from the big house to afford privacy yet close enough to make access to its enjoyments convenient. The building has survived intact and is a useful and successful tribute to the two friends. In the entrance hall on the ground floor are three mahogany boards that are inscribed with the history of Stringer Lawrence's military achievements. The lettering is as visible and legible as the day it was created.

The relationship of the two men began when Robert Palk was appointed by the Company as a chaplain to Fort St David in Madras. Stringer Lawrence was a seasoned soldier who had won a reputation in many campaigns for steadiness and reliability under fire. He was appointed by the Company to recover a potentially disatrous military situation against the French in the rapidly developing Carnatic region.

The Carnatic, a region of Southern India, between the Eastern Ghats and the Coromandel Coast was originally the country of the Kanarese; historically important as a rich and powerful trading centre and today part of Tamil Nadu State. It was a place of fabulous wealth and offered prospects for trade unequalled in the world. In the eighteenth and nineteenth centuries India was the place where young men were driven to make their fortune. In 1746 the great Eastern trading companies were active, enterprise was under threat and difficulties proliferated.

It was against this background that Stringer Lawrence arrived in India in 1748, with the rank of major and the reputation of a successful leader. Robert Palk was appointed naval chaplain to Admiral Edward Boscawen on the Namura, bound for India. He arrived at Fort St David in 1748, at the time when the French were in control of Fort St George in Madras.

Major Lawrence was allocated a difficult task. The company was suffering from the perceived superiority of the French militia of the *Compagnie Française pour le Commerce des Indes Orientales*. This was a commercial enterprise founded in 1664 to compete with the British and Dutch East India companies in the East Indies, originally planned by Jean-Baptiste Colbert and chartered by King Louis XIV for the purpose of trading in the Eastern Hemisphere. Lawrence was required to build and reform the inadequate militia so as to provide the muscle required by the East India Company to support its activities in both India and in China where trade was fast developing.

Major Lawrence first met Robert Palk in 1751. It was a happy meeting. Lawrence had been captured by a French patrol and released under the *Peace of Aix-la-Chapelle* whereas Palk was enjoying promotion within the company. It was a friendship that was to last until the death of Stringer Lawrence, in London, on 10 January 1775.

The stories of Palk's and Lawrence's lives were very much the story of immense trading successes following the capture of Pondicherry from the French.

The East India Company (EIC), originally chartered as the Governor and Company of Merchants of London trading into the East Indies, and often called the Honourable East India Company, was an English and later (from 1707) British joint-stock company formed to pursue the valuable trade with the East Indies but which ended up trading mainly with the Indian subcontinent, North-west frontier province and Baluchistan. The East India Company traded mainly in cotton, silk, indigo dye, salt, saltpetre, tea and opium. The Company was granted a Royal Charter by Queen Elizabeth in 1600, making it the oldest among several similarly formed European East India Companies.

The partnership of Robert Palk and of Stringer Lawrence brought together the military know-how of the soldier and the business expertise of a cleric turned entrepreneur. Lawrence was termed later by Robert Clive 'The Father of the Indian Army' because of his success in transforming a ragbag amateurish rabble into an efficient fighting service. Palk, never completely suited to life as a cleric, used his considerable intelligence and acumen as the arch negotiator who was able to steer the Indian princes and rulers into commercial contracts of formidable size and profitability. Many of those serving the EIC were not averse to serving themselves personally by operating private trading concerns as a sideline, often whether or not such activity was permitted by the rules of the company. Many were prepared to accept valuable gifts and patronage from the local rulers even if this was expressly forbidden by the company. As a result the more successful company servants returned to England to live out their remaining days with what was euphemistically described as 'a competence'. Robert Palk knew well how this system worked and, though he vigourously denied any wrong-doing or transgression of the company rules, was able to retire as Governor of Madras with a fine fortune that enabled him to live in luxury for the rest of his life.

So it was, that, when both returned to England in retirement, it was Robert Palk who had accumulated enormous wealth and Major General Stringer Lawrence who returned with a 'competence'. When he died Lawrence left most of his estate to Robert Palk, including his house in Bruton Street, London which served as Palk's London home for the remainder of his life. Out of regard for his friend Robert Palk named his eldest son Lawrence.

II
India before the English, 1482

The Mogul Emperor Baber (of Turkish descent 1482 - 1530) invaded India in 1526 and was eventually succeeded by his grandson, Jelaleddin Mahmomet Akbar (1542-1605) who reigned for 49 years.

He was probably the greatest of the Mogul emperors, who conquered all of Northern India and Afghanistan and who extended his rule as far south as the Godvari River. The Moguls were Muslims who ruled over a Hindu majority. He was tolerant but strong in military terms, but, after his death, his empire started to decline.

Then started the rule of Aurangzeb (1658-1707), who became emperor in 1658. Mogul control in south India came under pressure with the increase of attacks by the Hindu Maratha princes. Aurangzeb, who lacked Akbar's religious tolerance, imposed special taxes on Hindus, destroying their temples and forced them to convert to Islam. Soon after Aurangzeb's death, the empire crumbled creating a void which a number of european countries attempted to exploit.

Bahadur Shah I (1707-12), was more tolerant but he was unable to reverse the Mogul decline. His effort to collect taxes or jizya became ineffectual. He also attempted to control the Rajput states of Amber and Jodhpur, but was unsuccessful. He did not succeed in dominating the Hindu Marathas who were never defeated by the Moguls. However Mogul rule persisted in the south.

Between 1707 and 1761 the southern provinces rose against Delhi and they became increasing independent from the central authority both economically and politically. Through trade in local raw produce and artifacts, these provinces became virtual kingdoms. Bengal, Bihar, and Avadh in Northern India were among the new independent regions where these developments were most apparent. Their rulers became independent warlords recognizing the Mogul Emperor in name only.

Part of the Indian subcontinent came under the control of European colonial powers, through trade and conquest. Alexander the Great came in 327–326 BC when he established satraps in the north though they quickly crumbled after he left. The Romans had sea-born trading interests in India. The spice trade between India and Europe became one of the drivers of trade attracting European powers to India when the Netherlands, England, France, and Denmark established trading posts in India in the early 17th century. As the Mughal Empire disintegrated in the early 18th century the Maratha Empire in turn became weakened after the third battle of Panipat. The unstable Indian states which emerged were increasingly open to manipulation by the Europeans through dependent "friendly" Indian rulers.

After the decline of the Roman Empire's trade with India, the Portuguese were the next Europeans to arrive in May 1498. The first successful voyage to India was by Vasco da Gama in 1498, when he arrived in Calicut, now in Kerala, where Saamoothiri Rajah gave him permission to trade in the city.

In 1502 the Portuguese Empire established the first European trading centre at Kollam, Kerala and in 1505 the King of Portugal appointed Dom Francisco de Almeida as the first Portuguese viceroy in India, followed in 1509 by Dom Afonso de Albuquerque. In 1510 Albuquerque conquered the city of Goa, which had been controlled by Muslims. A feature of the Portuguese presence was their promotion of the Catholic Church. The Jesuits played a fundamental role, and to this day the Jesuit missionary Saint Francis Xavier is revered among the Catholics of India.

The Portuguese established a chain of outposts along India's west coast and on the island of Ceylon in the early 16th century and Portugal's northern province included settlements at Daman, Diu, Chaul, Baçaim, Salsette, and Mumbai. The rest of the northern province, with the exception of Daman and Diu, was lost to the Maratha Empire in the early 18th century.

In 1661 Portugal was at war with Spain and to obtain support from England had agreed the marriage of Princess Catherine of Portugal to Charles II with a dowry that included the city of Bombay. This was the beginning of the English presence in India.

The Dutch East India Company established trading posts and controlled the Malabar southwest coast (Kodungallor, Pallipuram, Cochin, Cochin de Baixo/Santa Cruz, Quilon (Coylan), Cannanore, Kundapura, Kayamkulam, Ponnani and the Coromandel southeastern coast (Golkonda, Bimilipatnam, Kakinada, Palikol, Pulicat, Parangippettai, Negapatnam) and Surat. The Dutch also established trading stations in Travancore and coastal Tamil Nadu as well as at Rajshahi in present-day Bangladesh, Pipely, Hugli-Chinsura, and Murshidabad in present-day West Bengal, Balasore (Baleshwar or Bellasoor) in Odisha, and Ava, Arakan, and Syriam in present-day Myanmar (Burma). Ceylon was lost at the Congress of Vienna in the aftermath of the Napoleonic Wars, where the Dutch having fallen subject to France, saw their colonies raided by Britain. The Dutch later became less involved in India, as they had the Dutch East Indies (now Indonesia) as their prized possession.

At the end of the 16th century, England and the United Netherlands formed private joint-stock companies to finance the voyages: the English (later British) East India Company, and the Dutch East India Company, which were chartered in 1600 and 1602 respectively. These companies concentrated on the valuable and lucrative spice trade. The close proximity of London and Amsterdam across the North Sea, and the intense rivalry between England and the Netherlands, inevitably led to conflict between the two companies, with the Dutch gaining the upper hand in the Moluccas (previously a Portuguese stronghold) after the withdrawal of the English in 1622, but with the English more successful in India, at Surat, after the establishment of a spice factory in 1613.

III
Fort St. George, 1639

The English East India Company in Fort St. George had been developing the opium export trade with China since 1730. This trade was unlawful in China from 1729 but it helped finance the trade imbalances from the British imports of tea, that resulted in outflows of silver from Britain to China.

The French also established a trading company at Pondichery on the Coromandel Coast in south eastern India in 1674. Other French settlements were Chandernagore in Bengal, north eastern India in 1688, Yanam in Andhra Pradesh in 1723, Mahe in 1725, and Karaikal in 1739. The French were constantly in conflict with the Dutch and British in India.

At the height of French power the French occupied large areas of southern India and the area lying in today's northern Andhra Pradesh and Odisha. Between 1744 and 1761, the British and the French repeatedly attacked and conquered each other's forts and towns in southeastern India and in Bengal in the northeast. After some initial French successes, the British decisively defeated the French in Bengal in the Battle of Plassey in 1757 and in the southeast in 1761 in the Battle of Wandiwash, after which the British East India Company was the supreme military and political power in southern India as well as in Bengal. This is the period that is described in this book when the battles fought by Stringer Lawrence (then, after he became unwell, by Robert Clive) supported by an efficient accounting and adminstrative system devised and operated by Robert Palk. This combination enabled the failing British interests of 1746 to become the dominant trading and political force in the Indian sub-continent up to independence in 1947.

Denmark was another minor colonial power to set foot in India. It established trading outposts in Tranquebar, Tamil Nadu (1620), Serampore, West Bengal (1755) and the Nicobar Islands (1750s). At one time, the main Danish and Swedish East Asia companies together imported more tea to Europe than the British did!

The East India Company (EIC), called the Governor and Company of

Merchants of London, traded into the East Indies as joint-stock company formed for pursuing trade with the East Indies but which ended up trading mainly with the Indian subcontinent, north-west frontier province and Balochistan.

It traded mainly in cotton, silk, indigo dye, salt, saltpetre, tea and opium and was granted a Royal Charter by Queen Elizabeth in 1600, making it the oldest among several similarly formed European East India Companies. Shares of the company were owned by wealthy merchants and aristocrats. The government owned no shares and had only indirect control. The Company eventually came to rule large areas of India in 1757, after the Battle of Plassey, which lasted until 1858 when, following the Indian Rebellion of 1857, the Government of India Act 1858 led to the British Crown assuming direct control of India in the era of the new British Raj.

On 10 April 1591 three ships sailed from Torbay, England around the Cape of Good Hope to the Arabian Sea on one the earliest of the English overseas Indian expeditions. One of them, the Edward Bonventure, then sailed around Cape Comorin and on to the Malay Peninsula and subsequently returned to England in 1594. In 1596, three more ships sailed east and all were lost at sea. Two years later, on 24 September 1598, another group of merchants having raised £30,133 in capital, met in London to form a corporation. Later they increased their capital to £68,373, and began again, this time successfully.

In 1609 King James renewed the charter for an indefinite period, including a clause which specified that the charter would cease to be in force if the trade turned unprofitable for three consecutive years:

> Upon which assurance of your royal love I have given my general command to all the kingdoms and ports of my dominions to receive all the merchants of the English nation as the subjects of my friend; that in what place soever they choose to live, they may have free liberty without any restraint; and at what port soever they shall arrive, that neither Portugal nor any other shall dare to molest their quiet; and in what city soever they shall have residence, I have commanded all my governors and captains to give them freedom answerable to their own desires; to sell, buy, and to transport into their country at their pleasure. For confirmation of our love and friendship, I desire your Majesty to

> command your merchants to bring in their ships of all sorts of rarities and rich goods fit for my palace; and that you be pleased to send me your royal letters by every opportunity, that I may rejoice in your health and prosperous affairs; that our friendship may be interchanged and eternal.

The Company was led by one Governor and 24 directors, who made up the Court of Directors. They, in turn, reported to the Court of Proprietors which appointed them. Ten committees reported to the Court of Directors.

The Company created trading posts in Surat and, by 1647, the Company had 23 factories, each under the command of a factor or master merchant and governor if so chosen, and had 90 employees in India. The major factories became the walled forts of Fort William in Bengal, Fort St George in Madras, and the Bombay Castle.

In 1657, Oliver Cromwell renewed the charter of 1609, and brought about minor changes in the holding of the Company. The status of the Company was then further enhanced by the restoration of monarchy in England. In an act aimed at strengthening the power of the EIC, King Charles II provisioned the EIC with the rights to autonomous territorial acquisitions, to mint money, to command fortresses and troops and form alliances, to make war and peace, and to exercise both civil and criminal jurisdiction over the acquired areas.

In September 1695, Captain Henry Every, an English pirate on board the Fancy, reached the Straits of Bab-el-Mandeb, where he joined five other pirate captains to make an attack on the Indian fleet on the annual voyage to Mecca. The Mughal convoy included the treasure-laden Ganj-i-Sawai, reported to be the greatest in the Mughal fleet and the largest ship operational in the Indian Ocean, and its escort, the Fateh Muhammed. The pirates gave chase and caught up with the Fateh Muhammed some days later and meeting little resistance, took some £50,000 to £60,000 worth of treasure.

Every continued in pursuit and managed to overhaul the Ganj-i-Sawai, who put up a fearsome fight but it too was eventually taken. The ship carried enormous wealth and, according to contemporary East India Company sources, was carrying a relative of the Grand Mughal, though there is no evidence to suggest that it was his daughter and her retinue. The loot from the Ganj-i-Sawai totalled between £325,000 and £600,000, including 500,000 gold and silver pieces, and has become known as the richest ship ever taken by pirates.

In a letter sent to the Privy Council by Sir John Gayer[3], then governor of Bombay and head of the East India Company, Gayer claims that:

> It is certain the Pirates did do very barbarously by the People of the Ganj-i-Sawai and Abdul Ghaffar's ship, to make them confess where their money was.

When the news arrived in England it caused an outcry and a combined bounty of £1,000 was offered for Every's capture by the Privy Council and East India Company, leading to the first worldwide manhunt in recorded history. The plunder of Aurangzeb's treasure ship had serious consequences for the English East India Company. The furious Mughal Emperor Aurangzeb ordered Sidi Yaqub and Nawab Daud Khan to attack and close four of the company's factories in India and imprison their officers, who were almost lynched by a mob of angry Mughals, blaming them for their countryman's depredations, and threatened to put an end to all English trading in India. To appease Emperor Aurangzeb and particularly his Grand Vizier Asad Khan, Parliament exempted Every from all of the Acts of Grace (pardons) and amnesties it would subsequently issue to other pirates.

The prosperity that the officers of the company enjoyed allowed them to return to Britain and establish sprawling estates and businesses, and to obtain political power. The Company developed a lobby in the English parliament. Under pressure from ambitious tradesmen and former associates of the Company (pejoratively termed Interlopers by the Company), who wanted to establish private trading firms in India, a deregulating act was passed in 1694.

This allowed any English firm to trade with India, unless specifically prohibited by act of parliament, thereby annulling the charter that had been in force for almost 100 years. By an act that was passed in 1698, a new "parallel" East India Company (officially titled the English Company Trading to the East Indies) was floated under a state-backed indemnity of £2 million. The powerful stockholders of the old company quickly subscribed a sum of £315,000 in the new concern, and dominated the new body. The two companies wrestled with each other for some time, both in England and in India, for a dominant share of the trade.

It quickly became evident that, in practice, the original Company faced scarcely any measurable competition. The companies merged in 1708, by a tripartite indenture involving both companies and the state. Under this arrangement, the merged company lent to the Treasury a sum of £3,200,000, in return for exclusive privileges for the next three years, after which the situation was to be reviewed. The amalgamated companies became The United Company of Merchants of England Trading to the East Indies.

By 1720, 15% of all British imports were from India, nearly all passing through the Company, which reasserted the influence of the Company lobby. The license was prolonged until 1766 by yet another act in 1730.

This was the background to the most important career opportunities available to young men of the 1740s. If they were the eldest sons of the gentry they might inherit and run estates and live in comparative opulence. If they were second sons they might be educated to become, for example, clergymen. There were opportunities in the Civil Service though most of these required considerable patronage and expense. But what if none of these opportunities was available? The literature of the eighteenth and nineteenth centuries is full of stories of misery and want endured by those who had insufficient means to fund a career. The professions and trade remained an option but to enter these required both funding and influence. The premium demanded of a prospective shop assistant could be beyond the means of many genteel families. There always remained a military career and commissions in the army were available for those who had the contacts and influence to command entry. For most, though, the army or the navy represented a hard apprenticeship followed by a sharp pyramid of promotion prospect.

There was another option for those whose relatives possessed influence. The East India Company offered an attractive career to those who could beg and borrow their way into it. There were many routes to entry; some involved joining the militia formed by EIC to protect its interests and, after 1757 being a member of a British Army regiment involved in India would do as well. The most important junior posts in the company were those described as "writers". These were the minor clerical posts on offer to talented and qualified young men offering an opportunity to progress up the ladder of promotion to well paid career jobs. A famous example of a young man taking this route to promotion was Robert Clive in 1749.

There were hidden benefits available to those who reached senior company positions. These took the form of either presents offered by native traders looking for the lucrative trading contracts offered by the company or private trades arising from the individual's own initiative. It is this opportunity to increase the company's remuneration by entrepreunerial activity that became such an attractive proposition for a young man. He might leave England with £2 in his pocket and return 10 or 15 years later with £60,000 in his bank account. The objective, then, was to return home with what was described as a competence capable of comfortably funding the remainder of one's life.

By no means did everyone lucky enough to be recommended for company service achieve this objective. Life could be dangerous in India. Everywhere there were conflicts as native groups and European interests squabbled over trade and the results could be extremely nasty for both military and civilians who got on the wrong side. Coupled with this the climate was often dangerous to those not used to the heat and diseases that proliferated. Medical services were primitive and to contract a serious disease or condition often meant near-certain death.

Also the ability to get on with colleagues was paramount because a senior was capable of terminating a promising career for the most trivial of reasons.

On the other hand the rewards of modest success were impressive. Good progress ensured that a wife would consider your proposition and her family would probably agree the marriage. Incomes were usually enough to permit family life at a good level. The rewards of high success were dazzling. Robert Clive returned to England with a huge fortune obtained, he always maintained, by legitimate means. Always he wished to convey the impression that he accepted no presents from the Indian princes. Where then did his wealth come from? Despite his protestations much of it emanated from the patronage he offered.

The same can be said of Robert Palk who returned to England in 1767 with sufficient wealth to purchase the whole of a Haldon Hill estate of 60,000 acres and the village of Torquay with enough change to purchase a country seat and many other properties. He also averred that he accepted no bribes or payments from illicit trading activities. Where did all his wealth come from?

The company was alive to the problems posed by senior employees who conducted private trades and commissions on their own business. Since it seems all the senior company managers were to some extent trading for their private benefit it had to be the Court of Directors in London who acted to outlaw the practices of accepting presents, commissions or bribes. They still permitted certain trading arrangements where these had been personally licensed and this still afforded huge profits to be amassed by a lucky few.

An example of the dangers and pitfalls involved in this is presented by the case of Warren Hastings who was sent to India as the company's senior executive. When he returned to England with a fortune he was challenged in the courts for accepting presents contrary to company policy. Though acquitted, after four years of legal defence he had completely exhausted his wealth.

To those not so fortunate as to occupy a position of seniority where presents and favours could be demanded as of right, it could be difficult to accumulate a competence. Major Stringer Lawrence was not supposed to be wealthy when appointed to command the company's forces in 1747. He had fought around the Mediterranean for many years and in many campaigns and was 49 when he arrived in India. His talents were those of a military man with a thoughtful and successful approach to command. When he left India in 1767 he had pensions and presents from several sources and enough to fund the purchase of a London house in Bruton Street. When he died he left what he possessed mostly to Robert Palk and family.

IV
Competition between England and France, 1742

Britain and France became bitter rivals in India and frequent conficts between them took place for control of colonial possessions. In 1742, fearing the expense of a war, the British government agreed to a deadline for the licensed exclusive trade in India until 1783, in return for a further loan. Between 1756 and 1763, the Seven Years' War diverted Britain's attention to consolidating its territorial possessions in Europe and in America.

The result of the Industrial Revolution was that Britain surged ahead of its European rivals and demand for Indian commodities was boosted by the need to sustain the troops and the economy during the war and by the increased availability of raw materials and efficient methods of production. Britain experienced higher standards of living and its spiralling cycle of prosperity, demand, and production influenced overseas trade. EIC became the single largest player in the British global market. It reserved for itself an unassailable position in the decision-making process of the Government. William Henry Pyne notes in his book The Microcosm of London (1808) that:

> On the 1 March 1801, the East India Company increased from £5,393,989 to £15,404,736 and their sales increased since February 1793, from £4,988,300 to £7,602,041.

Saltpetre used for gunpowder was an example of the trade goods of EIC.

Sir John Banks negotiated an agreement between the King and the Company and began his career by arranging contracts for victualling the navy which he did for most of his life. He knew Samuel Pepys and John Evelyn and obtained a substantial fortune from the Levant and Indian trades. He became a Director and later, as Governor of the East India Company. He invented the auction procedure for his goods:

> for the King 'at the price it shall sell by the candle' that is by

auction where an inch of candle burned and as long as it was alight bidding could continue."

The agreement included with the price: an allowance of interest which is to be expressed in tallies.

This was something of a breakthrough in royal prerogative because previous requests for the King to buy at the Company's auctions had been turned down as not honourable or decent.

After the Seven Years' War resulted in the defeat of the French forces this stunted the influence of the industrial revolution in French territories. By the Treaty of Paris (1763), France regained the five establishments captured by the British during the war (Pondichéry, Mahe, Karikal, Yanam, and Chandernagar) but was prevented from erecting fortifications and keeping troops in Bengal.

Elsewhere in India, the French were a military threat, particularly during the War of American Independence and up to the capture of Pondichéry in 1793 at the outset of the French Revolutionary Wars without any military presence.

With the gradual weakening of the Marathas in the aftermath of the three Anglo-Maratha wars, the British also secured Ganges-Jumna Doab, the Delhi-Agra region, parts of Bundelkhand, Broach, some districts of Gujarat, fort of Ahmmadnagar, province of Cuttack (which included Mughalbandi/the coastal part of Odisha, Garjat/the princely states of Odisha, Balasore Port, parts of Midnapore district of West Bengal), Bombay (Mumbai) and the surrounding areas, leading to a formal end of the Maratha empire.

Hyder Ali and Tipu Sultan, the rulers of the Kingdom of Mysore, offered much resistance to British force. They sided with the French during the war and continued resistance with the four Anglo-Mysore Wars. Mysore finally fell to the Company forces in 1799, with the death of Tipu Sultan.

In the 18th century, Britain had a huge trade deficit with Qing Dynasty China and so in 1773, the Company created a British monopoly on opium buying in Bengal. The opium trade was illegal in China so Company ships could not carry opium to China and therefore the opium produced in Bengal was sold in Calcutta on condition that it be sent to be smuggled into China from Bengal by traffickers and agency houses such as Jardine, Matheson & Co and Dent & Co. in amounts averaging 900 tons a year. The proceeds of the drug-smugglers landing their cargoes at Lintin Island were paid into EICs factory at Canton and by 1825, most of the money needed to buy tea in China was raised by the illegal opium trade.

Though the Company was becoming increasingly bold and ambitious in putting down resisting states, it was becoming clear that it was incapable of governing the vast expanse of captured territories. The Bengal famine of 1770, in which one-third of the local population died, caused distress in Britain. This led to the passing of the Tea Act in 1773, which gave the Company greater autonomy in running its trade in the American colonies, and allowed it an exemption from tea import duties which its colonial competitors were required to pay.

When the American colonists, who included tea merchants, were told of the act, they tried to boycott it, claiming that although the price had gone down on the tea when enforcing the act, it also would help validate the Townshend Acts and set a precedent for the king to impose additional taxes in the future. The arrival of tax-exempt Company tea, undercutting the local merchants, triggered the Boston Tea Party in the Province of Massachusetts Bay, one of the major events leading up to the American Revolution.

Under this provision governor of Bengal, Warren Hastings, became the first Governor-General of Bengal, and had administrative powers over all of British India. It provided that his nomination, though made by a court of directors, should in future be subject to the approval of a Council of Four appointed by the Crown. Hastings was entrusted with the power of peace and war. British judicial personnel would also be sent to India to administer the British legal system. The Governor General and the council would have complete legislative powers. EIC was allowed to maintain its virtual monopoly over trade in exchange for a biennial sum and was obligated to export a minimum quantity of goods yearly to Britain.

The East India Company was the first to record the Chinese use of orange-flavoured tea leading to the development of Earl Grey tea. EIC introduced a system of merit-based appointments that provided a model for the British and Indian civil service.

V
The French in India, 1664

The *Compagnie Française pour le Commerce des Indes Orientales* was founded in 1664. It was planned by Jean-Baptiste Colbert and chartered by King Louis XIV for the purpose of trading in the Eastern Hemisphere. Resulting from the fusion of three earlier companies, the 1660 Compagnie de Chine, the Compagnie d'Orient and Compagnie de Madagascar it was led by De Faye, who was joined by two directors belonging to the two most successful trading organizations at that time: François Caron, who had spent 30 years working for the Dutch East India Company, including more than 20 years in Japan and Marcara Avanchintz, a trader from Ispahan, Persia.

The first French voyage to the Indies in 1603 was captained by Paulmier de Gonneville of Honfleur and Henry IV authorized the first Compagnie des Indes Orientales, granting the firm a 15-year monopoly of the Indies trade. This precursor to Colbert's later Compagnie des Indes Orientales, however, was not a joint-stock corporation, and was funded by the Crown.

The initial stock offering quickly sold out, as courtiers of Louis XIV recognised that it was in their interests to support the King's overseas initiative. The *Compagnie des Indes Orientales* was granted a 50-year monopoly on French trade in the Indian and Pacific Oceans, a region stretching from the Cape of Good Hope to the Straits of Magellan. The French monarch also granted the Company a concession in perpetuity for the island of Madagascar, as well as any other territories it could conquer.

The Company was able to establish ports on the nearby islands of Bourbon and Île-de-France (today's Réunion and Mauritius). By 1719, it had established itself in India, but the firm was near bankruptcy. In the same year the Compagnie des Indes Orientales was combined under the direction of John Law with other French trading companies to form the Compagnie Perpétuelle des Indes. The reorganised corporation resumed its operating independence in 1723.

With the decline of the Mughal Empire, the French decided to intervene in Indian political affairs to protect their interests, notably by forging alliances with local rulers in south India. From 1741 the French under Joseph François Dupleix pursued an aggressive policy against both the Indians and the British until they were defeated by Stringer Lawrence. The final and decisive battle was won by Robert Clive at the battle of Plassey. Several Indian trading ports, including Pondichéry and Chandernagore, remained under French control until 1954.

The Company was not able to maintain itself financially, and it was abolished in 1769, about 20 years before the French Revolution. King Louis XVI issued a 1770 edict that required the Company to transfer to the state all its properties, assets and rights, which were valued at 30 million livres. The company was reconstituted in 1785 and issued 40,000 shares of stock priced at 1,000 livres apiece. It was given monopoly on all trade with countries beyond the Cape of Good Hope for an agreed period of seven years.

The agreement, however, did not anticipate the French Revolution, and on 3 April 1790 the monopoly was abolished by an act of the new French Assembly which enthusiastically declared that the lucrative Far Eastern trade would henceforth be "thrown open to all Frenchmen". The company, accustomed neither to competition nor official disfavor, fell into steady decline and was finally liquidated in 1794.

A *Popular History of France From The Earliest Times Volume VI. of VI.* by Francois Pierre Guillaume Guizot (Trans. Robert Black 1898), contains a description of the defence of French interests at the time when Major Stringer Lawrence arrived in India.

The influential French personality was Dupleix who became Governor General of the French establishment in India, and the military rival of Stringer Lawrence and later, Robert Clive.

Dupleix was born in Landrecies, France. His father, wishing to bring him up as a merchant and to distract him from his taste for the sciences, sent him on a voyage to India in 1715 on one of the French East India Company's vessels. He made several voyages to the Americas and India, and in 1720 was named a member of the superior council at Pondichéry. He displayed great business aptitude and, in addition to his official duties, made large ventures on his own account, and acquired a fortune. In 1730 he was made superintendent of French affairs in Chandernagore. In 1741, he married Jeanne Albert, widow of one of the councillors of the company known to the Hindus as Joanna Begum. She proved of great help to her husband in his negotiations with the native princes.

He became, in 1742, governor general of all French establishments in India and succeeded Dumas as the French governor of Pondichéry. His ambition was to acquire territories in India and for this purpose he developed relations with the native princes and adopted oriental splendour in his dress and surroundings. His native troops, called sepoys, were trained as infantry men and that also included the Hyder Ali of Mysore. Danger to British interests and power were partly averted by the bitter mutual jealousy which existed between Dupleix and Bertrand François Mahé de La Bourdonnais, French governor of the Isle of Bourbon (today's La Réunion).

When the city of Madras capitulated to the French following the Battle of Madras in 1746, Dupleix opposed the restoration of the town to the British, so violating the treaty signed by La Bourdonnais. In 1747 he sent an expedition against Fort St David, which was defeated on its march by the Nawab of Arcot, ally of the British. Dupleix succeeded in winning over the Nawab, and again attempted the capture of Fort St David, but did not succeed. A midnight attack on Cuddalore was repulsed at a great loss to Dupleix.

In 1748 Pondichery was besieged by the British, but in the course of the operations news arrived of the peace concluded between the French and the British at Aix-la-Chapelle. Dupleix next sent a large body of troops to the aid of the two claimants of the sovereignty of the Carnatic and the Deccan. In 1750 the Subadar of Deccan gave the Alamparai Fort to the French as a token of his appreciation of the services of Dupleix and the French forces. The fort was later captured by the British and destroyed.

Then ensued the battles that culminated in the domination of the British after Plassey. The conflicts between the French and the British in India continued until 1754, when the French government, anxious to settle peace, sent a special commissioner to India with orders to supersede Dupleix and, if necessary, to arrest him. Dupleix was compelled to embark for France on 12 October 1754.

Jeanne Albert died in 1756.

Having invested his private fortune in the implementation of his public policies, Dupleix was ruined. The government refused to support him, and he died in obscurity and want on 10 November 1763.

Says Voltaire:

The Curate and the General

> The fate of France has nearly always been that her enterprises, and even her successes, beyond her own frontiers should become fatal to her.

and this was certainly true in Canada, America and India. The defaults of the government and the jealous colonists, in the 18th century, spawned the military defeats which were to cost the French nearly all their colonies.

More than a hundred years previously, at the outset of Louis XIV's reign, and through the efforts of Colbert, marching in the footsteps of Cardinal Richelieu, a India Company was founded for the purpose of developing French commerce, which had been shrouded in wealth and grandeur. The Company nearly failed and it was only revived by the efforts of M.Law. It paid no dividend to its shareholders, who benefited only from tobacco revenues granted by the king, though its directors lived a life of magnificence where they were authorised to trade on their own account. Bolder than his colleagues, Joseph Dupleix endowed France with a flegling empire in India. He became head of the French establishments at Chandernagore after he had improved the city and constructed a fleet, whilst acquiring for himself an immense fortune. He was then sent to Pondichery as governor general when the war of succession to the empire broke out in 1742.

Dupleix and his wife, had been secretly forming a network of communications that informed them of the many intrigues of the petty native courts. Madame Dupleix, a Creole, was brought up in India, understood many of its dialects and so was able to assist her husband in the campaigns that followed.

Good relations existed between Dupleix and the governor of Bourbon and of Ile de France, Bertrand Francis Mahe de La Bourdonnais, when, in September, 1746, the latter appeared with a small squadron in front of Madras, already a principal English settlement. Commodore Peyton, who was cruising in Indian waters after having been beaten twice by La Bourdonnais, kept at a distance, left the town feebly fortified and the English, who had counted on the Nabob of the Carnatic, also did not receive the assistance expected. They surrendered at the first shot, promising to pay a ransom for Madras, which the French retained as security until the debt was discharged. La Bourdonnais received from France this order "You are not to keep any of the conquests you make in India." At the time the white town was occupied solely by Europeans and English settlements whilst the black town was inhabited by a mixed population of natives and foreigners and by traders or artisans.

Chests containing the ransom were taken aboard the vessels of La Bourdonnais which made sail for Pondichery. The governor of Bourbon was in a hurry to get back to his islands. Autumn was coming, tempests were threatening his squadron and Dupleix was disputing the terms of the treaty for the ransom of Madras because he had contrary instructions to raze the city and place it in the hands of the Nabob of the Carnatic. Guizot writes:

> La Bourdonnais, in a violent rage, about to be arrested by order of Dupleix, put the governor-general's envoys in prison amd the conflict of authority was aggravated by the feeble and duplicious instructions from France. Suddenly a huge tempest destroyed part of the squadron in front of Madras and La Bourdonnais, flinging himself into a boat, had great difficulty in rejoining his ships; he departed, leaving his rival master of Madras, and adroitly prolonging the negotiations, in order to ruin at least the black city, which alone was rich and prosperous, before giving over the place to the Nabob. Months rolled by, and the French remained alone at Madras.

Dupleix decided to violate a promise given by La Bourdonnais and quashed the capitulation of Madras for which he had not agreed the conditions. The report of the quarrel and the interpretation by Dupleix, would eventually ruin his rival in Paris whom he had vanquished in India. On arriving at Ile de France, La Bourdonnais learned that a new governor was there. His dissension with Dupleix caused the Company to appoint a successor. Guizot again:

> Driven to desperation, anxious to go and defend himself, La Bourdonnais set out for France with his wife and his four children; a prosecution had already been commenced against him. He was captured at sea by an English ship, and taken a prisoner to England. The good faith of the conqueror of Madras was known in London; one of the directors of the English Company offered his fortune as security for M. de La Bourdonnais. Scarcely had he arrived in Paris when he was thrown into the Bastille, and for two years kept in solitary confinement. When his

innocence was at last acknowledged and his liberty restored to him, his health was destroyed, his fortune exhausted by the expenses of the trial. La Bourdonnais died before long, employing the last remnants of his life and of his strength in pouring forth his anger against Dupleix, to whom he attributed all his woes. His indignation was excusable, and some of his grievances were well grounded; but the germs of suspicion thus sown by the unfortunate prisoner released from the Bastille were destined before long to consign to perdition not only his enemy, but also, together with him, that French dominion in India to which M. de La Bourdonnais had dedicated his life.

Meanwhile Dupleix grew more powerful. On the 30th of August, 1748, Admiral Boscawen laid siege to Pondicherry and stopped outside the fort of Ariocapang.The troops disembarked but could not dig trenches beyond the swamp that protected the town. Dupleix who commanded the French batteries was wounded on 6th of October and his place on the ramparts was taken by Madame Dupleix alongside her future son-in-law, M. de Bussy-Castelnau, Dupleix's military lieutenant. Guizot says:

> The fire of the English redoubled; but there was laughter in Pondichery, for the balls did not carry so far; and on the 20th of October, after forty days' siege, Admiral Boscawen put to sea again, driven far away from the coasts by the same tempests which, two years before, had compelled La Bourdonnais to quit Madras. Twice had Dupleix been served in his designs by the winds of autumn.

The peace of Aix-la-Chapelle put an end to war between the Europeans and made Dupleix gloomy despite the order of the Riband of St. Louis and the title of Marquis, that was recently granted by the King. Worse, he had been obliged to restore Madras to the English. At Surat both East India Companies were established. On the coast of Malabar the English at Bombay, and the French at Mahe; on the coast of Coromandel the English held Madras and Fort St. George, the French Pondichery and Karikal. The principal factories, as well as the numerous dependent establishments were defended by European soldiers and Sepoys.

The Great Mogul, sovereign of all India, was selling titles without taking any part in the fighting. Dupleix took the side of Chunda Sahib, in the Deccan, against their rivals supported by the English but the French battalion sent by Dupleix to the aid of his allies found that a ball had killed the Nabob. That same evening, Murzapha Jung was proclaimed Soudhabar of the Deccan, and granted the principality of the Carnatic to Chunda Sahib, at the same time reserving a vast territory to the French Company .

Dupleix was delighted and Pondichery was ready to welcome him. Dupleix dressed himself in the magnificent costume of a Hindu prince and went with his troops to meet him. Both entered in a palanquin to the sound of cymbals and French military music. A throne awaited the Soudhabar, surrounded by the Afghan chiefs, who were claiming their reward. By now a third of India was obedient to Dupleix. The Great Mogul sent him a decree of investiture and demanded, from Princess Jane, the hand of her youngest daughter (who had previously been promised to M. de Bussy). Dupleix well knew the frailty of human affairs, and the dark intrigues of Hindu courts.

The successes of Dupleix frightened King Louis XV and his feeble ministers and angered the British who were faltering and badly managed. Guizot says:

> At Versailles attempts were made to lessen the conquests of Dupleix, prudence was recommended to him, delay was shown in sending him the troops he demanded. In India, England had at last found a man still young and unknown, but worthy of being opposed to Dupleix.

In Stringer Lawrence the British had discovered a champion. Undemonstrative and friendly with a ready gift for humour and beloved of his officers and troops, Lawrence set out to defeat Dupleix by the simple tactic of playing to his personality. Too late, Dupleix found out that he had underestimated his rival. Finally, however, it was Lawrence's protege and friend, Robert Clive, who would prove to be Dupleix's nemesis.

Meanwhile war in the Carnatic still continued. Muhammed Ali, Chunda Sahib's rival, had for the last six months been besieged in Trichinopoly and the English had several times attempted to raise the siege. Troops' morale was good as demonstrated by their declaration:

> Give the rice to the English; we will be content with the water in which it is boiled.

A body of Mahrattas, allies of the English, then came to raise the siege. The British pursued the French and Chunda Sahib as they retreated and, under Stringer Lawrence, broke the siege of Trichinopoly and released Mahomet Ali. Chunda Sahib, shut up in Tcheringham, was handed over to his rival by a Tan j ore chieftain whom he trusted. He was put to death and the French commandant, a nephew of M.Law's, promptly surrendered to Stringer Lawrence. Guizot writes:

> The dismay at Versailles was great, and prevailed over the astonishment. There had never been any confidence in Dupleix's projects, there had been scarcely any belief in his conquests. The soft-hearted inertness of ministers and courtiers was almost as much disgusted at the successes as at the defeats of the bold adventurers who were attempting and risking all for the aggrandisement and puissance of France in the East. Dupleix secretly received notice to demand his recall. He replied by proposing to have M. de Bussy nominated in his place. "Never was so grand a fellow as this Bussy," he wrote. The ministers and the Company cared little for the grandeur of Bussy or of Dupleix; what they sought was security, incessantly troubled by the enterprises of the politician and the soldier. The tone of England was more haughty than ever, in consequence of Lawrence's and Clive's successes. The recall of Dupleix was determined upon.|
> The Governor of Pondichery had received no troops, but he had managed to reorganise an army, and had resumed the offensive in the Carnatic; Bussy, set free at last as to his movements in the Deccan, was preparing to rejoin Dupleix. Dupleix wished to preserve the advantages he had won but Saunders refused to listen to that. The approach of a French squadron was signalled; the ships appeared to be numerous. Dupleix was already rejoicing at the arrival of unexpected aid, when, instead of an officer commanding the twelve hundred soldiers from

France, he saw the apparition of M.Godeheu, one of the directors of the Company and but lately his friend and correspondent. "I come to supersede you, sir," said the new arrival, without any circumstance; "I have full powers from the Company to treat with the English."

The British were not deceived. They insisted that Dupleix's recall was made a condition of a cease fire. Louis XV. and his ministers showed no opposition and the treaty was concluded, restoring the possessions of the two Companies just as they were before the war, with the exception of the district of Masulipatam. The British gave up some small forts and a few small towns of little importance; France ceded their empire of India. When Godeheu signed the treaty, Trichinopoly was on the point of defeat. Bussy was furious, and would have left the Deccan but Dupleix ordered him to remain there whilst he embarked for France with his wife and daughter. Dupleix's life's work had been destroyed in just a few days by the stupidity of his country's government. The fortune he had acquired during his great enterprises was invested in the service of France and the revenues he built to finance his advance were all seized by Godeheu.

Amazingly, France welcomed Dupleix's arrival as a triumph. Dupleix wrote:

La Bourdonnais

> My wife and I dare not appear in the streets of Lorient because of the crowd of people wanting to see us and bless us.

Guizot again:

> ....the comptroller-general, Herault de Sechelles, as well as the king and Madame de Pompadour, then and for a long while the reigning favourite, gave so favorable a reception to the hero of India that Dupleix, always an optimist, conceived fresh hopes. "I shall regain my property here," he would say, "and India will recover in the hands of Bussy."

However, he was just as mistaken about justice as he was about the determination of the French government. Dupleix's wife died at the end of two years, worn out with despair. Dupleix lobbied ministers with projects for India and all his ideas were finally vetoed by order of the king.

Persecuted by his creditors he exclaimed a few months before his death:

> I have sacrificed youth, fortune, life, in order to load with honour and riches those of my own nation in Asia. Unhappy friends, too weakly credulous relatives, virtuous citizens, have dedicated their property to promoting the success of my projects; they are now in want. I demand, like the humblest of creditors, that which is my due; my services are all stuff, my demand is ridiculous, I am treated like the vilest of men. The little I have left is seized, I have been obliged to get execution stayed to prevent my being dragged to prison!

Dupleix died on the 11th of November, 1763, the most striking, if not the last or most tragic victim of French enterprise in India.

VI
The Seven Years' War, 1754 - 1763

Meanwhile the Seven Years' War had started and the whole of Europe had joined in the contest. The French navy, feeble in spite of the efforts that had been made to restore it, lost battles on every sea. Count Lally-Tollendal, descended from an Irish family which took refuge in France with James II, went to Count d'Argenson, minister of war, with a proposition to reduce British power in India. Lally had served with distiction in the wars of Germany and had seconded Prince Charles Edward in his brave attempt upon England. The directors of the India Company asked M. d'Argenson to entrust Lally with king's troops promised for the expedition. M. d'Argenson said to them:

> You are wrong, I know M. de Lally; he is a friend of mine, but he is violent, passionate, inflexible as to discipline; he will not tolerate any disorder; you will be setting fire to your warehouses, if you send him thither.

The directors, however, insisted, and Lally set out on 2nd May, 1757, with four ships and a body of troops. Some young officers belonging to the greatest houses of France served on his staff.

Lally's passage was a long one and British re-enforcements had preceded him by six weeks. On arriving in India, he found the arsenals and the magazines empty and Pondichery alone fourteen million francs in debt. Meanwhile the enemy was pressing on all fronts.

Lally marched to Gondelour (Kaddaloue), which he carried on the sixth day and he invested Fort St. David, the most formidable of the English fortresses in India. The first assault was repulsed because the general had neither cannon nor oxen to draw them. He hurried to Pondichery and had natives harnessed to the artillery trains. Fort St. David was taken and razed. Devicotah, after scarcely the ghost of a siege, opened its gates. Lally had been hardly a month in India, and he had already driven the English from the southern coast of the Coromandel. Lally wrote:

> All my policy is in these five words, but they are binding as an oath—No English in the peninsula.

He had sent Bussy orders to join him for an attack on Madras. So the brilliant courage and heroic ardor of M. de Lally had triumphed over the first obstacles but soon his recklessness was about to lose him the fruits victory. He said to the directors in Paris:

> The commission I hold means that I shall be held in horror by all the people of the country.

He had aggravated his critical position and the supine French government had made fatal progress amongst its servants.

Count d'Ache, who commanded the fleet, had refused to second the attempt upon Madras. Twice, in Indian waters, the French admiral had been beaten by the English and so he set sail for the Ile de France, where he decided to winter. Now Pondichery was threatened, and Lally found himself in Tan j ore, where he had hoped to recover the considerable sum due to the company. He had attacked a pagoda, thinking he would find treasure, but the idols were hollow and worthless. The pagoda was in flames and the hapless Brahmins were still wandering round their temple. The general took them for spies, and had them tied to the cannons' mouths. The danger that Pondichery faced forced M. de Lally to raise the siege of Tan j ore.

Meanwhile, Lally was angered by shortage of money; he attributed this to the ill will and dishonesty, of the local authorities. He wrote, in 1758, to M. de Leyrit, Governor of Pondichery:

> Sir, this letter shall be an eternal secret between you and me, if you furnish me with the means of terminating my enterprise. I left you a hundred thousand livres of my own money to help you to meet the expenditure it requires. I have not found so much as a hundred sous in your purse and in that of all your council; you have both of you refused to

> let me employ your credit. I, however, consider you to be all of you under more obligation to the Company than I am, who have unfortunately the honour of no further acquaintance with it than to the extent of having lost half my property by it in 1720. If you continue to leave me in want of everything and exposed to the necessity of presenting a front to the general discontent, not only shall I inform the king and the Company of the fine zeal testified for their service by their employees here, but I shall take effectual measures for not being at the mercy, during the short stay I desire to make in this country, of the party spirit and personal motives by which I see that every member appears to be actuated to the risk of the Company in general.

In the midst of distress Lally led his troops to Madras and won the Black Town. An officer under his command says:

> The immense plunder taken by the troops had introduced abundance amongst them. Huge stores of strong liquors led to drunkenness and all the evils it generates. The situation must have been seen to be believed. The works, the guards in the trenches were all performed by drunken men. The regiment of Lorraine alone was exempt from this plague, but the other corps surpassed one another. Hence scenes of the most shameful kind and most destructive of subordination and discipline, the details of which confined within the limits of the most scrupulous truthfulness would appear a monstrous exaggeration.

Lally in despair wrote to his friends in France:

> Hell vomited me into this land of iniquities, and I am waiting, like Jonah, for the whale that shall receive me in its belly.
> The attack on the White Town and on Fort St. George was repulsed; and on the 18th of February, 1759, Lally was obliged to raise the siege of Madras.

The animosity, which Lally provoked in India, was destined to cost him his life and his honour. Scarcely had he arrived in England, ill, exhausted by sufferings and fatigue, followed even in captivity by the reproaches and anger of his comrades in misfortune, he was accused of treason; and he obtained from the English cabinet permission to go to Paris. Lally said: I bring hither my head and my innocence.

There he remained for nineteen months without being examined. When the trial commenced in December, 1764, there were one hundred and sixty charges, nearly two hundred witnesses and the trial lasted a year and a half. He claimed the jurisdiction of a court-martial, but this was rejected and when he saw himself confronted with the dock, the general suddenly uncovered his white head and his breast covered with scars, exclaiming, "So this is the reward for fifty years' service!" On 6th May, 1766, his sentence was at last pronounced. Lally was acquitted on the charges of high treason but found "guilty of violence, abuse of authority, vexations and exactions, as well as of having betrayed the interests of the king and of the Company." When the sentence was being read out "Cut it short, sir," said the count to the clerk, "come to the conclusions." At the words "betrayed the interests of the king," Lally drew himself up to his full height, exclaiming, "Never, never!" He was insulting his enemies, when, drawing a pair of mathematical compasses from his pocket, he struck it violently against his heart. But the wound did not go deep enough and M. de Lally was destined to drink to the dregs the cup of man's injustice to man.

On the 9th of May, at the close of the day, the valiant general mounted the scaffold on the Place de Greve. Permission was refused to the few friends who remained faithful to him to accompany him to the place of execution and there was only the parish priest of St. Louis en L'Ile at his side.

For fear of violence he was gagged like the lowest criminal as he mounted the ladder, knelt without assistance and calmly awaited the death-blow. "Everybody," observed D'Alembert "everybody, except the hangman, has a right to kill Lally." Voltaire's judgment, after the subsidence of passion and after the light thrown by subsequent events upon the state of French affairs in India before Lally's campaigns, is more just: It was a murder committed with the sword of justice.

Timeline for Stringer Lawrence

1697 Mar 6 Born in Hereford
1717 Ensign in Clayton's Regiment 14th of Foot

Campaigns:
- 1719 Glenshiel
- 1727 Defence of Gibraltar
- 1745 Flanders
- 1745 Highland rising - Culloden

Indian career :
- 1747 Nov EIC appoints as commander Fort St George
- 1747 Feb embarks for Madras
- 1748, Lawrence lands at Fort St. David aged 49
- 1747 Taken prisoner by French
- 1748 Released under Treaty of Aix-la-Chapelle
- 1749 Clive first comes to notice of Lawrence

Years of service in India shared with Robert Palk:
- 1750 Lawrence meets Robert Palk
- 1750 25 Sept Lawrence resigns and leaves for England,
- 1750 Mar returns to Madras to relieve Trichinopoly,
- 1753 - 1755, Lawrence defends Trichinopoly.
- 1754 Lawrence commissioned Lieut. Colonel
- 1758 Lally captures Fort St. David; advances on Madras.
- 1759 Apr Visits England for his health
- 1761 Returns as Major General with Robert Palk
- 1763 - 67 Palk appointed governor of Madras

1766 Lawrence returns from India to England
1766. Lawrence retires.
1775 Jan 10th Lawrence dies

Part Two
Stringer Lawrence in India

VII
Stringer Lawrence 1747 - 1766

The only positive knowledge we have of Stringer Lawrence's parentage comes from the baptismal register in the Church of All Saints at Hereford, which shows that on 27th February, 1697, Stringer, the son of Mr. John Lawrence and his wife Mary, was baptised. In the All Saints' burial register it is recorded the burial of Michael Stringer took place on the 13th November 1698 and so it is reasonable to assume that Stringer was the maiden name of Lawrence's mother.

The coat of arms on Stringer Lawrence's monument in Westminster Abbey (ermine, a cross ragul gules) is almost identical with the coat of arms granted to Sir John Lawrence, Alderman of London, and Lord Mayor in 1664, in which year the grant of arms was made (ermine, a cross ragul gules, a canton ermines).

The archives of the City of Hereford, which were partly destroyed in the Civil War, show that there was a family of the name of Lawrence living in Hereford in the 17th and 18th centuries. In 1625 a James Lawrence was Mayor of Hereford.

A memorandum signed by the Parliamentary officer, Colonel John Birch, shows that a "Mr. Lawrence" was fined six pounds for being disaffected to Parliament.

In 1660 James Lawrence, junior, gentleman, was admitted to the freedom of the city, and became Mayor in the following year. In 1682 John Lawrence, apothecary, and in 1702 John Lawrence, brewer, were admitted to the freedom of the city. One of these could well have been the father of Stringer Lawrence. In 1707 William Lawrence, brewer, in 1714 Humphries Lawrence, gentleman, of Leominster, in 1761 Samuel Lawrence, brewer, were all admitted to the freedom of the city.

What we know is that Stringer Lawrence, at the age of 19, joined Colonel Clayton's regiment, founded in 1719. This later became the 14th of Foot.

It is probable that Lawrence saw action in the Highlands during the first two years of his service and also that he served with the regiment in the battle of Glenshiel which took place on June 10, 1719 during what was known as the "Little Rising" when a small force of Spanish soldiers (only around three hundred of whom reached Scotland) landed at Lochalsh to form a nucleus for a rising of the Highland clans. The only battle of this rising occurred between a government army led by General Wightman and Jacobites under the 10th Earl Marischal at Glenshiel. The Jacobite cause was supported by France and occasionally Spain. Cardinal Alberoni on behalf of Philip V of Spain sent five thousand men to aid the emerging rising.

Less than a thousand men assembled to be led by John Cameron of Lochiel, Captain and Chief of Clan Cameron, along with Lord George Murray and the Earl of Seaforth. A reported one hundred and fifty Cameron men were among the assembled Jacobites. Eilean Donan Castle became their supply base while they headed off for Inverness through the Great Glen. The army's plan of action was to advance upon and capture Inverness.

The Hanoverians were aware of their moves and attacked Eilean Donan Castle from the sea, destroying it with cannon fire of three warships. General Wightman came from Inverness and confronted the Jacobites at Glenshiel on the 10th of June. The forces were well matched and the battle continued for hours with no clear victor. When expected Jacobite support from the Lowlanders failed, spirits fell completely. The rising was abandoned and the Highlanders dispersed to their homes and the Spaniards surrendered to Wightman. Lochiel, after skulking for a time in the Highlands, made his way back to exile in France.

Stringer Lawrence was a newly recruited subaltern and ensign, the most junior commissioned rank in the army (the equivalent of a second lieutenant today), who would carry the colours into battle as the rallying point for the troops.

Over the next few years the regiment was regularly engaged in and around the Mediterranean culminating in the Defence of Gibraltar in 1727. The action started after the the vigorous Spanish bombardment of the Rock when reinforcements arrived. On 1st May the Governor, the Earl of Portmore, arrived with ten companies of the First Guards and the 14th Regiment (Clayton's or the West Yorkshire Regiment – later the Duke of Wellington's Regiment). Room was made for the new reinforcements by moving troops south. One of the few sorties of the siege occurred just before the arrival of Lord Portmore. An ingenious plan was devised by Clayton though it failed due to the gunners acting too soon:

> This morn: early 2 Sergeants each having ten Men sally'd out to the very Trenches, call'd to the Enemy and had them advance, at the same time gave them two Volleys which was the Signal appointed by the Governor who was on the battery to give the word, but the Gunmen whose business it was to begin, being either drunk or mad, or both, over eager fired away without the sign, and so spoiled the project. The Sergeants did their duty well and allarm'd the whole army and Trenches, so that there was beating to arms immediately, which was what we wanted, for when they had been form'd in a Body then our guns shoul'd have done great execution, but the Gunner's Rashness let them know the Stratagem so they dispers'd.

The recently arrived British reinforcements allowed the garrison to maintain the batteries, re-mount the guns and return fire. Lord Portmore, in an attempt to boost the morale and productivity of his infantry turned labourers, increased their pay from eight pence to a shilling a day. On 15th May, the commander, de las Torres, trying to make a point, sent a Flag of Truce to the Governor, with a "Compliment to inform his Lordship that they have not begun the Siege, and that as yet they were only trying their ordinance, tho' they yesterday sent us, most part into the Town, 119 Bombs and near 1500 Balls and keep still a most dreadfull firing."

Nevertheless, the firing from the Spanish guns began to slacken. After several days' continuous fire the Spanish iron cannon began to burst, whilst the better brass cannon began to drop at the muzzle from overheating. The besiegers were also beginning to suffer from a lack of supplies owing to the poor Andalusian roads.

> Had we found ourselves in such a position as to be worthy of being asked our opinion of the enterprise before the siege began, as we are now to be worthy of being consulted by your Excellency over its prosecution, we would have voted on nothing more than a diversionary tactic overland ... [the geography and defences of Gibraltar] all combine to make a counter-attack so manifestly unbeatable

So ended the siege of Gibraltar at which the reputation of Stringer Lawrence, now a captain in the regiment, was first recognised.

After many more years in several naval conflicts, Clayton's regiment of marines is reported in Flanders in 1745. At issue was the Hanoverian succession. The most celebrated anecdote of the battle relates to Sir Charles Hay, a captain in the 1st Foot Guards. On reaching the brow of an incline the columns confronted the French line of Foot. Opposite the 1st Foot Guards were the Garde Francaise. This French regiment had given way at Dettingen and in their precipitate retreat had tipped up one of the bridges of boats. Many had drowned.

Sir Charles Hay is reputed to have doffed his hat and bowed to the French officers saying:

> We are the English Guards. We remember you from Dettingen and intend to make you swim the Scheldt as you swam the Main.

The alternative story is that Sir Charles Hay said

> Messieurs les Gardes Francaises, s'il vous plait, tirez le premier.

Hay was wounded in the battle.

The next campaign fought by Clayton's was, as part of the army sent north under the Duke of Cumberland, at the battle of Culloden that took place also in 1745. Between 1,500 and 2,000 Jacobites were killed or wounded, while government losses were much lighter with 50 dead and 259 wounded. The aftermath of the battle and subsequent crackdown on Jacobitism was brutal, earning Cumberland the sobriquet "butcher". Efforts were subsequently made to further integrate the comparatively wild Highlands into the Kingdom of Great Britain whilst civil penalties were introduced to weaken Gaelic culture and attack the Scottish clan system.

So, Stringer Lawrence, at the age of 49, had reached the rank of major and was earning a reputation as a commander in the field. Col Biddulph, writing in 1901 about the military exploits of Stringer Lawrence, explains he wishes to set the record straight and thereby to do justice to the man he believes was largely responsible for the success of the East India Company and who did so much to lay the foundation of the Indian Empire by the end of the 18th century. This is in contrast to the popular view that the famous Robert Clive was to be credited with the victor's laurels assisted in a junior capacity, by Eyre Coote.

Major General Robert Clive, and Lieutenant General Sir Eyre Coote have been justly celebrated as the famous commanders who won the crucial battles

Robert Clive

in India but beside them there were a number of officers, anything but inferior to them in military terms, who as majors and captains or even as subalterns commanded armies in the field, won important victories, conducted sieges and carried on successful operations, especially during the period 1750-1757, often against superior numbers and always under the greatest of difficulties, whose names have now passed into oblivion:

> ...stouthearted but utterly forgotten Englishmen, who, at great odds and with small means, sustained the fortunes of their country in many a hazardous predicament by their devoted bravery and steadfast perseverance.

Some of their deeds have been described by Orme but without local knowledge of places and conditions Orme can be difficult to read. His narrative of fifteen years' warfare is sometimes diffuse. The enemies against whom the British armies fought were worthy foes. In statesmanship there was nobody in authority on the English side who could match the Frenchman, Dupleix. He was well supported by his Government and commanded superior resources to those of the English. Despite this Dupleix was no soldier. His colleagues, La Bourdonnais, Bussy and Lally were excellent generals. In addition they endured much less interference from their local government.

The French troops were more numerous and better equipped than the English though their native commanders were frequently incompetent (though Hyder Ali was as fine a military leader as India has ever produced) but the numbers and resources they brought into the field made them formidable enemies. The fighting was often vicious. The Indian leaders had strong fortresses, powerful artillery, and thousands of horsemen, against whom were matched the slow-moving English infantry supported by guns drawn by oxen.

Sepoys, described as the the sweepings of the seaports, were gathered by sharks and the press who were not allowed to recruit openly. Orme describes a newly-arrived batch in 1752, as being the very men with whom Clive won the battles in Covelong and Chingleput. Sometimes there were Swiss mercenaries, who often deserted wholesale to join the French ranks. Easy victories were never available in India against the French in the 18th century. English successes in India were largely due to the fine qualities of the subordinate officers when given detached commands.

VIII
Stringer Lawrence arrives in India, 1748

The India known to Lawrence was divided into a number of successor states to the Mughal Empire. Over the forty years since the death of the Emperor Aurangzeb in 1707, the power of the emperor had fallen into the hands of provincial viceroys or soobedars. The chief rulers on the Coromandel coast were the Nizam of Hyderbad, Asaf Jah I and the Nawab of the Carnatic, Anwaraddin Muhammed Khan. The Nawab nominally owed fealty to the Nizam, but often acted independently. Fort St. George and the French trading post at Pondichey were both located in the Nawab's territory.

Through the 17th and early 18th centuries, the French, Dutch, Portuguese, and English had vied for control of various trading posts, and for trading rights with local Indian rulers. The European merchant companies raised bodies of troops to protect their commercial interests and to influence local politics to their advantage. Military power was rapidly becoming as important as commercial acumen in securing India's valuable trade and increasingly, it was used to gain territory and tax revenue.

This is the background to the appointment of Lawrence by the East India Company. One of the difficulties faced by the directors was the slow communication between London and the Indian outposts coupled with the very long journey times for officers before they could reach their commands. This meant that there had to be much reliance upon the local governments which in turn resulted in frustration felt by commanders in the field. A prime example of this was the news of the fall of Madras when the English had all been taken prisoner. Lawrence was some 11 months into his voyage and had to wait for news. The Directors appointed a new governor, and a Council, of which Lawrence was made the third member but his work in the Council was confined to military advice and duties. Lawrence's voyage included a visit to Batavia, before making the Coromandel coast. Probably there they received news of the fall of Madras at the Cape, and went to Batavia to await further intelligence.

In January 1748, Lawrence landed at Fort St. David, then expecting an attack by the French. After the fall of Madras, the Fort St. David officials had taken on the administration of the Company's affairs on the coast and very easily the English might have lost their last foothold in Southern India. Two attacks since the fall of Madras, had been foiled rather than defeated. Biddulph writes:

> Lawrence's first care was to form a camp outside the walls. This led to the detection of a plot among the native officers of Peons, who were in secret correspondence with Dupleix. The presence of the English fleet on the coast prevented any French movement against the place for a time. Lawrence employed the interval in reorganising the companies of Europeans, and introducing a system of military law. The reorganised companies were seven in number, consisting each of one captain, one lieutenant, one ensign, four sergeants, four corporals, three drummers, and seventy privates. The lieutenant of Lawrence's company was called captain-lieutenant, and ranked as a captain. In the field, these companies acted together as a battalion, but ten years elapsed before they were formed into an administrative battalion in quarters. In the same way, the peons (those in servitude to a master for debt) were organised in companies, and, eleven years later, in battalions. It was in such humble beginnings that the Anglo-Indian army had its origin. Six months after Lawrence's arrival, Dupleix took advantage of the absence of the British squadron to make another attempt against Cuddalore.
>
> The French military, from Pondicherry, appeared within three miles of Cuddalore on the morning of the 17th June. Lawrence had been warned, and withdrew the guns and garrison to Fort St. David, about a mile distant, announcing that he did not consider Cuddalore tenable. Directly night fell, he brought back the garrison and guns. At midnight the French advanced with scaling ladders, and were received with such a fire of grape and musketry that they flung down their arms and retreated to Pondicherry without making any further attempt.

Two months later, Lawrence was involved in the same disaster that he

had previously inflicted on the French. On receipt of the news of the loss of Madras, the Directors in London decided to send Admiral Boscawen to Pondichery on an expeddition that that sailed from England in November, 1747. On the flagship was the Rev'd Robert Palk, making his first visit to India.
For the purposes of the expedition, twelve independent companies, each of one hundred rank and file, were formed by drafts from different regiments, Artillery was added, and the whole force consisted of about 1,400 men. Some time was wasted in an abortive attempt against Mauritius. On the 29th July, the squadron arrived off Fort St. David, the troops were landed and, on 8th August, they began to march to Pondicherry.

The operations by land and sea, led by Boscawen, were complex and failure was blamed on his ignorance of land warfare. With marines, sailors, and a Dutch contingent from Negapatam, the European rank and file amounted to 3,720 men. Lawrence's authority only extended to the Company's troops, which formed a fifth of the whole force, not counting sepoys.

The first attempt was made against Ariancopang, a detached fort two miles from Pondicherry. Without information, without reconnaissance and without scaling ladders, seven hundred men were marched to the attack, with the inevitable consequence. One hundred and fifty men were killed or wounded and some of the best officers among the English troops were also killed and all without the slightest advantage gained.

Siege operations against Ariancopang were begun and a battery was opened with very little effect. Law, who commanded the French in Ariancopang, made a sudden sortie with a mixed force of infantry and cavalry against a part of the line held by sailors. The sailors were struck with panic at the sight of the cavalry and fled. The panic communicated itself to the regular troops, and the whole of the entrenchment was abandoned.
Biddulph says:

> Lawrence, who commanded in the trenches that day, refused to fly, and was made prisoner as a result. The same day the magazine in the fort was blown up by accident, forcing the garrison to retreat into Pondichery. On the 30th August, Boscawen arrived at Pondichery. After an abortive month the seige was abandoned. One thousand and sixty-five soldiers and sailors had died and an enormous quantity of ammunition had been wasted.

Orme observes:

> There are very few instances, of late years, of a siege carried on by the English with less skill than this of Pondichery.

In November, news was received of the cease fire in Europe and Lawrence was permitted to return to Fort St.David on parole, pending ratification of the Treaty of Aix-la-Chapelle, which restored Madras to the English. Biddulph writes:

> The establishment of peace left both English and French stronger in military resources in India than they had ever been before. The French could now, with impunity, interfere in the politics of the Deccan and Carnatic courts which greatly increased their political influence. This they proceeded to do.
> Boscawen was ready to retrieve his failure against Pondicherry and agreed with the Company's officials to support the cause of a Tan j ore prince who had been living under the Company's protection. This Tan j ore claimant made promises and gave assurances that his appearance in Tan j ore territory at the head of an armed force would be the signal for thousands to join the force. In return for assistance in gaining the throne of Tan j ore, he undertook to cede Devicotah to the English.

At the end of March, 1749, four hundred and thirty Europeans, with a thousand sepoys and a small siege train were despatched against Devicotah, under command of Captain Cope. The force reached Devicotah with only three days' provisions in hand and, after a series of errors in which the troops were only saved from destruction by mistakes made by the Tan j oreans, Cope was glad to make his way back to Fort St. David.

The English were by this time disillusioned about the influence of their protégé, but thought it necessary to wipe out the reproach of their failure by a second expedition, which was entrusted to Lawrence. This time success attended their efforts.

The details of this action are of little interest except that this was when Clive first met and impressed Lawrence. A breach was made and Clive volunteered to lead the storming party. The sepoys held back, and Clive's little party of Europeans was cut to pieces; Clive was almost the only one that escaped. Lawrence at once made a second assault at the head of his whole European force and Devicotah fell. The Tan j ore ruler was glad to make peace and Devicotah was ceded to the English.

The acquisition of Devicotah was not good for the Company. It was their first deliberate attempt at territorial gain without acting in self-defence. They ignored the Tan j ore prince whose help they used and Boscawen, on receiving news from Madras, returned to England.

Stringer Lawrence had become the acknowledged general in the field and was appointed by the Directors as Chief Commissioner to take over in Madras. Many of the survivors of the troops Boscawen had brought out with him entered the service of the Company. Eleven subalterns were transferred to the Company's service and were retained on the half-pay list when they returned to England. Among them were two officers, John Dalton and James Kilpatrick, who served in India with distinction. In a memoir, Captain Dalton, known as the Defender of Trichinopoly, wrote:

> In spite of peace having been established in Europe, the English and French in India were soon opposed to each other with rival claimants in contention for the thrones of the Deccan and the Carnatic. In March, 1750, Lawrence, with six hundred Europeans, joined the camp of Nazir Jung, the Soobadar of the Deccan, who was opposed by rival pretenders to the Soobahship and the Nawabship of the Carnatic, supported by a force of 2,000 French under d'Auteuil, the brother-in-law of Dupleix. It was the first time, since the establishment of peace, that English and French troops had been opposed to each other and d'Auteuil tried to

intimidate Lawrence by a bit of bluff. Sending him a flag of truce, d'Auteuil expressed his desire that no European blood should be shed and, as he did not know where the English were posted, he would not be to blame if any shot came in their direction. Lawrence replied that his post would be known by the English colours carried on his flag-gun; that he was just as averse to spilling European blood, but if shot came his way he would certainly respond. In order to try Lawrence's mettle, d'Auteuil fired a shot over the English camp. Lawrence at once answered it with three guns, "and saw they were well pointed." d'Auteuil, with a mutiny amongst his men, retreated that night, sacrificing his guns and gunners.

But Lawrence's relations with Nazir Jung were unsatisfactory and he shortly marched his troops to Madras where there were wide-ranging changes among the officials. Floyes, the governor, and Holt, the next senior, had been dismissed from the service and Saunders was summoned from Vizagapatam to take charge at Madras. For four months, Lawrence was made provisional governor at Fort St. David.

Before Saunders' arrival, Lawrence's relations with the provisional Government at Madras were strained. The old problem reappeared. Interference was permitted in military policy by civil officers whose real expertise was the management of the Company's commerce. In June, 1748, the power to convene a court martial had been given to Lawrence by the Directors, but the power of overriding him was vested in the Governor and Council.

In 1750, the Court of Directors sent orders for the withdrawal of Lawrence's powers, but it was found impracticable to do this. He was also dissatisfied by the failure of the Company to enforce discipline. He had no real authority over his men, and his pay was miserably small.

On the 25th September 1750, he resigned the Company's service, and sailed for England a month later. The Directors then acted with an alacrity that they had not previously shown. They packed Lawrence back to India before he had been two months in England with the title of Commander-in-Chief of all the Company's military forces in the East Indies, at a salary of £500 per annum, to which was added a yearly allowance of £250 in lieu of diet money, servants, horses, and all other privileges and perquisites. He was also commissioned to form a company of artillery at Fort St. George.

The most challenging part of Lawrence's career was about to begin. On the 14th March, 1752, Lawrence landed in Madras and assumed command of the army that was ready to march under Clive's control. A political committee of the Council was formed consisting of three members including Stringer Lawrence. Meanwhile during his absence the unofficial war between the English and French, acting for the rival claimants to the Nawabship of the Carnatic, had started, and Clive had gained prominence by his feats at Arcot and Covripauk. However, there was discontent among the officers who had not been paid the agreed allowances, and so troop discipline was poor.

Three days after landing, Lawrence, with 1,500 men, of whom 400 were Europeans, marched to relieve Trichinopoly, where Mahomed Ali, the English claimant to the Nawabship together with a small English force under Captains de Gingens and Dalton had been besieged for seven months by a French force under M. Law, (the French officer into whose hands Lawrence had fallen prisoner at Ariancopang) and a large native force under Chunda Sahib, the French protégé. Biddulph writes:

> In Trichinopoly there was a Mahratta force under Morari Rao, the chief of Gooti, in the pay of Mysore, and a contingent from Tan j ore, whose ruler had, for the time, cast in his lot with Mahomed Ali. On the 26th March, Lawrence arrived within twenty miles of Trichinopoly. Morari Rao was in secret correspondence with the French, unknown to

Lally at Pondicherry

Lawrence. Law and Chunda Sahib were encamped on the south bank of the Cauvery, about five miles east of Trichinopoly from where they were instructed to prevent Lawrence's force from reaching the garrison. Several useful positions were open to Law for opposing Lawrence at the various rivers Lawrence was obliged to cross before arriving within striking distance of the besieged town; but Law neglected all these opportunities and, instead of moving to meet Lawrence, he decided to hold the ground on which he stood. Ten miles from the allied camp, Law had occupied Coiladdy, where the Cauvery divides into several branches, with about six hundred men, where he had formed a battery commanding Lawrence's route at point blank range. Lawrence's march was directed along the strip of land between the two southern branches of the Cauvery, using the protection this provided. It was his intention to strike southwards across the southernmost branch, before engaging Coiladdy: but his guides misled him, and he suddenly found himself under the fire of the battery. Twenty Europeans were killed, and much confusion caused among the baggage before he could extricate himself. Continuing his march, without further interruption, Lawrence halted that night about ten miles from Trichinopoly. The next morning, 28th March, Lawrence resumed his march, having been joined in the night by a hundred Europeans and fifty dragoons from the garrison.

While he marched on the fortified rock of Elmiseram, another detachment from the garrison, under Captain Dalton, consisting of two hundred Europeans and four hundred Sepoys with four guns, arrived at the Sugarloaf Rock. Dalton continues his account:

> M.Law had drawn up his force, with his right resting on Elmiseram, and his left back against the Cauvery at Chucklipolliam. Lawrence's desire was to reach Trichinopoly without a fight so he marched southwards rounding Elmiseram where he was joined by Dalton. He halted to rest the troops who were suffering greatly from the heat, while Morari Rao and his Mahrattas from the city pretended to skirmish with the French. News was received that the whole French line, with their allies, were advancing so Lawrence pushed forward Clive with a small detachment of

Europeans and some guns, to take buildings that Law had not occupied, while he moved in support. A fierce cannonade of nine guns on the English side started against twenty-two on the French. The next day Lawrence sent Dalton with a small force against Elmiseram (an isolated rock with a fortified temple on the summit). A small party of grenadiers, attempting a night attack without orders, were beaten back, but the French surrendered on the following morning. Fifteen Frenchmen, thirty Sepoys, and two guns, one of them an 18-pounder, were captured. Two days afterwards, Dalton and the grenadiers captured another gun that Law had posted in a small building on the island, commanding the bathing place used by the principal leaders of Mahomed Ali's army. Dalton hid his men behind an old wall on the bank of the river and at noon, when the guards were asleep or engaged in cooking, the grenadiers forded the river and captured the gun before it could be fired twice. This gun was then brought across the river, under cover sent to cover their retreat.

IX
Lawrence and Clive foil the French, 1754

The success of these actions made a great impression. Until then, the operations of the English had been feeble with the exception of Clive's deeds at Arcot and Covripauk and the French had carried all before them. Now the French were forced on the defensive and the English were the attackers.

Morari Rao now stopped the treacherous correspondence he had been conducting with Chunda Sahib. But Law's position on the island was extremely strong owing to the watercourses with the huge stone temples that stood in walled enclosures. Law had only to keep communications open with Pondichery.

Lawrence now took Clive into his confidence by proposing to split the force, sending half north of the Cauvery to intercept Law's communications with Pondicherry. Hazardous as this was Clive at once agreed.

When the scheme was explained to Lawrence's native allies, they refused to have any part of it, unless Clive was given the detached command. This worried Lawrence, who had all along intended to give the command to Clive, but he did not wish officers senior to Clive to decline to serve under him, He need not have worried.

On the night of the 6th April, Clive, with four hundred Europeans, seven hundred sepoys, four thousand native horse, and eight guns, passed the Cauvery, and occupied Samiaveram, where they dug in. M.Law countered by sending troops to occupy Munserpet. Consequently, a detachment sent by Clive to dislodge them was beaten back with some loss.

But the enemy was weak and retired to Pitchandah. Clive followed up his advantage by capturing Lalgoodi, where Law had a large magazine of supplies. Meanwhile, Dupleix, alarmed at Law's retreat to Seringham, had collected all the men he could spare from Pondicherry, and sent them, under d'Auteuil, to reinforce Law. d'Auteuil reached Ootatoor, thirteen miles northeast of Samiaveram, on the I4th April, and sent messengers to Law advising him of his intention to reach the Cauvery by a night march.

One of his messengers was captured by Clive, who marched the same night to intercept him. d'Auteuil received news of Clive's march, and fell back on Ootatoor. Clive then also returned to Samiaveram. Clive's movement to intercept d'Auteuil was obvious to Law on the following day, but he did not see his return. Law then sent a small party of eighty Europeans, forty of whom were English deserters, and seven hundred sepoys to surprise Clive's camp at Samiaveram, while he was engaged with d'Auteuil.

They reached Clive's camp at midnight and. with the help of English deserters, passed themselves off on Clive's sepoys as a reinforcement from Lawrence. The story was believed and they were conducted through the camp, where, reaching Clive's quarters, they opened fire on the buildings in which Clive and his soldiers were asleep. There ensued five or six hours of confusion, in the course of which Clive had several narrow escapes. Twice he was alone in the midst of the enemy, mistaking them for his own men but his courage and presence of mind saved him. He was then shot at while parleying with the enemy, who were in the building in which he had been sleeping.The two men beside him were killed.

When daylight came the French became aware of the failure and surrendered. The French sepoys attempted to retreat but were cut down and slaughtered to the last man by Clive's Mahrattas. Had Law sent a larger and better commanded force, he might have been successful in cutting off Clive's whole detachment.

The leader of the deserters was Kelsey, who had been given a commission in the French Army by Dupleix. He was the man who had tried to assassinate Clive during the parley for surrender. Lawrence ordered him to be hanged.

This produced a strong complaint from Dupleix, who urged the Madras Council to send Lawrence to Europe to meet charges of bad faith.

Dupleix could now see that in Lawrence he had a formidable enemy. Law, who remained encamped at the western end of the island, now only retained the small post at Pitchandah, north of the Cauvery. At the eastern end of the island he had an important magazine at Coiladdy. d'Auteuil remained at Ootatoor.

It would have been sensible for the two French commanders to execute a pincer movement around Clive's detachment, while Lawrence was engaged south of the river. However, they were intent upon joining together on the island.

Lawrence sent his Tan j ore force to capture Coiladdy, which he did on the 26th April. The loss of the supplies stored there began to affect Law's force. The next move was made against d'Auteuil. Events had shown that it was important not to weaken the force at Samiaveram, so Lawrence sent Dalton across the river with 150 Europeans, 400 sepoys, 500 Mahratta horse and four guns to attack d'Auteuil. Dalton's account continues:

> On the evening of the l0th May, Dalton reached a point within two miles of Ootatoor. Before setting up camp he sent a party of Europeans and sepoys to dislodge the enemy from the small village to his front. Dalton's men succeeded but pushed beyond the village, without orders, and found themselves face to face with d'Auteuil's whole force. After a brief skirmish, in which they lost an officer they fell back to the village, and held it till Dalton came up. The sun had set, and Dalton worked on d'Auteuil's fears by a bold move in the failing light. Keeping his guns in front of the village, with a few men to give the appearance of strength, he sent his whole force of infantry, in two parties, to fall simultaneously on both flanks of d'Auteuil's force. d'Auteuil thought he had to do with the whole of Clive's force, and retreated precipitately to Ootatoor, followed closely by Dalton. Further conflict was prevented by d'Auteuil's cavalry, who having cut in on Dalton's rear were driven off by Dalton's Mahrattas. The same night, d'Auteuil evacuated Ootatoor, and fell back eighteen miles on Volcondah, abandoning a great quantity of ammunition and stores. Dalton's march towards Ootatoor had been seen from the island, but was taken to be part of Clive's force. Law now crossed the river to attack Samiaveram, and found himself confronted by Clive in a strong position. After some skirmishing, he recrossed the river to Seringham. Two days later, the river rose to prevent Dalton from rejoining Lawrence. Dalton placed his detachment at Clive's disposal, and offered his own services as a volunteer, to prevent any dispute arising from his rank. Lawrence,who had already made a lodgement on the island, now ordered Clive to attack Pitchandah. Clive's guns first broke up Law's camp, forcing him and his allies to take refuge about the Jumbakistna temple and Pitchandah fell after two days' bombardment. The siege of the island was now complete, every part of it being exposed to artillery fire. Lawrence then crossed over to the island at Chucklipolliam and dug a trench right across the island, east of the Jumbakistna temple, forcing

Law and Chunda Sahib to meet him at the Seringham temple. Heavy guns were brought up from Devicotah.

The force of Europeans with Lawrence on the island were only half the number Law had at his disposal, so a direct attack was impossible even if only because the frequent rising of the river made it very difficult for Clive to provide support.

While he waited for guns from Devicotah, Lawrence sent Clive in search of d'Auteuil. On the 12th May Clive found d'Auteuil a few miles south of Volcondah. The English sepoys, had outmarched the Europeans and were now so full of spirit that they attacked and drove d'Auteuil into the town. The Europeans assaulted the gateway and, before morning, on the 29th May, d'Auteuil had surrendered with his whole force, consisting of 100 Europeans, 400 sepoys, 340 horse, three guns and a great quantity of stores, including 800 barrels of powder and 3,000 muskets.

Chunda Sahib's people, seeing which way the battle was going and being short of provisions, started to leave him. In despair, he entered into negotiations with the Tan j ore General for a free passage but was instead made prisoner. On the 3rd June, Law surrendered, with 35 officers, 785 Europeans, of whom 60 were sick or wounded, 2,000 sepoys and 45 pieces of artillery. Chunda Sahib was put to death by the Tan j ore General on the very same day. All this happened without a pitched battle.

A notable feature in the campaign was the fine military spirit developed among the sepoys under Clive at Arcot. Orme says:

> It is indeed difficult to determine whether the English conducted themselves with more ability and spirit, or the French with more irresolution and ignorance, after Major Lawrence and Captain Clive arrived at Trichinopoly.

Dupleix, whom Mills styles:

> the most audacious contemner of truth that ever engaged in crooked politics.

accused Lawrence of having ordered Chunda Sahib's death ; and Dupleix's friends accused Lawrence that he could have saved him if he had wished.

The truth was that Lawrence was in no position to dictate to his native allies because the English were only auxiliary to the war and their views had no weight except in the actual fighting. Mahomed Ali, the Tan j oreans, the Mysoreans and the Mahrattas, all wished to capture Chunda Sahib to further their own political purposes and so were against allowing any of the others to take him prisoner.

Lawrence had offered to settle the dispute by taking charge of the prisoner, but the confederates agreed that he should not be kept by the English. Wilks states that Chunda Sahib was put to death at the instigation of Mahomed Ali because his death was the only solution that would prevent a quarrel among the allies. Not a scrap of evidence has ever been shown that Lawrence was aware of the proposal until afterwards. It was on Law's advice that Chunda Sahib chose to run any risk rather than surrender himself to the English. The accusation comes with bad grace from Dupleix, in view of the fact that he wished to imprison Chunda Sahib for life and at that very time held a firman, secretly obtained from the Nizam, setting aside Chunda Sahib, and placing the Nawabship in the hands of the French.

Law's conduct in retreating to Seringham has been the criticised, but Lawrence considered it the correct step at the time. Its effect on Law's native allies was certainly strong but Law was to blame for not opposing Lawrence's march to Trichinopoly.

This episode was a real shock to the French and Dupleix changed his plans. The arrival of the annual fleet from France brought reinforcements and by intrigue he sewed dissension between Mahomed Ali and his native allies. He claimed the right to act in the name of the Emperor of Delhi in proclaiming Reza Sahib, Chunda Sahib's son, Nawab of the Carnatic.

Two months after Law's surrender, the French inflicted a defeat on an English force. The Madras Council, elated by their recent success resolved to take Gingee, an exceptionally strong fortress held by the French, about forty miles from Pondichery and seventy-five from Madras.

Lawrence, who was at Fort St.David, set out for Madras to try to dissuade Mr. Saunders from the undertaking, because of the fortifications, the difficulty of sending supplies to the besieging force, the necessity of settling affairs at Trichinopoly and the inadequacy of the English forces. All such arguments were ignored. On July 26th, Major Kinneer, an officer new to the country, arrived before Gingee with 200 Europeans and 2,000 of the Nawab's troops. Dupleix sent an equal force from Pondichery, under his nephew, M. de Kerjean. Kinneer marched to meet de Kerjean, who waited at Vicravandi, twenty miles southeast of Gingee, with the river to his front.

The English guns, commanded by a French deserter, were badly handled and their attack repulsed. Kinneer was wounded, and many officers and men killed but Kinneer managed to bring out the rest of his men to Fort St. David. The expedition had no chance of success and soon Kinneer died of illness brought on by disappointment.

M. de Kerjean was then sent by Dupleix, with every available man, to blockade Fort St. David. His force amounted to 450 European Infantry, 1,500 sepoys, fourteen guns, and 500 native horse. Among the arrivals from Europe, 200 Swiss troops in English pay had reached Madras. Half of them were despatched in open boats to Fort St. David. Lawrence strongly urged that the men should not be sent in open boats but the Council overruled him. It was part of the unwritten code that governed the acts of the two Companies that while their nations were at peace there should be no hostilities at sea. But Dupleix, though he might have hesitated to attack a ship, was ready to snap up defenceless troops in open boats. As the Swiss passed Pondichery, he intercepted them and took them prisoner.

Lawrence, who was ill at the time, embarked with the rest of the Swiss for Fort St. David. His force consisted of 400 Europeans, 1,700 sepoys, and eight or nine field guns, together with three or four thousand representing the Nawab's troops. de Kerjean, finding he was about to be attacked, broke up his camp and retreated to Bahoor, followed by Lawrence. The next day, the French force moved back to the boundary hedge marking the limits of Pondicherry.

According to war rules of the time, Lawrence was prevented from following into French territory and instead attacked those French outposts that were outside the boundary hedge in the hope of bringing them to battle. Seeing that de Kerjean had no intention of leaving his position under the walls of Pondicherry, Lawrence decided to lure him out. Feigning he could not advance, he returned to Bahoor. De Kerjean allowed himself to be coerced by Dupleix into following Lawrence and set up camp two miles from Bahoor.

Before daylight, on the 26th August, Lawrence moved in to attack. The force was led by sepoys and, unusually, the European battalion was kept in reserve. In every action the decisive blows were always struck by European troops so it was essential to know how the French battalion was disposed before the English became too engaged. The English sepoys then opened fire whilst the Europeans continued their advance with shouldered arms. As daylight came, the French battalion was seen with their right resting on a high bank, and their left covered by a stretch of water. The English battalion formed up opposite, and advanced under a heavy fire of cannon and small arms. The records of war show that one line or the other usually gives way. In this skirmish the French withstood the shock, and the two lines crossed bayonets without flinching.

After a few minutes of hand to hand fighting the English grenadier company and the two platoons next to them broke through the French centre. At this the whole French line gave way and fled. The Nawab's cavalry, instead of pursuing, galloped off to plunder the French camp, so that the French were allowed to escape. However, de Kerjean with 15 officers and 100 Frenchmen were taken prisoner, and a great number killed; maybe 100 by the bayonet. Eight guns, with all the French ammunition and stores, were captured. Of the English battalions 4 officers and 78 men were killed and wounded, mostly by the bayonet, so close was the fighting. In his gratitude to the English, Mahomed Ali remitted the ground rent of twelve hundred pagodas a year hitherto paid for Fort St. George and thereafter the East India Company held the fort free of charge.

Lawrence was now reduced to inaction by the difficult attitude of the Mysore Durbar and the Mahrattas still under the influence of Dupleix's intrigues. As a result Lawrence was engaged in little fighting and much marching, during which the Mahrattas plundered friend and foe impartially, until sickness among his troops forced him to return to Cuddalore.

The Directors in London were not aware of what was going on in the South of India when they sent instructions to Lawrence to proceed to Calcutta, to advise about the fortification. Lawrence was too busy to go and continued his service on the Coromandel coast.

Once again Lawrence sought to relinquish his command. There was discontent among the troops who remained unpaid and suffered low morale. He complained that he was not allowed to make use of the powers conferred on him by the Directors. For example the Governor sent him orders for military movements without informing him of his plans or listening to his opinion and made appointments and promotions among the troops without consulting him.

In November Lawrence formally relinquished command, but was persuaded to resume it after an interval of only three weeks.

Stringer Lawrence as pictured in the Hereford Times

X
The siege of Trichinopoly, 1753

In January, Stringer Lawrence was again engaged, in the neighbourhood of Cuddalore, against the French now under M. Maissin, with their allies the Mahrattas, who had declared themselves against Mahomed Ali and the English. On 8th January, he took three guns from the Mahrattas. The French were dug in before Lawrence's camp at Trivadi, in an unassailable position and all his efforts to force an engagement were unsuccessful. For four months the two armies were in sight of each other and a number of skirmishes took place between the English and the Mahrattas, in which a lack of cavalry placed Lawrence at a disadvantage.

The Mahrattas showed energy, but the French troops were kept in reserve probably discouraged by recent reverses. It was Dupleix's tactic to hold Lawrence on the coast while his plan was working at Trichinopoly. On the 1st April, while protecting a convoy from Fort St. David, Lawrence was attacked by a large Mahratta force supported by a French battalion.

Stringer Lawrence quickly accepted the challenge, and a brisk engagement ensued, during which the Mahratta leader, Morari Rao's brother, was killed, and the French battalion retreated. Having his convoy to protect meant that Lawrence was unable to follow up his advantage. Two days later, he bombarded the French camp, but without success. Lawrence was relieved from his dilemma by urgent news from Trichinopoly, which caused him to move his operations there.

Mahomed Ali's affairs in Trichinopoly had been going very badly following Law's surrender. To secure the Mysore alliance Ali had engaged by treaty to surrender Trichinopoly to the Mysore Durbar, without the knowledge of the English, and without any intention of making good his promise to them. The Tan j ore chief had withdrawn, tired of the contest and Ali, without money or supplies, found support only from Dalton, who had been left at Trichinopoly with 200 Europeans and 1,500 sepoys following Law's surrender.

Before commencing open hostilities, the Mysore leader tried to dispose of Dalton but the plot to assassinate him and efforts to seduce his sepoys had no success. Two emissaries, with the Mysore regent's papers in their possession, were captured by a native officer and blown from guns. An attempt was made to recruit Poverio, a Neapolitan in the Nawab's service, but Poverio betrayed the plot. The Mysore Regent immediately put a price on Poverio's head.

Lawrence was kept informed and proposed that Dalton should seize the Mysore Regent and Morari Rao, by surprise, but the Madras Council disapproved of his idea. Mill remarks that the Council should have followed Lawrence's advice both in this and in surrendering Trichinopoly to Mysore, according to the original agreement with Mahomed Ali.

> Delicacy would have been less violated in one instance, by following the advice of Lawrence, and prudence would have been more consulted by following it in both.

It was at this juncture that Morari Rao, the Mahratta leader, who wanted Trichinopoly for himself and who had thrown in his lot with Dupleix, joined Mahomed Ali's enemies. Dalton explains:

> Now the Mysoreans began to intercept the entry of provisions into Trichinopoly and open hostilities started. Permission was sent from Madras to treat the Mysoreans as enemies. The Mysore army camped on the island of Seringham, the scene of Law's surrender. Dalton resolved toattack their camp and at 10 o'clock at night on the 23rd December, 1752, he crossed the river, and attacked the Mysore camp. The action was completely successful, and Dalton returned to the city after killing a great number of the enemy, with only twenty killed and wounded.

From then on Trichinopoly was closely invested by the Mysore general, who with 8,000 men, camped at Fakeer's Tope, south of the city. Dalton forced him to retire and return to Seringham. Provisions were running short, and Dalton was obliged to ask Lawrence for assistance. Lawrence had been anxious about the safety of Trichinopoly, but still the Council took no action. On the 11th April Lawrence wrote :

> If Captain Dalton is to be reinforced, and his situation seems to cry aloud for it, 'tis time to determine something, for the rising of the rivers (and

> that season is approaching) will put it out of our power to assist him.

News from Trichinopoly reached Lawrence at Trivadi, near Cuddalore, at 10 o'clock at night. On the 20th April, leaving 650 men at Trivadi, 150 of whom were Europeans, he marched, at six hours notice, to Fort St. David to collect supplies. Renewing the march next day, he entered Trichinopoly on the 6th May, just seventeen days after Dalton's message.

Sickness and desertion on the march had considerably reduced the number of Lawrence's Europeans, 100 of whom were unfit for duty and were carried into hospital on arrival. His force, including the original garrison, consisted only of 500 Europeans, 2,000 sepoys, and 3,000 of the Nawab's horse and artillery of 10 field guns and two eighteen-pounders.

In taking this decision to march to Dalton's aid, Lawrence acted without permission of the Madras Council. It is evident that the long forced stay near Cuddalore was against his wishes. This brought the dispute between Saunders and himself to the fore. The bickerings between them had not ceased, and Saunders had gone so far as to accuse Lawrence of neglecting the Company's interests.

This time the Council not only approved his march, but also disclosed their policy as he had so often requested. From this time on there was agreement between Lawrence and the Governor.

Directly Lawrence's withdrawal from Trivadi was known to Dupleix and without waiting for intelligence reports, he despatched M.Astruc with 200 Europeans, 500 sepoys, and 4 guns to Trichinopoly. Dupleix's plans now depended on winning at Trichinopoly.

Biddulph writes:

> The day after Lawrence's arrival at Trichinopoly, Astruc, a general of considerable ability, joined the Mysoreans in Seringham and assumed command of the whole force. With such a numerical superiority his success seemed assured. The country in the neighbourhood of Trichinopoly was particularly favourable to M.Astruc. North of the city the Cauvery River divides into two branches to form the island of Seringham, an area capable of holding his whole force. South of the city, at a distance of between two and four miles, are the strong semi-circular

positions known as Elmiseram, French Rocks, Sugarloaf Rock, Golden Rock, Fakeer's Tope, Five Rocks and Weycondah which together make up favourable positions for attacking Trinchinopoly. For thirty years Trichinopoly had been the objective of various armies in Southern India. Few places have been the scene of such continuous fighting as the country for ten miles round Trichinopoly from 1732 to 1760.
Lawrence was now poorly supplied. His best chance lay in active defence, and in being able to win over the Tan j ore Chief, who was still neutral. He was also at a disadvantage through lack of cavalry. The Nawab's 3,000 horse were unable to face the Mysore and Mahratta cavalry led by Hyder Ali and Morari Rao.

Giving his troops three days' rest, he set out to dislodge the French and Mysoreans from Seringham. The engagement was mainly an artillery one. First a charge of Rajpoot cavalry was repelled by the English sepoys but Lawrence was forced back to camp after the troops had been on standby for twenty hours whilst having suffered only a very slight loss. The result of the day's operations had been to show that in Astruc he had an able enemy. Lawrence abandoned the idea of dislodging the enemy from Seringham, and concentrated upon obtaining supplies.For the purpose, he moved to Fakeer's Tope, two and a half miles from the city to prevent being encircled, and sent parties of sepoys to secure provisions. He remained in htis position for five weeks, without being able to bring the French to battle, or to receive more than provisions sufficient for daily consumption. He had become dependent upon Chief of Poodoocottah, who was friendly to Mahomed Ali and whose territory extended to within a few miles of Trichinopoly known by his family title of Tondiman.
Meanwhile, affairs were going badly for the English in other parts of the Carnatic. Trivadi, where the garrison was captured by the French and the defeat at Arcot were bad enough but every chieftain or soldier of fortune had set up his standard and was ravaging territories that were still allied to Mahomed Ali. Dupleix, whose battle plan was centred on Trichinopoly and importantly on the capture of Mahomed Ali, discouraged the

Mahrattas from joining in and instead prevailed on them to join Astruc, to whom he sent 300 hundred more Europeans and 1,000 sepoys.

On receipt of these reinforcements, Astruc left Seringham, crossed the Cauvery, and camped on the plain to the west of the city near Weycondah. His force consisted of 450 Europeans, 1,500 well-trained sepoys, 11,500 Mysore and Mahratta horse, two companies of Topasses (Portuguese native Christians), and 1,200 sepoys in the Mysore service and 15,000 badly armed, undisciplined footmen, more used to plundering than fighting.

Lawrence had at his disposal 500 Europeans, 2,000 sepoys, of whom 700 were engaged in collecting and sending in supplies, and 100 of the Nawab's horse. Lawrence's lack of cavalry was made worse by Mysore and Mahratta horsemen led by two first-rate leaders - the Mysore cavalry under Hyder Ali, and the Mahrattas under Morari Rao.

Two miles south-west of the Fakeer's Tope were the Five Rocks hills where Lawrence maintained a sepoy guard to keep the route open for supplies. By this time Lawrence was ill and had gone into the city to recover. Astruc, finding the Rocks undefended, advanced during the night and bombarded the English camp. Lawrence, under pressure, held the position during the day and then that night withdrew his camp behind a hill closer to the city.

Astruc brought his whole force to the Five Rocks, cutting off Lawrence from the Tondiman's country, and from his detachment of 700 sepoys. Lawrence's position was now perilous. The enemy's position and numbers made it impossible for him to order an attack. Astruc was determined to run no risk and it seemed that Lawrence, who was short of supplies, must surrender. Half a mile from Lawrence's camp and nearly a mile from Astruc's was the Golden Rock, where Lawrence maintained a guard of 200 sepoys. Astruc saw that if he could gain this post he would force Lawrence into the city so he could continue the siege.

At daybreak, on the 26th June, he attacked with a mixed force of Europeans and sepoys and, in spite of gallant resistance on the part of the defenders, overwhelmed them, killing or taking prisoners before Lawrence could assist. The French battalion formed up behind the rock, with the French guns posted at the base and opened fire. The whole Mysore army was drawn up a gunshot distance to the rear, while the Mahrattas dashed about in small detachments, threatening the flanks and rear of the small English force.

Lawrence's position was by now even more desperate. A number of his sepoys were in the city to buy rice and 200 of them had been killed. After providing for the safety of his camp, he could only muster 300 European infantry, 80 artillerymen, and 500 sepoys. With this force he advanced to within a short distance of the Golden Rock before the outpost was overwhelmed. Retreat meant probable defeat but it would be sheer madness to attack such a strong position. As usual Lawrence chose the brave option. Among his excellent qualities was the power to inspire confidence in a few words as he explained the situation. His officers agreed with his plan while the men expressed delight for "a knock at the Frenchmen" who had been so long out of their reach. Ordering the grenadier company to assault the rock, Lawrence moved with the rest of his little force round the base, to attack the French battalion head on.

Scrambling up the rock, with fixed bayonets holding fire but cheering as they moved, they hit the French defenders so hard that they fled headlong down the reverse side of the Rock. The French defenders did not see the attack and had wheeled to meet Lawrence. In this way they exposed their right flank to the fire of the English grenadiers who were now in posisiton on the rock. Lawrence drew up his force at twenty yards from the French line. In spite of M. Astruc's efforts, his men were astounded to be attacked by an enemy that seemed beaten just moments before. Under musket cover they quickly retreated. A bayonet charge converted this into panic and they fled leaving three guns in Lawrence's hands. The Mahrattas tried to retaliate and though some of the grenadiers fell under their sabres they were soon forced to withdraw with heavy losses.

Morari Rao's nephew was killed in the action. He had cut down one of the grenadiers but the man's comrade who was loading his musket, fired his ramrod through his body. After the action Lawrence sent the body back to the Mahrattas in his own palanquin. The French fell back to the Mysore lines and kept up an ineffective cannonade. For three hours Lawrence remained at the foot of the rock, expecting an attack. He formed the hollow square, with captured guns and about seventy prisoners in the centre, and deliberately marched back towards his camp. When he was hardly hardly clear of the rock, the whole of the enemy's cavalry, of upwards of 10,000 in number, charged furiously.

Of course this was a well-tried tactic. Several times the Mahrattas had succeeded in overwhelming detachments of infantry by dashing in after first drawing their fire. But the English battalion and sepoys stood firm and not a shot was fired. The square halted and the guns poured grape shot into the massed Mahrattas until they broke ranks and left in complete disorder. The small band of heroes marched back to camp with the spoils of victory.

No braver feat of arms was ever performed. The first result of the victory produced dissension between the French and their allies. Astruc handed his command to M. Brenier, and returned to Pondicherry. Lawrence obtained fifty days' provisions and leaving Dalton with a small garrison, marched towards Tan j ore, thirty miles distant. His object was to induce the Tan j orean Chief to supply cavalry, and to meet reinforcements on its way from the coast.

Meanwhile Brenier closely invested the City and had he decided to act decisively might have taken it. But Dalton's vigilance, together with occasional sorties, prevented such an attempt.

Lawrence had won over the Tan j ore Chief, who provided 3,000 horse and 2,000 matchlock men with reinforcements of 170 Europeans and 300 sepoys from Fort St. David and he then marched to within ten miles of Trichinopoly. However, Brenier was determined to intercept him and occupied strong positions south of the City from Weycondah to Elmiseram and the Golden and Sugarloaf rocks, about half a mile apart, were strongly held by the French infantry supported by guns.

On the 8th August, Lawrence resumed his advance. Though encumbered by thousands of bullocks he still had the huge advantage of knowing the disposition of Brenier's forces as provided by Dalton. The key obviously was the French control of the Golden Rock so Lawrence formed up as if he intended to attack the Sugarloaf Rock. Brenier fell for the trap, and left the Golden Rock to strengthen the threatened position. Lawrence detached his grenadier company, with 800 sepoys, to seize the Golden Rock - a movement not seen by the French commander until too late to prevent it. This was Lawrence's great skill as a military commander in the field. Time and again he demonstrated that a careful appraisal of the enemy strength supported by intimate knowledge of the geography could be used to mislead the opposition. His mastery of the tactic of offering battle in one direction followed by a real thrust in another was what made Stringer Lawrence such a difficult enemy.

Brenier dispatched 300 Europeans to strengthen the small party he had left at the Golden Rock and a thousand cavalry to attack the English infantry on the way. But the grenadiers kept up a rolling fire on the horsemen and, reaching the Golden Rock, drove the enemy down and raised their colours at the top before the infantry detached by Brenier could engage them. Instead of making an effort to recover the position, they then occupied the high ground between the two rocks, and opened a withering fire with four guns on the Golden Rock positions. Brenier, instead of moving his main body to support his detachment as perhaaps he should have done, remained near the Sugarloaf, while Lawrence moved his whole force to the Rock itself.

An artillery duel ensued in which the English battalion suffered losses. This was the signal for Dalton to leave the City with two field guns and a detachment to attack the rear of the enemy's cavalry, who quickly broke up and galloped off. Seeing Brenier's main body still stationary, Lawrence sent the grenadier company and 200 Europeans with 300 sepoys to harry the French detachment. The officer instructed to attack sent back word that he could not proceed without cannon so Lawrence galloped up, dismissed the officer and and took command himself. They were received with a heavy fire, which killed Captain Kirk of the Grenadiers. Captain Kilpatrick then took command of the grenadiers, asking them, if they loved their Captain, to follow him and avenge his death.

> Actions on the spot have generally a very great effect, when delivered from a person whose spirit and courage is known.They roused in an instant and swore they would follow him to hell, and avenge Kirk's death.

as Lawrence afterwards wrote, describing the affair. The French broke and ran off to Weycondah, overcome by Dalton's guns, leaving three field pieces in Lawrence's hands.

Brenier, although it was now much too late, moved up his main body. Seeing Lawrence's whole force advancing, his men lost heart and, without waiting to exchange shots, ran to the shelter of the Five Rocks, exposed as they went to fire from English guns at the Golden Rock. Sadly. the Tan j ore horse, who might have destroyed them, refused to pursue and so the battle ended.

Lawrence marched back into the city with his convoy and the captured guns. Of the French, about one hundred Europeans were killed and wounded and of the English, about forty killed, principally by artillery fire.

In the course of the action Lawrence's palanquin bearers had strayed out of line and were snapped up by the Mahrattas. Lawrence sent to recover it, but the French had already sent it to Pondichery, where Dupleix had it paraded through the streets as proof of Lawrence's defeat and death.

During Lawrence's absence from the city Dalton had been closely blockaded in Trichinopoly. There a French officer, feigning himself to be a deserter, gained access to the town, in order to communicate the weak places of the defence to Brenier and to provoke an outbreak of the French prisoners. He was detected, and hanged after Lawrence's return.

A fortnight later, Lawrence moved against Weycondah, where Brenier had concentrated his force and built fortifications. The French abandoned the position without resistance, and camped at Mootachellinoor on the Cauvery, leaving a gun and some equipment in Lawrence's hands. Here Brenier was joined by a strong reinforcement under Astruc, consisting of 400 Europeans, 2,000 sepoys, six guns, and 3,000 Mahratta cavalry, together with a great number of irregular infantry. The English were again as much outnumbered as they had been at any time during the war. Astruc again assumed command. and the French prepared to attack. Reoccupying the original positions of the Five Rocks and the Golden and Sugarloaf Rocks, they dug in and restarted a blockade. This was a mistake because the tactic did not make use of his great superiority of force. Lawrence quickly responded by moving into the open plain, south-east of the French Rock, to assist the convoys coming from Tan j ore, while he awaited reinforcements

> For eighteen days the two armies faced each other, about 2 miles apart on the open plain, without so much as a bush between them. Each side could plainly see what was going on in the other camp. The difference in morale between the two armies is illustrated by the fact that the English were camped on the open plain, while the superior numbers of French had their front covered by trenches.

On the night of the 18th September, Lawrence seized a hillock between the camps, brought an 18-pounder out of the city, and opened fire on the French camp who promptly detached a party against the gun. A fire fight ensued, under cover of which the expected reinforcements, consisting of 237 Europeans and 300 sepoys, under Captain Ridge, joined Lawrence. With Ridge also came Captain Caillaud, who was destined to succeed Lawrence, and who was to outwit d'Auteuil on this same ground four years later. Having nothing to gain by further delay, Lawrence took the offensive. His troops were in high spirits, but with three days' provisions only quick and decisive action was required.

Leaving his tents in the city, he drew up his little army at the Fakeer's Tope at daybreak on the 20th and offered battle. M. Astruc did not accept the challenge so Lawrence sent for his tents, and pitched camp. Lawerence writes:

> All the while the cannonade from the 18 pounder was maintained that they might think we had no other view than that of disturbing them in their camp with our shot. This lulled them into a security.

After dark, the tents were sent into the city and preparations made to attack. Lawrence's force consisted of 600 European infantry, in three divisions, 100 European artillerymen with 6 guns, 2,000 sepoys, and the Tan j orean cavalry and matchlockmen. At four in the morning of the 21st September, the army started, marching in three divisions in column, guns to either flank and sepoys following in two lines in rear of the guns with the Tan j ore cavalry bringing up the rear.

The object of first attack was the Golden Rock on which Astruc had posted 100 Europeans, 600 sepoys and two guns, with two companies of Topasses. It was a bright moonlight night, but clouds hid the moon as the force moved out so that they arrived within pistol shot of the rock before they were discovered. They poured in a volley as they rushed to the assault with such spirit that the enemy fled without even waiting even to fire their two cannon which were ready loaded with grape shot. Without waiting longer than was necessary to disable the guns, the force advanced again, the Europeans in line, with the sepoys on either flank.

The French trench was in front of their camp, but the adjoining native camp was open to attack. Lawrence's plan was to penetrate the native camp to turn the flank while the Tan j ore horse with some matchlockmen moved against the French front threatening to attack. With drums beating, portfires lighted, and the sepoys' native instruments at full blast, the British force advanced with loud cheers into the Mysore camp, spreading panic. Nine French guns were brought into action but in the dark all they did was harm to their native allies. The sepoys kept up continuous fire and the Europeans marched in with fixed bayonets and shouldered arms.

As day was breaking, the Mysore camp was cleared and the French battalion was seen drawn up in line with a large body of sepoys on their left flank, while another large body, directed to cover their right flank was posted on the Sugarloaf Rock. Reforming as they advanced and reserving fire, the English infantry were received with a volley at twenty paces, which caused some loss. Captain Kilpatrick, leading the grenadiers on the right of the European battalion, was seriously wounded. The result was that the French sepoys on the left broke and fled under the fire of the English sepoys. Caillaud, who had taken Kilpatrick's place, seized the opportunity and wheeled up the right division of the European battalion to attack the uncovered left flank of the French battalion. They poured in heavy fire and followed with the bayonet, rolling them up at the centre. Then the remainder of the English battalion attacked from the front.

The French retreated in disorder despite Astruc doing his best to rally them. The English grenadiers were there again before they could reform so that the whole French force dissolved and ran off in disorder.

The overthrow of the French battalion was completed in ten minutes. The English sepoys on the left, who had taken no part in the action so far, pushed on to the Sugarloaf Rock, which they carried defeating and dispersing the French sepoys posted there. The whole affair scarcely lasted two hours.

Seeing the defeat of the French, their native allies dispersed in flight. The whole plain was covered with the retreating enemy, who were estimated at 30,000 footmen and 16,000 horse. In wild confusion the great mass of fugitives mingled with elephants, camels and bullocks, fled as best they could towards Mootachellinoor, not stopping till they had crossed the Cauvery to the island of Seringham,

The Tan j ore horse then amused themselves with plundering the French camp as was their wont. M. Astruc, with nine officers, and 100 Frenchmen, eleven pieces of cannon and all the tents, equipment and ammunition of the French camp, remained in Lawrence's hands. Dalton says:

Dalton took twenty-one French prisoners and sixty-five more were found straggling in Tan j ore territory. A number were knocked on the head by the country people, as they wandered in the woods. 200 of them were killed or wounded in the engagement and the Mahratta horse alone saved the French European infantry from total destruction. A thousand of the French native allies were killed and wounded. Of the English, six officers and seventy men were killed or wounded, among the latter being Lawrence himself. Kilpatrick, in spite of being shot through the body and receiving several sabre wounds from Mahratta horsemen as he lay on the ground, survived to fight again.The action was decided entirely by the infantry and the English guns were never engaged, while the French guns were so badly served that they onlyinflicted damage on their own allies.

Lawrence followed up his victory by laying siege to Weycondah, that sameevening. Early on the 23rd, before the breach was ready for assault, the English sepoys, seeing some of the garrison escaping, broke away from their officers and tried to attack. Finding this impracticable, they made for the gateway. A sergeant of sepoys, "a resolute Englishman," whose name is not remembered, clambered up and planted the colours of his company on the parapet. He was quickly joined by some of his men, the gate was opened, and those outside rushed in with such fury, with the bayonet, that the garrison flung down their arms and surrendered.

Then Lawrence, after sweeping a large quantity of supplies into the city, where he left a small garrison, marched for Tan j ore, where his presence was needed to counteract the intrigues of Dupleix.

XI
Renewed French Assault on Trichinopoly, 1753

In November 1753, a French reinforcement of 300 Europeans and 1,200 Sepoys, under M. Maissin reached Seringham. Their arrival was kept secret, to put the Trichinopoly garrison off their guard. Then at three o'clock in the morning of the 28th November a determined attempt was made to surprise Trichinopoly. A select body of 600 Frenchmen, led by an English deserter, crossed the ditch, and seized a detached battery without alarming the main garrison. To succeed thay had only to blow in a small side gate.

Elated by their success, the French disobeyed orders, and commenced firing. The alarm was given to Kilpatrick, who was in command but who was still confined to his bed with wounds. His orders to his subaltern, Lieutenant Harrison, were coolly obeyed.

Lawrence writes;

> The picquet and reserve hastened to the rampart and opened fire. By great good fortune, the guide and both powder bearers were killed and the French, stuck between the outer and inner walls, were unable to advance or retreat and were exposed to a merciless fire as soon as daylight permitted. They were glad to surrender. A number attempted to leap into the ditch when they found the attack had failed. Few escaped without serious injury but some were carried off by their friends who had remained outside. Eight officers and 364 men were taken prisoner, one officer and twenty four men killed, and a number wounded.

Thus "French petulance" as Lawrence called it, saved Trichinopoly from the greatest risk during the war. The acute phase of the struggle was at an end. Lawrence could defeat the French, but he could not drive them away, backed up as they were by some of the best cavalry in Southern India.

Dupleix was now at the end of his resources and attempted to come to an arrangement with the English, hoping to win by diplomacy what he had failed to win by force. In January, 1754, commissioners from both sides met at the

Dutch settlement at Madras but their views were found to be irreconcilable. On the English side the commissioners laid down a basis of negotiation that Mahomed Ali should be recognised as Nawab of the Carnatic and that the Tan j ore Chief should be guaranteed the peaceable possession of his kingdom. The French terms were based on the recognition of Salabut Jung as Soobadar of the Deccan, and the rejection of the claims of Mahomed Ali. They also produced Sunnuds from Salabut Jung, appointing Dupleix commander in all the countries south of the River Kistna, and granting him Arcot and Trichinopoly. This was supported a Firman from Delhi confirming the grants made by Salabut Jung. The English held this document to be a forgery, as it probably was.

Apart from the Moghul Firman, which, after all, had only academic value, the position of the English in Southern India would have become untenable had they agreed to the French demands. The conference was broken up eleven days after it began.

Negotiations by the Mysore Regent were now opened with the English for the possession of Trichinopoly. The Madras Council wished Lawrence to conduct the negotiations but he excused himself on the plea of poor health though in reality it was because he disapproved of the conditions. He held the opinion that Mahomed Ali should be forced to observe his promise to deliver Trichinopoly to Mysore, and he did not cease to express his regret that the attempt had been made to keep Trichinopoly after promising to cede it.

The Madras Council held a different opinion. They now made the absurd proposal that Trichinopoly should be held by the English till the other articles of the proposed treaty with Mysore were carried out and that a certain proportion of Mysore troops should be introduced into the garrison. Lawrence bluntly wrote to them :

> Give me leave to tell you the proposal is absurd and impracticable.

The negotiation, after dragging on for a long time, came to nothing. While this was happening Lawrence was camped at Trichinopoly, confronting the French Force in Seringham, now under M. de Mainville. The country for a great distance round had been denuded of supplies of every kind by the warfare of the two previous years and Lawrence was now dependent for provisions on Tan j ore. These were usually brought in by the Tan j ore merchants to

Tricatopoly, eighteen miles east of Trichinopoly, from where they were escorted in by detachments from Lawrence's camp. This duty was one of great fatigue and risk to Lawrence's small force which was saddled with a number of French prisoners. There were sufficient English troops to spare to strengthen his force but the Council chose to keep them on the coast.

In the middle of February 7th a more important convoy than usual was on its way from Tricatopoly. Lawrence had sent out a detachment of 230 Europeans, about 500 sepoys and 4 guns, under Captain Grenville, to bring it in. Grenville had orders to keep his force together and, if attacked, to take up a position and defend himself until Lawrence could come to his aid. De Mainville had intelligence of this convoy and detached 400 Europeans, 6,000 sepoys and 7 guns with 8,000 Mahratta horse to intercept it.

On the morning of the 15th February 1754 Grenville had reached a point between Elmiseram and the river when he was attacked. Disregarding his orders, he had distributed his men on both sides of the convoy along its whole length. On seeing the enemy, he made no attempt to get his men together or to take up a position, and the whole detachment was overwhelmed by the Mahrattas, almost without striking a blow. The French troops only came up in time to save the lives of some of them. Men, guns, supplies and money were lost, and Grenville paid for his error with his life. Lawrence also lost that splendid company of grenadiers that he had formed with such care and often led to victory. Of the 230 Europeans lost, 138 were prisoners, only thirty-eight of them being taken unwounded. Of the eight officers present, four were killed and three wounded.

This disaster worried Lawrence enormously. He was no longer able to send parties to bring in convoys from Tan j ore, and was obliged to depend on the Tondiman's country for supplies. He was oppressed by serious illness and concerned about success because of the insufficient means at his disposal.

To protect the convoys he was reliant upon a gallant native soldier, Mahomed Yusuf, of Nellore who had entered the Company's service under Clive, at the beginning of 1751, at the head of a small body of his own men. Lawrence describes him as

> An excellent partisan brave and resolute, but cool and wary in action. He was never sparing of himself. A born soldier and better of his colour I

never saw in the country. He always prevents my asking, by offering himself for everything, and executes what he goes about as well and as briskly as he attempts it.

On Lawrence's recommendation Yusuf was granted a commission as commandant of all the sepoys in the Company's service. Lawrence's communications with native authorities were conducted through an interpreter, a Brahmin named Poniapa, whose position made him privvy to important secrets. Poniapa entered into a secret correspondence with the Mysore Regent with the intention of being asked by Lawrence to negotiate a termination of the war. This Lawrence did with the result he provided a plausible report though having secretly agreed with the Regent to betray the English. He also revealed the difficulties in obtaining supplies. He then demanded of Mahomed Yusuf that an incriminating letter from the Mysore Regent, addressed to Mahomed Yusuf, should be dropped in the English camp. The letter was read to Lawrence by Poniapa. Lawrence was deceived and Mahomed Yusuf was arrested and his fate sealed had not the man who dropped the letter been discovered in time. Poniapa was confronted with the Brahmin who confessed the truth.

Poniapa was blown from a gun by sanction of the Madras Council and Mahomed Yusuf was exonerated. But the narrowness of his escape and the danger of serving people who were at the mercy of interpreters made a lasting impression on Mahomed Yusuf that bore evil fruit eight years later.

On 12th May, 1754, Lawrence detached a party under Captain Caillaud, consisting of 120 men with 500 Sepoys and 2 guns, to escort the convoy coming from the Tondiman's country. de Mainville had intelligence of the convoy and sent a detachment of troops with some Mysore horse and four guns to intercept it. The Mahrattas, were absent having quarrelled with the Mysoreans the day before. Caillaud left camp at four in the morning, with

Trinchinopoly

Mahomed Yusuf reconnoitring in front. Suddenly, Yusuf's horse neighed, and was answered by others. Riding to the top of a bank, Mahomed Yusuf was met with a ragged volley disclosing the ambush. In the dark, the French were posted below a bank so Caillaud sent patrols against both flanks who drove them from cover with the loss of a few men and a tumbril of ammunition. A message was sent to turn the convoy back until daylight. When the firing was heard Captain Polier joined Caillaud to bring their force to 360 Europeans, 1,500 sepoys, and 110 English troopers with 5 guns.

Lawrence was ill in the city at the time and could not move though he insisted on being carried to the ramparts from where he could see the combat. French reinforcements had also arrived, bringing up their force to 700 Europeans, 50 dragoons, 5,000 sepoys, 10,000 Mysore horse and 7 guns. Polier, who was a Swiss officer, real name Polier de Bottens, retreated in the face of such odds and for a mile his party moved steadily, harassed by French cannon and musketry until they were able to take cover under a bank. Two of the guns had been disabled and Polier was wounded, and obliged to hand over the command to Caillaud.

Caillaud faced the advancing French and opened heavy fire of grape shot from two guns while the sepoys were drawn up to protect the left flank and rear against cavalry. The guns were served well and the French battalion halted, waivered and began to retreat. Caillaud advanced and fired a volley, which threw the French into panic.

They fell back followed by their sepoys and Mysore allies and Caillaud was able to resume his march. 6 of his 9 officers were wounded and 55 soldiers and 150 sepoys were either killed or wounded.

The French were becoming disheartened by their many failures to take Trichinopoly and instead turned to ravaging the territories of the Tondiman and of Tan j ore. However they were able to do little damage beyond destroying the dam of the Cauvery river which was a blow to the prosperity of Tan j ore. Then a Tan j ore force of 1,500 men was overwhelmed by Morari Rao.

Lawrence immediately marched to Tan j ore where he reinstated the Tanjore commander who had been displaced through Dupleix's intrigues. Here he remained some weeks, and received a reinforcement of Europeans and sepoys while waiting to be joined by the Tan j ore army.

On the 16th August, Lawrence and his allies camped six miles west of Elmiseram. His force now comprised 1,000 European infantry, 200 Topasses,

3,000 sepoys, and 14 field guns. The Tan j ore force added 2,500 cavalry, 3,000 infantry, and a few guns.

Meanwhile de Mainville was hovering round Trichinopoly without making a serious attack. On the 16th August he received orders from Pondichery to pass command to Maissin who had moved from Five Rocks to intercept Lawrence. His force consisted of 900 European infantry, 400 Topasses, a number of sepoys, 8 guns, and 10,000 Mysore horse under Hyder Ali. On the 17th August Lawrence was able to seize a deep watercourse and high bank between French Rock and Elmiseram which Maissin had failed to occupy. Together with Hyder Ali his plan was to draw the English force towards Five Rocks when Hyder Ali would seize the chance of attacking the convoy.

The plan nearly succeeded. Lawrence, seeing the French drawn up on his left, accepted the challenge, and advanced in two lines. A fierce cannonade ensued in which the French suffered a good deal and retired to put their tactic into action and, as the opposing lines were on the point of exchanging fire, they retreated towards Five Rocks. Lawrence was preparing to follow, when he received news of Hyder Ali's attack on his rear. As a result of impatience, Hyder Ali had moved too soon. Leaving some of his cavalry to keep the Tan j ore horse engaged he galloped round French Rock and was driven off only after capturing thirty-five carts laden with arms, ammunition and equipment.

The separate French attack, from the island of Seringham, was met by a sortie from Trichinopoly under Kilpatrick, who drove them back to the island without loss. Maissin, who had orders not to risk a general engagement, offered no further opposition, and Lawrence entered Trichinopoly with the loss of only one officer and fifteen men.The French had a hundred Europeans killed and wounded.

Three days later, Lawrence moved to the Fakeer's Tope, in the hope of an engagement but the French had had enough and set fire to their camp and retreated to Mootachellinoor, leaving the road open for Lawrence's supplies. That evening Elmiseram was invested by the Tan j ore troops which surrendered two days later.

Finding the French dug in at Mootachellinoor, Lawrence moved to Warriore. By now the French had little confidence and in spite of the strength of their position, now covered by flooding from the Cauvery on both flanks, abandoned the entrenchment by night and retreated across the river to Seringham. Further operations were suspended on account of the rainy season.

In October, news of a truce, preparatory to a peace, was signalled between the French and English Companies, and Dupleix was recalled. Lawrence received notice of the grant to him of a sword of honour, worth £750, by the Court of Directors. It can truly be said that the services Lawrence rendered his country, in 1752 and 1753, were exemplary and he fully deserved the honour. In 1751 French power in India was at its zenith. A French Nizam ruled at Hyderabad and a French Nawab was predominant in the Carnatic. From the Nerbudda to Cape Comorin the whole country was under French domination. Had Dupleix triumphed at Trichinopoly, the expulsion of the English from Madras and Fort St. David would have been certain. Lawrence's victories turned the tide and brought about the withdrawal of Dupleix, in whom France squandered the services of the best statesman she ever sent to India.

Within seven years the fortunes of the French in India were irretrievably reversed. Dupleix had repeatedly assured the French Government that the British were on the brink of capitulation; one more effort was required and all the wealth of India would be within their grasp. But defeats and disappointments destroyed Dupleix's credit in France and he was recalled to end his days in disgrace and ruin just a month before the first Royal regiment from England landed in India. M. Cultru, in his study of Dupleix, states that it was the defeat of Law in 1752 that had a decisive effect on Dupleix's career, by destroying his reputation in France. All his previous successes were forgotten.

But some doubt that the death of Chunda Sahib was more disastrous to Dupleix's policy than Law's surrender was to French armies. Chunda Sahib's ability made him a better candidate for the Nawabship than Mahomed Ali and after his death Dupleix failed to find any worthy claimant to the Carnatic throne through whom he might prosecute his dreams of aggrandisement, until he was able to assume the government himself. In the following year, the French with their Mysore and Mahratta allies were far stronger in the field than the English, and had every prospect of regaining the prestige they had lost through Law's defeat.

The East India Company now realised that, if they wished to protect their hugely valuable and growing trade, they had to fight for it. The territorial expansion that followed was forced in their own defence.

XII
The English Army arrives in India, 1756

So important had the Indian trade become to England that it was decided that the defence of the national interest must not be left in the hands of a company militia. It is probable that Lawrence and Robert Palk had much to do with this decision. The King's army must now get involved.

When the 39th Regiment arrived in India, Lawrence received notice that the King had promoted him to Lieutenant Colonel in the East Indies though this did not mean he had command of troops in the field. He held the appointment of Commander-in-Chief under the Company but the command of the Royal troops was dependent on seniority and Adlercron, who commanded the 39th, was senior to Lawrence by date of commission.

Lawrence refused to serve under Adlercron, and so retained only the command of the Company's troops. For two years his work was chiefly administrative. When the news in 1756, of the capture of Calcutta by Sooraj-ud Dowla, preparations for an expedition for its recapture were made and Adlercron was promptly set aside owing to his want of experience of the country, and his independence of Company's officials. The result was that when ill health prevented Lawrence from taking command Robert Clive was selected in his place.

In April, 1757, the French tried again, because the Seven Years' War had started in Europe and this gave them the motive to succeed in India.

Their first move was another attempt to capture Trichinopoly. On the 12th May, d'Auteuil, with 1,150 Europeans and 3,000 sepoys, occupied Seringham, and three days later started to shell the city. Caillaud, who held the command at Trichinopoly, was away besieging Madura, which had been seized by Mahfoos Khan. Consequently Trichinopoly was held only by 165 Europeans and 700 sepoys under Captain Joseph Smith who had also to keep 500 French prisoners. Of course their release was one of d'Auteuil's objects. For ten days the garrison was shelled and threatened with assault; the news of Caillaud's approach caused d'Auteuil to retire to intercept him, by occupying the old positions at the Five Rocks, Fakeer's Tope,and the Sugarloaf.

Caillaud, with 120 Europeans and 1,200 sepoys, marching without artillery or tents, had arrived within twelve miles of the city when he received Smith's messengers telling him of the disposal of d'Auteuil's forces. At the same time he detected the presence of d'Auteuil's spies in his camp. He pretended not to recognise them while keeping them under surveillance and proceeded as if to pass between Five Rocks and the Sugarloaf Rock. After satisfying himself that the spies had gone off to carry the news to d'Auteuil, he changed direction and striking eastward emerged from the woods opposite Elmiseram. The whole plain was a deep swamp under rice cultivation and d'Auteuil, believing it to be impassable, had not stationed a guard there. After seven hours of forced march without a single shot being fired Caillaud reached Chucklipolliam on the Cauvery. At daybreak a salute of twenty-one guns announced to d'Auteuil that he had been outwitted. He immediately struck camp and marched for Pondicherry.

The Council had already sent Adlercron with what troops the Presidency could muster to Smith's relief. Adlercron's movements were so slow that he took six days to cover thirty miles, and he was still at Ootramaloor when the news of Caillaud's arrival in Trichinopoly reached him. He then marched on Wandiwash and captured the Pettah. Seeing no chance of success against the fort he then fell back to Ootramaloor to await instructions.

The Council was displeased with Adlercron and ordered him to return to Madras. A French force, under Saubinet, had reached Wandiwash before Adlercron started for Madras and occupied Ootramaloor a few hours after he left it. Adlercron, without informing the Council, or preparing to oppose the French, continued his march to Madras. The French immediately advanced on Conjeveram, which they burned though they failed to take the Pagoda, which was stoutly held by Sergeant Lambertson and two companies of sepoys.

The Council now realised the mistake in leaving the fertile Paliar valley to the French and ordered Adlercron to take the field again.

During his three years in India, Adlercron was a continual source of embarrassment to the Council. He was a dull, incompetent man who was puffed up with a sense of his own importance as commander of the King's troops, His instructions before leaving England had not been shown to the company directors which ensured a clash of authority. The Council in Madras were annoyed. They had been deprived of the experienced Stringer Lawrence and were worried about operations directed by Adlercron. For three years their efforts had been directed to getting the use of Adlercron's troops without Adlercron. Likewise Adlercron was determined that his troops would not be employed unless he had the command. The services of the 250 men of the 30th, who had helped to recover Calcutta, were only secured on the understanding that they were to act as Marines under the Admiral. Adlercron's incompetence and obstructiveness, and his seniority of rank, threatened to paralyse all military operations in India.

At a time when the presence of every British soldier was worth his weight in gold, the Company had asked the Crown to recall the 39th Regiment, merely to get rid of Adlercron. But 18 months would elapse before the representations of the Madras Council bore fruit.

In this dilemma, Lawrence, who had hitherto refused to serve under Adlercron, now offered to accompany him as a volunteer. Making his way, by sea, to Fort St. David, he took a hundred men from the garrison there, landed at Madras, and joined Adlercron near Chingleput. The army marched for Ootramaloor, where it remained for forty days, within a few hours' march of the French, without a shot being fired. In a letter written by Adlercron at this time, dated Ootramaloor 10th June, 1757, he says :

> What increases my confidence of success is that I am assisted with Colonel Lawrence, who is not only deservedly esteemed for his military capacity, but has a thorough knowledge of the situation of the country. This gentleman is in such favour with the Company's managers that, in order he might have command of the army, the Committee had the assurance to propose my staying at Fort St. George to assist them in their Councils, which they have always hitherto kept private from me.

It apparently never occurred to Adlercron that Lawrence had waived his objections to serving under him to be at hand to keep him out of trouble.

It seemed impossible to bring the French to battle except at a disadvantage. There was much sickness among the troops, so, on Lawrence's advice, the army fell back on Conjeveram at the end of July.

At the end of 1756, the 39th were ordered to embark for England, and Lawrence once more became the senior officer in India. Several officers and 350 men of the 39th transferred their services to the Company.

For the first two years of the war, the English forces in Madras were reduced to act on the defensive. Every available man who could be spared had been sent to Bengal with Clive. Fortunately, the French did not take advantage of this and only pursued secondary targets whilst awaiting the large armaments that were promised from France.

In the meantime, Bussy seized the English factories in the Northern Circars. When reinforcements reached Pondicherry, the French overran the Carnatic, snapping up all the strongholds in native hands, and took Chittapet from the English.

At the end of April, 1758, Lally arrived at Pondichery with a powerful fleet commanded by d'Ache, field guns and troops and power over the whole of the French troops and possessions in India. The English were weak and had been forced to retire from their conquests in Southern India. Trichinopoly, Arcot, Chingleput and Conjeveram alone remained to them, besides Madras, Fort St. David and Cuddalore on the coast. Within five weeks of Lally's arrival, Cuddalore and Fort St. David were captured, and Lally determined to march on Madras.

But d'Ache refused to support him with the fleet, and money was tight. To remedy this, Lally determined to attack Tan j ore. He laid siege but, at the end of three weeks, was forced to return to Pondichery. D'Ache, too, was beaten in his encounter with Pocock, off Tranquebar, and left the coast. Before doing so he seized a Dutch ship even though France and Holland were at peace and thus obtained money for Lally to equip his army.

On the 12th December, Lally appeared before Madras and occupied the town. Lawrence, at St. Thomas's Mount, fell back before the French advance. As before, on entering the fort, command of the troops devolved on the Council. The Council placed the defence of the fort to the Governor, Mr. Pigot, recommending him to consult Lawrence on all occasions, and to assemble a council of the superior officers of the garrison if necessary. Thus responsibility for defence was Lawrence's, who had under him an able body of officers appointed by himself over the past ten years. Three of his best officers remained outside Fort St. George: Caillaud and Preston to carry on a partisan warfare against the French rear, and Joseph Smith, who held Trichinopoly, where the French prisoners exceeded his small garrison of invalids by five to one. Mahomed Yusuf, of Nellore, also did good service in partisan warfare against the French.

Lawrence's garrison comprised 1,600 Europeans (including officers), 64 Topasses, 89 Coffrees (natives of Madagascar and the East Coast of Africa) and 2,220 sepoys. Nine hundred of the European infantry belonged to Colonel Draper's regiment, the 79th, that had just arrived from England. There were also about 140 men of the Royal Artillery.

The occupation of the town by Lally was the signal for the French troops to seek booty and drink. Their disorder and drunkenness was fully predictable and a sortie against them was prepared. Six hundred men with two field pieces were placed under Colonel Draper who entered the town before he was discovered by the French and put the opposition to flight. French reinforcements arrived, and confusion followed. The English troops were separated, and Draper, with only four men, was in brief possession of a battery of French guns. Saubinet, one of Lally's best officers, was killed, and d'Estaing was taken prisoner; but the English were obliged to return to the fort in face of the additional reinforcements brought up by Lally, after suffering a loss of fifty killed, 30 wounded and 103 taken prisoner with six officers killed and three wounded. The French lost of 200 killed and wounded, besides four officers killed and twelve wounded. The loss of Saubinet and the capture of Count d'Estaing were seriously felt by Lally at the start of the siege.

On the 2nd January, the French batteries opened, and the siege started in earnest. Sallies were made from time to time with some success and in one of them, Major Brereton, of the 79th, captured two guns and brought them into the fort. A welcome supply of powder was also obtained because the French had dispatched three native boats with fifty barrels of powder from Madras, with a French soldier in each boat. The boatmen disarmed the French and brought the powder into the fort, for which they were paid full value.

On the 30th January, the *Shaftesbury* managed to run the gauntlet of the French blockading ships, and landed a much-needed supply of specie and military stores. Meanwhile, Caillaud, Preston and Mahomed Yusuf had continued warfare against the French communications. Caillaud had succeeded in raising a force of about 4,700 natives, with which he fought an indecisive action at S.Thome on the 10th February.

On the 16th February, Pocock's fleet sailed into the roadstead, just a few hours before Lally's intended assault. The condition of the garrison was now so much better than that of the besiegers that it is doubtful if any assault could be successful. Lally was determined not to risk it. He broke camp and the next morning the retreating French columns were visible from the walls of the fort. So ended the most intensive siege that had yet occurred in India and it proved to be the last serious bid for an Eastern Empire by the French. Fifty-two French guns and a quantity of stores were found in their trenches. The English loss amounted to 33 officers, 559 Europeans, and 346 sepoys killed, wounded and prisoners. The fort was so well supplied that it was calculated there were enough stores to stand another siege. All the operations of the defence had been managed by Lawrence. Mr. Pigot had had the good sense not to interfere and had helped in directing the distribution of supplies.

Reinforcements from England brought the strength of European troops in Madras to over 1,700. The Council again thought they should act and, again against Lawrence's advice, they sent him towards Conjeveram, which was occupied by Lally. But Lawrence's army was badly off for transport, and the Council had no money to maintain the troops in the field. They were now as anxious to bring back their troops to Madras, as they had been to send them out.

Lawrence pointed out the evil of retreating in face of the enemy, though he had considered the move towards Conjeveram a mistake. To strengthen the Council's indecision, he left the army and came to Madras. His health had by now completely broken down and he made known his intention of returning to England.

A few days later, in April, 1759, he sailed, with the intention of never returning to India.

On his arrival in England, the Directors granted him an annuity of £500. In September, 1760, the Directors voted statues to Lawrence, Clive, and Pocock:

> That their eminent and signal services to this Company may be ever had in remembrance.

XIII
Return of Lawrence to India, 1761

This was not to be the end of Stringer Lawrence in India. On the 3rd October, 1761, Lawrence, yielding to the requests of the Directors, again took his seat in the Madras Council, having returned to India in the *Fox*. By this time, he had won the support of Council to the extent that his responsibility was much improved.

He was again made Commander-in-Chief of all the Company's forces in India and, to ensure that he should not be superseded in the field by any colonel of King's troops was promoted to Major General in the East Indies, by the King. He was given a seat in Council at Madras, next to the Governor, with power to vote generally being restricted to military subjects only. His salary was fixed at £1,500 a year, and it was ordered that, in the event of his visiting Bengal, or any other place where there was a Council, he was to be granted a seat on the Council Board it being particularly mentioned that he was to take precedence over Colonel Coote.

Hitherto, personal staff had not been provided for senior military officer except in the field, but Lawrence was now granted an aide-de-camp and a brigade major so his work became mostly administrative. The power of the French in India had been finally broken and Caillaud, Carnac, Coote and Adams were dealing effectively with the situation in Bengal. However. Lawrence had still to deal with the treachery of his old Brahmin interpreter. Since 1756 Mahomed Yusuf's loyalty had fallen under suspicion and in 1761, at the insistence of the Council, the Nawab appointed him Governor of Madura and Tinnevelly. Before long he gave trouble, and he aimed at independence.

He collected arms and men, strengthened the fortifications of Madura, and, at the end of 1762, invaded Travancore territory without authority. Two months later he openly hoisted French colours and had over 25,000 men in his pay, among them 200 Europeans under a French officer, Flamicourt. At the same time a certain M. Mandave, living at the Danish settlement of Tranquebar, announced himself as the representative of the French Government, and called on the Madras Council to stop threatening Mahomed Yusuf. He asserted that Madura had been ceded to the French by Mahomed Yusuf, and that the cession must be recognised under the suspension of arms just concluded between the two nations. Also Flamicourt was acting under orders. The Madras Government was greatly embarrassed by these claims, but, on addressing the Danish authorities M. Mandave concluded his connection with the French in Madura, and left India.

Lawrence advised immediate action, and a force of 9,900 men was assembled at Trichinopoly, under Colonel Monson, to march on Madura. Mahomed Yusuf 's enterprising character quickly showed because on the 11th August he attacked a reconnoitring party of sepoys, and drove it back with a loss of 150 men killed and wounded. On the 3rd September another reconnoitring party was driven back, with the loss of one European officer killed and sixteen or seventeen Europeans killed and wounded. Monson's artillery was so inferior that he was forced to raise the siege in November and to camp six miles away from Madura.

Mahomed Yusuf took advantage of this to open communication with the Governor and Lawrence and liberal terms of amnesty were offered, though he refused.

In April, 1764, the siege was renewed under Major Charles Campbell and on the 24th April, five redoubts were taken by storm. Batteries were opened and, on 26th June, an assault was delivered and repulsed, with the loss of two officers killed and eight wounded. Some 150 Europeans and 50 natives were killed and wounded and Major Preston died of his wounds.

Campbell turned the siege into a blockade until scarcity and discontent forced the garrison to consider their own safety. Mahomed Yusuf was seized and confined by M. Marchand, the French commandant, who surrendered next day. On 15th October, Mahomed Yusuf was hanged as a rebel against the Nawab.

Lawrence's final year in India was probably the pleasantest of his life. He possessed the full confidence of both the Directors in London and colleagues in Madras, and was the closest friend of the Governor, Sir Robert Palk, to whom he stood second in Council.

Little has been said so far about Lawrence's relationship with Robert Palk, largely because Lawrence's achievements were military and his life was lived in the trenches, redoubts, sieges and camps throughout the region. But crucial was his reliance upon his great friend who throughout was working his way to prominence in the Council and in the whole Company. Palk was that rare person who could persuade and organise a huge organisation to do what he wanted and what Palk wanted above all else was the opportunity to organise huge trades without the inference of the French. From the time he arrived as a divine in the company's service with the Boscawen's expedition of 1747 until he finally left India as Governor of Madras, his was a career of continuous promotion and appointment to senior and influential posts in Council. When he met Lawrence he knew that he had made a friend who needed his assistance to create an efficient fighting force. So it was that he reorganised the payment systems and by this helped to improve poor morale in the fighting forces. Lawrence with Palk sat in Council and worked with him up to the time he retired.

It was in April, 1766, that he said farewell to India and was succeeded, as Commander-in-Chief, by Caillaud who, in turn, was succeeded by Joseph Smith. Mahomed Ali Khan, whose rule over the Carnatic had been secured by Lawrence, showed his gratitude by obtaining permission from the Company to grant Lawrence an annuity of 3,750 pagodas a year (about £1,500). The money was paid by the Directors, until Lawrence's death in London on l0th January, 1775.

When Lawrence died his remains were taken to Dunchideock, near Exeter, where the Haldon Belvedere was added to the Haldon House Estate and erected to his memory by Sir Robert Palk.

If the best General is the one who makes the fewest mistakes, Lawrence's name occupies a high position on the honour list of commanders. To describe him as only a master of strategy would be wrong. He was so much more than that. There was little place for strategy in the warfare in which he was engaged and so his talent was largely tactical. The Council kept strategy jealously in their own hands but against Law and de Kerjean in 1752, and by his transfer of operations from Trivadi to Trichinopoly in 1753, Lawrence showed a grasp of strategical principles that would have won success on a larger field.

The armies he led were out of all proportion to the issues they decided. They were always of inferior quality. How bad they could be, at times, as shown at Volcondah, in April, 1751, during Lawrence's absence from India, when, under such officers as Kilpatrick and Clive and Dalton even, the

European companies behaved in such a cowardly way that they had to be marched away from the field of operations.

Lawrence had that supreme gift of a great commander in being able to motivate his men at critical moments, while he commanded their confidence. In the field, he showed the qualities of a great commander, though opportunity to exercise them on a larger scale was denied him. Never forcing a battle without need, he struck with all his force and with the greatest daring when the opportunity occurred. His decision taking was ever carried out without faltering, and always with the best results. Especially he possessed the gift of misleading and confusing his enemy as to his intentions

In council, his judgment was as sound as it was in the field. The civil government regretted when they had not followed Lawrence's advice. Had one of those minds that reaches the right conclusion easily and unerringly.

d'Auteuil, Law, de Kerjean, Astruc, Brenier, Astruc again, Maissin d'Auteuil, Lally, indeed every French leader who crossed swords with him retired defeated from the combat, or had to yield himself a prisoner.

Macaulay writes of Lawrence as being

> ...gifted with no intellectual faculty higher than plain good sense...

but leaves it to be inferred that Lawrence's triumph over Law was as much due to Clive as to his own efforts. In this he was no doubt misled by Clive's biographer, who writes of Clive "placing himself" under Lawrence when Lawrence returned to India in March, 1752. Clive had, at that time, only just sprung into notice by his feats at Arcot and Covripauk. His merits were challenged, and his successes were often put down to good fortune. Clive, was disliked by colleagues which found expression in an address to Lawrence. Had Clive refused to serve under Lawrence, he would have been required to abandon a military career and return to his writership. Instead of Lawrence being indebted to Clive, it was Clive who, at that time, owed his advancement to Lawrence.

In the operations that crushed Law and d'Auteuil, Lawrence took Clive under his wing and listened to his advice. Considering their difference of age and rank at the time this is a proof of the acuity of Lawrence's character. He would have hesitated to divide his forces had he not gauged Law's over-caution and lack of enterprise and had he not recognised Clive's capacity to carry out his orders.

Clive made no move except under Lawrence's orders. However, probably because much of the fighting was done by Clive, his name stands out more prominently than Lawrence's during the two months' campaign. Events showed that Lawrence was well able to act by himself. Clive was not at Bahoor, nor was he in India when Lawrence fought Astruc and Brenier, Morari Rao and Hyder Ali, on the battlefields of Trichinopoly in 1753. The operations of that year alone are sufficient to establish Lawrence's reputation.

Yet, Lawrence's military triumphs have been overshadowed by Clive's, though Clive was never matched against a French commander of like capacity. But Stringer Lawrence was so quiet and unassuming, that his genuine merit might easily pass unobserved.

Few things are more characteristic of Lawrence than his personal relations with Clive. When he arrived in India, totally ignorant of the country, at an age when most men have difficulty in adjusting to new circumstances, it would not have been surprising if he had mistrusted a masterful, headstrong, young man of twenty-two, who had only established at that time a reputation for love of fighting. But Lawrence quickly recognised Clive's genius, and reported to his superiors that Clive's successes were not due to good luck, as many imagined, but to real merit.

When the expedition was prepared to avenge the horrors of the Black Hole of Calcutta, ill-health alone prevented Lawrence from taking the command. Lawrence, not Clive, would have triumphed at Plassey had Lawrence's health permitted him to assume the command.

Throughout his career in India the relationship between Lawrence and Clive (who quarrelled with almost everybody else), were most cordial. When the East India Company voted a sword set with diamonds to Clive, he refused to receive it unless a similar honour was paid to Lawrence and, when Lawrence retired to England, Clive, who had become rich and powerful, bestowed on him an annuity of £500 from his private means. Nothing is more honourable to Clive than the deference and consideration with which he treated Lawrence at all times and nothing testifies better to Lawrence's character than the ungrudging regard paid him by Clive.

Since Lawrence's day many illustrious names have been added to the roll of our Indian officers. None among them has a better claim to be remembered than Stringer Lawrence, the Father of the Indian Army.

On his death, the Directors of the East India Company voted a sum of £700 for the erection of a monument to his memory in Westminster Abbey in recognition of their gratitude for his eminent services. It bears the following legend :

DISCIPLINE ESTABLISHED. FORTRESSES PROTECTED.
SETTLEMENTS EXTENDED. FRENCH AND INDIAN ARMIES
DEFEATED
AND
PEACE CONCLUDED
IN THE CARNATIC.

With a carved representation of the fortified rock of Trichinopoly.

General Stringer Lawrence

Timeline for Robert Palk

1717 - 1798
1717 Born at Lower Headborough Farm, Nr Ashburton, Devon
1717 Baptised on December at the Old Mission House, Ashburton.
1739 Graduates from Wadham College, Oxford University
1739 Ordained at Exeter Cathedral by Bishop Weston
1739 Held two curacies in Cornwall at Egloskerry and Launcells
1747 Appointed chaplain by the East India Company
1747 Joined Admiral Boscawen's expedition to India
1748 Chaplain at Fort St David
1750 Resigned and started for England
1750 New opportunity offered in Bombayto
1751 Returned Fort St David
1751 Meets Stringer Lawrence
1752 Appointed Lawrence army paymaster
1753 Member of Council
1759 Returns to England
1761 Returns to India with Stringer Lawrence
1761 Third of Council with the duties of Export Warehousekeeper.
1763, 1763 Palk assumed the office of President
1764 Suppression of Yusuf Khan's rebellion in Madura
1766 Treaty of Hyderabad
1767 Palk resigns the Chair and reaches England on the 13th July, 1767
1767 Retires from EIC
1767 MP for Wareham
1768 - 74 MP for Wareham
1782 Appointed Sir Robert Palk
1798 Died at Haldon House, Dunchideock, Devon

Part 3
Robert Palk in India 1747-1767

XIV
The Palks of Ashburton, Devon, 1717

Robert Palk came of yeoman stock established at Ashburton, Devon, says Col. H. D. Love, in his report to the India Office on the Bannatyne Collection in 1922, produced at their request. The family homestead was Lower Headborough, the first farm out of Ashburton on the road to Buckland-in-the-Moor within half a mile of the town.

His father Walter Palk, born in 1686, was of yeoman farmer stock and his mother, Frances, was the daughter of Robert Abraham. Walter Palk supplemented his income by acting as a carrier of serge, from the cloth mills just down the road, over Haldon Hill to Exeter. Walter had three children, Walter, Robert and Grace. It was Robert who was to bring the family fame and fortune.

Doubts have arisen in some journals as to the exact birthplace of Robert Palk because, although there were Palks recorded as living at Ambrooke in the late 15th century, in 1717 the Neyle family apparently owned Ambrooke. Robert Palk mentioned Ambrooke in reference to his line of descent, and some historians have assumed that was where he was born. Educated at Ashburton Grammar School, he was sponsored by his godfather (who was also his maternal uncle) Robert Abraham, to attend Wadham College, Oxford, graduating in 1739.

In 1679 Walter Palk, of Ashburton, left the reversion of his lands to his nephew Walter (b. 1659), son of Thomas Palk. This second Walter was succeeded by his eldest son Walter (b. 1686), his other children being Jonathan, Thomas and Grace. The third Walter married Frances Abraham at Buckland-in-the-Moor, and had three children, Walter (b. 1714), Robert (b. 1717), the subject of this book, and Grace. The fourth Walter married in succession Thomasine Widdicombe, of Priestaford, Ashburton, her sister Mary Widdicombe, and Mary Mugford, by all of whom he had children.

Robert Palk married Anne Vansittart, and his sister Grace became the wife of Richard Welland.

Two of the Welland boys, nephews of our Robert Palk, served in India.

Among the numerous offspring of the fourth Walter were Walter (b. 1742), afterwards M.P. for Ashburton ; Robert (b. 1744), who joined the Bengal civil service ; Thomas (b cir. 1750), who came to Madras a cadet, but was later transferred to the civil service ; Grace, who married Nicholas Tripe of Ashburton ; and Jonathan, vicar of Ilsington. Mention is made also of two brothers, Lieut. Thomas Palk and Ensign John Palk of the Madras army, who appear to have been grandsons of one of Sir Robert Palk's uncles. They died together while campaigning in the Northern Circars. Other Indian connections of Sir Robert were Thomas Abraham, a Bengal civil servant, who was a member of his mother's family, and several of the Vansittarts, his wife's relations.

It is said that Robert Palk was born at Ambrooke, in the parish of Ipplepen, which was the property of the Neyle family, but the statement needs verification. Certainly he was baptized at the Old Mission House, Ashburton, on the 16th December, 1717. He received his early education at Ashburton Grammar School, a very ancient foundation, matriculated at Wadham College, Oxford, in 1736, and graduated three years later.

After being ordained deacon the Revd. Robert Palk was appointed a naval chaplain, and in 1747 he accompanied Boscawen's expedition to the East Indies as chaplain to the Admiral. Boscawen, on the 15th of July, was made rear-admiral and commander-in-chief of the expedition to the East Indies. On the 29th of July 1748 he arrived off Fort St. David, and soon after laid siege to Pondicherry; but the sickness of his men and the approach of the monsoons led to the raising of the siege. He arrived at Fort St. David in July, 1748, and was present at the unsuccessful siege of Pondicherry.

In November, news reached India of the Peace of Aix-la-Chapelle, but though hostilities ceased, the fleet remained on the Coast. At the beginning of the following year an incident occurred which determined Palk's future career.

The Rev. Francis Fordyce, the Company's chaplain at Fort St. David, a notoriously quarrelsome and ill-tempered man, publicly insulted Robert Clive, and blows were exchanged between them in the streets of Cuddalore. An enquiry was held by the Governor and Council with the result that Fordyce was suspended as being " a meddling mischievous person."

Palk sought the approval of the Directors, and the Admiral consented to his transfer. This "very worthy and able Divine " assumed his new duties on the 1st April, 1749.

Meanwhile the Directors sent out the Rev. George Swynfen as a second chaplain for the Coast, and though they approved of Palk's appointment, decided that their own nominee should be the senior.

In October, 1750, the fleet sailed for Bombay en route for England, and Palk accompanied it with the intention of formally resigning His Majesty's service and obtaining a regular engagement from the Company. On reaching Bombay in March, 1751, he heard of Swynfen's death, and returned at once to Fort St. David, where he was reinstated. Fort St George, which had been in the possession of the French from 1746, was restored in 1749, and in April, 1752, the seat of Government was transferred from Fort St. David to Madras,

Palk accompanied the President and Council to Madras. In December, 1751, the Directors, having heard of Palk's departure in the preceding year, but not of his return, nominated two chaplains for the Coast, the Rev. Samuel Staveley and the Rev. Thomas Colefax. The arrival of these gentlemen in June, 1752, left no vacancy for Palk.

The Madras Government, however, quickly found another place for him. The Consultation Book for August contains the following :

> The account of the army in camp having been kept in an irregular manner, which creates confusion, 'tis agreed that the Rev. Robert Palk be appointed Paymaster and Commissary in the Field at the rate of 10s. a day salary and Rs. 5 a day

At this juncture Colefax died, and Palk continued to perform clerical duties intermittently in addition to his special work. That work brought him into intimate relations with Major Stringer Lawrence, who commanded the army operating against the French in the southern districts. On two occasions, in April, 1753, and May, 1754, Palk was sent to the Court of Tanjore, where he successfully negotiated with the Raja for aid in troops and money. In January, 1751, he was deputed with Henry Vansittart to meet the French commissaries at Madras and arrange a suspension of hostilities. No agreement was then effected, but at the end of the year Palk and Vansittart went to Pondicherry and returned with a provisional treaty of peace.

The Government in Madras were so well satisfied with Palk's political work that they presented him with a diamond ring to the value of 1,000 pagodas.

At this period Robert Orme, the future historian of the war with the French in India, was a member of the Fort St. George Council. The following extract from a confidential letter, dated 26th October, 1755, addressed by him to John Payne, one of the Directors, throws light on Palk's character and duties :

> Mr. Palk, a gentleman left in India by Mr. Boscawen and made chaplain at St. David, was, at the time I left India, in high favour with Mr. Saunders; he was one of his family. It is long since this gentleman had thrown aside the learning of ancient or Christian books to study the tempers of mankind, in which he is indeed a great proficient, and as great a one in adapting himself to them, I must say, with decency. His character as a clergyman admitted him to the conciliation of disputes, and where he did not succeed, his intentions were rewarded with the graceful name of a Peace Maker. I had perceiv'd various instances of his address in the management of persons at variance with another, and supressed what was my rising sentiment in favour of the general one. Mr. Palk was chosen by Mr. Saunders to go to camp, under the name of a Commissary design'd to retrench expences, but with the real view of softning and managing Colonel Lawrence's warm and sudden temper in the contests then subsisting between him and Mr. Saunders, How well he fullfilled this commission I would williingly throw a veil over, but the facts are known to all, and do not seem disavowed by himself. He received from Colonel Lawrence most beneficial employs in the camp, and by his means in other services, which have, in the time of my voyage, set him independant in the world with at least 10, 000/. from the two he came with into India. And from a month after his arrival in camp, Mr. Saunders rcceived no further tokens of his attention or respect. And Colonel Lawrencc became all in all with Mr. Palk. The influence which I have

above described Mr. Palk to have over the greatest part of the community of which he is the pastor shone forth eminently now in their notions of the Governor. Mr. Palk blamed him : all the world did so too. Mr. Palk gave witness to a more than heroick character in Colonel Lawrence : he became immediately a hero of the first order."

Then ensued a lengthy series of campaigns, particularly during 1752-1754 in the Carnatic that cemented the bond between Stringer Lawrence and Robert Palk. Lawrence experienced difficuly with the ruling company council and in this Palk was able to assist with a growing reputation for fair and competent administration. It has been said that Lawrence won the battles and Robert Palk won the peace that followed thus leading to beneficial treaties and successful trade arrangements. Palk had an early premonition that if trade was to succceed then the company must fight for it.

Lawrence and Palk met Nawab Muhammad Ali at Arcot in August, 1755. and attended him at his triumphal entry into his capital. In the preceding February the Directors had nominated a Select Committee of eight members at Fort St. George to communicate with their own Secret Committee on military and political topics, and they settled that the first vacancy be filled by the Rev. Robert Palk.

An opening occurred by the death of Colonel Caroline Scott, Engineer General, and Palk occupied it in September. In December, however, the Court with accustomed vacillation decreed that he should confine himself to Church work and be posted to Fort St. David.

Sir Robert Palk

Photo courtesy Mrs Tom Fenton and Iain Fraser

On receipt of these instructions in 1756, Palk announced his intention of leaving for England, but asked for time to wind up his affairs. With the sanction of Mr. Pigot's Government he remained at Fort St. George until August, 1758, exercising his various functions as chaplain, paymaster of the forces and member of the Select Connnittee.

In company with Orme, Palk sailed in the *Grantham*. The ship was captured by the French, who landed the passengers at the Cape and released them on parole. Palk reached England in 1759, bearing letters from the Nawab of Arcot to the King and the Company. His personality, ability and address produced such an effect on the Directors that they penned the following lines in their despatch of the 15th February, 1760 :

> We have fixed upon Mr. Robert Palk to succeed Mr. Pigot in the Government whenever it shall become vacant by the resignation or decease of that gentleman, being fully convinced his ability and experience will be of great service to the Company both before and after his succession to the Government, especially as affairs are at present circumstanced.

On the 14th November, 1760, arms were granted to "Robert Palk of Headborough in the County of Devon", and in the following February he married Anne, daughter of Arthur Vansittart of Shottesbrook Park, Berks., and sister of his old friend and former colleague Henry Vansittart, who had mean while become Governor of Bengal.

Palk sailed in March, 1761, with Major General Stringer Lawrence as a fellow-passenger and arrived at Madras in October, and took his seat as Third of Council with the duties of Export Warehousekeeper.

On the resignation of Governor Pigot on the 14th November, 1763, Palk assumed the office of President, occupying the Chair until the 25th January, 1767. His administration was popular and comparatively peaceful, the chief events being the suppression in 1764 of Yusuf Khan's rebellion in Madura, and the occupation of the Circars, followed by the Treaty of Hyderabad, in 1766.

Clive had obtained a free gift to the company from the Mogul, in 1765, of the five coast districts north of the Kistna which were known as the Northern Circars. They were ruled by Nizam Ali, Subahdar of the Deccan, who had granted one of them, the Guntur Circar, to his brother Basalat Jang. Brig General John Caillaud, Lawrence's successor, took possession of the districts without serious opposition in 1766. The Nizam was naturally aggrieved at his deprivation of territory, and prepared to invade the Carnatic. Palk, a man of peace, deemed it prudent to placate him, and Caillaud negotiated a settlement at Hyderabad. By the Treaty of the 12th November, 1766, the Madras Government agreed to pay an annual rent of eight lakhs of rupees for the Circars, to leave Basalat Jang in possession of Guntur for the term of his life, and to afford aid to the Nizam in the settlement of his own affairs. This last vague condition led, after Palk's departure, to war with Haidar Ali. Palk resigned the Chair to Charles Bourchier in January,1767 and sailed for England in the *Lord Camden*, accompanied by his wife and two children, Anne (Nancy) born in 1764, and Lawrence, so named after Palk's friend the General, born early in 1766. The ex-Governor reached England on the 13th July, 1767, and was well received by the King and the Court of Directors.

His long residence in India had enabled him to acquire considerable wealth. While placing the interests of his employers first, Palk had not neglected his own and the fortune with which he retired was not all derived from his official emoluments. As Paymaster of the Army and the holder of a bullock contract granted him by Clive, he had had early opportunities of making money, and those opportunities increased with his advancement in the service.

He was interested in private trade, a practice which was recognised by the Company, The custom of the time permitted the surreptitious receipt of presents by all public servants who could command them. Palk admits in one of his letters that he accepted gifts of money from prospective renters of lands, but he takes credit to himself for never having solicited a present

The Nawab had much to gain from a Governor, and though Palk resisted pressure to attack Tan j ore, he rendered valuable aid at Madura, and Muhammad Ali probably attested his gratitude in the usual manner. The conclusion of treaties furnished other facilities.

According to John Andrews, a senior civil servant who was deputed in January, 1760, to arrange terms with Haidar, Palk received a lakh (100,000) of pagodas from the Nizam and Gaillaud obtained Pags. 60,000 for negotiating the Treaty of Hyderabad of 1766. At the time the currency was the Pagoda for which the exchange rate into sterling was variable.

After visiting his relations in Devonshire, Palk took a house in Spring

Gardens, and entered Parliament as member for Ashburton. In 1761 he purchased the Haldon estate near Exeter.

The house had been built by Sir George Chudleigh about 1720. After his death in 1738 the property passed in succession to Sir John Chichester, Mrs. Basset, Mr. John Jones and Mr. William Webber.

A friend writing to Palk in December, 1769, congratulates him on the cheapness of his purchase, and mentions that Mr. Webber had given Mr. Jones £11,500 for it. Palk made many improvements ; laid down floors of Indian redwood, planted trees in the park, and gradually acquired adjacent land. A daughter Catherine (Kitty) was born to the Palks on New Year's day, 1768, and another, named Emelia, in 1771. Both died during adolescence.

Though he never joined the Company's Board, Robert Palk exercised influence on Indian affairs through Stringer Laurence, Sullivan and other friends. When not following the pursuits of a country gentleman at Haldon he resided in London, where he occupied a house in Park Place, St. James's, moving in 1775 to Bruton Street after the death of Lawrence.

He re-entered Parliament in 1774 and represented Ashburton until 1787. His great friend Stringer Lawrence was his frequent, if not permanent, guest until the General died in London in 1775.

Lawrence was buried in the church of Dunchideock close by Haldon, which contains a monument to his memory. Palk commemorated him by erecting a turreted and battlemented tower or belvedere, triangular in plan, on the summit of Haldon Hill, and is now known as the Haldon Belvedere.

The principal room on the lowest of its three floors contains a codestone statue of Lawrence, and mural tablets are inscribed with a recital in English, Latin and Persian of his military exploits. It was at Haldon House that a conference took place in September, 1776, between Robert Palk, George Vansittart, General Caillaud, Mr. Pechell and Colonel Macleane to discuss the conditions to be obtained from Lord North as the price of resignation by Warren Hastings of the office of Governor General.

On the 19th June, 1782, Robert Palk was created a baronet. His only son Lawrence, after leaving Oxford, travelled on the Continent and some of the son's amusing letters (q.v.) written in the course of the tour have been preserved. During his absence from England in 1786 his eldest sister Anne became the wife of Sir Bourchier Wrey, Bt., and the youngest, Emelia, died. Lady Palk expired in 1788 at the age of 50. Her husband survived her ten years.

Sir Robert was buried in Dunchideock church, but his remains were removed many years later to a vault outside the building. A simple tablet near the monument to Stringer Lawrence records the names of himself and eight members of his family.

Stringer Lawrence also features in the Ballantyne collection.The earliest is an autograph letter from Colonel Stringer Lawrence to Admiral Charles Watson, Commander-in-Chief of the East India squadron, dated Fort St. George, 8th October, 1755, embodying Lawrence's "Narrative" of his campaigns of 1751-1752. The letter, which is bound in book form, contains 221 quarto pages of manuscript.

Admiral Watson, who had brought out Adlercron's Regiment, the 39th Foot, in 1754, was at Madras on the date of the letter, and he sailed two days later for Bombay on a mission to suppress the pirates of the Malabar coast and to destroy the stronghold at Gheriah or Viziadrug of their chief Angria.

The Haldon Belvedere

XV
The Robert Palk archive, 1755 - 1783

The reader may be confused by some of the terms used liberally in the letters that follow. The following short explanations may be helpful in the understanding of how the various systems, financial and political, worked in Palk's time.

The first of these is the comewhat confusing descriptions of the money and negotiable instruments that were in use to lubricate the trades made by members of EIC (and the EIC itself) and also to return funds to England when the expected and eagerly awaited time for retirement came.

Starting with expectations: a ***competence*** was the term used to describe the degree of success achieved by the company servant and also to indicate when enough wealth had been gathered to allow a comfortable living for oneself and the family. In Palk's time this amounted to around £40,000. Considerably more than this was achieved by Palk which some estimates put at £120,000 and by Clive who undoubtedly exceeded £250,000. Warren Hastings also accumulated great wealth though he had to spend all of it to defend against accusations of fraudulent trading.All these sums are amounts in 1750 currency. How were these amounts collected and transferred to England? The letters that follow contain a number of different ways of calculting monies due.

British East India Company coins were minted in England and shipped to the East. The word 'Cash' was adopted from Sanskrit karsa, a weight of gold or silver of weight 83.30 grams. East India Company coinage had both Urdu and English writing on it and in 1671 the directors of EIC ordered a mint to provide coinage. In 1677 this was sanctioned by the Crown, the coins, having

Henry Vansittart

received royal sanction were struck as silver Rupees; the inscription runs “The Rupee of Bombaim, by authority of Charles II.”

Coins were also being produced for The East India Company at the Madras mint. The currency at The Company’s Bombay and Bengal administrative regions was the Rupee. At Madras, the Company's accounts were reckoned in “pagodas”, “fractions”, “fanams”, “faluce” and “cash” when the rupee was adopted as the unit of currency for the Company's operations, the relation between the two systems was 1 pagoda = 3-91 rupees and 1 rupee = 12 fanams.

The Pagoda was a unit of currency, a coin made of gold or half gold minted by Indian dynasties as well as the British, the French and the Dutch. It was issued by various dynasties in medieval southern India. There were two types of pagodas coined by foreign traders. The most valuable was the Star pagoda, worth approximately 8 shillings, issued by the East India Company at Madras. The second was the Porto Novo pagoda, issued by the Dutch at Tuticorin and also by the Nawabs of Arcot, and worth about 25% less than the Star pagoda.

Bills of exchange are financial documents that require the individual or business that is addressed in the document to pay a specified amount of money on a date that is cited within the text. Considered to be a negotiable instrument, the date for the demand to pay generally ranges from the current date to a date within the next six calendar months. Derived from the French word *allonger*, to draw out, the allonge is a small piece of paper that is appended to a contract or other form of negotiable instrument to provide room for an authorized signature that functions as an endorsement for the document, when there is no space for endorsements on the actual document. Along with space for authoritative signatures that function as additional endorsements, the allonge also often allows room for the high points of the agreement to be reviewed in an abbreviated form.

Often referred to in the correspondence is the Opium trade which has been known in China since the 7th century where it was used for medical purposes. It was not until the 17th century that the practice of mixing opium with tobacco for smoking was introduced into China by Europeans. The import of opium into China stood at 200 chests (annual) in 1729, when the first anti-opium edict was promulgated. This edict was weakly enforced, and by the time Chinese authorities reissued the prohibition in starker terms in 1799, the figure had leaped; 4,500 chests were imported in the year 1800.

The ***betel nut or leaf*** trade is often mentioned since this was a most profitable way of making money aside from EIC business. Farms existed for its production as authorised by the ruling princes who often demanded supplies of betel for their own domestic purposes. Woe betide any farmer who failed to provide adequate supplies for the Nabob! From the World Health Organisation:

> The betel (Piper betle) is the leaf of a vine belonging to the Piperaceae family, which includes pepper and kava. It is valued both as a mild stimulant and for its medicinal properties. Betel leaf is mostly consumed in Asia, and elsewhere in the world by some Asian emigrants, as betel quid or *paan*, with or without tobacco, in an addictive psycho-stimulating and euphoria-inducing formulation with adverse health effects

Finally the ***respondentia bond*** is defined (US Legal website):

> Hypothecation of a ship's cargo is called respondentia and is effected by a ***respondentia bond***. A respondentia bond is a loan upon the mortgage or hypothecation of a ship's cargo and generally, it is only a personal obligation on the borrower. It is not a specific lien on the goods unless there is an express stipulation in the bond. In case of loss, the loan amounts to an equitable lien on the salvage.

The correspondence was reviewed by Colonel Dove, in 1922, when he concluded his report to the India Office with an acknowledgement to the then owner of the collection Mrs. Bannatyne, in placing the documents at his disposal and affording facilities for their examination and study.

The collection of letters starts with an early letter from Stringer Lawrence writing as a Lieut. Colonel. It encloses Lawrence's personal account of his campaigns; written in October 1755 dated only a year before Lawrence left India to return to England. The letter is directed to Admiral Watson probably at his request. It contains a valuable first-hand account of the many actions fought by Lawrence The letter was retained by Robert Palk as a reminder of the campaigns in which he and Lawrence did so much to preserve and improve the East India Company's trade.

Lieut. Colonel Stringer Lawrence to Charles Watson, Esqr., Rear Admiral of the Red, and Commander in Chief of all His Majesty's Ships employed in the East Indies. 1755, October 8th. Fort St. George:

> Sir,
> I beg leave to present you with an account of my campaigns in India. The better to make the cause of the war understood I shall begin with a short account of the first rise of the troubles here ; the state of affairs when I left India at the end of the year '50 ; what happened during my absence and after my return in March '52, unto the end of the year '54, when a cessation of arms took place between the two nations.
> My narrative, Sir, will, I am afraid, savour more of the soldier than the historian, but I submit my stile and actions with all my heart to your inspection. Your good nature, I know, will make large allowances, and your judgment in correcting, at the same time it improves, will be a mark of your esteem and regard, which I shall at all times think myself highly honoured with. The Mogul Empire is divided into three Departments. I shall only treat of the one in which we have been concerned : it is to the southward and called the Deckan. The government of this third is appointed by the Mogul himself ; and by a power delegated from his Prince, he names the Nabobs to govern the different Subahs in his Principality.The Deckan has seven Subahships, which are named as in the margin. The capital of the Province is Aurengebade : the three last Subahships are comprehended under the name of the Carnatick, in which we have endeavoured to support the Nabob Mahomed Alice Cawn.

Lawrence's narrative was probably written and presented during the long sea voyage home and later printed by R. O. Cambridge in his Account of the War in India, 1750 to 1760. London, 1761. Lawrence's letter terminates thus:

> The day after the suspension of arms, proclaimed 11th October, 1754 was declared I left the army and came down to the Settlements, not the same man in constitution as when I left them, after a campaign of two years and seven months, and never absent from the field but six weeks in the whole time. A truce for a year and a half, or till we could receive answers from Europe, succeeded the cessation. Since that time our troops have some times been employed in settling the country and assisting the

Nabob to collect his revenues. I have now gone through my narrative, in which my constant endeavour has been to give a true description of our military transactions for the amusement and perusal only of a few particular friends, who, I hope, will make allowances for the want of a proper stile and correctness. If the subject is clear and easily understood, the end proposed is fully answered. I am, with the greatest esteem. Sir, your most obedient humble servant,

S. Lawrence

Mr Pye tells Robert Palk that he has arived safely in January 1758. The sense of relief is palpable. The sea voyage from India could be very long and dangerous. Mr Pye has been charged with the encashment of Robert Palk's Indian investments and here he reports on progress made to date. In 1759 Palk was returning to England and would not return to India until 1761. The size of his fortune was of the greatest importance to him for his new life in England. John Pye was one of four Navy Agents in July, 1757.

Mr Pye to Robert Palk 1758, February 5th. Bombay.

My dear Friend,

I have the pleasure to acquaint you of our arrival here the 23rd of last month, all well, and that in a day or two we embark on board the *Swallow* for Gombaroon, from whence we go in the *Success* to Bassorah; but as I have very little time to spare now, will proceed to commune with you on business.
Your Respondentia Bond on Capt. James I leave with Capt. Hough to be received the 13th instant, being then due. Your chest containing by your instructions ten thousand sonnauts, but by ocular demonstration only nine thousand nine hundred and ninety five, I have sold by Capt. Hough's advice for nine thousand five hundred and ninety five Bombay rupees. I have settled your account with Hough & Spencer to the 31st January last, and inclose you a copy of it, by which you will see the ballance due to you is thirteen thousand seven hundred sixty three rupees and fifty reas,

and that your Gheria prize money and Doidge's Respondentia on the Liveley is included in it.

The Governor and Council will give Hough bills for all the money we want, but not time enough for me to take one with me ; but I shall leave instructions with him to send two of your bills home by two of the European ships which depart in about' a month. Your bills will be made payable to Charles Brett. As soon as I get home I will see Brett, and commune with him on your affairs. No account can be given of the 400 rupees paid to Smith, late supra cargoe of the Grampus. The china of Japan and the third of a leager of arrack given you in former days by Henry Doidge, Esq., are safely deposed in a godown in the Tank House under the charge of George England. Observe your jars are not separated from the rest ; either you or King of the Cumberland.

I humbly apprehend amounts to pounds sterling 4,162/ 4/ 6, which you are morally certain of getting home this year ; so as it can't be better, why you must e'en be content 'tis well as it is — *Si fortuna vestra te tormento*. Let *sperato te contento*. Ives and Doidge send their best wishes. Mr. Shannon deserted us at Cochin, and one Mackintosh is come in his room. Alms goes with us, as does young Pigot.

I am sorry to tell you, in regard to your hopes of Doidge's drawing on you for forty thousand rupees, that Captain Hough having lain out for our and Mr. Stevens Squadron more money than was left here, there is no such thing as any prize money to be got ; so nothing can be done in that affair under Mr. Hawke and General Mordaunt on a secret expedition. The *Chesterfield, Portfield* and *Edgcote*, Indiamen, arrived at Limerick in June last. The *Syren*, sloop, Dick King, arrived in England the beginning of June, by whom the Company knew of the capture and recapture of Calcutta. The *Experiment*, man of war, engaged and took a French privateer of 36 guns and 400 men. Mr. Fox is Paymaster of the Forces. The Duke of Newcastle at the head of the Treasury, and I think Mr. Legge is Chancellor of the Exchequer.

Adieu, and believe me with all sincerity your faithful friend, &c.

John Pye.

PS Doidge says 'tis doubtful whether he shall write to you or no. His head achs ; he has a great deal to do. To be sure we have led fine lives since we have been here. Pemble is a fine fellow at 3 in the morning, and laughs heartily at the story of Cousin Swinney. Pray give my best wishes to Capt. Smith

In 1760 Palk was resident in Devon and writes to William Fergusson in terms that are somewhat unclear because the original letter from Palk no longer exists:

William Fergusson to Robert Palk, Esqr., at Mrs. Ray's in Tavistock Row, Covent Garden. 1760, November 10th.

I am favoured to-day with your letter of the 4th, and shall write to the two gentlemen in the north concerning the subject of your letter. They are not at all punctual in their answers ; for though I wrote them repeatedly of the necessity of returning an answer to the Gruffees at Fort St. George, and to Mr. Smith at Canton, and transmitted them the letters and accounts you sent me, desiring after perusal they would be pleased to send me back the same, or copys of them ; and that they would either write what answer they thought proper or leave it to me to do it, yet I have not received any answer from them.
Since it appears inconvenient that Miss Munro should go in the same ship with you, I shall agree to her going with Capt. Glover or with any other you shall approve, since there are other ladys going out with her in the same ship.
Mr Pye writes another letter that throws light on the subject of how and where to invest the proceeds of personal trading (a practice condoned by the Company). The reference to the South Sea Company is a famous example from the world of high yielding but risky investments available in 1760: As to what stocks it may be best to lay out the money in belonging to our Gruff, I cannot determine. Only I am afraid that trusting to the new supplys will be attended with delay and other inconveniences, especially as none of us are likely to be in London ; and therefore I should prefer either South Sea or Bank Annuitys, which always keep pace with the other Stocks, and are not liable to the same uncertaintys as the new supplys. When I recieve Mr. Munro and Mr. Robertson's answers, you shall be acquainted with them.

XVI
A letter from the King, 1762

There follows a letter from the King written to Lawrence in 1762 at a time when Lawrence was a member of council. There are marginal notes by Lawrence starting with names of the Subahships in the Deckan ; Aurengebade, Kandees, Barraud, Berampoore, Golcondah, Ahamad Nagar, Vizapoor ; the three last comprehended under the name of the Carnatick. The Carnatick is part on this side of the river Kitshna to Cape Comorin, and Golconda is on the other side of the river to Aurengebade : the whole goes under the name of the Deckan.

The letter was duplicated to Robert Palk who saved it to his archive. It did not contain good news! The details reveal the complex nature of the dealings between the French and British following the campaigns of 1752 - 54 and in 1759 by Robert Clive. Robert Palk was much involved in the administration and legal side of these:

Order for Restitution in the East Indies, 1763, March 16th. Court at St. James. To our Trusty and Welbeloved Major General Stringer Lawrence, Brigadier General William Draper, Colonel Eyre Coote, or to the Officer Commanding any Part of Our Land Forces in the East Indies, or to the Commanding Officer in any Islands or Places which shall have been taken possession of by Our Army.

George R.

> Trusty and Welbeloved, We Greet you well. Whereas a Definitive Treaty of Peace has been signed at Paris, on the Tenth Day of February last, by Our Minister Plenipotentiary and Those of Our Good Brothers The Most Christian King and The Catholick King to which The Minister Plenipotentiary of Our Good Brother The Most Faithful King acceded on the same Day ; And Whereas It is stipulated by the Eleventh Article of the said Treaty that Great Britain shall restore to France, in the Condition

they are now in, the different Factories which that Crown possessed, as well on the Coast of Coromandel and Orixa as on that of Malabar, as also in Bengal, at the Beginning of the year 1749 ; And that His Most Christian Majesty shall restore, on His Side, all that He may have conquered from Great Britain, in the East Indies, during the present War ; And will expressly cause Nattal and Tapanoully in the Island of Sumatra to be restored ; And Whereas it is stipulated in the Twenty Third Article of the same Treaty that all the Countries and Territories which may have been Conquered, in whatever Part of the World, by the Arms of Us and of the Most Faithful King, as well as by those of the Most Christian and Catholick Kings, which are not included in the present Treaty either under the Title of Cessions or under the Title of Restitutions, shall be restored without Difficulty and without requiring any Compensation ; And It being further stipulated in the Twenty Fourth Article of the said Definitive Treaty that the Factories in the East Indies shall be restored Six Months after the Exchange of the Ratifications of the present Treaty, or sooner if it can be done. Which Ratifications were exchanged on the 10th of this Instant March ; Our Will and Pleasure is that You do, pursuant to the Stipulations above recited, deliver or cause to be delivered to such Commissary or Commissaries as shall be named and authorized on the Part of our Said Good Brother The Most Christian King to receive the same, any of the Factories under Your Command which are to be restored to France in the Condition they are now in, agreably to the Stipulations of the Eleventh and Twenty Fourth Articles of the Definitive Treaty abovementioned, and also that You do deliver or cause to be delivered to the Commissary or Commissaries duely authorized to receive the same any Countries or Territories which may be to be restored to France or Spain in Consequence of the Twenty Third Article of the said Treaty ; And it is Our further Will and Pleasure that you should take the necessary Measures with the French Commissaries that Nattal and Tapanoully in the Island of Sumatra, and all that France may have conquered from Great Britain in the East Indies during the present War, be restored agreably to the Stipulations of the said Eleventh Article of the Definitive Treaty, as well as with the French and Spanish Commissaries for the Restitution of any other Conquests which may have been made upon Our Establishments in the East Indies by the Arms of the Most Christian and Catholick Kings, and which are to be restored in Consequence of the Twenty Third Article of the said Definitive Treaty; And that the same be restored at the same Time that Restitution is made of any Conquests which have been made by any of Our Forces under Your Command upon the French or Spanish Establishments. And for so doing this shall be Your Warrant. Given at Our Court at St. James's the Sixteenth Day of March, 1763, in the Third Year of our Reign.

By His Majesty's Command,
Lord Egremont (a Secretary in Bute's ministry of 1762).

A begging letter written by Brother Salvador to Palk in 1765 was an appeal to the governor of Madras, as Palk had now become, asking for assistance for the establishment:

Brother Salvator a Sanctis D'fonseca to Governor Palk, Madras. 1765, Sept. 27th. San Thome.

Most illustrious and invincible Governor, Lord Palk
With the greatest respect I throw myself at your Lordship's feet and approach, in the only possible way by means of this letter, to kiss your hand and enquire after your health. If that be good, I have no doubt that your Lordship will be crowned with yet higher honours due to the gifts and virtues which you possess ; for, as I have always heard, all men acknowledge your piety, power and greatness. When I arrived on this coast, I went to your Lordship's residence on six occasions to deliver a letter of recommendation from Dom Loppo ; but being unable to obtain speech with you, I gave the letter to M. de Landreset, the senior officer of the Portuguese forces at Goa, that he might deliver it by other hands. For your Lordship's satisfaction I will now be brief. I was sent out as the head of the Missions of the Spiritual Province of Portugal in the kingdoms of Jamseylon, Achem and Queda. I accordingly remained on your coast to supervise necessaries coming from Portugal and Goa, so that the missionaries in the said kingdoms might carry on their appointed work.

> Being myself quite worn out by persistent sickness, and being at present without means of subsistence, I suffer much. Like a lonely sojourner in Jerusalem I find myself in this place, where the power and honour of my kinsmen in Portugal are of no avail by reason of distance and my vow of poverty — a vow I find difficulty in observing in this country. Hearken therefore, my lord, to the counsel of Christ and the Apostle St. Paul, who says. It is more blessed to give than to receive.
> In time, by the love of Christ, and for the honour and salvation of your soul, I humbly beseech your Lordship to bestow alms on me according to the measure of your greatness and charity. And I will ever pray to the utmost of my power for your illustrious house, that God will guard you and deliver you from your enemies for many years to come, so that you may attain to immortal glory. Amen. God knows with what shame I expose my necessities to you. But forgive me, my Lord. Your most humble servant and true well-wisher with all my heart ; now and always, and at all times and in every place I will remember you as your petitioner,

Frater Magister Salvator a Sanctis D'Fonca. San Thome, at the hospice of St. Ritta 27th September, 1765. The outer cover carries a wax seal displaying a full length figure with aureole, and two acolytes below. The seal is inscribed. The cover is addressed thus :

Illustrissimo Gobernatori de Madrasta Domino Palco, Deus cum custodiat ad multos annos in Madrasta. " De Sancto Thome."

The Nawob Walajah writes to Governor Palk in 1766 enclosing a number of letters for the king and the East India Company, three years into Robert Palks's governorship of Madras, extolling the merits of Stringer Lawrence and announcing a financial transaction:

Nawab Walajah :Honble. Robert Palk, Esqr., Governor. [Endorsed in Palk's hand] Nabob's Letters to the King and Company per Pacific, 3rd April, 1766.

> Enclosed I send you a letter to the Company enclosing one for his Majesty, which I desire may be translated into English, and the copies sent to me that they may accompany the original and be clearly understood.
> I know you will highly approve of my doing this justice to General

Lawrence, of whose glorious actions you have so often been an eye witness. Be pleased also to repeat my attachment to the Company and my entire dependance, and above all I desire that what I have said concerning the General may be strongly recommended to the Company.
Enclosure No. 1

To the Honble. The Chairman and Gentlemen of the Direction of the East India Company:

The many and great obligations I am under to General Lawrence induce me to request you will be pleased to present the inclosed letter to his Majesty, whom God preserve. I send a copy for your perusal. You are too well acquainted with General Lawrence's eminent services to need a particular explanation. I have therefore only further to request that he may receive from you annually on my account on the 1st of January in Pagodas, which shall be repaid here on that day to your Governor and Council ; and I desire you will prevail on him to accept this from me as a gratefull acknowledgment to my great benefactor. By his Majesty's favor, your powerfull assistance and his signal successes, peace and plenty have been happily restored to my country. It is therefore equitable that he should reap a part of the fruits of his own labor. He is grown old with toil, but his glorious actions will never dye.
By means of Lord Clive the Mogul Patcha has conferred on me great honors and made my Government independent of the Deckan, chiefly out of regard to my attachment to the Company. Thus under your favor and protection my Government is firmly established, and I am free from all manner of apprehension. May your prosperity and your fame ever increase.
What can I say more ?

Enclosure No. 2.
To His Most Excellent Majesty George the 3rd, &c., &c.

I had the honor of addressing your Majesty by Admiral Cornish and

Colonel Monson, and now the departure of General Lawrence, a servant of your Majesty as well as of the Company, induces me again to express my gratitude for the very great assistance I have on every occasion received from the unwearied vigilance and distinguished abilities of this excellent officer, whose sword has been often my only protector in the day of battle ; who for years together kept the field against a numerous ennemy, and by his courage and conduct surmounted every difficulty ; who comforted me continually in my distress, and with a spirit and perseverance peculiar to himself was almost the only man in Indostan that never dispaired of my cause. No doubt Your Majesty is well acquainted with his important services, disinterested character and extraordinary merit, which are not to be described within the compass of a letter, but which I and my family above all others are bound to acknowledge. May your Majesty never want such an Officer to command your Armies. I have desired he Company to represent my firm reliance on your Majesty's protection, and to present this letter, intended to express my deep sense of your royal favor in giving me such assistance as I have found in General Lawrence.
May your Majesty's reign be long and happy.
What can I say more?

Letter written in 1766 by the the Secretary to the Court of Directors to Major General Stringer Lawrence announcing the pension awarded to Lawrence as he retired from India for the final time. 1766, December 4th. East India House.

It is with great pleasure I inform you that the Court of Directors yesterday came to an unanimous resolution that the annuity of five hundred pounds setled upon you for life, which ceased by your resignation thereof on returning to your station as Commander in Chief of the Company's forces in the East Indies in 1761, is to be continued from the time of your leaving Fort Saint George for England, when your allowances for the above mentioned station ceased. Most sincerely wishing the Bath may have the desired effect,
I remain, Sir, your most obedient humble servant,

Robt. James, Secretary.

Sea voyages to India were not to be taken lightly. Stories abound of shipwreck, pirates, French Men o' War, disease (of which small pox was ever present), tiny cabins and high prices. Journey times of up to 12 months were regularly required and changes to destination were ever possible. The following letter gives a feel for the conditions abord the packet *Osterly.*

Henry Moore to the Honorable Robert Palk, Esqr. 766, December 18th, Ship Osterley, near Anjengo:

> As the *Osterley* is now standing into Anjengo road, I write you half a dozen lines from on board her to advise you of our arrival thus far. I hope they will salute you and Mrs. Palk in good health. Mr. Vansittart was well in Burlington street the middle of March last. Should the *Anson* and *Devonshire* be arrived with you, you must have heard of him much later.When we were at Cadiz we heard of the arrival of the Admiral Stevens at Lisbon in ninety days from Bengal : she arrived there about the middle of April. We sailed from Cales [Cadiz] the 3rd of May, but the repairs we got there proving ineffectual, we were obliged to put in to Saint Salvador upon the coast of Brazil, where we arrived under the 13th of June with a leak of five feet an hour. I need not to Mr. Palk paint our distresses. Heaving down, and the giving our crazy ship a new bottom detained us at that place untill the 20th of September. We have since continued quite tight, and are all very healthy, nor has any accident taken place during the remainder of the voyage except the carrying away topmasts and other trifles of that nature. Thanks to Providence, our voyage now draws near a conclusion. When I embarque on another outward bound one I hope it will use me no worse than this has done. I beg my respects to Mrs. Palk.
>
> Henry Moore.

XVII
Company Friends, 1767

One of Palk's great friends and a valued colleague for many years was William Martin Goodlad, a Madras civil servant of 1761, who was Secretary in the Civil Department. He was a protege of Palk, who was a friend of the Goodlad family. There are many letters from him in the collection. Palk was now a very wealthy man and the liquidation of his investments was a preoccupation for many of his correspondents. Letters often addressed the political situation in detail and the mentions of Indian rulers and their states can be confusing. Obviously the state of peace was important as was the methods employed for encashing debt. This is a copy letter retained by Palk in his files.

[Endorsed] "Letter from Mr. Palk, 25th January, 1767, dated on board the Lord Camden, Captn. Nathaniel Smith, in Madras Road on the day he embarked for Europe. 1767, January 25th. On board the Lord Camden, Madras Road

Dear Goodlad,
I am much obliged to Mr. Bourchier and you for conveying the intelligence of Mr. Powney's safety. At any rate he is likely to make a better voyage than I had reason to expect.
As I think I know the goodness of your heart fullwell, I could never doubt of the sincerity of its sentiments. I freely acknowledge that I have often felt a most particular satisfaction in your success and well known improvement, and those sentiments of honor and uprightness which I know will never fail to be your constant companions ; and you can have none that you ought to be fonder of. There is no good fortune that can possibly happen to its greatest favorites that I do not most heartily wish you, and it will at all times give me pleasure to hear from you, or to be instrumental in promoting it. Mrs. Palk sends her most affectionate wishes, and I am, dear Goodlad, unalterably your sincere friend,

Robert Palk.

Though he was away from the Company in India Robert Palk retained his contact with the directors in London but he did not join the board. He was known as most approachable and effective in arranging situations for his friends and their families. The following is such an example:

In 1767 Ensign Carpenter writes to Robert Palk to thank him for past favours received and asking him to use his influence to retrieve a difficult situation:

Ensign J. Carpenter to Robert Palk. 1767, January 25th. Tritchinopoly.

> Give me leave to assure you that it is not in my power to express the sense I have of the very kind letter you honoured me with, or how much I am obliged to you for the favours you have shewn me. I most gratefully thank you, Sir, for your intentions to join my friends at home with your endeavours to recover the rank my former commission gives me.
> Mr. Webber was the gentleman that gott me first appointed. Last year my friends sollicited and procured me the interest of Mr. Cruttendon and Mr. Harrison, both of which gentlemen expressed the greatest desire of serving me, and, I am persuaded, did every thing in their power then towards it. They likewise applied, Sir, to Mr. Barrington, Mr. Savage, Mr. Scrafton and Mr. Wheeler, and engaged those gentlemen's interest in my behalf. As my present situation deprives me of the hopes of acquiring any thing farther than a maintenance suitable to the character we are in a great measure obligated to support at the expence of every thing valuable to us, and subjects me to such disagreeable inconveniences as to deprive me of serving me [sic] with that chearfulness necessary to our duty, I have wrote my friends that my whole welfare depends on the success of their endeavours in the strongest manner I were able ; but as you, Sir, know the very great difference between my present situation and that of those gentlemen who were appointed Lieutenants at the same time, or even those gentlemen who were then made Ensigns, notwithstanding they arrived in the country but a few months before me, I flatter myself. Sir, that it will be in your power to get me restored to the rank I am conscious to myself of never having deserved to be deprived of, and which I should be happy to shew myself not unworthy of possessing. This is the only hope I have. Sir, of ever seeing again my friends with pleasure or persuing with satisfaction the service I am engaged in. Most

sincerely wishing you and family health and every happiness,
I am. Sir, your ever obliged and obedient humble servant,

J. Carpenter.

Good news about his wife's family for Robert Palk written by George Vansitart, Bengal civil service, younger brother of Henry Vansittart, father of Palk's wife. There were many Palks and Vansittarts serving in India both before and after Rober Palk himself.

George Vansittart to Robert Palk, Esqr. Duplicate. 1767, February 15th. Madras.

Dear Palk,
Two or three days after your departure I received letters from Russell and Campbell congratulating me on my being appointed Resident at Midnapoor, and Campbell informs me that for this step I am entirely indebted to Lord Clive, who himself proposed it to the Board without solicitation, or even my name being mentioned to him. This is a favour which I little expected from his Lordship ; my obligation to him is therefore the greater, and I think that I may now with much propriety make him the acknowledgement which you proposed by way of advance towards a reconciliation. You know I am sensible that in some respects I have acted wrong ; I have no objection therefore to the making of such an acknowledgement on a motive of gratitude for the favour he has conferred on me, although, as there have been causes of complaint on both sides, I could not prevail on myself to do it through fear of his power. Inclosed is a letter to him on the subject. Consult with Harry concerning it, and if you and he approve it, let it be delivered. We shall set out in a day or two for Bengal. The John and James schooner is to have the honour of carrying us.
Yours very affectionately,

George Vansittart.

On 19 February 1767 Robert Palk, the nephew of our Robert Palk, writes a formal letter giving thanks for the treatment he has received and bringing him the latest news since Robert Palk, senior, had already left India for England. He then tells his uncle of his prospects for a better job. In the letter there is a harrowing account of what happened when smallpox broke out on board ship. Unhappily this was an all too common occurence.

Robert Palk jun. to Robert Palk, Esqr. 1767, February 19th. Fort St. George.

Dear Sir,

I embrace this opportunity of enquiring after your health and to thank you for your bountifull kindness to me. I hope that my future conduct will be such as to meet with your approbation, and that I shall have it in my power to make some return for the care you have taken of me from my infancy. I hope you will continue to favor me with your friendly advice, which hitherto has been of infinite service to me, and I do assure you it will always be gratefully received and acknowledged. I most sincerely wish you and Mrs. Palk may have a pleasant passage, and a happy meeting of your friends in England.

Lord Clive quited his Government the 26th ultimo in the evening, and embarked on board the Brittannia very much out of order. Before he resigned the Government a great many promotions were made, and amongst the rest George to the Chiefship of Midnapore. If nothing better offers for me after my arrival in Calcutta, I intend to ask to be appointed his Assistant, if he approves it. At present George tells me I had better wait for something better, but I should be very well satisfyed with that and the prospect of succeeding him in that employ some years hence. As George is in a great hurry to get down, we have taken our passage on the John and James schooner, and are to set out from Trivatore the morning after to-morrow.

Mr. Pybus has had a severe attack of his old disorder since your departure, which made him resolve to follow you on the *Anson*, Captain Linox, who arrived here four days ago, but the people on board have the smallpox to such a violent degree that numbers have died of it, and Mrs. Pybus insists on his not going on that ship, both on his own account and the child's. I believe he will be persuaded to wait till October. Captain Richardson has come off with flying colours. It appeared in the course of the examination that cloth was on board, but the captain and officers knew nothing of it. In short, the blame was thrown on the doctor, who died before the ship arrived at Bengal, and the purser, who told the Committee appointed for the enquiry that, since the blame was laid to him, he would not take up any of their time in contradicting it ; so it ended in Captain Richardson's being requested to dismiss him, which he did, and made the purser an acknowledgement for his great good nature. Mr. Mackey's account of their transactions at Teneriffe and Richardson's don't agree at all, notwithstanding Mr. McKey wrote him what he had said about it. The *Pigot* is expected here every day. On our journey to Gingee, being the fourth person, I was under the necessity of playing at cards, and by bad management and ill luck was a considerable looser, which drove me to the necessity of applying to Mr. Morse for Pags. 100. By a letter I have just received from my father I understand my brother is coming out on the expected ships, but he doth not tell me whether he is coming here or to Bengal. Should he not come out in the Service, I hope you will interest your-self in getting him appointed to Bengal. All your friend[s] at this place are well, and every thing goes on just as you left them. I desire my compliments to Mrs. Palk, Mr. and Mrs. Van and the General, and am with great respect, dear Sir, Your most obliged and obedient humble servant,

RoBT. Palk.

A sample of the betel nut

XVIII
Indian Traders and officials, 1767

Chocopah was a frequent Palk correspondent and usually provided interesting information regarding local conditions of trade. Chocapah Chetti was a merchant dealing with the Company and responsible for managing trades in various commodities. He writes in 1767 to inform Robert Palk about deals in cloth and other items:

Chocapah Chetti to the Honourable Robert Palk, Esqr. 1767, March 3rd. Fort St. George.

Honourable Sir,
I shall be extreamly glad to hear of your Honour and family's safe arrival in England and enjoyment of a perfect health in that delightfull country. Since your Honour's departure Mr. Bourchier carrys on his government in good order, and every thing going on at the same terms [as] when you

Warren Hastings

was here. The Company's broad cloth on the 27th of last month [was] put up at publick outcry at the Sea Gate on the usual terms, and sold about 30 lotts, each lott consisting [of] 5 bales, 3 bales of Auroras, one bale Popinju, and one bale ordinary red, and in some lotts one bale ordinary yellow, at 585 to 591 Pagodas per lott, and some Purpatanues at the usual prices, and the remainder they could not sell at that time. Mupral Kistnayah, farmer of Beetle and Tabacoa, having insulted with the Nabob and made demand [for] dutys for the trifling Beetle and Tabacoa bought for his Excellency's use, which the Nabob represented to the Governour and Council ; and then the Governour and Council examined this in consultation, and said to the said Mupral Kistnaya that he is not fit to be that farmer any longer, and took away the said Cowle from him, and gave that farm to one Vidyanado Modely, who was agent to Pushpunado Nainar sometime, and one Moodu Kistna Modely, the late Arrack farmer, for four years and five months from 1st of this month, at twenty three thousand agodas for every year. I shall be extreamly obliged to your Honour if you will be pleased to remember your old and faithfull servant Chocapah, and recommend him to your friends both here and coming up from thence.

We have not received any further news from Manilah, what they have done with our ship and cargo ; and if we are permitted to send our ships there to trade, it will be a very good thing for the merchants at this Settlement.

Since your Honour's departure, here is nothing materials that I can write to your Honour, but the Governour and Council deferred the new contract for the Honble. Company's Investment for the present year untill first April

Chocapah.

In 1767 Mrs Powney writes to wish Robert Palk well upon his final return to England. She also warns that her son may have a problem. Mary Powney, daughter of Capt. George Heron, master mariner and marine surveyor, was the widow of Capt. John Powney, master mariner. She died a centenarian in 1780.

Mrs. Mary Powney to Robert Palk, Esqr. 1767, March 12th. Fort St. George.

Dear Sir,
From the long acquaintance I have had the happiness to have with you flatters my hopes that you will pardon the intrusion of a few lines from an old friend to assure you of the greatfull sense I shall always retain of the friendship and many civilities you have so kindly, dear Sir, shewn me, and that my prayers will be constant for your safe arrival in England and the continuance of all blessings to you and yours. I hope some time before this reaches, you will be enjoying yourself in your own country. Pray present my respects to General Lawrence and Calliaud, and believe me to be with much affection, esteem and respect, dear Sir, your most obliged friend and humble servant,

Mary Powney
P.S. Sir, I have the pleasure to acquaint you of my son Will being safe and well at Malacca. Since, I hear he was arrived at Tellecherry and was going to Bombay, and I am afraid it will be a ruiness Voyage.

It seems that the departure of Robert Palk from the territory caused consernation amongst the merchants that he left behind. Two of them write to explain their problem with the Nabob because they were not sufficiently generous with presents of beetle for him and his wife.

Mooperala Kistnia and Rama Kisna to Robert Palk, Esqr. 1767, March 15th. Fort St. George

Sir,
I hope this will find you safely arrived in England, and that you and your family have had the enjoyment of a perfect health and that you will not forget your old faithfull servants who begin already to feel the want of your protection. Two days after your departure the Nabob delivered a petition to the Governor and Council accusing me of want of respect to him, and other trumped up storeys that I demanded dutys from him on beetle and tobacco brought for his household use. You may well remember, Sir, that I once informed you that on the Begum's arrival there

was large quantitys of beetle demanded, of which the under servants made a job by selling at the market ; and you was pleased to order me to acquaint Nazeeb Cawn to take just so much only as was wanted for the use of the Nabob's family, and accordingly 45 bundles of beetle (instead of 60) was determined to be sufficient for every day's expence ; and at the same time I shewed him the account of the beetle supplied to that time, amounting to twelve thousand fanams, which he said he would see about. No more past between the Nabob and me untill the day after your departure, when some tobacco being imported for the Nabob was, according to custom, brought to my godown. The third day after it was brought, and when my Peons carried it to Nazeeb Cawn, they carried also a memorandum at his own request of the dutys thereon, which amounted to a pagoda and odd fanams, and of this the Nabob made a handle as if I had slighted and made little account of him ; and the Governor and Council was pleased to reprimand me very much for it, and determined that it was a sufficient cause to forfeit my cowl, and the farm was disposed of to Vaydanadum and Moodukisna conicopoly on the 23rd ultimo for twenty three thousand pagodas per annum for the remainder time that I was to have enjoyed it. I delivered your letter of recommendation to Mr. Bourchier before the determination of Council, but it produced no favourable effect. I would not have given up the affair so easily had not Mr. Morse seemed very desirous that I should be rid of this business. Besides, I was very sensible that I could have got no redress here, and that the only way to have righted myself would have been to have pushed the matter further ; but to a person of my time of life it would be too troublesome and vexatious. Upon desiring Mr. Bourchier's advice what was best to be done, whether we should put in an answer into the Council, he told me the Nabob was so irritated that there was no other method of pacifying him but to surrender up my right quietly : that the Nabob had thoughts even of taking away the grant of the village that was allowed for the support of Ramaniaka's charity choultry at Checrecoad, and that it was with difficulty he (Mr. Bourchier) dis[s]uaded him from it. The diamond business is growing worse and worse every day, and if the Gentlemen in England don't stop [the] making of remittances, they will lose a great deal. The prices at Moonimadgoo is risen since the purchase for last ship, and the demand for diamonds increases daily. Gocul laughs when he is asked for the 5,000 pagodas of diamonds he promised you to give Mr. Morse for this ship, nor can Mr. Morse have any remedy whilst he [is] supported by gentlemen in station. Diamonds are carried now to Bengal and Surat, as there are people now who purchase at those places for Europe. We desire you will recommend us to your friends in power here that we may always have their protection. We wish only to live a quiet life. Please to present our humble respects to Mrs. Palk. We are very gratefully, Sir, your most obliged servants,

Mooperala Kistnia

A personal leter to Robert Palk from George Vansittart showing the stresses that attended senior company servants.

George Vansittart to Robert Palk, Esqr. 1767, March 16th. Calcutta.

Dear Palk,
Inclosed is a duplicate of my letter of the 15th of February. A strong north-east wind detained us at Madras from the 20th to the 27th. We arrived here the day before yesterday, and the day after to-morrow I set out for Midnapoor, where I shall be very well contented to remain quiet and undisturbed for some years. I believe I may be saved the trouble of a trip to Europe even if their honours in Leadenhall Street should take it into their heads to dismiss me in consequence of our last year's rebellion; for I have been positively assured by people who I should think must know that in such case the Committee will recommend me to be reinstated, and in the mean while continue me in the service till their further pleasure can be received. I am at present on perfectly good terms with all our rulers, and intend to adopt some of your prudential maxims. What with 30,000 rupees which we have lent to Russell, and the 20,000 which we are to pay to Robin, your balance will be but a trifle. We shall keep it in our own hands at 8 per cent, till we have a good opportunity of remitting it. My love to Mrs. Palk and the little ones. Yours affectionately,

George Vansittart

A letter of thanks from Mrs Casamajor following Palk's return to England for the last time. It illustrates again the many genuine friendships made by Palk throughout his time in India.

Mrs. Rebecca Casamajor to Robert Palk, Esqr. 1767, March 16th. Fort St. George.

My dear Sir,
As no distance of place can ever decrease the respect, esteem and gratitude that is due from me, I hope you will excuse the liberty I take in troubling you with a few lines to assure you of my ardent wishes that it may salute you in your native land after a short and pleasant voyage in health and a continuance of all other blessings. I suppose by this time you have reached the Cape or pretty near it, and hope Mrs. Palk and the little ones will be much benefited by its fine air and all other refreshments.
As you, dear Sir, have so great a number of friends to write you all occur[r]ences, I shall only mention, what I know will give you pleasure, that our new Governor goes on very well under the weight of government, in great spirits, and with much polit[e]ness and chearfulness entertaining his friends and company. I hope he will continue in health and strength to acquit himself to the satisfaction of all his well wishers. Give me leave to present my son's best respects, and that I am, with all acknowledgments and regard, dearest Sir, your affectionate and much obliged humble servant,

Rebecca Casamaijor

XIX
Colonel John Call reports, 1767

Formerly Chief Engineer and a member of the Madras Council, in 1767 Colonel John Call sends news in the letter kept as a copy by Palk. The political interest shown by Palk to his friends in India indicates his work when in post. This interest continued up to the ending of his business contacts which ran out (or letters were not retained) in 1783. He was always treated by those in office as a very effective channel of communication with the directors in London.

Colonel John Call to Robert Palk, Esqr. Duplicate. 1767, March19th. Madras.

My dear Friend,

As I persuaded myself you will impatiently expect to hear of the progress of the Confederacy against Hydre Ally, so I take up the pen with the greater pleasure to give you the state of our military as well as civil transactions since you left us.

Very soon after Colonel Smith arrived at Eiderabad, which was the 15th or 16th January, the Subah pitched his tents without the city, and in a few days proceeded towards the Kistnah, which he crossed the 18th ultimo, having spent some time in settling with the Polygars on his route. The 19th Captain James Fitzgerald's battalion and Lieut. Povery's detachment joined Colonel Smith, who had been very uneasy at the delay of our troops ; but he will be obliged to wait much longer for those from the Circars, because it was found necessary to reduce the Zemindars of Peddapore and Samilcotah, which kept Major Thomas Fitzgerald's detachment till the 15th February, and the 9th instant he was only advanced as far as Sangaverum near Eiderabad, so that it will be the 25th instant or perhaps the end of the month before he can possibly join the Subah, who on the 26th ultimo was just entering the country of Adony. The troops from hence and Vellore were delayed in the beginning of February by exceeding heavy rain, which laid all the country under water and made it the 18th February before they joined at Lalapett. From thence they were to cross into the Cadapah country at a pass called Mungalpettah, but having been disappointed of provisions from Arcott, it was the 11th instant before they crossed the hills, and they are now only near Cadapah, from whence you may judge it will be the end of the month before they can join the Subah's army. Mahadarow with his Marattas was early in motion and made very rapid advances to the southward, so that his troops entered the country of Adony and begun to plunder it by the end of January. After some threats and a little burning and fighting, which we suppose was by the Subah's connivance, Bazalet Jing settled with Mahadarow, and the Marattas proceeded towards Sera. One of Hydre Ally's Generals met them with a considerable body of horse, but he was defeated, made prisoner, and all his guns and baggage taken. Another smaller body met the like fate, and the Marattas by the last accounts we had were besieging Sera or Sirpi with their main body, while the rest scampered all over the country. Hydre Ali during all this time is at Syringapatam, either collecting his forces or endevoring to compromise matters for money. The latter, it is said, will take place, because it is not the intention either of the Marattas or the Subah to remain on this side of the Kistnah longer than the month of May. Allarmed at the apprehension of this event, and that all our project will be frustrated, we are going to send James Bourchier to make representations both to the Subah and Mahadarow how impossible it is to effect the overthrow of Hydre Ally in any year if they only cross the River Kistnah in January and recross it in May. For Hydre Ally, aware of this, need only garrison the places in the Sera Country and those of his late conquest north of the ancient Mysore country, and keeping behind Syringapatam with his main body, will never have any thing to apprehend but the burning and ruining part of the open country. Whereas if we proceed hand in hand and continue our operations during the whole year, there is no doubt but the expedition may be accomplished. Mr. Bourchier is also to endevor to bring about a formal Treaty between the Subah and Mahadarow, for which I lately drew out the enclosed reflections and articles. This Treaty we esteem absolutely necessary, for we cannot discover that any agreement at present subsists, and it is said that the Marattas proceeds on in the manner they do that they may have the first plundering of the country and possession of what places they can take. This is a system that must bring on disputes, and will save Hydre Ally if not prevented. The Marattas, it seems, are jealous of the large force we are sending to the Subah, and from the delay of our troops conclude we never meant heartily to enter into the operations against Hydre Ally. In a conversation yesterday with the Maratta Vakeel Mr. Bourchier endevored to remove that opinion, and assured him it was so much our intention to proceed to the utmost extremity against Hydre Ally that if Mahadarow would either continue himself on this side the Kistnah during the year, or leave Gopall Harry with 10,000 horse, we would do all we could to persuade the Subah to persist, and exert our utmost efforts to expell Hydre Ally from the Mysore country. The Vakeel seemed much pleased with the assurance, and declared his master wished for nothing so much as to continue the expedition with us, and he would immediately acquaint him of our resolutions. Thus stand affairs at present, and the prospect of accomplishing our views in the ruin of Hydre Ally is very unpromising.

The Subah affects to say that the reason so little has been done is owing to the delay of our troops, which he expected would have joined him the beginning of February ; that therefore nothing can be done this year, and it will be better to take a sum of money for the present, and return again early next year on a better plan of operations. To this it may justly be answered that unless the troops employed against Hydre Ally continue their operations the whole year, it will be impossible to remove him from the Mysore government, because he has nothing to do but put good garrisons in his frontier places and avoid a battle with his main body. Three or four months will then soon be spent, and there ends all his fears. Whereas if Sera, Chinnabollarum, Bengalure and the other countries and places north of the Mysore country be first taken, and the united forces proceed in a body to Syringapatam, Hydre Ally must either try his fortune in the field or lose the capital, and therewith all his power and influence. I shall only add that we shall use every argument we can suggest to induce the Subah and Mahadarow, either in person or by part of their troops, to continue the campaign during the whole year ; and if we find they are determined to return in May, we must take care not to let our expences exceed the money agreed to be paid the Subah, and we shall know better what dependance to place on such Allys hereafter. To say that the Nabob hath contributed all in his power by suggestions and jealousys to break our connections with the Subah would be advancing what I have no proof of, but if one may judge from conversation and appearances, he certainly does all he can to disgust us with Nizam Ally, and to bring about a closer alliance with the Marattas, in hopes, I suppose, by their means to share in the conquests to be made on Hydre Ally. However, he will be mistaken, for except the country of Dindegull and other places on this side the hills, he never shall have possession of any other while I can help it. The disturbances in the Tinnevelly countrys still continue. Major Flint, after taking two heavy guns from Polamcotah and a quantity of stores proper for a siege, marched against the Etavaram Polygar, which lays near Veypar on the east of that province. He breached the Fort and assaulted it, but was again repulsed with loss. He then determined to blockade it, but the Polygars making a sally in the night and being roughly treated, they abandoned that place, Pannyallum Crutch and Veypur, and fled no one knows where ; at least we shall probably hear no more of them till our troops are recalled. On the west side of the province the rebell Polygars are still very numerous and in possession of many places, such as Shatore, Rajapollam, Collangoody and Nadcutch, so that while they remain there is no chance of peace. Considering therefore that keeping Major Fhnt's party always in the field, and that party not being sufficient to crush the rebells or protect the country, will not only incurr a considerable expence, but the Nabob will still suffer the loss of great part of his revenues, we have resolved to send 200 Europeans more to join Major Flint's party, some sepoys and guns, intending that the whole shall be 400 military with 6 guns and 2,000 sepoys of the Company's, besides the Nabob's troops and the Auxiliarys of Tanjore, Tondeman and the Marawar. Donald Campbell, as the next eldest officer to Colonel Smith, is to command, and part of his regiment is gone from Vellore. The Nabob has been very pressing for this party to be sent, and by some hints occasionally let fall he seems to have in view the quarrelling with the two Marawars and taking their country. However, to prevent such a measure he has been positively told that while he keeps Madurah it is necessary these people should be his friends, and Donald Campbell has instructions not to enter the Marawar country under any pretence, nor suffer any of their places to be attacked.

His operations are to be confined to the rebell Polygars, and these he is directed to extirpate, to demolish every fort, to make severe examples of those he takes, and to establish a cantonment in such part between Madurah and Polamcotah as will best answer the purpose of keeping the country in peace. Donald's knowledge of these parts and the honesty of his disposition will answer our purpose in sending him, and soon put an end to the troubles.

About the middle of last month the Nabob came to the Fort, and having desired to speak to Mr. Bourchier and me, confessed to us that he was quite tired with troubles raised and complaints made to him every day by his managers in the countrys of Warriarpollam and Arielore. He therefore desired that we would again take those places under the Company's protection and raise another battalion of sepoys out of his troops at these places for the defence of them, but to be commanded, disciplined and paid by the Company, though made good at the end of the year by him. He then said he would withdraw or dismiss the rest of his troops, and leave the suppressing Polygars and establishing peace and security entirely to us, in which he said he hoped the King of Tanjore would give more effectual and ready assistance. As we hoped a tryal made of these plans of reconciling the Nabob's management of the revenues with our command of the forces might induce him to come more readily into the same measure for the Tinnevelly country, and by degrees dismiss all his sepoys, or at least turn over the best of them to the Company, we very willingly agreed to his proposal and have chosen Captain Mathews with two subalterns of the best dispositions and characters to form this new battalion, to be called the 16th, and to settle the country. Captain Mathews has very particular instructions for his behavior, and is fully acquainted of our hopes and views, and we have such an opinion of his honor and good temper that we flatter ourselves we shall be able to convince the Nabob that good men under proper orders are capable of protecting instead of injuring his affairs.

After much trouble and some altercation with the creditors, we got the form of a general Assignment and new bonds agreed to, and having collected in all the outstanding bonds and calculated the interest to the 31st January, new bonds were made out for even sums of money, and all the odd pagodas, fanams and cash paid off, so that we find the Nabob's real debt to his private creditors the 1st January, 1767, amounts to 55,800 Porto Novo and 22,29,650 Star Pagodas. To discharge this the Nabob has engaged that his Naib at Arcott shall remit us from certain countrys during this year 8 Lacks of pagodas, and that the King of Tan j ore shall pay us his tribute, so that we are to have above 9 lacks of pagodas. All this is very well, but three months of the year are nearly elapsed and not one single pagoda is yet come to our hands, nor can I say when these will. The Gentlemen from Bengali who are creditors write in very strange terms, and tax the Council here with having been very arbitrary and gone much beyond the Company's orders, and add that they are allowed by the regulations there to take the usual interest till the 30th April, and after that 12 per cent., which they expect to have, or else demand immediate payment of their money. This is very fine in speculation : I may as well insist on it that I should have 8 per cent, for my money in England because I live at [a] place where it is the common rate of interest. And as to demanding their money, why every body else would do so could they get it. It is necessity that has pointed out the present regulation to put every body on a footing, and not any orders of the Council, and I do firmly beheve that all the wise heads in India could not have devised a more equitable or simple method than we have established. The Nabob now knows what he owes and to whom (which he never did before) and every body knows how much he owes and the measures taken to pay oft his debts fairly and equally to all as the money comes in. We keep an open diary of our proceedings and a regular sett of books open to the inspection of every creditor, so that the most obstinate may be convinced of the justice that is done them.The Nabob has sent part of his baggage to the Mount and proposes to leave us about the 23rd instant. It is high time he was gone, for he never will be easy himself nor let others be so while he stays here and listens to every tale that is brought him. Nazeabeaur Cawn has been playing some tricks at court, and he has got the Subah to forbid the Nabob's Vakeel from going to the Durbar or from going near Colonel Smith. This same chap too affects to assume the management of all our affairs, and lets Colonel Smith know just what he pleases. The Nabob is much displeased at this, and begs we will get him removed, for he will otherwise spoil all his and our affairs. The fifth lack is not yet gone either in bills or money, nor do I hear when it is to go.

Lewin Smith hath recovered half the old ballances from Hussein Ally, and therewith supplyed the northern factorys with Madrass pagodas,which we cannot get here at any rate. He is now at Setteavaram settling with Sittaramrauze, but it seems that chap is very untractable, and does not seem inclineable to pay even two lacks of pagodas for the Chicacole Circars. The first point Lewin sticks on is bills for the 3rd Kist of last year, and he says he hopes to get them in a day or two. Then he will proceed to the conditions of this year. Sittaramrauz wants assistance to reduce more Zemindars. This we are determined not to give, for the more powerful he is made by our means the more troublesome he will prove to us hereafter, and I think I see already that he must be reduced next year or the latter end of this. We have made Bandarmalanka an independant factory of Mazulipatam, and given Whitehill leave to send one of the servant[s] to Madapollam in hopes of getting more cloth. Sulivan is gone with him as an assistant. Charles or James Bourchier will tell you a long story of the Vizagapatam Investment. I fear that part of the Camden's cargoe is in the same condition ; if so, it may spoil the sale of all the other goods ; therefore it should be hinted to the Directors to examine the Vizagapatam bales. The discovery has retarded the dispatch of the ship much, and given us abundance of trouble, for some of the Council attend every day to examine every bale and every piece. Nor is this all the inconvenience we have to apprehend, for many other bales from the northward not being arrived, we fear we shall not have tonnage enough for the Pigot.

We have yet received no further news of our Manilla ship, nor of the sepoys from Zoloo. The Minerva from Pegu is just come into the road, but I cannot say what kind of voyage she is likely to make. The Swan, after many perils and adventures, got safe to Malacca, and from thence sailed to the Malabar coast, where, we hear, she arrived the middle of January, and Will Powney was then very well. The Devonshire's packet and recruits were landed at Anjengo and sent to Palamcotah, from whence we received our letters, and among them several for you, which Mr. Morse took in charge. This ship was at anchor in our road during part of the gale of wind, and suffered much in the masts and rigging, so that she was obliged to bear away for Galle after trying to reach Madrass again.

I have now written all the publick news I can recollect. As for private anecdotes I have none but such as you will have elsewhere, especially of George, who left us about three weeks ago. A sly chap he was never to drop an hint or let me discover by any means what he was about. Though I knew it very soon, yet we never exchanged a syllable on the subject to the time of his embarking from Bengali. Poor James was greatly hurt at first, and is still very dolorous, though he declares he will not think of any closer connection.

Government seems to set very easy on our Friend. He is very desirous of making every boddy happy, and of pleasing. I ease him as much as possible of all military plans and details, and indeed I am never happier than when I can be of use to him or the publick. I shall be perfectly easy till I hear from you or see Mr. Du Pre arrive, and then I shall consider about returning to England, but I will do nothing rashly. My concerns in

Lord North by Nathaniel Dance

> the Nabob's hands will keep me at least till the end of next year, let what will happen, for I must get home some more money.
> Lord Clive writes me, just as he was preparing to embark, that he should endevor to send Dupre to Bengali if he was not appointed to this place before his Lordship got home. For my part I am as indifferent about it as ever I was about any event of my life, and I think I should rather rejoice than repine at a good reason for going home.
> I hope you have found England every thing you expected or could wish it. Perhaps the introduction of Mr. Pitt — I should say Lord Chatham — and Lord Shelbourne to the Ministry may have brought Mr. Sulivan again into the direction, and consequently Mr. Van. I wish all my friends well and happy, and I know of none who partake more sincerely of my best wishes than you and Mrs. Palk, to whom I desire my most respectful compliments, hope all the little family is well, and desire you will believe me, my dear Sir, your most oblige[d] and affectionate
>
> John Call

The Memorandum enclosed by John Call, with the last letter, describes the personalities and arrangements in force during the campaigns. The writer knows that Robert Palk needs this detail to discuss affairs with his other contacts such as the Company directors.

> We are now entering on a very interesting and expensive expedition, but the expence will be well laid out if the grand object can be accomplished. This object is the entire overthrow of Hydre Ally Cawn, who has usurped the government of the Maysore country, and being at the head of a large body of forces, in possession of a considerable treasure and revenues, and ambitious of extending his conquests, appears ready . to take the first opportunity of invading the Carnatick and disturbing the tranquility of that part of the country which it is our principal care and interest to maintain and preserve in peace. The Marattas, it is imagined, are equally desirous of reducing Hydre Ally's power, and fortunately for us Nizam Ally Cawn, subah of the Decan, hath desired that the assistance of our troops, which we are bound by treaty to give him, shall immediately be

employed for the same purpose. Nothing could tally more exactly with our own interest and inclination at this juncture ; and though we ought to be exceeding cautious how we contribute to aggrandize the power of the Marattas, yet as it is not possible for us to act against them in conjunction with the Presidency of Bengal, agreeable to Lord Clive's grand plan of reducing the Maratta power in general, till we have reduced Hydre Ally and secured peace to the Carnatick while we are employed elsewhere, so on this occasion we must temporise and seem to fall in with the views of the Marattas, who are the avowed and natural enemies of Hydre Ally.
The grand point we have to obtain at the first setting out is to bring about a formal Treaty between the Subah and Marattas, by which the pretensions of each party may be ascertained, and the disposition of the conquered countries fixed. For unless this is done it is hardly possible that two powers acting from different motives and independent year he had married Emelia, daughter of Nicholas Morse, late Governor of Madras. He was a member of Mr. Pigot's Council in 1758, and in the following year was nominated Governor of Bengal in succession to Clive. Vansittart assumed office in July, 1760, and ruled Bengal, until 1764, when he returned to England. He purchased a house at Greenwich and property in Berkshire. Entering Parliament in 1768, he was elected a Director of the East India Company in 1769, and was appointed one of three Commissioners to effect reforms in India. The Commissioners sailed in the Aurora in September, 1769, and the ship was never heard of after she left the Cape in December, of each other should persist in the prosecution of an enterprise where many events may be expected to embroil them with each other, or to divert one of them from the undertaking. With us it is quite different : we only seek to procure tranquility for the possessions we have, and we think that point cannot be obtained while Hydre Ally Cawn continues to govern the Mysore country. No offers, no concessions, no opposition ought to divert us from our purpose if it can be effected : on the other hand we had better never engage in it unless we can make sure of our Allys and fix them steady in the same pursuit.
The Subah, it may be supposed, will be the most easily prevailed on to abandon the expedition, provided Hydre Ally makes large offers of money, because the Subah's treasury is quite empty, and there is a strong

party at his court, who, actuated by the same motive, will plead strongly in favor of Hydre Ally. Should we discover this to be the case, and the Marattas continue firm, we must endevor to form a closer connection with them, for it may be regarded as certain that with their assistance the object of the expedition may be accomplished though the Subah should not take any part therein. Nay, more, it is highly probable that the Subah, seeing us and the Marattas determined to persist, will rather fall in with our views than risque the loss of his importance by withdrawing from the Alliance. But should the Marattas, either by the force of money or from a political motive founded on the apprehensions they may entertain of ours and the Subah's designs against them after the downfall of Hydre Ally is effected, be induced to accommodate matters with Hydre Ally, and, while the Subah is engaged on the expedition, form designs on any part of the Decan or threaten the Carnatick with an invasion, it is beyond a doubt that we shall be obliged to relinquish the enterprise. This event then is to be guarded against by every precaution we can suggest, and in order to accomplish the establishing a Treaty, as well as to reconcile all jealousys and apply in time proper arguments to prevail on both parties to adopt our sentiments, it appears highly necessary that some person of consequence should be sent to attend the Subah and Mahadarow while Colonel Smith is engaged in his military operations, who by his address and attention to every turn and event may manage both parties in such a manner as to keep them steady in prosecuting unanimously the expedition against Hydre Ally.

One maxim must be laid down as positive and without deviation (viz.) That as little territorial possession as possible be ceded to the Marattas, and in case the cession of some part annot be avoided, then it should be in that part of Hydre Ally's possessions most remote from the Carnatick, that they may not become our neighbours. To obviate any discontent on this head, a larger sum of ready money must be given by he Subah, and the future choute be engaged to be punctually paid.

On these principles it is to be wished that the following articles could be agreed to between the Subah and the Marattas under our guarantee.

1st. The contracting Powers, assisted by the English forces, shall mutually and vigorously act in conjunction against Hydre Ally Cawn till he falls in action, is made a prisoner, or quits the government of the

Maysore country and all other countries he has usurped ; and neither party shall withdraw their forces or make a separate peace without the consent and approbation of the other party.

2nd. Whatever forts or towns may be taken during the course of the expedition shall be garrisoned and kept by the Subah's troops till disposed of as hereafter stipulated ; and in case any treasure is found therein or otherwise taken, it should be equally divided between the contracting parties.

3rd. When Syringapatam is taken and the country of entirely reduced, the government of it shall be restored to the ancient family of the Rajah upon their agreeing to pay annually a tribute or peshcush to the Subah of lacks of rupees

4th. The country dependant on Sera or Sirpi being an ancient domain of the Subah of the Decan, he shall be at liberty to appoint whom he pleases to the government thereof, and fix the peshcush at what sum he thinks proper.

5th. The country lately conquered by Hydre Ally Cawn from the Queen of Biddanore shall be given up (if it cannot be avoided) to the Marattas, to be by them restored to the late family that governed, on such terms as they can agree on.

6th. All the other countrys and districts on the Malabar coast conquered by Hydre Ally shall be restored to the late possessors on such conditions as the Subah shall think proper ; unless under this article the Subah, in return for the services we may have rendered him, shall so manage that the English Company may have certain grants and privileges near Calicut, Tillichery, Onor, or at other places most convenient for their trade.

7th. The country of Bangalure, that of Chinnaballabaram, and that formerly possessed by Mararow near Cadapanattam shall be disposed of as the Subah shall think proper, and the peshcush to be paid for them shall be settled by him

8th. The country of Dindegul shall be restored and ceded in perpetuity to the Nabob of the Carnatick as a dependance on Trichinapoly, and all the countrys on the east of the hills, such as Ahture, Chilnaick, Gegadevy, Vaniambady, &c., and all the passes near them, shall be put into the said Nabob's hands and ever hereafter be deemed a part of the Carnatick

Payen Gatte, in consideration of his having paid part of the seapoys with the English troops on this expedition.
9th. That part of the country taken by Hydre Ally Cawn from the Cudapah Nabob shall be restored to him, and the peshcush of that country fixed on reasonable terms, provided he assists with all his troops on the expedition.
10th. A provision of some country, either what he at present holds, or elsewhere to a larger amount, shall be made for Mararow in consideration of his services, if he assists against Hydre Ally.
11th. Bazalet Jing and the Nabob of Canoul shall acknowledge the Subah's sovereignty over the countrys they now hold, shall always be obedient to him, and pay annually such a sum for peshcush as the Subah shall agree to.
12th. In consideration that Mahadarow faithfully agrees to all the above articles, and assists the Subah to establish his authority over the above countries, he shall be paid at the end of the expedition the sum of lacks of rupees, and shall receive annually from that time as a lawful choute one fourth part of all the peshcush the Subah receives from the countries south of the Kistnah.

John Call

XX
Transferring profits to England, 1767

Relatively large sums of money and other goods were traded personally, presumably with the agreement of the Company though often enough perhaps not. Officials and even directors presumably saw nothing wrong with private enrichment through commissions, presents and trading.

Very large sums were converted from local currencies - rupees, pagodas and bulses of diamonds into pounds sterling but only with considerable difficulty and at very large discounts. There were local banks prepared to effect the tranfers but the transactions were sometimes shady. The reason that payments and bills were were accepted was because this was preferable to seeing a bad debt emerge.

Colonel John Call to Robert Palk, Esqr. 1767, March 21st, Madrass.

My dear Sir,

By the *Anson* I have sent you, on your own account and risque, with some diamonds of my own and Gocul's 2,000 Pags. worth, the produce of which will be paid you by Mr. Cotsford, and you will also receive herewith a bill at 8s. 9d. the pagoda for 1,800/, being an equivalent for Pags. 4,114 more, which you run the risque of home ; so that your whole risque on the Anson is Pags.6,114 , and would have been about 8,000 Pags. but that I was obliged to spare some to Mr. Morse in return for some he gave you on the Camden. If any more diamonds come in before the Pigot sails, which I imagine will be in fifteen days at farthest, I shall endevor to send some on your account, or to get bills.

The remains of your money advanced to Gocull for diamonds is Pags. 7,885 32, which you may be assured I will get in diamonds or bills as soon as possible, or make him pay the interest between the dispatch of the Pigot and the October ship.

The Marattas, it seems, have taken Sera, Meddighery, formerly belonging to Morarow, and Ranibeddalure, where the Queen of Biddanore was confined, and are now advancing to Syringapatam. I only wish they may continue their measures, and that we may not quarrell by and bye with them to take out of their hands what they thus lay hold of before we and the Subah join them.

Lewin Smith hath got Soucar bills from Sittaramrauze for his third kist of last year amounting to 11 lacks of rupees, but he still writes that he is apprehensive he shall not prevail on the Rajah to pay two lacks of pagodas for the next year without assisting him with troops, which we are utterly against and hope to avoid.

Mr. Law some time ago returned to Pondichery, and the moment he landed put Mr. Bayellan and all or most of the Council under an arrest for their very refractory conduct during his absence. He brought Nicolas and other Councillors back with him to occupy their places, and it is said he is determined to send them all home on a ship now ready to be dispatched from Pondichery. We hear they have at present no money to advance for an Investment. I can recollect nothing more to add but to repeat my assurances of being, my dear friend, your very obliged and affectionate

John Call

[Enclosure.] Gocull Tarwaddy to Messrs. John Call and William Cotsford, General Post Office, London. Exchange for £1800 at 8s. 9d. and 30 days. 1767, March 21st, Madrass.

Gentlemen,

Thirty days after sight of this my second bill of exchange (my first and third of the same tenor and date not being paid) and upon the safe delivery to you of two bulses of diamonds sealed with my seal and marked No. 17 and 19, value as per invoice sent you Pags. 19,204 please to pay to Robert Palk, Esq., or his order, at whose risque so much of the said bulses of diamonds is to be conveyed to you, the sum of eighteen hundred pounds sterling out of the produce of the said bulses of diamonds. But in case of the loss of the said bulses or any part thereof, you are then only to pay to the said Robert Palk, Esq., or his order, at the rate of 8s. 9d. for every pagoda's worth of diamonds of my concern delivered to you according to the price in the invoice, and you will place the whole of this transaction to the account. Gentlemen, your most obedient humble servant,

Gocull Tarwaddy.

There were dangers in conducting the trades, as vividly described by a previous colleague. Palk is kept informed even though he has left for England. Charles Bouchier is now Goveror of Madras. He has many snippets of gossip to offer, not least the competition between James Bouchier and George Vansittart for the same lady. There is again reference to pipes of Madeira which were the wines of choice for the navy. Most of the ships bound for home or the Indes called in at Funchal where there were many old friends and colleagues living in retirement. Madeira wines (Sercial - nearly fermented completely dry; Verdelho - fermentation halted - characterized by smokey notes and high acidity. Bual (also called Boal) - medium-rich texture, and raisin flavours).

Charles Bourchier to Robert Palk, Esqr. 1767, March 22nd, Fort St. George.

My dear Friend,
I am almost too late to send you even a line by this ship, the *Anson*, though she has been detained much longer than I expected by a lucky discovery of some torn and darned cloth in some Vizagapatam bales overset in the surff, which led us to an examination of some others, and to our astonishment above a 6th part of their whole Investment has been found in that condition, which is above 130 bales. We thought it therefore most prudent to land near 300 bales that had been shipped on board, and they being in the same state with the rest, it is well we did so, or we might have incurred severe resentment from home. I think they will not disapprove this proceeding, though it has occasioned the ship's detention, as such a quantity of torn cloth must have prejudiced the sale of the rest, and the freight on it would have come to as much or more than the demorage incurred by the delay.
I have had scarce a leisure hour since you went, so much has the ceremonials on my coming to the Government, the correspondence with officers on command, frequent visits to and from the Nabob, who is still

here, and much other business engrossed my time and attention. You must forgive me therefore if I do not give you a detail of our political affairs since your departure. This I am the less anxious about, as Call tells me he has wrote you fully on the subject. It is one I must own I am not fond of, but our engagements with the Soubah have led us into such a scene that it will require more of my attention than any other part of the Administration. His Excellency can't avoid still shewing his enmity to the Soubah, but as I have already found that being a little austere sometimes, and insisting on his compliance with what is right, has a proper effect in keeping him within bounds, I hope to prevent his being so ridiculous as to let his idle conduct be known so as to reach the Souba's ears. I have indeed, my dear friend, a heavy burthen to support for some time. I have, however, the pleasure to tell you my friend Call is kind enough to assist me very essentially, and I hope, if I enjoy my health as well as I do at present, I shall rubb through it tolerably well and see you at furthest in the year 1770.

At the Nabob's desire I have sent you a letter from him inclosed. He imagines Mr. Van Sittart can explain it, and therefore would not have it wrote in English.

I send you one also for Mrs. Palk from Miss Stonhouse. I believe it is on a subject that you little imagine, and that it will therefore surprize you both. I confess to you I wish she had never made her appearance in this Settlement, for she gave me much uneasiness before you went on account of my brother's attachment, and this has been much increased by George Van Sittart' s paying his addresses to her, which he did within a week after you was gone. After he had in a manner engaged her consent, which, however, I must say she told him she would not give without I approved it, he came to talk with me about it. I candidly made him acquainted with my objections, indeed as freely as I did my brother, and assured him, as I was persuaded it would give you and Mrs. Palk uneasiness, I never could concurr in it. He endeavored all he could to induce me to determine otherwise ; but as you and Mrs. Palk seemed averse to my brother's being so attached, I could not imagine otherwise than that you will be much more affected at George's desire to be so intimately connected with her. I therefore persisted in assuring him I could not alter my resolution, which he took in very good part, as he said he perceived it proceeded from the affection I bore you and Mrs. Palk. In what manner he represented it to the young lady I can't say, but she has never even hinted to me a word of what had passed between her and George. Since he left us I have heard that they are so farr engaged that, if he is not ordered home for his behavior to Lord Clive, which he suspects may happen, he is under a promise of marrying her. I have taken an opportunity of letting her know that I imagined such a step would not be looked upon by you and Mrs. Palk as a handsome return for your kindness to her here. This has in some measure embarrassed her, but still I find she thinks her honor is too farr engaged with George to retract with credit to herself ; that is, according to my idea of the matter, that she would not willingly have you and Mrs. Palk displeased, but finds it too good a match to be relinquished ; and if you are so, she can't help it. I may be too severe in my sentiments of her possibly, and I shall be sorry if I am so, but I can't divest myself of the opinion I once told you I had of her, that she is mistress of too much art for so young a woman, and in many circumstances relating to her conduct I am confirmed in it, as are many other people here. I shall leave no endeavors untried to prevent their coming together that I can decently pursue, persuading myself that you and Mrs. Palk will be pleased if I succeed. Poor Jim cannot divest himself of the prejudices he had in her favor long before you went away, although he yielded to my persuasions and yours to decline all thoughts of her for a wife ; indeed he has been more affected since George became her admirer than before, arising both from his affection for you and Mrs. Palk, and his regard for the young lady, and what will be the end of it I don't know. I wish he may not run away with her from George, and yet he is so different from what he used to be that I had rather see him married to her than that he should continue under so great an anxiety of mind as he now does. At the same time I shall be extreamly sorry if she is ever married to George, for I much doubt from the short acquaintance they have had together if they have realy much affection for each other, and she seems to be ill calculated to make a discrete wife for so careless a chap as George is. In short, my dear friend, the whole affair has perplexed and vexed me to a very great degree, and I am not likely to be relieved from this situation for some time. I sincerely wish you and Mrs. Palk may suffer much less about her than I have done. I have desired

Mrs. B. will send me no more female recommendations, and I must entreat the same favor of you and Mrs. Palk. Of the two pipes of madeira you left here to be sent home, Capt. Lennox has taken one, as will Richardson the other. Lennox's receipt is inclosed, and as he is a very obliging, good kind of man, I cannot avoid, as it is [his] particular request, recommending him to your kind offices if it should at any time lay in your power to assist him in geting a good voyage.

As you was so kind to give me leave, I have desired Mrs. B. and Cotsford to consult you in the disposal of some money I remitted home by the Camden and now do by the Anson, and I shall be obliged to you to favor them with your advice on the occasion. There are great complaints of the bad quality of the diamonds now sent, which makes many people apprehensive they will sell very ill. In this you are interested as well as myself. If they should do so, how are we to get home any more of our money at a better exchange than 7s. 8d.? Pray favor me with your sentiments about this matter.

My being obliged to neglect Mrs. Palk by this conveyance concerns me much, but you are so powerful and an advocate that I doubt not you will readily prevail on her to forgive me. Let me beg you will assure her that, although I make but an awkward figure in her place at the head of the table, a remembrance of her civilities is too strongly imprinted in my mind for me ever to think otherwise than that I am under the greatest obhgations to her, and my best wishes always attend her. Be assured, my dear friend, I have as deep a sense of gratitude for your innumerable favors conferred upon me, and can never cease to acknowledge myself your most sincerely obliged and affectionate

Chas Bourchier

[P.S.] The *Pigot* will sail in about ten days or a fortnight.

XXI
Updates from William Goodlad, 1767

The faithful William Martin Goodlad keeps Robert Palk up to date with political events and, as usual, there are financial transactions to be considered.

William Martin Goodlad to Robert Palk, Esq.1767, March 22nd, Fort St. George

Dear Sir,
I embrace the very first opportunity, my dear Mr. Palk, of returning you my unfeigned thanks for the favors you heaped on me during your stay in India. There is not, I assure you, a day passes but they occur to me, nor do I ever reflect on them without earnestly wishing you will give me some opportunity of shewing the grateful sense I must ever retain of them nothing material has occurred in the Company's affairs since your departure, and the operations going forward will be so much better related by your other correspondents that I shall avoid troubling you with anything on the subject.
I have received a bond from the Nabob for the thousand pagodas he promised to Withecombe's father. It becomes due the 1st February, 1768, and bears interest at 10 per cent. As you left me no instructions concerning it, I know not whether you would chuse the whole to be remitted when it becomes due, or whether the bond is to be renewed and the interest only sent home annually. I beg you will write me on this subject. I shall remit the first year's interest without waiting your reply. There is one circumstance, my dear Sir, on which I must beg your advice. I remember you once mentioned to me that the reduction of the Nabob's interest would be a considerable drawback to my mother's income. It struck me so much that I could not make an ingenuous reply, for you must know that I have never allowed her more than 8 per cent, and my

reasons were these : — When my mother offered me this money, it was with a view of being of service to me as well as herself, and she repeatedly wrote me that she should be well satisfied with 8 per cent. When I put it into the Nabob's hands I concluded the risk to be mine, and therefore never wrote her that it was there. I declare solemnly that, had the Nabob failed, I should have thought myself accountable for the money (as indeed I do to this moment), and I so far concluded the interest to be mine that I remember to have once wrote her that I cleared 12 per cent, by the money. I beg, my dear my Mr. Palk, you will favor me with your opinion on this matter. If you think the 20 per cent, should go to my mother, I will chearfully pay it, for I shall be then convinced that I have acted wrong, though without any intention of doing so. It will, I confess, be some disappointment to me, but I would pay fifty times the sum rather that it should be imagined I could entertain a thought of keeping to myself what is the right of another. The dispatch, which we thought would be nothing, has proved very heavy, and fagged me confoundedly. It is in a good cause, and I shall probably continue writing in the same post these ten years.

I flatter myself this will find you happy to the utmost of your wishes, rewarded with ease and tranquility after a scene of care and trouble. You know not, my dear Mr. Palk, how well I wish you. I beg you will present my respectful compliments to Mrs. Palk, and believe me with real esteem and regard your infinitely obliged and obedient humble servant,

W. M. Goodlad

In the next month there is more news from Chocopah about the state of trade.

Chocapah to the Honourable Robert Palk, Esqr. 1767, April 3rd, Fort St. George.

Honourable Sir,

I had the honour to write a few lines under the date of the 3rd of last month per ship Anson. Last Monday the Governour and Council was pleased to settle the present year's contract for the Honourable

Company's Investment the same as last year, but only took the long cloth medlin from Dessoo Reddy and gave to Mootamary Chitty. Dessoo Reddy and Moota Chitty have not behaved well in their duty of bringing their cloth agreeable to their contract. The Governour and Council was pleased to tell me in consultation that I have behaved very well, and they are willing to give me some more articles, but there is none at present, and therefore I must be contented with the Salempores fine, the same as last year.

We have not yet received any further news from Manilah, which we expect every day. The Nabob still remains in the Company's Garden, and it seems that he will go to Trichanoply in a day or two.

Chocapah.

Military success was the key to commercial gains and John Call seeks to bring Palk up to speed on events and their consequences.

Lord Rockingham

Colonel John Call to Robert Palk, Esqr. 1767, April 6th, Madrass.

My dear Sir,
By this ship you will receive a duplicate of what I wrote you by the Anson. 1 believe I shall not be able to get any more diamonds to send you till next October. If any should come they will be sent partly on your account to Mr. Cotsford and my father as before.
All the detachments of our troops having been very near the Subah the 25th ultimo. Colonel Smith waited on the Duan and acquainted him that he was very uneasy at the Subah's dilatory manner of proceeding, and the reports which were spread of his intention to return very soon to the Decan and to make up matters with Hydre Ally. He therefore desired to be informed without evasion what were the Subah's real intentions, that he might judge how far it was consistent with his orders to conform thereto. After many excuses the Duan declared that the Marattas having deceived the Subah and already plundered all the country of what was to be got, and the season of the year being far advanced towards the period of repassing the Kistnah, the Subah for these reasons was resolved to accept Hydre Ally's offer of money if he would pay 50 lacks of rupees, and proposed to defer the prosecution of the expedition till next year, when he should set out much earlier. This was an event we most apprehended would ruin all our project, and you may imagine the Colonel was very much chagrined. He urged a thousand arguments to induce the Subah to persevere, and above all assured him that there never was a finer body of troops sent out of the Carnatick than we had sent out on this occasion, and that perhaps it might not be in our power to assist him so effectually another time. Both the Duan and Subah seemed deaf to all that could be urged, and only replyed that the Marrattus had always deceived them, and that in future they would entirely be guided by our advice, being persuaded of our real inclination to support the Subah's authority. Thus Aiatters stand with Jo and the Subah ; but we do not yet give up the point, and James Bourchier with Stracey sets out to morrow to try whether he can be more successful in the persuasive strain, or else to insist on the Company's possessions and the Carnatick being included in any arrangement that may be made with Hydre Ally.

About the same time we received Jo's letter a Vakeel arrived from Mahadarow, acquainting us of his master's success in taking Sirpi and all the country north of Bengalure, asking Choute for the Carnatick, and expressing a surprise that we should have joined the Subah with such a powerful body of troops without acquainting his master. To the first part we replyed that we were very glad to hear of his master's success ; to the second, that we never should consent to pay any Choute for the Carnatick after the King and the Subah had confirmed it as an Ultumgan or free gift to Serajah Doulah, and after we had fought so much to maintain it in its present state : he would therefore do well to touch no more on that subject. To the third we observed that the Subah had assured us of a solid and firm agreement made between him and the Marattas to attack Hydre Ally, and that we had readily joined him in consequence, and even acquainted Mahadarow of our intentions, though he affected to be surprised at it. The Vakeel then complained of the Subah's dilatoriness, and said that his master, finding the Subah was resolved to make up matters and return, had been necessitated to adopt the same plan, though much against his inclination.

We told the Vakeel that we had still hopes of engaging the Subah to persevere, and therefore desired he would write his master to defer the intended accommodation and wait till our army came up. To this he observed that his master could not depend on the Subah, but was apprehensive that with ourssistance he intended to quarrell with the Marattas. If we would engage to join Mahadarow and act with him, he would readily stay and prosecute the expedition to the utmost we could wish, without retaining any countries in his hands. After much other discourse it appeared clearly that Mahadarow was very suspicious of the Subah's designs, and would not wait till he came near him, but that he would be very glad to have our friendship, and act, as the Vakeel expressed it, under our orders. There is no saying what quantity of truth there is in all these declarations, but that we may lose no opportunity of coming at the designs of the Marattas, I am to set out privately tomorrow under pretence of visiting and providing for the defence of the passes, and when arrived at Cadapanattum or Palameleru, Mahadarow himself, as the Vakeel says, but I suppose some person deputed by him, is to come thither and communicate to me the Marattas' real intentions, and if anything can be effected to gain our point against Hydre Ally, I hope to accomplish it without interfering with the grand plan laid down by Lord Clive.

If both the Marattas and Subah (with whom we are determined not to break, and risque the tranquility of the Circars) are resolved to go back next month, we shall then so far change our project as to endevor to bring about a peace between the Subah and Hydre Ally exclusive of the Marattas ; to confine him to the ancient Mysore dominions, settle the future Peiscash, and engage him to assist us against the Marattas if there should be occasion hereafter.

Mr. Bourchier seems a good deal affected with this disappointment of his hopes, and many of the members of the senate cry out, ' I said it would come to this, and a pretty figure we cut truly.' For my part I think very differently, and see nothing more in it than this : — The Subah by treaty is entitled to our assistance ; he asked it, and we gave it to him. He told us he should attack Hydre Ally, and we rejoiced because it coincided with our interest. We even went farther and sent a powerful body of troops, hoping by that step to engage the Subah to root out Hydre Ally entirely ; but he never promised us any such thing, and perhaps never intended to do more than draw a sum. If then we are disappointed, we have nothing to blame but our own sanguine hopes, which flattered us that everything would go on as we would have it. Another time we must endevor to know what we are going about before we set out ; and at present comfort ourselves that we have faithfully adhered to our engagements and have 7 lacks of the Subah's to make good the expence, besides 10 lacks of rupees left clear to the company out of the Circar revenue, Lewin having at length let the Chicacole country to Sittaram and Ragorauze for 8 lacks of rupees clear of charges. We are forming a party of observation at Vellore, and I propose to reconnoitre Gegadevy and Vaireambady, so that if a good opportunity offers, I have leave to attempt to gain possession of these places.

The Nabob goes away in three days to Arcott. His money begins to come in from the 1st instant to pay his private creditors, and I hope he will not fail in his engagements. He is still as jealous as ever of Nizam Ally, and at variance with all his own family.My respects to Mrs. Palk. I have not time to say more than that I am, my dear friend, your most obliged and affectionate

John Call.

There follows a letter representative of the many that Robert Palk received asking for his help in gaining promotion in the Company. Robert Palk was so well regarded by the directors and his previous colleagues that a word of support in the right ear could produce excellent results. We have no way of knowing how successful these appeals really were because very few copies of the letters Palk wrote in reply exist today. However, from the effusive responses Robert Palk evidently delivered the goods.

George Purnell to Robert Palk, Esqr. 1767, April 7th, Fort St. George.

Sir,
I take the liberty to trouble you with enclosed duplicate of my last respects to you of the 22nd of last month, and now beg leave to repeat my most earnest request that you will interest yourself and influence your friends on my behalf. I present my humble respects to Mrs. Palk.
George Purnell.
P.S. Sir, Since writing the above I have transcribed sundry letters from Mr. Morse, dated the 2nd instant, to his correspondents in England, wherein he acquaints them of his design to withdraw from business after the dispatch of the ship in March, 1769. It is therefore most humbly submitted to you, Sir, whether, for divers reasons too obvious to need repeating, it be not the more necessary to make immediate application to your friends in my behalf, lest any delays might be prejudicial to my interest. I flatter my self. Sir, that you will be so good [as] to excuse this sollicitude in me
G. Purnell.

Robert Palk [jun.] to Robert Palk, Esqr., London. 1767, April 7th, Fort William.

Dear Sir,

I deferred writing to you by Captain Howe as I was in the hope of having something satisfactory to write you regarding myself. When I left Madras I thought I should not meet with any difficulty in getting appointed George's assistant to Midnapore in case nothing better offered. On my arrival here I found that vacancy had been filled up by one three years younger in the service than myself. I was told on my arrival that gentleman should be removed if possible to make room for me, but now I am told it can't be done. I have been assured by persons to whom you have recommended me that I shall be provided for the first opportunity ; so that I can give you no better account of myself than that I am living in Calcutta at a great expence without anything coming in.

When I arrived here I found the money you lent me laying dead in your attorney's hands, notwithstanding the particular request of George that it should be employed to the best advantage. I am now employing it to the best advantage, but I fear I am rather too late to expect much from it this season.

Mr. Kelsal is appointed Chief of Dacca in the room of Mr. Cartier, who resides in the Presidency as Second in Council.Two of our brigades are marched towards Illiabad on a report of the Abdallah's coming down from Delly against us by the particular desire of Shuja Dowla, as it is asserted, who in all probability will join them against us.

I will (for many reasons) defer writing any thing of the state of affairs here in this Settlement, &c. You will hear from other hands how matters go on. I hope you will not forget to send me Chambers's Gardenner's Dictionary. Mrs. Plowman has been delivered of a child, and is so ill that the doctors think she will not get over it. I desire my compliments to Mrs. Palk, and am with great respect, dear Sir, your most obliged and obedient servant,

RoBT. Palk.

P.S. I wrote to you and Mrs. Palk, before I left Madras, by the Anson.

12th April, Mrs. Plowman is no more.

XXII
The Nabob's debt is settled, 1767

The Nabob had acquired enormous debt and there were many who believed he would not or even could not pay. It is with considerable relief that he finally seemed able to meet his obligations.

James Johnson to Robert Palk, Esqr. 1767, April 11th, Fort St. George.

Sir,
You kindly promised to use your influence in my behalf with the Court of Directors for my admission into their service, and though I have little pretence to such an act of friendship from you, the encouragement you ever gave me induces me to solicit your good offices.
The Nabob's debt is at last settled. The amount of the new bonds is Porto Novo Pags. 55,800 and Star 22,29,650. Payments of the revenues began the first instant, and 29,000 pags. and a bill for a lack and ten thousand rupees are already received. 'Tis imagined when the Tanjour tribute of 4 lacs of rupees are received there will be money sufficient to make a general dividend of 10 per cent. Mr. Ross, who you know is busy in all affairs but his own, has endeavoured, contrary to the general voice of the creditors, to obstruct the proceedings of the trustees and alter their plans. His remonstrances were too unreasonable to merit even an answer. Some bales of Vizacpatam cloth were in landing accidentally damaged. Being opened, it was discovered that a very considerable part was torn. All the bales being examined were found in the same condition. John Davidson, the Warehousekeeper, we fear will bear the whole censure at home. His letter on the subject, far from vindicating him, acquaints the Council with more truth than prudence that inexperience makes him unfit for that employ.
I must not forget to thank you for your promise to Goodlad of recommending us to the Coral consigners. I think it a valuable branch of business if early entered into, and it cannot be very desirable to persons high in the service, as you have already experienced. I desire you will

present my compliments to Mrs. Palk.

Jas. Johnson

A military progress report, this time from John Stone, with news of the actions taken against Hyder (Hydre) Ali and the Morattas. As each territory became available for trade and as the agreements were made there were business opportunities. It has been said that the English were rapacious in stripping the sub-continent of most of its gigantic wealth!

John Maxwell Stone to Robert Palk, Esq. 1767, April 15th, Fort St. George

Dear Sir,

I could not avoid by this conveyance enquiring after your's, Mrs. Palk's and your family's health, particularly as it gives me at the same time an opportunity of expressing the sense I have of the many obligations I am under to you. With regard to publick affairs, I make no doubt but you will have a full account of them from Mr. Bourchier and Mr. Call. I shall, however, do myself the pleasure of acquainting you with the most material occurrences since you left us.

The detachments from Veil our and the Circars, on account of the many unforeseen difficulties they met with from the badness of the roads, could not, by the last advices, have joined the Soubah before the 10th instant. Mr. James Bourchier set off from hence a few days ago for the Soubah's Court to assist Colonel Smith in endeavouring to prevail on him to persevere in the expedition, as he has already given proofs of his backwardness under pretence that it cannot be finished in time to return before the rising of the Kistna. He had only advanced as far as Aydrugure on the northern confines of Hyder Ally's country, and it is much to be feared a small sum of money will induce him to march back without even attempting any thing to Hyder Ally's prejudice.

Maudharow, on the other hand, has been very active, having already over-run great part of the Biddenore country, taken Shirpi and several other places, and was marching towards Bengalore. He has had large offers from Hyder Ally, who remains at Syringapatnam, to withdraw, but what his intentions are we know not. The different conduct of Nizam

Ally and the Morattas was a convincing proof that they had not agreed on any settled plan of operations, and indeed Ruccun Ud Dowla acknowledged as much to Colonel Smith. It was therefore a part of Mr. Bourchier's and Colonel Smith's instructions to bring them if possible to some certain determination with regard to their proceedings, as well as concerning the disposal of the countries that may be conquered from Hyder Ally, regarding which such proposals were laid down as were thought would be agreeable to both parties. After all, it is much to be apprehended that Hyder Ally will escape for this time on paying a sum of money, as the Soubah's poverty, with the rapaciousness of his ministers, will probably, in spite of every argument that can be urged, induce him to make up matters and return. Lest this should be the case, a detachment of 200 infantry, four guns and a battalion of sepoys is ordered to be posted near the passes to oppose Hyder Ally, who will, if he has leisure, most probably attempt to disturb the Carnatic. Or, if the expedition goes on, and Hyder Ally should be obliged to withdraw his troops from any of the posts near the passes, we may get possession of such as it may be of importance to secure.

This is the present state of affairs. A few days more will, it is hoped, determine the fate of the expedition. The general observation is how necessary it was that the Soubah and the attas should have been brought to some fixed and settled plan before General Caillaud left Hydrabad, as Maudharow has not been within 200 miles of the Soubah since Colonel [Smith] joined him, and the Soubah seems so much incensed at the Morattas having got the start of him, that it will probably be difficult to bring them to act with that unanimity so necessary for insuring success. The Circars of Ellore, Rajahmundry and Mustaphanagur are entirely settled in peace, and all the Zemindars have been brought to acknowledge the Company's authority. The Chicacole Circar is lett for eight lacks of rupees for the present year. Sitteramrauze has only taken the district of Vizianagram ; the other part of the Circar is lett to one Ragorauze.

Mrs. Stone continues in but an indifferent state of health. She joins in the sincerest wishes for your's, Mrs. Palk's and your family's health and happiness, and in best respects to General Lawrence, with him who is, with the greatest gratitude and esteem, dear Sir, your most obliged and obedient humble servant,

J. M. Stone.
P.S. I need not say how happy I should be in receiving a line from you. My little girl is very well, but I cannot prevail on Mrs. Stone to let me accept of your exceeding kind offer.

John Pybus, another of Robert Palk's old friends, brings Palk up to date with progress in suppressing Hyder Ali. He also is concerned about Nabob payments.

John Pybus to Robert Palk, Esqr. 1767, April 15th

My dear Friend,
Having finished all my publick business for this ship, I am come out here to spend a few days with my good woman and her boy before she takes leave of this delightful retirement, which must now be soon, for the weather begins to be uncomfortably warm. I had hopes of His Honor's company to celebrate with a few more friends my dear little Patt's birthday, but he has yet many letters to write to England, which will detain him in town, where he suffers from the longshore winds and wishes for an opportunity of getting relief from this purer air. His Excellency the Nabob, with much seeming reluctance, left us the day before yesterday for Arcot, where he proposes making a short stay and then proceed[ing] to Tritchanopoly. Money comes in but slowly from him for discharging his private debts, and you may suppose his creditors are consequently clamarous. The vicinity of the Morattas has given the Nabob some disquiet (though I think he has nothing to fear from them) and the apprehensions of an incursion into this country from those maroders alarm people whose only hopes of recovering their fortunes from the desperate state in which they at present consider them are wholely founded on it's tranquillity. Call has, I make no doubt, given you a minute detail of all military and political transactions since you left us. He is at present on the look out at Cuddapanatam Pass for a Vakeel from the Moratta Mahadarow in hopes of diving into his designs. His progress in the Mysore country has been very rapid and success astonishing,

having taken Sirpi, Medgeri and many other small forts from Hyder Ally without the least opposition. The Queen of Biddanore and most of the principal people of distinction belonging to that country were prisoners in Medgeri, and have been set at liberty by Mahadarow. Hyder Ally is in Siringapatam preparing for a vigorous defence should the place be attacked, which will depend on the Subah's resolves. James Bourchier is gone to him with a view of leading him on, but Colonel Smith seems to apprehend the influence of Hyder Ally's money will be more powerful than all the arguments which he or James can urge. The Morattoes, we heard some time ago, were about settling for a sum of money, but as they still continue their ravages 'tis plain no treaty can yet have taken place. Todd has had a most laborious, tedious and fatiguing march from Vellour towards the Subah. He moved the 23rd February, had not joined Colonel Smith the 5th instant, and judged it would be still six or seven days before he could. Fitzgerald with the detachment from the Circars joined Smith the 2nd. Want of provisions has been an universal complaint from all quarters, and as the Morattas have scoured the whole country through which our troops are to march if they move farther south, and the Subah's army consists of a most numerous rabble, I think this will prove an insuperable obstacle to our operations, unless by moving towards the passes it should be our power to furnish supplies of grain from this country. The Subah seems unwilling to remain south of the Kistna during the rains, and unless he does, all the past will be labor lost. Hyder Ally writes to us submissively and sues now for the friendship he before rejected. If we can make use of his fears to get possession of the forts which command the passes leading into this country, and to secure such priviledges for the Company on the Malabar Coast as the gentlemen there have sollicited, 'tis all we must flatter ourselves with hopes of from the expedition, and more, I fear, than we shall be able to accomplish. You know it never was a plan that I could think well of, but my best wishes for it's success have kept equal pace with those who were the most sanguine for it.

Donald Campbel is gone with a detachment from the garrisons of Vellour and Tritchanopoly to settle the southern countries, and Major Bonjour is out with a party to prevent if possible any incursions from the Morattoes through the passes.

Smith has settled with Sittaramrauze for the Cicacole country at eight lacks, and soucar security has been given for the third kist of last year. Nothing more from the northward since you left us.
A sad discovery has been made of negligence in embaling the Vizagapatam Investment, and I fear that part which went by the Lord Camden was in no better condition. We have exculpated poor old Smith, and Davidson is ordered up. Humanity has saved him from dismission, which he well deserved.
Madge wrote to me to endeavour to get home for him a chest of table china intended as a present for Colonel Monson, which he said you would clear from the India House. Capt. Lennox of the Anson was so obliging as to carry it. The mark or any thing else relating to it I am ignorant of, but I suppose Madge has wrote to you about it.
George Vansittart, you will no doubt have heard from other hands, has made a bold stroke for a wife, but James Bourchier seems still to maintain his influence with the young lady, and 'tis yet a doubt who will be the happy man. I shall leave this subject to be treated on more at large by those who know more of the matter than I pretend to do.
You will by this time, I suppose, be about leaving the Cape, where I think it likely you would meet Lord Clive if he recovered his health. India affairs would afford you a large field to expatiate on. He, you and Van must go hand in hand, and take upon you the whole management of the Company's concerns at home, and then some regular plan and system may be laid down for conducting them abroad, where they begin to require very able heads and honest hearts for supporting with honor and advantage the whole vast superstructure which has been so suddenly and successfully raised.
Impediments may prevent the execution of our plan for leaving India in October next ; so that, let what will happen, you may be assured of seeing me in England about this time twelvemonth. We are looking out hourly for a ship from Europe, and are told that Du Pre may be expected as a successor to Mr. Bourchier. Such an appointment after a service of four and twenty years would hurt me, I confess, because 'twould be disgracieux to go home under so disagreeable a circumstance ; but so much is my heart set upon being with my young family that no consideration upon earth shall keep me another year in India if my boy is

able to undertake the voyage, which I thank God we have at present great encouragement to hope will be the case, as he continues stout and jolly, and is almost weaned already. I shall hope the pleasure of finding a letter from you either at the Cape or St. Helena in my way home, for I shall be anxious to know how poor Mrs. Palk passed the first two or three months of her voyage, which must, I think, have tried her patience, spirits and constitution unless that unhappy woman you carried with you was either soon relieved from her misery or recovered ; and I am most heartily vexed to think she should have had so little feeling or consideration for her mistress as not to have accepted the offer made her of being accommodated here. Mrs. Pybus desires most affectionately to be remembered to you, and joins with me in the same to Mrs. Palk. I hope your dear little ones got well over the voyage. Our kind compliments if you please to Harry Van and his family and General Caillaud

John Pybus.

Ananda Pillae

XXIII
The China Trade, 1754

There follows a commentary on the relations that the Company and others had with China and the difficulties they faced. The tea trade with China resulted in a payments imbalance in England and as a direct result there was an outflow of silver of large proportion. Consequently any trade in the other direction was much welcomed by the government. Unfortunately one of methods chosen to correct the balance of payments resulted in the healthy or unhealthy trade in opium, sold in packets the size of cannon balls. This was much to the disgust of the Chinese authorities who did all they could to bring the trade to an end.

The complexity of business in the region in which Robert Palk was evidently involved are obvious from the content of the next letter.

It is also clear that the tentacles of the East India Company were into every business opportunity in the Levant which possibly explains why the directors took such a lenient view of employees who conducted private business. The government at home was also supportive for the same reasons.

This is why England started to become so powerful as a seafaring nation and ready to fight to maintain her trade advantages.

George Smith came to Madras as a free merchant in 1754, and subsequently spent several years in China and he writes to explain why difficulty arises in respect of one transaction.

We have to imagine Palk's response to unwelcome news.

George Smith to Robert Palk, Esqr. 1767, October 30th, Fort St. George.
(Received per *Hector*, 22nd April, 1768.)

Sir,

I did myself the pleasure of writing you by the *Glaten*, Capt. Doveton, whom I fell in with in the Straights of Banca last January, and informed you of my fortunate escape from Manila and the treatment I had met with there. The Nabob writes the Company on this subject, and sends them a copy of my memorial and an estimate of the losses arising to him from the iniquitous measures of the Spanish Governor, which amounts to Spanish dollars 144,650, which if paid we shall make a good voyage. I am not so sanguine in my expectations as to hope for this sum, though no more than we have a just claim for, yet I think the justice of the Catholic King will order us a restitution of the presents extorted from us and the ship's demurrage during her illegal detention in his port. If the Company views this matter in its proper light, it will appear interesting to them, because they have not only a large duty on the goods provided and sent to Manila, but out of the specie, the produce of said goods, they are supplied with silver for China ; and if this is not imported from Manila or Europe all the rupees in the country will be drained for China, and in a short time none to be had, which would be attended with serious consequences unless they send silver to Canton from England, which they have not done for some years past. In this view I hope they will regard the matter, and apply to his Majesty for his good offices, through his minister at the Spanish Court, for redress of our losses, and that the trade be put on a more certain footing in future ; that is, to obtain permission for the Nabob to send his ships to Manila under the direction of such Europeans as he may appoint ; for if the Catholic King employs foreigners in his service, why may not the Nabob ? I hope you will use your influence to bring this about by the Company, as well as with his Majesty's ambassador at Madrid. Various circumstances have prevented me from making remittances to you either from China, Batavia or Madras, but I have told Mr. Morse that I would pay him the sum I owed you on demand, or continue it at interest untill I could remit it to you. I hope you will pardon any disappointment which may arise to you from this money's not being paid in England when due, as it arose from a series of events which I could neither foresee nor prevent. I have however the satisfaction to inform you that the sum I owe you is as good as any in India, malgre Dom Joseph Raon, whom if he had succeeded in his avaritious views would not have incapacitated me from paying my debts. I therefore account myself rich.

I received from the General of Batavia the greatest marks of politeness and civilties, and obtained a valuable and well assorted cargo at that port to the amount of 70,000 rix dollars, and could the *Sultanissa* have carried goods for all the silver on board her, I could have had them, and no questions asked. But all the advantages I expected from this indulgence were frustrated by Capt. Scott's want of judgement and experience in steering an improper course for Ceyloan, which obliged us to bear away for Atcheen, finding it impracticable to fetch any part of this coast, not even Point Palmeiras. We were so far to the East of Ceylon when in its latitude, and blowing hard, the south west monsoon having broke on us the 18th May, we were obliged to bear away for Atcheen, which we could not fetch, so were forced to go to Queda, which we reached in great distress. We arrived here only the 21st September, and unfortunate as our voyage has been, I hope we will still get our principal concern if the Sultanissa can get a freight to Bombay from Bengal, where she is now gone ; and I hope Mr. Russell will be able to obtain this for us. If the Catholic King is just and generous we will get the interest on our capital. The money which you lent Messrs. Jourdan, &c., I have delivered to Mr. Morse : this sum and that lent Capt. Scott I was unable to remit during my voyage, and I could not think of leaving it in the hands of any person at Batavia where a man to day exists and tomorrow is no more until October, when it would be received into the Company's cash.

I brought several curious pieces of Japan ware and china from Batavia, and made a tender of some of them to Mr. Morse for you, but he told me that you had been amply supplied before you departed from hence.

I am favored with a most friendly letter from Mr. Vansittart this season, wherein he very kindly desires me to communicate my views as to myself, should not my Manila voyage have answered my expectations. I have taken the liberty of hinting to him that I should be greatly obliged to him for an introduction into Mr. Morse's house on his return to Europe or etiring from business as I intend residing here until I can go home on the terms I have always proposed for myself: £20,000 realized in England is the extent of my present wishes, and but for Dom Kaon, I should now have been of this value. As matters have turned out I must labour some years more so have dropt my thoughts of seeing England so soon as I hoped ; and now I have my hands at the oar I must even pull away untill I have got my vessell into port.

Mrs. Munro desires her compliments to you and Mrs. Palk, and says she

hopes you have assisted in getting Aurora sent to her under care of a proper person. I have received Bob's dividend of the Nabob's debt to him, and will continue to receive any more which may be made him, which I fear will be but small and slowly paid. His mother is very anxious about hers, and no wonder, as almost all her money is in those funds. It will, I hope, in time be paid off.
I was happy to hear of your and Mrs. Palk's safe arrival at St. Helena, and hope this will find you happily setled in Old England, where that you may live long in health and prosperity I most sincerely wish.

George Smith
P.S. The money I had in the Nabob's hands was fortunately paid off in the currency of 1766 as my bonds became due.

John Calland has encountered unfairness in his relationships with Company managers and is distressed. He appeals to Palk to intervene.

John Calland to Robert Palk, Esqr.1767, November 3rd, Fort St. George

Sir,
The many friendly offices I have received from you, added to the assurance you gave me on leaving India, induces me to take this opportunity of writing you, as it will inform you of a circumstance the most interesting to me that has ever yet happened, since it not only effects [sic] my character but future expectation, and has badly rewarded me for so many years' service
You can be no stranger to the malicious disposition of the gentlemen that I had for my Counsel at Cuddalore, who by encouraging every thing that could oppose me and giving ear to every story that was told them without foundation or enquiry, I must greatly attribute what has happened, flattering themselves that if they could but get me removed, their frauds would not be detected
Shortly after your leaving Madras, the old Investment being at an end, a new one was to commence, when I proposed, as the most effectual means of making the Merchants fulfill their future contracts, a penalty of 10 per

cent, on failure. This the Merchants consenting to, a few days after were called to execute them ; but instead of complying, not only refused doing of it, but denied having agreed to any such thing. As a letter had been wrote to the Presidency immediately on our engagement, I was under the necessity of representing this behaviour, when the merchants were directly ordered up to Madras. But previous to their setting out, Mr. Dowsett sent for Irshapah Chitty, the leading man of the whole and asked him what he had done to me to occasion my being so inveterate as to occasion my writing to Mr. Bourchier in particular against him, to take away his Palankeen and turn him out of the contract. This had the effect which was expected and desired of enraging this man against me, and by that means the others from his influence over them.

Dowsett having obtained leave, hurried to Madras to represent to Mr. Bourchier that Irsappa Chetti was the cause of the trouble. When the Merchants arrived the Governor was of course extreamly angry with

Amsterdam
East Indiaman

them, but in particular with this Irshapah Chitty, and laid the whole blame on him for the trouble they had given. This confirmed him in what had been so falsely told him, and fearing the disgrace of having his Palankeen taken from him and turned out of the contract, and the others, not knowing what might happen to them, thought it advisable to fall on some method to appease the Governor's anger, and of course made their application to Narrain Pillah and Chocapah Chitty as having the ear of Mr. Pybus. What with preparations for the expedition to Golcondah and other matters, the Merchants continued for six weeks, if not longer, at Madras without anything further passing ; which gave them all the time they could wish in preparing and making good their story, and visiting Mr. Dowsett, who was all this time there with them, daily.

Eventually the Merchants were received by the Governor and Mr. Pybus, and directed to submit their complaints in writing. At the next Council meeting four of them handed in petitions, which were entered in the proceedings ; the remaining three said they had no cause of complaint. I was then ordered to Madras.

On my arrival I visited the Governor, who received me as he had always done and with the same deceit, his tongue saying one thing and his heart another. However, from the favourable reception I met Avith I freely told him every thing expressing my astonishment that any complaint whatever should be made against me by these people, as I had never given them any cause that I knew of, or ever heard they were dissatisfied. From the Governor I went to Mr. Pybus to pay my compliments, who, instead of receiving me with even common politeness or civility due to a stranger, absolutely insulted and abused me, comparing me to Governor Macraey, and telling me that if what the merchants alledged against me was true, and which he made not the least doubt of, I ought to be dismissed the service with infamy (for these were his very words and expressions.

Some days after my arrival the petitions were sent me by the Secretary (another advocate for the cause by his connexion with Dowsett and Cuming) ; to answer which I did accordingly ; but foreseeing that I should have the worst of it I went frequently and breakfasted with Mr. Bourchier, and desired him to accommodate the matter, since it must hurt me at any rate if such a thing appeared on record. But all was to no

purpose. His answer was, that as it was now in every one's mouth, the only way was to go through with it.
It's unnecessary to repeat what are in the proceedings, as I have sent them to Colonel Campbell with direction to get them drawn out in another manner, and to make the whole publick, since I not only think myself extreamly injured, but there isn't a person in the Settlement acquainted with the service but thinks so too. Suffice it to say that I hope you will use your influence with the Court of Directors on my behalf.
Though I intend to proceed to England, 'tis not by choice, but necessity that obliges me to it, and therefore shall perhaps be glad to return again if I can do it with credit.

John Calland.

The betel trade was important to Indian communities and resulted in the foundation of many farms engaged in its production. Erstwhile colleagues of Robert Palk inform him of their problems and of the state of local relationships
.

Mooperala Kistnia and Rama Kisna to Robert Palk, Esqr. 1767, November 4th, Fort St. George. Received per Hector, 22nd April, 1768.

Sir,
We had the pleasure of addressing you per *Anson,* and the duplicate of which went per Pigot, whereby you would have been fully informed about the Beetle and Tobacco farm is ended to us soon after your departure. Old Kistnia hinted to you several times that after your government this poor country and the inhabitants would not be so happay and quiet as during your time. Just it has happened accordingly, every body wishing for your goodness and care that lived in peace with all the Powers of the country ; whereas lately a small body of the enemy's horse rode up to the Governor's Garden House, burning and destroying all that came in their way. Numbers of poor innocent people from St. Thome, the

Mount, Conjeveram and other places were killed, wounded and carried into captivity without one soul going to their defence, which has occasioned such a general consternation in our Black Town that most of the inhabitants have sent out their familys to places of security, which is a great hinderance to all trade and business. God send us peace and quietness, for otherwise the poor country will be entirely ruined.It will give us great pleasure to hear of your safe arrival in England, and that you and Mrs. Palk and General Lawrence enjoy a good health, to whom please to present our most humble respects.

Mooperala Kistina and Rama Kisna

Nawab Walajah writes to General Stringer Lawrence in terms that show the great respect that he commanded by the time he retired to England,

Nawab Walajah to General Lawrence, Behauder, Hous Bur Jung. 1767, November 5th, Fort St. George.

Sir,

The Company's ship Hector being now under dispatch for England, I embrace with pleasure the opportunity of enquiring after your welfare, as well as to acquaint you of the receipt of your letter, with the tellescope which you was so extreemly good as to get repaired for me. I return you many thanks for the great care you have taken of it. I am sorry to acquaint you that the house and furniture you was so kind [as] to leave me at the Mount was plundered by our enemy, and particularly the cot you used to sleep upon and the diamond cut globe were entirely destroyed. The loss of these two articles gives me great concern ; but as this is a subject of which you will hear of from some of your friends, excuse me from mentioning it any further.

Believe me I shall be ever ready of embracing every opportunity that presents itself of serving you, as I shall be ever sensible of the many great obligations I lay under to you. Give me [leave] to conclude. Sir, by saying I am and ever shall be your sincere friend.

What can I say more ?

Palk writes to inform his friends of his new establishment in London and indicates that he will buy a country property. This purchase turned out to be Haldon House in 11,000 acres of hillside overlooking the Exe Estuary close to Exeter.

Copy letter: Robert Palk to William Martin Goodlad. 1767, November 15th, Spring Gardens. (Received 8th May, 1768, per *Watson*.)

> Dear Goodlad,
>
> By the ships lately arrived I have received two letters from you which gave me much satisfaction. I shall always expect and I shall always be glad to hear from you, as I take great part in your success and prosperity. I saw Mrs. and Miss Goodlad yesterday, and was happy to find your mother's health so well reestablished. She mentioned to me her intention of remitting you one thousand pounds, and I promised to give a bill for that sum whenever it was convenient to her. I am settled in a town house at least for three years, and whenever any thing offers to my likeing, I shall make a purchase in the country; for in this very expensive land it becomes necessary to get into a settled way of life as soon as possible. Capt. Martin has left a fine family, and in good time I hope we shall be able to send you one of them. We are selling out the India stock; by the present price the estate will be benefited upwards of two thousand pounds.
>
> I have been well received both by His Majesty and the Company. Mrs. Palk and the children are well, and I expect soon to have an addition to the family.
>
> So many gentlemen returning to the Council will not be very acceptable at Madras. Mackay's bar was also intended to be taken off, but that is dropt, for the present at least. Lord Clive has exerted himself for Mr. Call, but Mr. Dupre has carried it. Annual salaries are settled on the Governor and Council of Bengal, and perhaps at Madras. No European is to trade in salt, &c., and the Governor of Bengal is not to trade at all. Such regulations as these, however, cannot be lasting. I have endeavoured to get you Coral consignments, but with no success I fear. Tell Mr. Johnson that I am sorry to you that all my interest, with Lord Clive's added to it, cannot get my nephew out a writer. I hope, however,

we shall be more successful after the departure of the *Watson*.
I am, dear Goodlad, your affectionate and sincere friend,

RoBT. Palk.
P.S. Mrs. Palk sends you her best wishes.

An ill-spelled oddity follows, written in an unknown hand.
[To the Editor] " For the Morning Chronicle."
Not dated [1767]

You are desired to assure the writer off a false and scandalous letter in your paper off yesterday, addrest too L. S. Esq. and signed Pericles, that fame was never more mistaken than in what is alledged concerning 10,000 being given too procure a Government for a gentleman formerly in the Church. The appointment at that time met the general approbation. He had been long in the service, and without ever applying by himself or freinds too any Director had been made a member off the Select Committee, and had been ordered the publick thanks off the Company and a present as a mark off their approbation near the same time that General Laurance and Lord Clive had been rewarded and distinguisht. Mr. Palk almost at the commencement off the war on the coast of Caromandel had been deputed with General Laurance too consert measures for its success with the powers from whome assistance was expected, the Misoreans, Marattas, Tanjorins, Maravars, &c. He was in several campains with General Laurance, and in consert with him formed those military regulations which have effectually almost ever since kept down the great expence off the army on the coast of Caromandel. He kept the Rajah off Tan jour in friendship and alliance with the Nabob. He had the honour of being appointed to meet the French deputies at the congress held at Sadrass in the time of Mr. Dupleix, when with the assistance of Mr. Vansittart a forgery was discovered in the Mogul's Saned Ar. He was also deputed to conculde [sic] the truce with Mr. Godeheu, and his appointment to succeed Lord Pigot was never solicited on his part : it was freely and graciously offered, and given without fee or reward.

XXIV
Perils at sea, 1750

When times were quiet there was an opportunity for old scores ot be settled and new ones invented. In the army, officers occupied the forced period of inactivity themselves by fighting duels. Amongst the company's other servants there were disputes and challenges often designed to obtain promotions or preferment. In such cases Robert Palk was often asked to intervene. The Palk correspondence is full of such difficulties in which he is asked to side with the writer.

Now that Robert Palk is comfortably settled at home in his Devon constituency and his London home, he reflects upon the sea voyages undertaken by the Indian and Company servants. These were difficult experiences [as described by Keble Chatterton (a naval officer during the period 1924 - 1944)] who researched naval and Company records to provide details of the voyages made by Company servants and their families in both directions during the period 1750 to 1772. In his excellent book "The Old East Indiaman" he reports on the conditions that had to be endured by troops, Company executives and their wives and even very young children who ventured to make the journey.

The Company had developed a system for transferring employees to and from India that borrowed extensively from the Royal Navy. As Chatterton observes there could be problems. Owning fine ships, well crewed made the Company a target for the pressgangs (the *press*):

> The crews of the eighteenth-century East Indiamen were such skilled seamen, so hardened to the work of a full-rigged ship, so accustomed to fighting pirates, privateers and even the enemy's men-of- war: a favourite custom was to lie in wait for the homeward-bound East Indiamen, and when these fine ships had dropped anchor off Portsmouth, in the Downs, or even on their way up the Thames, they would be boarded and relieved

of some of their crew: to such an extent, sometimes, that the ship could not be properly worked.

The following letter sent by the Company to the Admiralty on 22nd December 1740 is typical:

> "Secrett Committee of the United East India Company do humbly represent to your Lordships that they do expect a considerable fleet of ships richly laden will return from the East Indies the next summer and do therefore earnestly beseech your Lordships that three or four of His Majesty's ships of good force may be appointed to look out for and convoy them safe to England."

It made little difference. The trade was so valuable to the nation that they were forced to make concessions. Convoys were organised to protect the large lumbering vessels from French privateers and even pirates.

These convoys took the East Indiamen even from the Thames down Channel as far as Spithead. Sometimes they picked the latter up only at the Downs, escorting them for several hundred miles away from the English coast out into the Atlantic. These merchantmen were similarly met at St Helena and escorted home, the men-of-war being victualled for a period of two months. Even if an East Indiaman was able to arrive singly and run into the Hamoaze (Plymouth Sound) on her way home, having successfully eluded hostile ships roving off the mouth of the English Channel, it was deemed advisable for her to wait at Plymouth until she could be escorted by the next man-of-war bound eastward to the Thames.

There were plenty of French privateers lurking around the Channel, and, at any rate about the year 1716, there were also Swedish privateers on the prowl in the same sea ready to fall upon any East Indiaman going in or out of the Downs. One notorious Swedish pirate was La Providence, of 26 guns. An Englishman, Captain North Cross, commanded her. He had been tried and sentenced to death for some crime, but he had succeeded in making his escape from Newgate, and had fled the country. He had crossed the North Sea and had obtained from Sweden letters of marque to rove about as a privateer. His crew were a rough crowd of desperados of many nations, and his ship was very fond of lying in Calais roads ready to get underway and slip across the English Channel as soon as an outward-bound East Indiaman was reported to be in the Downs.

Now, in the month of November 1717, the skipper of La Providence was lying in his usual roadstead, and tidings came to him concerning one of the Company's ships then in the Downs. The privateer was kept fully informed by means of those fine seamen, but doubtful characters, which lived at Deal. They were some of the toughest and most determined men, who stopped at nothing. The result is not known but pirates earned a good living and were encouraged to attack enemy shipping during the many wars of the eighteenth century.

To contract a passage to India was no mean undertaking and adventure was to be expected. After leaving the Downs the ship cleared the western mouth of the English Channel and then steered "W and to WSW." It took three months to reach the Cape of Good Hope, and even then it was not too far south to fall in with French men-of-war. After calling at Spithead outward bound they sailed passed the Needles.

A seaman went on board with his sea-chest, his bedding and personal possessions. Slackness could be firmly punished, as illustrated by the East Indiaman Greenwich.

This particular occurrence belongs to the year 1719 and happened when the watch had been called. As some of the men did not turn out as smartly as they ought, the boatswain took out his knife and cut down their hammocks, to their great discomfort and indignation. So infuriated in fact were the crew that they declined to go on the next voyage until the boatswain had been discharged.

The directors settled the size of ships required and the owners saw that they were supplied. The size of the crews were large, but wages were low and safety was the dominating factor allowing plenty of men in each watch for handling sail. Each ship carried about thirty guns and though both broadsides would not be fired at once half those guns would necessitate a good number of the crew. Indiamen could even act as warships if the need arose. Merchantmen frequently obtained letters of marque for acting against the ships of a nation and when during the year 1739 Britain declared war against Spain the directors of " The United Company of Merchants of England Trading to the East Indies" petitioned for "Letters of Marque or General Reprisals against Spain." The request was made on behalf of their ship, Royal Guardian, 490 tons, 98 men and 30 guns; and for other vessels of their fleet.

Crews were such seasoned men, and their commanders such determined fellows, that they formed really a most valuable reserve to the Royal Navy. They were not individually a match for the biggest of the enemy's battleships, but none the less they were equal to any frigate and of far greater utility to the King's service than any merchant liner would be today in the time of war.

The chief cargoes which East Indiamen took out to the East still included those woollen goods which had been sent since the foundation of the Company, and they continued to bring back saltpetre, but now tea was becoming a much more important cargo. In addition to that tea, which came home in the Company's ships and paid custom duty, there was a vast amount brought in by smugglers. This was because the East Indiamen brought back chiefly the better, higher priced tea, compelling the dealers to send to Holland for the cheaper variety. The East Indiamen's captains were not above smuggling and one of the methods was to wait until the ship arrived in the Downs. Men would come out from the Deal beach in their luggers and then take ashore quantities of tea secreted about their person. Goods (such as silk and tea) were dropped through the ship's ports into a smugglers' boat that had come out from the beach.

Other than men-of-war, these were the cream of ships that ever sailed the seas. On arriving at their port in India they were always saluted and their captains received great respect. Under the captain there were from four to eight officers in the bigger ships, who all wore uniforms, the duties on board being carried on just the same as in a man-of-war. However, some of the Company's servants were making handsome profits even when the Company itself was doing badly. Eastwick mentions the name of a purser who had such nice little perquisites out of his office that he left the service and became owner of a ship, which traded between London and Calcutta. She was a ship of no mean size, for she carried thirty cabin passengers and 300 lascars, together with a large mixed cargo of the value of £13,000. It is stated that one of the cabins cost four hundred guineas for the voyage.

Had it not been for the popular taste which the United Kingdom had now shown for tea, the Company's ships would have been compelled to cease trading with the East. When, in 1773, the Company's charter was once more renewed, a grant was made of a monopoly also to China. From about the middle of the eighteenth century the Company had become more of a military than a trading concern, yet the latter was anything but insignificant.

In the year 1772 the East India Company were employing fifty-five ships abroad, aggregating 39,836 tons. At home some thirty ships of an aggregate of 22,000 tons were being constructed. By 1784 the number of its ships at home and abroad was sixty-six. Keble Chatterton:

> The Company decided to build for its own use a number of bigger ships than they had been wont to use and thus those wonderful East Indiamen, for which the eighteenth century will ever be famous, came into being. They were of 1200 to 1400 nominal tons, though their real measurement was greater than this. Such ships began to be built about the year 1781, though in earlier days the ships had recently averaged between 400 and 500 tons, not exceeding the latter figure. The Company expressly forbade hired ships from calling at places other than those which it ordered, or to take any foreign coin or bullion, goods or provisions at any place short of her consigned port. Pepper was not to be shot loose between decks or the freight would not be paid for. If the ship should touch at St Helena or the island of Ascension she was not to sail without the permission of the Governor and Council. Nor was she to touch at Barbados, or any American port, or any of the western islands, or even Plymouth, without orders or some unavoidable danger of the sea, under a penalty of £500. The commander, chief and second mates were to keep journals of the ship's daily proceedings, from the time when she first took on cargo in the River Thames to the time of her return and discharge of her cargo in England. Wind, weather and all the remarkable transactions, accidents and occurrences during the voyage were to be noted in these journals, as also of everything received into the ship. These journals were to be delivered up to the Company afterwards, on oath, if required. No unlicensed goods were to be carried in the ship nor any passengers to be taken without permission. The ship was to have her full complement of men during the voyage, and none of these crews was to be furnished by the master or officers with money, liquor, or provisions beyond the value of one-third of what the wages of such seamen should amount to at that time.

The paymaster (who was appointed by the Company and owners jointly) was to pay the seamen's wives one month's wages in six. The commander was to have the use of the ship's great cabin, unless it were required for the Company's servants voyaging out or home. It was the duty of the part-owners or the master to send in the ship always the sum of £500 in foreign coins or bullion for use in the case of extraordinary expenses during the voyage. The commander was also to be supplied with £200 a month for paying wages and provisions while in India or China and whenever lascars were hired, the Company were to pay for their hire. When the East India Company had been granted a further extension of their monopoly they started a good trade with China, and had received fresh capital for their operations.

There was still trouble with the French. In the curious incident of the Lord Eldon being nearly captured right on the doorstep of her home this ship, an East Indiaman outward bound to India, had backed her sails and was lying off the Needles hove-to, awaiting passengers who had been delayed in joining her.

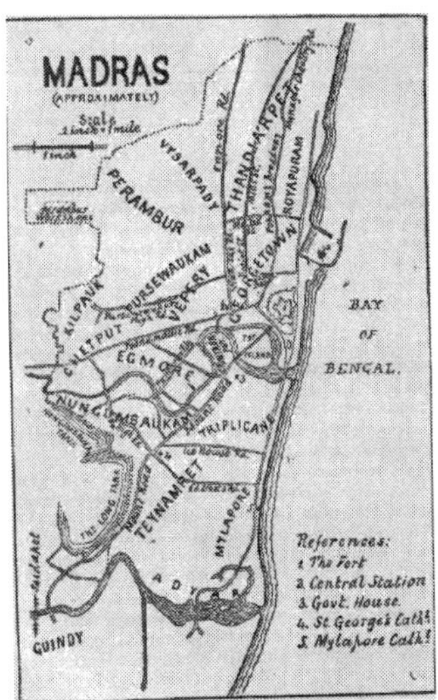

Madras

But whilst she was thus hove-to a sea fog suddenly came down. Not far off was a French privateer hovering about and this was the chance of a century. Under cover of this fog he approached the East Indiaman unobserved, so that he came right alongside. When the men on board the Lord Eldon discovered this big ship close up to them in the haze they were alarmed, but not for the obvious reason. It did not occur to them that she was a privateer, but assumed she was one of the King's ships and was now about to press the East Indiaman's crew into the navy. As the crew had no desire to come under impressment, they at once hid, with the result that the privateer's men had no difficulty in coming on board the Lord Eldon. The captain was below at the time and hearing a noise came on deck to see what it was about and then to his amazement found that his ship was in the hands of the enemy. However, he was not one easily to be daunted, even by such a surprise as this. His life was made up of things unexpected, and knowing that his men were well drilled he called to them to repel boarders. They at once responded to the command and came out from their hiding places, and after a sharp fight drove the invaders overboard. One Frenchman had even got possession of the Lord Eldor's wheel, but the East Indiaman's captain killed him by cutting off his head with one stroke of the sword. In a very short time the privateer, who was now more surprised than the crew of the merchant ship, hurriedly made sail and disappeared into the fog. The incident shows the fighting efficiency of the commanders and men of the Company's vessels at this period.

During the early part of the eighteenth century about fifteen of the Company's ships would sail to the East Indies from London, but this average gradually rose until, by 1779, there were about twenty vessels going out each year. The numbers increased to such an extent that in some years there were as many as forty and in 1795 as many as seventy-six made the voyage.

Passage times could be very long. One East Indiaman left the Thames in 1746 and after voyaging to the East returned to Scotland in 1748. She left England, September 20, 1746. Arrived at St Helena, December 25, 1746 left St Helena, January 14, 1747 and arrived at Batavia, April 19, 1747. She Left Batavia, June 9, 1747 and arrived in China, July 8, 1747. Left China, January 12, 1748 and arrived at St Helena, April 4, 1748. Left St Helena, April 25, 1748. Arrived off Scotland, July 9, 1748. Keble Chatterton writes:

The captain's "great cabin" was in the steerage, and he was forbidden to partition it off in any way without special orders from the Company. When a ship went into action, those canvas berths or cabins of the officers were taken down. As to the passengers' baggage, Gentlemen in Council were allowed to bring three tons or twenty feet of baggage, two chests of wine being included as part of this baggage if returning to India. Their ladies were allowed to take one ton of baggage if proceeding with their husbands: but if proceedingto their husbands, two tons. General officers were allowed the same as Gentlemen in Council, colonels were allowed three tons, but only one chest of wine, and so on down the scale. On East Indiamen the passenger would take on board a table, a sofa (or two chairs), and a wash handstand. In addition to bedding, sofa, table and two chairs, members of the Select Committee could take three tons of baggage, supra-cargoes of two and a half tons and writers proceeding to China one and a half tons. If there was no duty payable on the baggage it could be shipped at Gravesend but if otherwise it went aboard at Portsmouth. Other goods intended for the use of the passenger on the voyage, included musical instruments for ladies and books were allowed to be taken as baggage.

Life on board was organised. At 6.30 am the crew washed down decks and an hour later the hammocks were stowed in the nettings round the waist by the quartermasters. At eight o'clock there was breakfast and then began the duties of the day. The midshipmen slept in hammocks, but the chief mate and the commander were the only officers in the ship to have a cabin of their own. In no other ships outside the navy, excepting perhaps some privateers, was discipline so strict. The seamen were divided into two watches, the officers into three. The crew had four hours on duty and four hours off. There was always plenty of work to be done. After saying good-bye to the English coast cables had to be put away and anchors stowed for bad weather. Sails were set, men were sent aloft to take in sail and sheets and braces required trimming. In addition, ballast sometimes required shifting, sails had to be repaired, leaks stopped, masts greased, new splices made and so on. This was in normal voyages : but in the case of bad weather there was much more besides. On Wednesdays and Saturdays the 'tween decks were cleaned and holystoned.

The men were divided into messes of eight men, their allotted space being between the guns, where the mess-traps were arranged. The 'tween decks had to be kept scrupulously clean and were inspected by the commander and surgeon. No work was allowed to be performed on Sunday except what was necessary, though manuscript journals show that this regulation was not always respected. The crew were mustered in their best clothes and everyone that could be spared was present at prayers. Dinner was served at noon and the passengers were given three courses and dessert, but without fish. There was plenty of wine and beer and there was also grog at 11am and 9pm. Champagne was drunk twice a week. There was a cow carried, and later on a calf brought on board with its mother that became veal when the ship had crossed the line and was nearing India. In addition there were also ducks and fowls, sheep and pigs, so that the ship's boats and decks were often mildly suggestive of a farmyard. The ceremonies of crossing the line were kept up, and Eastwick has instanced dances and theatricals to relieve the monotony of the long voyage. Keble Chatterton:

> As for the ships themselves, they were all built of wood. From roughly 1775 to well on into the nineteenth century they were not only rigged, fitted out, manned and handled like the contemporary frigates of the Royal Navy, but they were, in the first place, built after their model, with one exception. The East Indiamen were a fuller bodied type, but the naval frigates, inasmuch as they were built for speed and not for cargo, could afford to have finer lines. A great deal of valuable room had to be wasted in the excessive amount of pig-iron ballast which these ships had to carry. To call them fast would not be truthful, but then there was no competition before the year 1814, and so there was little need to hurry, and they certainly were not driven. At the approach of night they snugged down, for there was no premium awaiting them however fast they made the voyage. If, however, they endangered the ship or damaged the cargo they would incur the East India Company's displeasure.
>
> One of the finest ships ever built for the Company was the famous East Indiaman Thames, a vessel of 1424 tons, with her general, massive appearance, the strength of her gear, the gun-ports, the decorative stern with its windows the East Indiaman with all her striking characteristics of

picturesque power. The West Indiamen were essentially more suited for trade, and their capacity for cargo was very great. They were mercantile craft pure and simple.

Though the ships were well found there could be accidents to add to the perils of disease, shipwreck, pirates and enemy action.

One of the greatest disasters which ever befell any of these East Indiamen was the loss of the Kent that carried soldiers and families bound for India. This was a fine new ship which had left the Downs on the 8th of February 1825. Favoured with a fine north-east wind the Kent made a quick passage down the English Channel and on the 23rd was out in the Atlantic pitching to the swell. Interrupted occasionally with bad weather the stately ship pursued her way across the Bay of Biscay for another five days, when a heavy gale from the south-west sprang up and the following morning the weather got worse. The fair wind which had brought them down Channel now headed them. The bigger sails were taken in, and others were close reefed. Topgallant-yards had to be struck and so violent was the gale that by the morning of the 1st of March the vessel was hove-to under a triple reefed main-topsail only. There was only the tiniest patch of canvas on her. She was rolling very badly and life-lines were run along the deck for the whole watch. For the women and children below, matters were alarming and unpleasant in those cooped-up quarters. So heavily did the Kent roll that at every lurch her main chains were well below the hold, so one of the ship's officers went down with a couple of seamen in case anything might have broken adrift and be endangering the hull. He took with him a patent safety lantern, but as the lamp was burning dimly, he handed it up to the orlop deck to be trimmed. He then discovered that one of the spirit casks had got adrift, and sent the two men to get some wood to wedge it up. Soon afterwards the ship gave a heavy lurch, so that the officer most unfortunately dropped the lantern. In his eagerness to recover it he let go his hold of the cask and there was a smash. Instantly the spirits reached the lamp and the whole of the after hold was ablaze. Here was a terrible position: a raging storm outside and a raging fire within. Clouds of smoke cameup the hatchway and were blown violently to leeward as the wind fanned the flames. The captain of the ship gave his orders and both the seamen and the troops worked their very hardest with buckets, pumps, wet sails, hammocks anything in fact that could be employed to put the fire out. But far from decreasing the conflagration it was spreading and smoke came up in volumes from all four hatchways. The captain now ordered the lower decks to be scuttled, the combings of the hatches to be cut and the ports to be opened, so that all the sea might have free entry. Meanwhile some of the women and several children unable to gain the upper deck had perished. As some of the passengers went below they met one of the mates staggering up the hatchway, exhausted and almost senseless. He reported that he had just stumbled over some dead bodies, who must have perished in the suffocating smoke. With difficulty the lower ports could be opened owing to the atmosphere, but when the passengers at last succeeded the sea came pouring in, carrying chests and bulkheads before it. Happily the tons of water which made their way into the hold checked the fury of the flames and decreased the possibility of explosion, which had been the greatest fear. But now the ship was fairly water-logged and fear of death from explosion gave way to fear of death by drowning. Efforts were therefore made to close the ports again, and batten down the hatches and stifle the fire. The occasion was terrifying in the extreme, for it was merely a question as to how long the Kent could last. Six or seven hundred human beings in the agony of suspense often more trying than physical pain itself were on the upper deck. Some had been suffering the pangs of seasickness for days, many had rushed up from below with no time to slip on warm clothes, others were seeking out husbands, wives or children. Some were saying their prayers, while some of the toughest seamen took up their positions immediately over the magazine in the hope that when the explosion came at any moment they might be blown into eternity without delay. The sea was winning, and suddenly the Kent's binnacle broke away and was dashed to pieces on the deck. This was taken as a particularly bad omen by some and the end was awaited. But just then the fourth mate decided to send a man up to the foretop in case a ship might be on the horizon. The man, after scanning the horizon, began waving his hat and shouting." A sail on the lee bow!" and the announcement was received with three cheers. Distress signals were made, minute guns began to be fired and setting the three topsails and foresail the Kent ran down to the stranger. This was found to be the brig Cambria, of 200 tons burthen, on her way from Falmouth to Vera Cruz with Cornish miners on board. After the Kent's signals had been hoisted there followed a further period of suspense. Had the brig seen the signals? Had the sound of the guns reached her in the violence of the gale? But presently the stranger was seen to hoist British colours and to crowd on all sail, in spite of the gale. Her captain was evidently determined to assist if he could. The crews and passengers were saved as the Kent foundered in the storm.

Such were the trials endured by the passengers who probably travelled back and fore at least twice during a Company appointment in India. Stringer Lawrence and Robert Palk made such journeys - Lawrence even twice in just over 12 months!

Grenadiers and sepoys

XXV
John Calland's problem, 1768

John Calland was an old friend of Palk who had run into difficulties with his commercial contracts. He appeals to Ropbert Palk for assistance in London.

John Calland to Robert Palk, Esqr. 1768, April 25th, Fort St. George.

Sir

It being the advice and opinion of every one acquainted with the Cuddalore Merchants' complaints against me, and the severe usage I have met with in consequence, that I renew by all means my application to you. I beg leave to enclose you duplicate of my letter per Hector, copies of the four petitions given in against me, my answer thereto and refutation of the whole, which are the material papers of the proceedings. The remaining part, containing little more than the examination of the witnesses. I have sent to Colonel Campbell, who will shew them to you if you will please to take the trouble of asking for them.

As Mr. Saunders will in all probability be Chairman when this affair comes under consideration, I cannot avoid looking upon it as the most propitious circumstance for me that could happen ; being in the first place a man of sense and who has a thorough knowledge of the service, and in the next that you are intimately acquainted with him ; from which I hope the complaints made against me will be so far mitigated that I shall be restored, by their being looked upon as malicious and ill-grounded, and merely in consequence of my imposing the penalty of 10 per cent, on failure of contract, and thwarting the ambition and evil practices of the most considerable Merchants, but Irshapah Chitty and Moodo Kistna in particular. Had I robbed or defrauded the Company (as it seems those who were in Council with me are judged to have done), or had the service in the least suffered, I should have thought myself justly deserving the treatment I have received. But on the contrary, did I not bring the Cuddalore Investment to fifteen hundred bales, which was more

by some hundreds than had been got for many years before ? Besides, is there a man in the service that can accuse me of ever wronging the Company the value of a fanam, or not doing my duty in every office I have been employed during the seventeen years of my servitude, which brought me the next to Council ?
I flatter myself you will interest yourself so far in my behalf with Mr. Saunders as to get justice done me and every prejudice removed by my re-instatement yet, should it happen otherwise, and the reward of so many years' diligent and faithful services be cancelled I shall then think it incumbent on me to use those materials I am possessed of in taking a laudable satisfaction of those men who have so cruely injured me. The materials I have got I have neither spared money or trouble in procuring, and which are such as, without ostentation or deceit, must inevitably ruin Mr. Pybus, and give such an insight into things as will hurt the servants in general.
Mr. Bourchier, I hear, accuses me of using him ill and being ungrateful. But sure, not upon reflection ? Let any one read my letter to him of the 23rd March, and the Merchants' to me a month afterwards, and be told the repeated sollicitations I made him to compromise the affair, to no purpose ; and then judge of the reason he has for saying so, and if I have not had sufficient cause and provocation for every thing I have said and ten times as much more. Words are nothing. 'Tis the actions of a man that another is to judge by, either of his friendship or sincerity. I hope for my own sake, as well as the invidious Mr. Pybus's, and in short every other person connected with the service, that you will use your influence with Mr. Saunders and others so as to make further proceedings unnecessary.

John Calland.

James Bourchier to Robert Palk, Esqr. 1768, May 2nd, Madrass.

Your favor, my dear Mr. Palk, from St. Hellena, contrary to your expectation, reached me in November before we could have any intelligence of your safe arrival in England, nor have we yet any further tidings of you ; but I will hope you are there, and happy to the extent of your wishes. Your friend poor Charles has had a very troublesome government almost ever since you left him in it : this confounded war has kept his hands full and his spirits harrassed, yet fortunately he has enjoyed great health. As I presume Call, whose genious lies in political narrative, has given you every particular of what has happened and what is to be expected, I will not touch on the subject. He with Mackay are gone as Field Deputies to assist the Nabob and Colonel Smith with their counsel, and I hope by a vigorous and spirited effort we shall subdue the Hydra.

The Gentlemen of Bengal, notwithstanding their boasted promises of an exertion of their assistance, have failed in the most essential point of mony, which will, I fear, force us to break in upon the China stock. However, nothing must now be spared to put an end to this war. If we succeed (as we have all the reason in the world to expect) in the down fall of Hyder Naigue, we shall secure stability to the Company's possessions on this and the Mulabar Coast, and root out a power, the only one indeed that could afford our neighbors (the French) any support in case of a rupture between our nations — an object in my opinion of the first importance. By the reports we have, and indeed they themselves confirm, they are collecting and disciplining a large body of troops at the Islands, which, depend upon it, they will augment by every vessell they can steal out thither. It therefore behoves the Honourable Twenty four to keep a very watchful eye on them, and to give us early intelligence of the first likelihood of trouble, as well as secure, by the Piscash they are to pay the Government, a formidable naval force to preserve to us the command of the seas. In that case they will put it in our power to divest the gentry of all they possess here ere they can be reinforced or even in a condition of defence.

Most probably I shall leave India ere there can be a war, yet I shall ever retain that attachment to the service, and Madrass in particular, as to wish the utmost success to their affairs. You will know our situation, my dear Mr. Palk, and the precautions that ought to be taken to preserve the well being of the Company abroad, and I make no doubt will give them every useful light that can tend to that desireable end. It's to be hoped the Company will earnestly endeavor to keep complete our military establishment. This has been a fatal season to many valuable young

officers as well as the private men ; it's therefore the more necessary we should be amply supplyed with recruits.
Our society of males continues much the same as when you left us, except the loss of poor Griffiths, who dyed after a long fit of illness the latter end of last month, much lamented by those who were intimately acquainted with him. Thomas and Stone are his executors, who will do the greatest justice to his estate. George Stratton is married to a Miss Lights that came out on one of the latter ships of last year : you may remember a brother of hers that came out a Writer the season before you went home. And Alexander Davidson, when he quitted the sub accountantship, asked leave to go to Bengal to establish a correspondence and of course to commence merchant, is returned with a wife, a Miss Pigot, you may remember formerly under the patronage of Phebe Graham. How he succeeded in the first scheme I have not heard. Pasley, Briggs and the two secretaries are very jolly, and hold you in grateful remembrance. I have given Mrs. Palk an account of all the females, so I shall refer you to her for particulars. Adieu, my dear Mr. Palk. Believe me, with all the gratitude a heart susceptible of the nicest feelings can possess, your ever affectionate

James Bouchier

Financial worries are again the subject of George Smith's letter in May 1768. Money exchanges from India to England were complicated by the lack of banks large or sophisticated enough to handle the international trade. Instead this was conducted sometimes in cash, sometimes by letter of credit, often by diamonds and always with substantial handing discounts. This was very much Robert Palk's area of expertise though even he could not liquidate all his investments before leaving for home. The correspondence does not reveal how much he was able to send home whilst still in the service of the company but by inference it must have been an enormous sum.

George Smith to Robert Palk, Esqr. 1768, May 7th, Fort St. George.

Sir,
I did myself the pleasure of addressing you by the *Hector,* informing you of the safe arrival of the Sultanissa Begam at this port the 20th of September, and of her being sent to Bengal, whence she proceeded to Bombay. The difficulty of remitting your money has been increased by the formation of an Association of diamond buyers, and Gocull and Nellacuntaker, though they had promised me as far back as October last to take from me each the sum of 5,000 pagodas at Respondentia on diamonds security, have broke through their promise in consequence of the above combination. Thus circumstanced, and no other channel but the Company's cash at 7s. 4d. open, what can I do ? I must have recourse to your good nature and friendship for a further credit. I have given Mr. Morse a statement of your moneys in China, which I hope to be able to remit shortly, as the silver of this country begins to be pretty well drained, and moreover the call for money here will soon be so great that the Company's cash in Canton must again be opened. By this ship comes a copy of a letter from the Governor of Manila to the Nabob, by which it plainly appears that what was done to me proceeded from suspicions of English property being under my management, and that the Uke treatment is menaced to any ship in the same circumstances with the Sultanissa ; from which it is evident that the Company should fall on some mode of securing the Manila trade from insult and even confiscation, or they must soon export bullion from Europe, which they will not for some time, I imagine, find convenient.
I refer you to your other friends here for a detail of the war, the peace with the Nizam, and the present operations against Hyder Ally : they will be better able to inform you of these series of events than I can possibly do.
Mrs. Munro desires her compliments to you and Mrs. Palk, and she hopes you have been so kind as to send out her daughter

George Smith.

Thomas Palk, son of Walter Palk and nephew of Governor Palk, arrived in the Dublin in 1768 and entered the Madras Army, but was subsequently transferred to the civil service. He must not be confused with his remote cousin, Lieut. Thomas Palk, who was serving in the Northern Circars. He now writes to give the latest gossip and provides a further insight into the perils of taking ship in 1768.

Thomas Palk to Robert Palk, Esqr. 1768, May 7th at Sea.

My dear Sir,
I now set down to write to all my particular friends. The man at the mast head spys land, where he has been to look out for a ship. We are now steering round the Cape, without the wind alters its point, and if it does, we shall certainly put into the Cape. I shall first begin to write to you, as I imagine we shall meet with some ship or other, for I would not miss any opportunity whatever of writing my friends an account of my health and welfare. We sailed from the Downs the 31st January, and after a troublesome passage of about three weeks, we made Teneriffe, from whence I wrote to you by a Dutch man that was first going to Cadiz and from thence to England. I can only mention one or two particulars. By the rolling I met with a terrible fall, that occasioned me the headache for several days afterwards, which I have felt since three weeks most severely. Several days together we were obliged to set on the deck to dine. You may easily judge. Sir, how great the motion was, but we have felt no such weather since, nor never do I desire to again.
At our landing at Teneriffe Mr. Wynch went to his friend's house and his family with him, and had there been room he would have introduced me to him, but I made him an apology.
Alexander, another who goes as a free merchant and me took a lodging at a French house during our stay. I at first often received invitations from my good friend Mrs. W. to walk out on their sharp flint stones, which she liked, and most generally on the terrass on the top of the house ; but afterwards when we were reconciled in respect to our intimacy, and found that my company was accepted of, I made free to introduce myself. On the day of our departure Mrs. W. introduced me to Mr.

Dupree. During the little time I picked a little acquaintance with him, and after about an hour stay I took my leave of him in company with Mrs. D. and Miss Monro, who are very well except Mr. D. He has carried the gout on board with him, but Mrs. D. is in great concern about her little child as the small pox is on board the Queen.

We sailed from Teneriffe the 7th of March, from which time we had surprizing good weather with constant fair winds. We are almost becalmed in the lattitude of 35 degrees south, which is something surprizing. We are not likely to have such weather as what was suspected we should. My good Mrs. W. has been under a great deal of chagrin on account of the death of her little child, which expired about a month ago. She has often been taken in fits since, more so than before, and has seemed to recover her spirits ; but Miss Flora has been unfortunately taken ill of a fever, and is again at present restored to her former health I hope. We had her company to drink a cup of tea with us in our little cabbin this afternoon, which we have often had and hope to again. She is a good little girl. Mr. Wynch has shewn me several very friendly marks, which I must keep up at all events.

Francisco has long been our waiting man, but is at present obliged to turn cook, which at first he was often complaining to me of ill usage ; but that is now all over, as the complaints have been presented to the Captain, who has been ill, but is now better again. I shall say nothing more particular at present till we get sight of a ship ; then I shall make a conclusion.

I remain, dear sir, your most dutiful and ever respectful nephew,

T. Palk

XXVI
Poor Griffiths dies , 1768

Sad events permeate the correspondence when the death of Palk's friend Griffiths was announced and his wealth required distribution to his widow and family

The Rev. John Thomas to Robert Palk, Esq. 1768, Sunday May 7th, Fort St. George.

Sir,
As you had poor Mr. Griffiths interest always at heart, I hope this letter relative to him will need no apology.
After a tedious and painful illness, which he bore with great resignation, he paid his last debt to nature the 25th of last month. His last sickness, which was a complication of diseases, the gout and palsy, with a disorder of the bowels, deprived him during the last fortnight of his life first of his memory and afterwards of his understanding. Happy for him in such circumstances that he was released out of his misery !
He has left every thing he possessed in India for the education and emolument of his two sons, which after the sale of his books and furniture may pobably amount to 7,000 pagodas. Mr. Stone and I, who are appointed his executors, intend employing this money here, except what may be expended on their education. For Mrs. Griffiths' support he has left a sum lent on Government security ; how much I cannot ascertain. The Revd. Mr. Richard Canning, senior, of Ipswich, is appointed guardian to his sons. It was always Mr. Griffiths' desire that both his sons should come out to this presidency in the civil service. You will pardon me. Sir, for embracing this opportunity of returning my most thankful acknowledgments for your favours to me at Madrass, a sense of which I hope ever to retain.

John Thomas.

William Martin Goodlad writes to comment upon the political situation still obviously so interesting to Palk. He provides the gossip: who has died, who engaged to be married and who is making the news. And the children in the settlement have been innoculated against smallpox!

William Martin Goodlad to Robert Palk, Esqr. 1768, May 12th, Fort St. George.

My dear Mr. Palk,

The *Admiral Watson* brought me your very affectionate letter of the 15th November, which afforded me a pleasure I cannot easily describe to you. Indeed, my dear Sir, I will ever remember your kindness to me with a grateful heart.

Your endeavours to procure me coral consignments were very obliging. Mr. Bourchier's strong recommendations have brought us one chest, and a promise of employment from two or three other dealers.

Enclosed you will receive a bill for £200, being two years' interest on the money you so very obligingly lent me. I have no directions from you regarding the money given by the Nabob to poor Withecombe's father. I would fain have got from him both principal and interest, but my endeavours were fruitless.

I wrote you of poor Cranch's death, and promised to administer to the estate and settle his affairs. This, however, I have been prevented from doing by his having made a will when at Batavia. Madge is the only surviving executor. The state of his affairs I know not, but imagine they will yield about 1,500 pagodas.

The next dispatches will, I fear, cut off all the creditors' resources from the Nabob for some time, as we have a hint about private interest clashing with the payment of his debt to the Company. Should the Court direct his discontinuing the payments to his creditors, I know not what they will say on the subject, or how they will reconcile such an order. There are some turbulent spirits amongst them not quite so ready to conform to commands as the President and Council are in general. Mr. Dupre, &c., returning to Council is, as you say, not very agreeable to the

Gentlemen here. For my own part it matters not. Andrews his appointment is the only thing that vexes me, for I profess a regard for the service, and I cannot but think him unworthy of it. Is there a probability even that a man will pay a proper attention to the Company's concerns who was totally lost to any care for his own ? And this is the man expressly sent out because it was necessary to strengthen the Council with sober and sedate people ! Fie on it ! Poor Ardley was with me just now, hopping about like a parcht pea. What vexes me is that Call should be put over my head, for 'tis disgracing me without answering any one end. The little man is really much hurt. He wants to get out of the Settlement, and will probably turn or endeavour to turn Smith from Vizagapatam. I think, however, he will not effect it.

With respect to politics, the Governor and Mr. Call, I suppose, write you fully. They will explain to you what is doing and what is intended, but can they tell you what has been done ? I most sincerely wish, for the sake of my worthy friend Mr. Bourchier, that a man of real capacity may arrive to take the command of the army. Smith, with a most amiable heart, has not an head for his station. It has been evident from the commencement of the war — too evident to us here. But will it be equally apparent to the Gentlemen at home that such has been the chief cause of our expending immense sums almost to no purpose ? I love Mr. Bourchier in my heart's core, and I therefore feel the more for the many unlucky events that have fallen out since he came to the Chair. You know the Governor full well, and must have been sensible of the influence Mr. Call would have over him. The latter is unsteady. He is very snug behind the curtain. When any of our actions (to speak in the military style) redound to our credit, he has the power to engross a great share of it : when the contrary, he knows on whose shoulders they will naturally fall. I would not lay open my thoughts on such subjects to any man but you, whom I shall ever regard as a father. If I am culpable, chastise me as you would a son. Poor Griffith died last month after a very lingering and painful illness. Captain McLean was killed some time ago. Stratton is married to Miss Light, and Miss Carter to Captain Gee.Mrs. Tom Powney has been innoculated, and is well again without being marked. Most of the children in the Settlement have undergone the same operation. Poor Donald Campbell lost two, the only ones that died.

I most sineerely hope the increase you expected in your family has proved to your satisfaction. I am particularly interested in the happiness of yourself and Mrs. Palk, and shall be ever, with the most grateful sentiments of esteem and regard, your ever affectionate and obliged servant,

W. M. Goodlad
P.S. I have delivered to Captain Mears the remainder of the letters you desired of me. The former part was sent by Captain Richardson of the Pigot, and I hope have got safe to you. By the next ship you shall have the translate of the Spanish arguments respecting the reduction of Sooloo. Adieu once more, my dearest Sir. Stone tenders his best wishes to you and Mrs. Palk.

Much correspondence is devoted to payments to Palk on account of interest due on loans he made them. The number, size and duration of such loans pay testimony to the considerable wealth Palk accumulated in his 20 years in India. Here is an example:

Laurence Sulivan to Robert Palk, Esqr Endorsed in Palk's hand 'Mr. Sulivan, concerning what I have advanced' 1768, May 19th, Great Ormond Street.

My dearest Friend,
If I have hitherto taken no notice (except in casual discourse) of the money I owe you, it is because I have expected from week to week, by clearing my self of India embarrassments, to have been in a capacity to do it ; but since my own honour with the interest of my friends have determined me to go deeper than ever, and consequently it will be convenient to me to delay the payment some months longer, I think it right (though by you not desired) that you have my obligation payable on demand, and which is now enclosed. The whole I make £4,108, viz., a bill on the Navy, £3,000 ; paid Mrs. Darvall, £1,000 ; paid Mrs.Wood,£108 ; Total £4,108.
What you have lately at times disbursed at Ashburton, let me know the amount and I will give an order on my bankers for the payment. I am,

with true and unalterable affection, my dear Sir, your most sincere friend and obedient servant,

Lau. Sulivan.

George Vansittart is a close relation of Palks's wife, Anne and he writes to warn Palk that his nephew may be in serious trouble. Not surprising because most of the company servants were desperately trying to line their pockets by any means - legal or illegal. It is impossible to believe that the directors did not know what was happening. All the great and the good who eventually made good and escaped to England - Clive, Palk and Warren Hastings - went home with enormous fortunes. All protested innocence of crooked dealings some with greater success than others.

George Vansittart to Robert Palk, Esqr. endorsed 'Received 2nd May 1769, per Valentine. 1768, September 6th, Midnapore.

Dear Palk,

I have received your letters in favour of Mr. Darell, and hope to see him when I go to Calcutta. I will also do what I can for Mr. Yarde, but cannot at present learn where he is.

I live much to my satisfaction at Midnapore, but the matter of profit is entirely changed by the Court of Directors' orders concerning salt, who choose rather that the benefit of that trade should be enjoyed by a parcel of Calcutta Banyans than by their own servants. Of three things I have now to determine which to prefer — spend more money than I can gain, improve my fortune by means which would be prejudicial to the Company, or trade in salt, &c., in spite of their orders at the risque of being dismissed from their service.

I am sorry to have a piece of very disagreeable news to communicate to you. Through the influence of bad example and bad advice your nephew has been led into a scrape, which I fear will be the means of his losing the Company's service. Upon his arrival at Cossimbazar he was appointed to the office of Buxey, and in consequence had the care of providing materials for the cantonments which are building there. In the management of this business his predecessors had been used to charge the Company 30, 40, 50 per cent, above the bazar price. Your nephew was unfortunate enough to continue the practice. A month or two ago it was discovered, and it is now under strict examination. I have sent Harry a copy of what he has been able to say in his defence: he will show it to you.

Mrs. G. Van. desires to be remembered. She was brought to bed of a boy the 19th of last month, and is now very well. My love to Mrs. Palk. I will write to her by the next ship. My congratulations to you both on the increase of your family.

Mr. Verelst talks of going home this season, and Mr. Cartier will succeed to the Chair. We are at present in peace, but probably shall not be so long : however, I will not go about to entertain you with politicks or news. I write fully and freely to Harry, and that must suffice. I am ever, my dear Palk, your very sincerely affectionate

George Vansittart

Thomas Vansittart is Palk's nephew and is a frequent and interesting military correspondent. More trouble is expected from Hyder Ali who cannot be brought to battle.

Thomas Palk to Robert Palk, Esqr. 1768, September 30th, Camp near Colar to the southward of Madras.

My dear Sir,

We arrived here the 13th July after a passage of six months, which I thought very long. Mr. Wynch behaved exceedingly well to me : I wanted for nothing. I came ashore at Madras in the boat with him and Mrs. W., who was very kind to me, more so than I ever could expect ; not the least vanity appeared in her. I was to have had a room in his house, but Mr. Goodlad insisted that I should be with him whilst I remained at Madras, which was about a fortnight, I being very busy preparing myself for camp. Goodlad is very much my friend and adviser. Mr. Goodlad recommended me to his worthy friend Captain Hector Mackay, with whom I live in camp, who advises in everything : he is a worthy man.

Ever since I have been here we have been running about the country after our hero Hyder, who wants to take our great guns that we are getting up to go against Bangolure, a very strong fort, one army being divided ; one army being in the road to Bangulore, and the other division watching Hyder's motions. We want to bring him to an engagement, but he is so artful a warrier he won't let us. He has, I hear, made proposals of peace to us, which is at present a secret, it being an uncertainty. It may be well enough for those that have made their fortunes, but as for the subalterns I know not what they will do. This is a life. Sir, that I am contented with and that I like very much, was I not so low on the list, but that is I hope to your certainty of getting me in the Civil list.

I assure you I meet with a great many friends here. Colonel Campbell is very kind to me ; he wanted me to live with him. He went to Colar sick on account of the ball he received in his body, but I fear it will hinder him from taking the field again. I need not tell you how much he is beloved here, which I imagine you are no stranger to. Colonel Smith is an exellent man. I often dine with him, as I shall to day. He is a man, which no one is unless he is sensible of feeling. How much my father is mistaken in the objection he had against my being in the army, that I should be more exposed to bad company. Here is, I own, good and bad, and very good genteel young fellows :therefore if I keep the bad company it is my fault.

I wrote to my brother at Bengal, but whether it will go safe I know not, as he is not at Calcutta. I had a letter from Tom Palk the night I got to camp, who is with Captain Madge. I hope that Mrs. P. is well and my little cousins.I remain, my dear Sir, your sincere and affectionate nephew

T. Palk.

[P.S.] Since I wrote you the former. I told you how happy I was with Captain Mackay, but since then I have lost him, lost him ; he is no more. In attempting to escalade the Fort of Malwagle on a high rock, that is an impossibility to perform ever. We took it by stratagem from Hyder, as did he again, but 'tis imagined by bribery ; but, however, Colonel Wood marched there immediately and ordered a party to storm it if possible, and my dear Hector would go a volunteer, and was obstinate enough not to be advised to the contrary ; but he got on the wall twice and was knocked off, and making the retreat my friend, whom I could venture to call so, was killed. What his friend Goodlad suffers is unaccountable, whom he made his executor.

Lieut. Thomas Palk to [Robert Palk, Esqr.] 1768, October 24th, Samalcotah.

Sir,
I hope you have duly received my last letter dated from Chicacole, in which I acquainted you of an expedition's being ordered to march against Hyderabad. We soon returned, as peace was made with the Nizam when we were within five days' march of his capital. Soon after our joyning Colonel Hart I was appointed his Aid du Camp, in which station I acted a very short time, as the command was taken from him by Colonel Peach, of the Bengali detachment.

Hyder Ally has been very troublesome ere since, although he has been worsted in every engagement. Colonel Wood has been excessive lucky in his conquests of late : he has taken several of Hyder's forts, in one of which he put about 6,000 people to the sword ; he indeed in general gives them little or no quarter. About the beginning of this month he attacked Hyder's whole army, which consisted of about thirty thousand horse and foot, with only 450 Europeans and three thousand sepoys. The action lasted five hours, when Hyder was obliged to retreat, leaving in the field about 2,000 foot killed, 100 horse, and several elephants and camels. On our side were killed Captains Villiers Fitzgerald and Hector Mackay, 2 ensigns and 63 private killed and wounded, and about 250 sepoys killed and wounded.

About two months since, on an alarum in our Morattoe camp. Captain Gee, who was Aid de Camp to Colonel Smith, was ordered to see what was the matter ; but the Morattoes, imagining him to belong to Hyder Ally cut him to pieces. He is greatly lamented. He married Miss Carter about 6 months before his death.

Cousin Thomas arrived some time since, but I have not as yet had the pleasure of seeing him as he is at present with Colonel Smith. He acquaints me by letter that he left all friends in Devonshire well. He seems to like a camp life very well, and says most of your friends behave

excessive kind to him. Young Mr. Smerdon was with us at this place (for a few days) about 2 months since, but is at present at Ellore under Lieutenant Colonel Tod's command. I am sorry to acquaint you that his behaviour has been very indifferent since his arrival. I shall defer giving any account of him, as Captain Madge tells me he intends writing you a long letter concerning him, and another to Mr. Smerdon to advise him to send for his son home.
I received a letter from cousin Robert about a month ago.He is still third in Council at Cossimbuzar. He acquaints me that Suraja Dowla is on the point of breaking out with the Company again, and that he has an immense army now in the field. It is also thought that the Nizam will not keep to his treaty long, for which reason Councillor Whytle is ordered on an embassy to Hyderabad to endeavour to prevent Hyder Ally's bringing him over, which it is conjectured would be the case unless Mr. Whytle settles matters There are three field officers and three captains arrived this season : one of the majors is dead since his arrival. It is reported several of the field officers intend leaving the country as soon as the war with Hyder Ally is at an end.
By letters from my mother and uncle this season they inform me of their having seen you at Ashburton soon after your arrival and of your kindness in promising to send my brother out as soon as of a proper age Be pleased to make my respects to Mrs. Palk, and to Mr. Palk and his spouse at Ashburton. I remain, with due regard and esteem. Sir, your most obliged and devoted humble servant,

Thomas Palk.
P.S. This last engagement with Hyder Ally is said to have been the warmest contested action that has happened since General Lawrence appeared on the plains of Trichinopoly : by which Colonel Wood has gained great honour.

XXVII
Communications with London, 1768

Communications between company servants and London were complicated by the need to send letters by sea and this caused problems. Here Robert Palk is responding in 1768 to letters of 1767. Where there were instructions to give regarding the encashment of bonds or recovery of credits the results could be seriously compromised. This is why someone in Palk's position required dependable and qualified representatives in India who could make decisions in his absence.

Robert Palk to William Martin Goodlad. 1768, November 1st, London. Received 18th May, 1769, per *Lioness*.

Dear Billy,

Your two last letters are of the 21st September and 6th November [1767], and we have since in some measure been relieved from our anxiety by some success against Hyder Aly, and the return of Nizam Aly to our alliance. This I hope will inable you sufficiently to lower Hyder Naig, and prevent his being troublesome in future.

Being but just returned from Devonshire, I have not lately seen Mrs. or Miss Goodlad, but I hear they are well. I have succeeded no better than last year in the consignment way. The trade is become so bad that they all talk of withdrawing their concerns ; therefore be careful how you meddle with diamonds, for in general they will not now bring seven shillings.

Your militia no doubt was admirably appointed, well disciplined and well commanded ; but with such light infantry as James Bourchier, Jos. Smith, yourself and Troutback should have marched out to the enemy and given them a fright, of which they would have been very susceptible ; but I suppose you were taken by surprise, and they were too quick in their motions.

Mr. Sulivan would not be dissuaded from trying his luck once more : the lists of Proprietors will be published in a few days, and then, if I mistake not, he will see clearly that, with all the split votes the Dutch could furnish, he has not the least chance ; and I shall be glad to see an end to all contest.
Nancy and Lawrence are well, and a little girl [was] born the first of this year. My nephew Tom being appointed a Writer, I desire that you and Stone will take him under your management and endeavor to qualify him for a good Company's servant. I forgot to say to his Honor the Governor that the General desires he will favor and protect Mr. Ballard, who went out a Cadet in the same ship with Mr. Alexander. I am ever, dear Billy, your affectionate and sincere friend,

Robt. Palk

George Vansittart to Robert Palk, Esqr. 1769, January 5th. On my way from Calcutta to Midnapore.

You will have heard of Plowman's unexpected death. I went to Calcutta to adjust our business, and made it over to Darrell and Hollond, with whom I have entered into partnership for commission business only. I did not before mention that your nephew had involved himself the deeper in his scrape by agreeing with the other Cossimbazar gentlemen to destroy his Bengal accounts at the time they were demanded from him by the Committee of Inquiry. This, however, was the case ; and this being considered, the Gentlemen of the Council have, I think, acted towards him with all the lenity which could be expected. Upon his delivering to them a just account of his profits, and acknowledging the impropriety of his conduct, they have allowed him an emolument of 15 per cent, upon the prime cost of the materials in consideration of trouble, risks and charges, and they have continued him in the service with only the restriction that he shall not be employed out of Calcutta till the Company's pleasure be known. It must now be your care and his other friends' in Europe to get his pardon confirmed and compleated. Mr. Verelst promises that both in his publick and private letters he will write strongly in his favour. The prime cost of the materials which he provided was about a lack of rupees : his profits about 60,000. I look upon Alexander to be the person to whom he is principally obliged for escaping so well.

I am ordered on deputation to Janoojee, the Moratta Chief at Nagpore,a trip of 400 or 500 cos. Shuja-ud-daula has agreed to a limitation of his forces, and we are now good friends again.

George Vansittart.

Palk worries about a request to return some of the presents he was made when in office. As usual he wants the whole affair to be covered up. Palk draws an interesting distinction between presents offered and demanded, which reveals a culture of bribery and corruption below the surface of apparent probity.

Robert Palk to William Martin Goodlad. 1769, March 17th. London. Received 3rd September.

My dear Goodlad,

In future I promise you to be a much better correspondent, which hitherto has not been the case. Interruption and dissipation are so much in fashion that it has been difficult in this great town to keep an hour to oneself. I have many friends besides yourself to whom I ought to make a better apology.

I have now before me your letter of the 12th May, which conveys to me the true state of affairs, that state which I always dreaded. To carry on such a war required the greatest abilities in the commanding officer, and the highest consideration in laying in provisions. Nizam was too long and too much distressed on his march to be of any service to the alliance ; and unless he could have been supplied with money, the consequence must be his getting it from Hyder Naig. I hope the ship which we daily expect will give us better advices. If we could have kept our ground at Onor, I should have concluded the war in a fair way of being finished. You have attributed our want of success to the right cause. Many here are of the same opinion, but those who have it only in their power to remedy that defect do not chuse to show the world that they could be mistaken. The Governor and Mr. Call have both incurred the displeasure of the Directors. When they leave for England, I request that Wynch, Morse and yourself may take their places as my attorneys. Withecombe's money you should remit to me as soon as you receive it. The Company would like to cut off the resources of the Nawab's creditors, but legal opinion is against them. They have appointed a secret Committee of Inquiry, which will be occupied two or three years, by which time I hope most of the Nawab's debts will be paid.

You may remember that I always shuddered at the Nabob's debt, and I shall be happy when I hear the creditors are out of danger.

Inclosed is a letter to Moodu Kisna, who is desired with you to settle a certain affair. Royala Punt, formerly Renter of St. Thome, Devecotah, &c., says he was turned out soon after my departure, and wants some presents which he made for that reason to be returned. I never in my life asked any man for a present, and those he gave me were so large that indeed they astonished me, viz., one thousand pagodas when he rented Munnimunglum from the Nabob's manager, one thousand when I came to the Government, and, long after he had taken the above farms for five years, I think six or seven thousand more — Moodu Kisna knows which. Of the latter sum I am willing to return him so much back as was unexpired of his term, dividing the latter sum into five ; but this must be done in a judicious manner, and that nothing of it may ever transpire. In short, more or less I leave it to you and Moodu Kisna to settle on any terms confidentially, and to receive the amount from my attornies, to whom I have mentioned it but very slightly. I am sure during my whole government I never sought or intended to oppress any man. And yet I apprehend some European must have forced him to make this demand.

I recommend my nephew Tom to your care and protection. The Directors promised he should be the first on the list, and they made him the last. In this country all is party, and poor Tom is involved, though his unkle never meddles further than to give his single vote.

I am ever, my dear Billy, your sincere and affectionate friend,

RoBT. Palk.

XXVIII
Warren Hastings is expected, 1769

Josias Du Pre brings a military progress report for Palk to see how the politics are shaping. By now it has become very clear, not only to the company but also to the goverment at home, that progress in the field leads directly to commercial success. The Company started with the need, militarily, to protect the trade but has now embraces a policy of increasing dependent territory to increase trade! The appointment of Warren Hastings was imminent and welcome.

Josias Du Pre to Robert Palk, Esq. 1769, June 15th. Fort St. George.

Dear Sir,

I will not attempt to give you an account of our unfortunate transactions in the course of the war ; you will have it at large, I dare say, from some of your other friends, and you will find that, far from depriving Hyder of the power of doing mischief, we have been brought to disgrace. Though our armies, with a good General at their head, may almost command victory over any country .enemy who will risk a battle, there are other ways by which we may be overcome. We may be ruined by expence. That the peace we have made will be blamed there can be no doubt ; ill success can never share any other fate. I am clear, however, all our circumstances considered, that there was no alternative but that or worse. We must now bend all our endeavors to restore our finances, which are reduced to worse, much worse, than nothing.

What? Is there to be no end to wars and rumours of wars in Leadenhall Street ? For my part I have been endeavouring to lay in a small store of philosophy on that subject ever since I was appointed. If I am permitted to stay here a few years, 'tis well, I will do the best I can ; and if I should be invited home, why that too will be well, for it will save me an infinite deal of trouble, which I fear, as things are, will procure but little honor and little profit. Your nephew, I understand, after having tried and very

well endured a fatiguing campaign, seems to prefer the sword to the quill. He has not yet made a decisive choice. He shall have my support in either, for I hear he has merit. Mr. Morse will always find me ready to give all the assistance that I can with propriety in your affairs or his own. I hope Mrs. Palk and your little ones enjoy good health. I wish I could send them a few rays of our sun. We could spare them, for I have never known so hot and dry a season. We are burnt to cynders. Mrs. D. sends her compliments ; she has lately presented me with another girl.
Mr. Ballard ! Thank God he is not here. I should be sorry not to take notice of any one recommended by General Lawrence. I am told that he is a very bad character : he got into some scrape here and fled to Bengal.
I beg leave to make my salam to General and Mrs. Caillaud.
Have some mercy, I pray you, upon poor America, or you will repent it by and by. Keep off a French war a few years longer if possible, that your affairs in the East as well as the West may be better prepared : — I am speaking now to the senotor. I wish you happiness. What can you wish for more !

Jos. Du Pre

Nick Morse gives a detailed account of the strengths and weaknesses of the company's military position and comments on the changes that are about to happen.

Nicholas Morse to Robert Palk, Esq. 1769, June 26th. Fort St. George

I am of opinion that Harry Vansittart's purchase of a house at Greenwich is well judged. His coming abroad again will depend on circumstances. The want of currency in Bengal is affecting both revenue and trade, and the Government there have ordered the coining of gold mohurs. The causes of the deficiency of silver are natural, and little improvement can be expected while the country remains disturbed. I regret the frequent changes in the ministry at home. Luxury and licentiousness were never at so great a high, and the nation in general [is] much altered for the worse. Mr. Bourchier talks of leaving India next January. The appointment of Mr. Hastings next to Mr. Du Pre I find had been determined in the Court of Directors. They are happy in having so worthy and capable a person in their service, as the present state of India requires those of such a character ; for though there has been a peace made with Hydro Naigue, yet there is no dependance on him ; but rather that he might joyn the French on any rupture with them, as it is certain there are connections between them, and it may be apprehended that Sujah Doulah might be ready to make use of any advantage of time and circumstances. The Morattas are powerful and always acting for interest ; and on the whole the English may esteem themselves happy if they can preserve what they have, to do which will require great care and circumspection, and to be prepared. Had a peace been made in September last, the Carnatic would not have suffered in the unhappy manner it has, nor Hydro boasted that it was now his time to do it. The terms are not yet made public, although concluded six weeks ago.

Mr. Call is far from being well, yet cannot resolve to go to Europe on this ship. He and the military have not agreed, and I think if the Deputies had not been sent it might have been better ; at least there would not have been so much uneasiness in the camp. As to the late war, much has been wrote to Europe by the Dutton, and as to the peace, there will be a great deal to say by this ship from different hands. The justices and jury at the last sessions had some disputes : the first sworn in were soon dismissed, and another set sworn in. Messrs. Majendie, Benfield, and Marsden are bound in recognisances of £1,000 to appear at the Court of King's Bench on Michaelmas Term, 1771.

The advices by the Egmont occasioned the Gentlemen at home to put some treasure on each ship bound to China, which was well judged. The supracargoes have liberty to draw for £200,000 on England and will greatly help persons in their remittances home of their money.

Your nephew, I believe, has not yet determined about the civil or military : I shall therefore refer you to him for an explanation. He seemed apprehensive that his allowances in the civil might not be equal to the other ; on which I assured him that your attorneys would make up that to him, which might be about [Pags] 12 more to his diet money, the Ensign's pay being, with the allowance, about 20 pagodas per month ; and that I did not doubt but you would hereafter order him some money to assist him in business. I have said much to him on the occasion, and endeavoured to persuade [him] not to miss the opportunity of being in the civil, as what you had obtained for him with some trouble, and as the best way of his getting forward in life. He is a very good lad, sedate and well disposed, and has given much satisfaction to his superior officers, and may do well in either way.

I have arranged matters with all the correspondents of the House, and shall relinquish business as soon as the accounts are closed, so the next despatch will be from Mr. Hollond and his associates. I am quite tired out, finding it impossible to satisfy every one. You are sensible of the trouble I have had, and the difficult times I have had to negotiate their affairs in, which others are not. I never kept back any money that could be remitted, and yet find some of them think we have.

Nic. Morse

John Maxwell Stone to Robert Palk, Esqr. 1769, June 27th. Fort St. George.

A peace was in April last concluded with the formidable Hyder : I wish I could say that we had compelled him to it. The particulars of all publick affairs you will no doubt have from Mr. Bourchier, whose situation for this long time past has been truly to be pitied. Vexations and disappointments seem to have been his constant attendants, though I am convinced no man could deserve them less if a truly good heart and ah earnest desire to promote the Company's interest could keep him free from them.

Your nephew Tom has been in some doubt whether to continue in the military or accept of the civil service. Indeed I was not surprised at it, as he seems to have a turn for a soldier's life, and during the last campaign, which has been a very severe one, has acquired his share of honor and the esteem of every officer in the army. He has, however, at last determined on the civil, and this day signed his covenants, though not without some reluctance.

J. M. Stone.

P.S. You will no doubt have heard of the death of our poor friend

Griffiths. Mr. Thomas and I have the management of his affairs, which, with your kind assistance to him, will I hope turn out a sufficient provision for his children. We expect one of them may arrive in India this season

Charles Bourchier to Robert Palk, Esqr. 1769, June 29th. Fort St. George.

I am infinitely obliged to you, my dear friend, for many of your most acceptable favors, and for so warmly espousing my cause with the Court of Directors. They did me but justice in believing that I was doing my best for them, as I can with truth say my sole view in continuing the warr was the interest and welfare of the Company ; and as the reducing the power of Hyder Alice was a measure strongly recommended by Lord Clive for the security of the Company's possessions in the Carnateck as well as the Nabob's dominions — a measure also repeatedly urged by the present Committee in Bengal, and which in my own judgment and of my colleagues here [was] of essential consequence to the Company's prosperity — I cannot help being vexed that they should think me and some others so culpable in adopting it when there was the greatest probability of carrying our point. I cannot however be surprised that they should be so much out of humor ; for accountable as they are now become to Parliament for all transactions, to avoid any reproach they may apprehend, they no doubt will load us with censure ; and should we escape it this year we shall inevitably be dismissed the next when they are acquainted how much the scene has changed since the Egmont left us, and with the distressful situation the Carnateck, the Nabob's and the Company's affairs have been reduced to by the continuance of the warr. I have therefore determined to leave India next January at all events, and hope to be happy amongst you and the rest of my friends in England towards the end of summer if the Directors will let me be at peace there ; but as I have reason to believe an ill Starr presided at my birth, I have apprehensions that they will give me some trouble after I am got home. We have at length happily put an end to the enormous expences occasioned by the warr by concluding a peace with Hyder, who, having led Colonel Smith a dance of near a month, had the address, after drawing him as far as Villaporum, to slip by him, and making a march of no less than 45 miles the first day, got so much ahead of our army that he reached the Mount three days before they got the length of Vendaloor. On his arrival there he wrote to me that he was come so near to make peace with us himself. In the extremities we were reduced to we gladly embraced the opportunity of opening the Conference again ; for the country being entirely at his mercy ; our army being incapable of protecting it or bringing him to a decisive action, and daily diminishing by sickness and fatigue ; the promised succors of horse by the Nabob and Mora Row not arrived, nor likely to be for some months, and our distress for money great ; our whole dependance being on the Nabob, who though he promised largely we had doubts of his performing ; and it being also the Company's positive orders to make peace, were under the necessity of doing it almost at all events. I will not trouble you with a detail of all that passed on the occasion, though I have been very particular therein to both Rous and Mr. Sulivan, and probably you may know from the latter.

I hope therefore you will be satisfied by my telling you that after five days spent in the most tiresome and vexatious discussions with the Vackeels that were sent in after Mr. Du Pre had been with Hyder one whole day at the Mount, the articles were settled of which you have a copy inclosed. Besides which, the Nabob was obliged to submit to consent that all of the Novoyt cast who were in the Carnateck should be permitted to leave it if such was their choice. As this article the Nabob thought affected his honor, it was agreed to be left out of the written treaty.

We also agreed, after the treaty was signed, to give up to Hyder some stores at Colar, as we understood from Captain Kelly, who commanded there, that the place could not hold out beyond the 10th April. As a fact, it held out until the treaty was signed, and we are therefore holding an inquiry into Captain Kelly's conduct. As you are well acquainted with the Nabob's rooted antipathy to Hyder, and how ambitious he is, you will not be surprised that he should be so very averse to our making the peace as he has expressed himself on several occasions. It is, however, very extraordinary that these foibles should so much get the better of his reason as to blind him to his own interest in the highest degree. He saw our united efforts could not prevent the daily ravages of his enemy, and that every hour we delayed coming to an accommodation subjected him and his wretched subjects to the severest losses without the least glimpse of hope that we could find any other means of preventing it than by concluding a peace ; yet he wished it could have been avoided ; would not consent to have his name inserted as a contracting Power ; and, though he promised to authorise us to act for him in making peace for the Carnateck by a letter, we have never yet been able to obtain such an authority from him. He has indeed been so very refractory lately that I have at times had infinite trouble with him, and I am very suspicious he has somebody he places a confidence in that puts false notions into his head, which induce him to act so very differently to what seemed to be his former disposition ; and who knows it may be the author of the curious pamphlet wherein you and I and Call are extolled for being such excellent cooks.

The apprehension that the Company will in time take his country into their hands (as has been done in Bengal) to clear off their debt, now no less than 12 lacks of pagodas, besides the expenses of the warr amounting to 14 lacs more (a sum you will be amazed at, and which I fear I shall be hanged for : however, so it is, and I must abide by the consequences) alarms him beyond measure and throws him into the utmost despair. He is nevertheless meditating at times the means to clear off his debt to the Company, and proritises to effect it in three years if peace subsists so long. Indeed I suspect he must have a hoard somewhere, as the Company and individuals assisted largely sometimes towards defraying his expenses, during which interval the revenues of the country were collected by him ; and this I am the readier induced to believe from his having at times talked of discharging his debt in even 18 months. Possibly if the Company propose any measures that may be dissatisfactory to him and that may increase the suspicions he has already entertained, he may exert himself and pay off what he owes them. With respect to the charges of the warr, notwithstanding he made an agreement with us, which is entered in Consultation, to bear them all, provided we left the management of the conquered countrys to him and the produce at the time they were so, with all the plunder taken, he now disputes the matter and says his agreement was conditional that we took

Seringapatam ; than which nothing is more untrue. We have left this circumstance to the Company's determination ; and as they had an interest in the war, which was begun in consequence of our possessing the Circars, they ought in reason [to] take to themselves some portion of the charge of it ; and I think that ought to be at least one third, as the value of their possessions bears about that proportion to the amount of the Nabob's.

Hastings's superceding Call is a mortifying circumstance. Call, however, will go home as soon as he possibly can settle his affairs, but I believe he will not do so before me.

I wrote you in duplicate by the *Dutton*, which my friend Carter carried, to put one packet on board any ship he might meet with in the voyage. I therein gave you a full account of Calland's malevolent intentions. What you mention of the letter you received from him and his declarations therein confirm my suggestions. I hope, agreable to what I proposed to you, that you have found means to prevent his executing his vile purpose; for in the humor the Directors seem to be at present a hint only from him will be sufficient to awaken all their suspicions, which may occasion such orders as will affect numbers both at home and abroad. Nothing has been done here yet relative to the enquiry ordered last year, as Ruccun ud Dowlah, the Souba's minister, who had the principal hand in concluding the Hydrobad Treaty, has been absent ; but as he is soon to return there, he will be applied to on the subject. I shrewdly suspect from advices I have seen that further scrutinies will be ordered this year from home, and I wish I may not have trouble thereby.

Rajahpundit is an infamous rascall, and so much involved in debt to the Nabob as well as others that he is now under confinement with the Nabob on that account. I have talked with Moodoo Kistnah and communicated what you desired of me to Goodlad : by the next dispatch. I shall let you know what has been resolved on ; hitherto nothing, as there has been little opportunity for it.

It has been with some difficulty your nephew Tom has been prevailed on to lay down the sword. He has been an Ensign some time, and being reduced from 17 pagodas to 8.23/. per month was a powerful argument against relinquishing it. He promised to make a good officer, being fond of his profession, but is convinced that his future prospects of advantage are more extensive in the civil than the military. He is a sedate, sensible youth, and much regarded in the corps he belonged to. Could he be assisted a few years with the addition of 10 pagodas per month to his writer's stipend, it would be very acceptable, and little enough to keep him out of debt, as you know.

By the way of China shall find means to make remittances to you my attorneys of at least £30,000 on account of myself and Jim ; and by the end of next year shall have in England, I hope, with what is already in your hands, about £60,000, the mode of remittance being already secured. How much more we are possessed of I am yet uncertain, but I have set tight to work as soon as the Thames is sailed to settle all my accounts and dispose of outstanding concerns.

I thank you for the house you have purchased for me, which according to Mrs. B.'s description of it must be a very excellent one. I wish the price may be not too great for my fortune ; but if it should appear to be so, I imagine I can always have it in my power to dispose of it without much loss.

Besides the vexation our late troublesome situation gave me, we have had further cause for it from the refractory behavior of a Grand Jury, who treated us so contemptuously on the Bench that we were at length put to the disagreable necessity of ordering three of them, Benfield, Majendie and Marsden, to prison because they refused to enter into a recognisance to appear and answer for their misconduct before the King's Bench. but which they were released from on signing the recognisance. They threaten us with great damages, which has occasioned us to be very particular in an address to the Court of Directors on the occasion ; and I am so much persuaded we have done no more than we can answer for that I am perfectly easy on the occasion. However, I shall be glad if you will make some enquiry into the matter at the India House, and write me a line to meet me at St. Helena in what light the matter is taken at home, as well as any other intelligence that materially concerns me.

Chs Bourchier.

XXIX
Palk is concerned about trade, 1769

Robert Palk to William Martin Goodlad 1769, November 5th. London. Received 1st May, 1770.

My Dear Billy,

Your letter of the 11th March recording the unhappy state of affairs on the Coast gives me the most sensible concern and uneasiness. We have gone on from victory to victory without reflecting how the whole was to be preserved and governed, and what fatal consequences a reverse must have involved us in. When Nizam Aly settled with Hyder, certainly we should have done the same. We should then have given all India a strong impression of our power, and probably have secured the Carnateck from future invasions. As it is, I dread and am very anxious for the next accounts.

Your kindness to Mr. Helling as well as my nephew has been very great. The latter I should rather have continued in the military, but his mother, reflecting on the loss of so many of his countrymen, will not hear of it ; and so I suppose he brings up the rear of the Writers, a piece of revenge in Direction which I did not deserve, and owing to those perpetual struggles at the India House, where the parties have for some years been violent to the last degree. At Mr. Vansittart's departure a Coalition had taken place, which lasted only a few days, but I still hope it may be renewed ; though I know little of the matter, being just arrived from a six weeks' tour into Devonshire.

On Bourchier and Call's coming away I have desired that Wynch and you may succeed them as my attorneys. I have another copy of the letter from Rajah Pundit, and hope that long ere now a proper gratuity has been made him, as I had rather be at any expence than that any man should say I had done him any injustice.

Great preparations I find are making to send you every assistance. I am sorry the loss of so many officers makes a reinforcement of them necessary. The General and Mrs. Palk remember you most cordially. I am ever, my dear friend, most affectionately yours,

Robert Palk

Lieutenant Thomas Palk to Robert Palk, Esq. 1770, January 12th. Condapillee.

Honoured Sir,
I expected my brother out the last season from what my mother acquainted me in her last letter, and the accounts I heard from cousin Thomas at Madrass. The latter informed me there was one of our name coming out on one of the ships. But I was agreeably disappointed, for I think he was then rather too young to set out in the world. But even though he had come out the last year in a military capacity, he would not have yet been an officer, for out of the 50 or 60 cadetts that arrived the last season there are not more than 6 or 8 have got commissions. I am still a lieutenant, and expect to continue so for some time, as there is now between me and a company sixteen. Colonel Wood, Captains Kelly and Orton were tryed the former was, I hear, charged with eight crimes. The sentence of the court is not yet made publick in general orders. Most of the 3rd Regiment has been stationed at Ellore ever since peace was concluded, under the command of Lieut. Colonel Tod. He will not remain there long it's thought, as Colonel Hart is expected there very soon.
About 5 months since I was ordered from Ellore with 4 companies of Captain Madge's battalion to the command of this garrison. Captain Madge at the same time marched with the remaining six companies and relieved Captain Bellingham from the command of Samalcottah.
The latter goes to command the Chicacole Circar. I have not been able to ascertain what effects were left by Mr. Mould, who was drowned from on board a vessell in Madrass roads. Mr. Bourchier resigns the chair to Mr. Du Pre about the end of this month.
When my brother arrives I shall ask Mr. Call to get him appointed to the 3rd Regiment, now in the Circars.
Captain Madge will inform you this season of young Mr. Smerdon's elopement from Madrass. He took a journey there about six months since

on purpose to endeavour to get him home on some of the last ships, but he went off before his arrival there, and has not since been heard of I believe.

Cousins Robert and Thomas are both very well. I keep a constant correspondence with them, and heard from each of them very lately. The latter informs me he has an intention of paying his brother a vissit this year with the two Mr. Stonehouses. Be pleased to remember me most affectionately to Mrs. Palk, and to Mr. Palk's family at Ashburton.

Thomas Palk

Warren Hastings is now in post and realises, if he did not before, that Robert Palk has the ears of the directors. He hastens to set out the political situation.

Warren Hastings to Robert Palk, Esq. 1770, January 29th. Fort St. George.

Dear Sir,

I have received your favor of the 23rd June by the *Lapwing*, and am much obliged to you for your good wishes. A part of these is happily accomplished. All wars are at an end, and if there is not the fairest prospect of the continuance of peace, there is a very hearty inclination to it and a determination to maintain it if possible on our side, which is the best security for it. Our people are yet sore of their late ill success, and are all more anxious to secure the Company's property than to extend their dominion or retrieve the reputation of their arms. There is certainly some defect, whether in our civil or military system I will not say, which ought to be removed before we engage in new wars, as I do not find that either Hyder Alice's abilities are of the first kind, or his horse equal to those of Shuja Dowla ; and I believe we have been successful against as powerful enemies, and with less than a fifth part of our present strength. A reformation in this point I shall hope for from the abilities and experience of our friend and his assistants. To explain the intimation in the beginning of my letter that we had not the fairest prospect of peace, I must add that we have been alarmed for some time past by formidable preparations made by all our neighbours, which have begun to shew their object by hostilities between Mahadebrow and Hyder Alice. Negotiations have been formed between them, and seem likely to take place by the payment of a sum to the former for the chout, and a further aid, it is said, for an expedition against the Payengaut. As the harvest, which has been very plentiful, is almost gathered, I hope we shall be provided both with grain and money to prevent the effects of their ravages if the Marattas should make us a visit.

It gave me an unspeakable pleasure to hear of the new commission granted to Mr. Van, and to find such a man as Colonel Forde joined with him. I cannot say I was so well pleased to see Scrafton's name with theirs, but a further reflexion has reconciled me to it. All parties will be better pleased with the measures taken by the Commissioners than if Mr. Van alone, or joined only with his friends, had formed them ; and Scrafton is neither illnatured nor hard to manage when he has no troublesome people about him. Forde will, if I mistake not, have a great ascendant over him. He is a reasonable and steady man, and Mr. Van, from his superior abilities and knowledge of the methodical part of business, in which I believe the others are deficient, will certainly take the lead in everything. I suppose the Commission will last during the period of Cartier's government, and our friend return to his former station. I know no other recompense the Company can make him for his trouble and the odium which the execution of such a trust will unavoidably draw on him. Bengal certainly requires such a ruler. The Company's affairs there have been declining very fast, and for their sake more than that of this Presidency, which stands in great need of such a reforming power also, I am most heartily glad the Company have adopted so wise a plan, the wisest they ever thought of.

Young Griffiths has always behaved very well. He is good natured and willing, and his parts such as will mend. He lives with me, and I have put him under Goodlad in the Secretary's office. I hope you will have interest enough to obtain his appointment upon the covenanted list, as I fear there will be strong objections to a public recommendation of him from hence. I had Mr. Bolton's promise, voluntarily given, for his appointment if he behaved well. He is now 15 years of age.

I have lived almost in the Council Chamber since my arrival. I cannot boast of having done much in it, as our attention has been mostly taken

up in clearing away the dirt of the late war. It seems to be the fate of the age we live in that all public acts shall be personal; and it has been my hard lot to arrive at a time when the whole Settlement was ready to take fire at every measure of the Government, partly from past discontents and partly from present interest. Among other disagreable things, the Board were under the necessity of bringing Colonel Wood to a court martial, of disapproving the sentence by which he was acquitted, and of dismissing him from the service. From the great opinion I have of Mr. Sulivan's integrity, I am sure he will applaud the conduct of the Board if he believes it to have been just, and be the first to confirm their proceedings. But as it is possible to be prejudiced when we think ourselves guided by motives of strict justice : as Colonel Wood is a relation of Mr. Sulivan and will take more pains to vindicate himself than others to convict him : and as the proceedings of the court martial are so voluminous as to frighten any man who sets a value on his time from an attempt to read them, I hope, if he has any doubts of the propriety of Colonel Wood's dismission, he will take the trouble to examine the facts on which it was founded, and that you will have so much influence with im as to persuade him to this. My regard for his friendship, and my desire to see the authority of this Government duly supported (and it much wants it) are my inducements for mentioning this, though I believe it unnecessary.
I beg you will present my compliments to Mrs. Palk and the General, who with yourself have my sincere and hearty wishes. I am, dear Sir, your obliged and affectionate humble servant

Warren Hastings.
P.S. It is necessary to advise you that I secured bills for the amount of my bond to Mr. Sumner, which will go by the March ship.

Thomas Palk to Robert Palk, Esq. 1770, January 31st. Fort St. George.

Honoured Sir,
I have now the pleasure to write you by the Britannia, Captain Rous, who is come down from Bengal to carry our present Governour, his brother and Mr. Call home, all of whom I shall feel much the loss of in many respects, particularly my good friend Mr. Call, who has treated me like a friend, which is rare in this country. I have lived with Mr. C. ever since I gave up the sword.
Since my taking up the pen I have through economy been applying to Mr. Bourchier, &c., to get me to a subordinate [station], and not to stay in this luxurious place. but the Governor told me it was your express desire that I should be kept in the office for three years, which is a long while to slave for a scanty eight pagodas a month.
In consequence of Mr. B.'s departure they have made me an allowance of twenty pagodas per month. It has been my whole study to live on the little I have, and likewise to be as frugal as possible. It may perhaps. Sir, be made appear to you that I have been extravagant, but my study has been the contrary I assure you.
With diffidence I venture to ask you for a loan, on which I shall of course pay you the usual interest.
I have already began to merchandise. I do not know whether it is through Mr. Call's recommendation or not ; I believe not, as my brother wrote long since to me on the subject of sending me consignments. I have accordingly received one from him by the Britannia containing three bales of Radnagor raw silk, which he says is a little for a beginning, so I expect more soon, and I intend to apply myself very strickly to business. The coming out of the Commissioners in the Aurora frigate make[s] everybody surprised it seems, as they will have it in their power to turn out and take in as they please. I hope not. If they do, it will be much longer than I imagine before I come to be of any rank who are [sic] the youngest servant on this Coast. Had you waited till the last election you might have got me at least at the head of the list. However, a certainty is better than an uncertainty. Your most dutiful and most obedient nephew,

Tho. Palk.

The problems of Smerdon are recounted by Thomas. He was letting down the side.

Thomas Palk to Robert Palk. Esq.1770, February 5th. Fort St. George.

I send this by the hand of Mr. Call.

You desired me in your letter by the Duke of Grafton to give you some account of that wretch Smerdon. I am sorry he should have come here under your recommendation. He stayed here about a month after he arrived, and I believe behaved tolerably well. He then went recommended to Captain Madge and stayed with him about two months, which he spent in drinking &c., &c., what is disagreeable for me to mention and much more so for you to peruse. Captain M. having tried every means and way to make something of him and took an immense deal of trouble, he was obliged to send him down here to Mr. , I forgot his name ; he came a free merchant recommended by you, who had promised to carry him to sea; but instead of waiting on that gentleman he has absconded, and no accounts have since been heard of him. He squandered away a great deal of money, which he has left for poor Madge to pay, which I believe he will do on account of Mrs. Smerdon's desire, who wrote him on the subject of lending him a little money, and his coming very bare here ; but without ever signing her name to the letter, so that he is in doubt whether he will ever be paid.

If you grant the loan asked for in my last letter, I would place the sum in the hands of my friend Mr. Morse, and be guided by his advice. Mr. M. begins to be tired of the world : he is settling his affairs, and intends retiring into the country ; I imagine to the Mount, as he is building a house there

William Martin Goodlad to Robert Palk, Esq. 1770, February 6th. Fort St. George

We are still in peace, and I hope likely to continue so ; though as yet I think it altogether doubtful whether we shall or not. Hyder and the Marattas are at present disputing the superiority. Some skirmishes only have hitherto happened, though a considerable part of his country has been laid waste by them. Should matters be compromised, I think it hardly to be doubted but the latter will pay us a visit ; but their exorbitant demands on Hyder give us some hopes that no accommodation will take place. He has sent to demand our assistance in consequence of the late treaty, and Vackeels from the other party are shortly expected to arrive. If there is a possibility of keeping the mid channel, we certainly shall ; at any rate every species of delay must be used without coming to any determination ; for it cannot be our interest to espouse the cause of either, especially in our present situation as to cash. It is a most difficult card to play.

I am exceedingly pleased with the appointment of the Commissioners on many accounts. Such extraordinary powers were absolutely necessary to regulate affairs in Bengal, where by all accounts the expenses, as well civil as military, but particularly the latter, have grown to a most enormous degree. The Commissioners, however, have undertaken one task which I most heartily wish they may accomplish with honour — I mean the regulation of our political system. It appears to me to be attended with so many difficulties, and those of such a nature that I much fear they will fail in the attempt. Can any plan be fallen upon for so regulating the system that the three Presidencies may co-operate ? I think not. Private letters inform us that restoring the Circars is to be another object of the Commissioners' attention. This there can be no difficulty in executing ; but why restore them ? The argument, I suppose, is that by keeping them our force is too much divided, and that in case of a rupture with the French such division would expose the whole of our possessions. It has weight, and for that reason our first principle, I think, should be to abandon them in case of such a rupture : but why give up at once a very considerable revenue (they will probably produce this year more than 5 lacks of pagodas, besides Cicacole), and by relinquishing these countries give the French the fairest opportunity they can have of firmly establishing themselves? I cannot persuade myself that the Commissioners will restore the Circars, even though they should have come out with that intention. I have acquainted you of the transactions of the Select Committee and Nabob's creditors in my former letters. These matters still continue on a very unsettled footing for the creditors will not rely on the Company for the recovery of what is due to them, and the

pressing demands of the Select Committee to have the Company's debt discharged in preference has prevented the Nabob from making any payments in discharge of his debt to individuals. There are amongst these some turbulent spirits. They address the Court by this ship, and have appointed attorneys to act for them in England. General Richard Smith is at the head of them. Fairfield, Calland, Affleck, Saunders, and, I think, nine others are in commission with him, but what their instructions are I know not. The creditors have hopes that the Commissioners will have it in their power to settle matters to the satisfaction of all parties ; and I most heartily wish it may prove so, since it will relieve the distresses of many, and restore harmony to the Settlement, which we have long been strangers to. At present discontent prevails in every countenance.
I told you of the Court Martial on Colonel Wood, and expressed my apprehensions that the charge of having appropriated to himself the provi- sions taken in the Coimbatoor country would appear too clearly for the Court to pass it over. I was, however, mistaken, for he was acquitted of every charge, though nine in number. But no sooner was the sentence known than the President and Council dismissed him from the service on a clear conviction that, though acquitted, the charges (or most of them) were proved beyond dispute by the evidence produced before the Court. The matter, as I take it, was thus : — the Court were convinced that several of the charges were proved, but they could not condemn Wood for many things which most of themselves had probably been guilty of, nor disapprove of his proceedings without acknowledging those perquisites to be illegal which they would fain establish as their right. The privileges of a Commander-in-Chief appeared therefore in great measure to depend on the issue of this affair ; and the President and Council found it necessary to assert their authority, and by dismissing Wood convince the whole corps that they would not allow of those abuses, which began to be regarded as dues to the officers in command. I have been told that this step has given great dissatisfaction, and that the officers in general complain loudly of the injury done to the service by the dismission of an officer on articles which he had been acquitted of by his judges but still I think the step was absolutely necessary ; and if the President and Council were at all culpable, it was in not publishing their reasonings on the proceedings of the Court., because in my opinion

conciliating the minds of the corps of officers and preventing as far as possible any discontent from getting possession of them is a point that should be materially attended to.

Verelst, I imagine, will be in England before this can reach you. His administration is greatly censured, and there are those who scruple not to say it was a compound of indolence and ignorance.

Mr. B., Call, James Bourchier, Debeck and Frieschman all leave us on the Britannia. Du Pre became Governor the 31st ultimo agreeable to the Company's orders ; but he has hitherto remained quiet in his new station, and there will be no meeting till Mr. B. has left us. Then we shall see what we shall see, and you shall know how we go on. I have before expressed to you what my apprehensions are. Hastings's amiable disposition has, however, in great measure eased them, and I am willing to hope that his mildness will prove a palliative to the rigour of the other.

Mr. B. and myself have been on the most friendly footing during his whole government. . His administration has been truely troublesome and unfortunate, and he now labours under the displeasure of the Court for faults which I cannot think were his own. To me it is past a doubt that our want of success has been in great measure owing to Call ; and I will frankly declare to you that I have seen sufficient of him most heartily to wish that he may never have the administration of affairs lodged in his hands. I will go so far as to say he has neither steadiness or abilities for such a post ; and after saying this you must not imagine you are reading the opinion of a prejudiced person, for Call and I have had no sort of dispute ; we have rather been on an intimate footing. I speak from conviction that he might make a good Counsellor, but that he would be a wretched Governor.

I have nothing to say to you on the subject of Madras news, except that Jack Hollond has brought a young wife from Bengal, who is more admired for her good sense than beauty, though in the latter she surpasses most of our females. But this is mere hearsay, for I have been so tied to my desk that I have not paid a visit for many months.

The matter which you wrote about to Moodu Kistnah and me still remains in the same situation. I wish I may not shortly have occasion to observe your instructions on that head. I have my fears however.

At last Robert Palk is at home in Haldon House close to the Plymouth to

Exeter road.

Robert Palk to William Martin Goodlad. 1770, March 15th. London.

Dear Goodlad,
The French are not likely, I think, soon to disturb you, for their situation in Europe is certainly more pitiful than ours. They have been obliged to make use of the sponge, finding it impossible to raise supplies sufficient to pay the annual interest of their debt. Oceans of people are gone this year to India, and I am at a loss to guess how they can all be provided for. However, the number is much less for Sulivan's opposing it. To sup- port a proprietary interest the Directors are in a manner obliged to over- load India. It is very uncertain which party will be triumphant this year in Leadenhall Street ; both sides seem to be sure of success. Whoever carries it, I should think it will be the last great struggle, and whichever way it goes I think your little brother will have a good chance of seeing you next year
In my last I told you we were on our journey into Devonshire, where I have at last, near Exeter, pitched my tent — in a good house and very pleasant country, close to the road when in good time you land at Plymouth.

RoBT. Palk.
P.S. Mrs. Mackay came home in good time to save the dismission of her husband.

On Hasting's mind is the transfer of wealth to England, again, this time by bulses of diamonds. The term refers to a bag used to measure the worth of precious stones. He is in this transacton with Mrs Ironside. The first worry about the fate of the *Aurora* is voiced by Warren Hastings. The ship carried Henry Vansittart back to India to try to recover his fortune lost through a riskly investment in company shares. The later correspondence with Laurence Sulivan, who also lost his money in the venture, makes clear the extent of the personal tragedy sustained by Robert Palk should the *Aurora* be lost.

Warren Hastings to Robert Palk, Esq 1770, April 3rd. Fort St. George.

Dear Sir,

I wrote to you by the Britannia, and at the same time acknowledged the receipt of your favor of the 23rd of June last. By this packet I have sent bills to my attorneys to enable them to discharge my bond to Mr. Sumner, and have directed them to apply to you to assist in settling that account, which is the last trouble that I shall have occasion to give you in this business. For that which you have already had, and the risque you have undergone in it on my account, I repeat my thanks.

I hope I shall have your excuse for the trouble which I am going to give you in an affair of another kind, having taken the liberty to consign two bulses of diamonds to you, one marked No. 1, the property of Mr. Hancock, the other marked No. 2, belonging to Lieut. Colonel Ironside. It was the only way I had of complying with the pressing solicitation of these gentlemen to remit money for the use of their families, as they had been disappointed of bills in Bengal. Having neglected to give proper directions to me concerning the consignments, their first application being for bills, they have made it necessary for me to request you to receive these commissions, as Mr. Hancock's attorneys can be but incompetent judges of the value of diamonds or the methods of disposing of them, and as Mrs. Ironside, like other ladies, is most probably acquainted with only one way of laying out jewels.

I do suppose that Mr. Hancock's attorneys will be glad to leave the disposal of his diamonds to your management. In that case I shall be obliged to you if you will dispose of them to the best advantage, and let them have the produce ; but if they should rather chuse to receive them unsold, be pleased to deliver them into their charge. I have only written to Mrs. Hancock upon the subject, by whose directions I request you will be guided. That lady, Francis Austen, Esq., and the Rev. Mr. George Austen are Mr. Hancock's attorneys.

The produce of Colonel Ironside's diamonds you will be pleased to pay to Mrs. Ironside, his lady. She is a relation of the General's, and of an amiable and deserving character. This will serve as an excuse for troubling you with her concern. I believe I shall have your ready permission

for the other.
The late arrival of the *Aurora* gives us all much uneasiness. I never knew any object in which the wishes of all men seemed so heartily to concur as in the coming of the Commissioners, and this may be the reason why we are so alarmed at their long passage, which is what ought to be expected from the difficulty of the navigation round Ceyloan at this time of the year, and would to God they were come! We are just arrived at the crisis in which I fear we shall be compelled to declare ourselves the friends or foes of Hyder or Mahdebrow. Both have been hitherto kept in expectation of our alliance, and that expectation only has, I believe, prevented the ravages of the latter. Griffiths is well, and goes on well. Pray present my compliments to Mrs. Palk and the General, and believe me to be with the truest esteem and regard, dear P, your obliged humble servant,

Warren Hastings.

Warren Hastings to Robert Palk, Esq. 1770, April 7th. Fort St. George.

Dear Sir,
I must trouble you again to desire that you will not sell the diamonds by an advance on the invoice price, which I understand is the usual method, because they are, I am assured, of a superior quality to most sent to England by this ship. You will be pleased therefore to open the bulses, and rate them by their quality when you dispose of them. Shall I beg the favor of you to send the enclosed to Lieutenant Douglass of the York man of war ? I cannot recollect a more particular direction to him. I am, dear Sir, your most obedient servant,

Warren Hastings

William Martin Goodlad to Robert Palk, Esq. 1770, April 8th. Fort St. George. Received 15th October.

My dear Friend,
We have been long looking out for the *Aurora*, and persuade ourselves that she must make her appearance very shortly. The *Stagg* arrived at Anjengo the 19th February, and we learn by her that the *Aurora* left the Cape between the 20th and 30th of December. According to the common course of passages she should be here now, yet the uncertain season makes us very little apprehensive for her, particularly as the Duke of Kingston was at the Cape at the same time, and ought by the same rule to have been with us.
Peace still prevails, and in my opinion we have little to apprehend for the present year. The season is already very far advanced, and the Marat- tas too much engaged with Hyder to trouble us. No compromise seems likely to take place between them, and the apprehensions of our joining Hyder will prevent their commencing hostilities as long as their disputes subsist. Each party would rejoice at our assistance, and 'tis possible the Marattas may endeavour to frighten us in order to obtain it ; but I cannot believe they will go further, and unless they do, I regard it as certain that we shall remain neuter. They have plagued Hyder confoundedly. May they continue to torment each other !
At present our prospect is very good. The Committee had, previous to Mr. B's departure, settled very advantageous terms with his Excellency for the discharge of his debts, and he has hitherto been very punctual in his payments. We shall be able to pay off our debt, assist China largely, and nevertheless provide an ample Investment. How different was our prospect twelve months ago !
Colonel Wood did intend to have taken his passage on the *Anson*, but his unfortunate disputes with the Board have prevented it, for they would not give him leave unless he would give security to stand the issue of the suits commenced against him in the Mayor's Court. He talks loudly of the injustice done him in many respects.
Matters have hitherto gone on very smoothly in the new government. Du Pre is very clever and calculated for business. We are punctual in every thing — registers closed, papers signed and dispatches delivered to an hour and my poor pate and fingers have paid pretty severely for many days past.
A storm is said to be brewing in Bengal, and 'tis probable the name of

Cossim will be once more familiar to us. The Gentlemen there, however, seem more alarmed with expectations of the French than from inland appearances; with what reason I know not, but I am sure we are not equally apprehensive here. That great preparations have been making at the Islands is certain, but in my opinion their views are more bent towards the entire conquest of Madagascar than this way.
Calcutta itself is in a deplorable way, and the want of money felt to a degree scarcely to be conceived ; individuals daily becoming bankrupts, property sold by the Mayor's Court for not a third of its value, and, what is still worse, grain so exceedingly scarce that the distresses of the country people are beyond all conception. The Nabob Syfe ut Dowlah thought to be past recovery in the small pox.

W. M. Goodlad
P.S. Pray, my respectful compliments to the General. The Nabob sent his annuity late last night

Duel: pistols at 20 paces

Robert Palk to William Martin Goodlad. 1770, June 16th, per *Dolphin* frigate. Received 20th February, 1771.

My dear Goodlad,

I join in all you say in your letters of 16th September and 19th November concerning poor Bourchier, and will only add the times have been very unfortunate. However, his reception will be more to his satisfaction than he expected. I only wish, instead of driving Calland to despair, he had moved him from St. David. I desire you will still continue your ap- plication concerning Withecombe's money.

I hope in God you will continue in peace ; but as long as we are to protect the Carnateck troubles will sometimes arise, and it will require the most prudent management to keep clear of them. I have, however, great expectations from Mr. Du Pre and Mr. Hastings, if more cooks do not spoil the soop, and the Commissioners at least do no harm. The only good these gentlemen can do, I judge, at Madras will be to soften the severity of the Company's orders concerning the Nabob's creditors. The Company cannot set aside the rights of the creditors ; and the whole can only be meant to shew at a General Court that the Directors have exerted themselves, and there I suppose it will end. However, entre nous, it seems surprising to me that the Governor and Council ever gave their sanction to such an Assignment, because the only inducement the Company could have in launching out their money to the Nabob seemed to be a just expectation that the Carnateck was bound for the security of re- payment. I very sincerely pity the poor Nabob, and wish there was any prospect of an end to his troubles. I often advised him, when he was bor- rowing such large sums, of the consequences which might hereafter follow.

I recommend you to correspond with Mr. Purling on the Company's affairs, as he is strongly supported by Lord Clive, and the present directors are now firmly established. I am writing on my way to Devonshire for the summer. Hint to my nephew, whose letters show marks of carelessness, that more thought is called for.

RoBt Palk

XXX
The loss of the Aurora, 1770

There is devastating news for Robert Palk's wife's family when it is realised that the *Aurora*, carrying George Vansittart's brother and his son is much overdue after leaving the Cape of Good Hope.

George Vansittart to Robert Palk, Esq. 1770, September 5th. Calcutta.

Dear Palk,
I must now communicate to you a piece of intelligence on which I cannot reflect without the deepest sorrow, and which will be equally afflicting to you. The *Aurora* left the Cape the latter end of December, and has no more been heard of. Faint hopes are entertained that she may still be safe; but for my part I must confess that I can flatter myself with none. A storm, a rock or fire have, I fear, deprived us for ever of our brother. I write by this ship (the *Lapwing*) to you and my eldest brother only, and to you two I leave the disagreeable task of informing my mother, Mrs. Harry Van, Mrs. Palk and the rest of our friends of this most unhappy event. I shall in future write fully to you whatever may occur to me rela tive to the transactions in Bengal as I used to do to Harry.
Councils are established at Moorshedabad and Patna for the management of the Dewanny revenues. Messrs. Becher, Reid, Lawrell and Graham compose the former ; Alexander, Vansittart and Palk the latter. Palk and I shall travel off to Patna in a few days. You will hear from your nephew that he is now a married man. Our little George Henry has been very dangerously ill, but by Mr. Hancock's good management is now recovered

George Vansittart.
P.S. Colonel Ironside is apprehensive of being superseded by Colonel

Lesly, and has desired me to request your interest in his behalf.

The dreadful famine in Bengal and Bahar is described by Robert Palk's nephew:

Robert Palk jun. to Robert Palk, Esq. 1770, September 8th. Calcutta

> I gratefully acknowledge the trouble you have taken to obtain my reinstatement in the service. Councils are nominated for Moorshedabad and Patna for revenue collection, and I am appointed to the latter with Alexander and Vansittart.
> George has told you in his letter how faint our hopes are of ever hearing of the Aurora. She left the Cape the 23rd of December, and has no more been heard of. The captain talked of making a short cut ; said the India-men took too great a circle in general. Our fears are that fire, a rock or something of the kind has for ever deprived us of poor Mr. Van — a cruel fate indeed ! His loss will be severely felt in India as well as at home. The Stag has been on her embassy to Persia, but I can give no ac- count of her proceedings there. She is daily expected from Madras with General Coote on board.
> We have had a most dreadfull scarcity in Bengal and Bahar this year. Many hundred thousand of poor creatures have died for absolute want. In many parts of the country there are not hands enough to cultivate the lands. My acknowledgments are due to Mr. Vansitart's father. I shall do my best for his son: indeed I have often endeavoured to bring him out of a strange unaccountable way of life, which has brought on him much misery and must in a few years end his existance. .
> I hope some of the ships of the season will bring me the books you promised to send, Millar's Dictionary and Hooker's History. You sent me a very handsome supply of books from Madras, and it is with infinite satisfaction I dedicate an hour or two every day to their study, which, to my shame I say it, is more than ever I did before. I correspond with my brother at Madras, who is now in joint house keeping with James Call, and have consigned goods to him. I have heard nothing of Mr. Yarde, who was in bad health when he left Calcutta to join the army. Mr. Becher

has been seriously ill, and intends making a sea voyage as his last resource. I have not yet communicated the most material piece of news regarding myself, and what will, I believe, surprise you much. You may remember how alert I used to be at Madras when in the company of Miss Stonhouse, the propensity I had to make myself a favorite ; but George's coming down cut off all my hopes. I have, however, allyed myself to the family by marrying the second sister. I fear you will think that by this act I have defeated your good intention of rendering me usefull to my friends at home ; but I give you my word. Sir, it shall be no obstacle to that end. I have no desire to see any of my sisters in India, but if you think proper to send either of them out, I shall give them a most sincere reception and take every care of them in my power. If either of 'em should come out, as well as I can recollect my youngest sister (Grace) is the best calculated.

Robert Palk
11th [Sept.] I have just received a letter from Mr. Morse giving hopes of the Aurora R.P.

A famine in Bengal kills hundreds of thousands of people when subsistence farmers die and crops fail and nothing is done to provide emergency rations. Disease and starvation were bedfellows in these times and regarded as natural disasters to be endured, observed and reported sympathically.

Thomas Palk to Robert Palk, Esqr. 1770, October 9th. Fort St. George.

I miss my friends who sailed in the Britannia, especially Mr. Call, with whom I lived from the time I quitted the army. I am now in the office under Mr. Goodlad, but should like to change to the Accountant's branch. From the intimate friendship that appeared to subsist between you and Mr. Hastings it was natural for me to expect he would pay some kind of attention to me, but to my surprise he never once asked me in his house ; though from one in his station, and so superciliously disposed, it is not extraordinary. Mr. Morse is exceeding kind to me and very much my friend.

I thank you for the allowance of Pags. 20 per month, which you have made me. My brother in Bengal has been very good in sending

consignments of raw silk to me and Mr. James Call jointly. He has lately been appointed to Patna.
I make no doubt. Sir, but you will be surprised to hear that he was, on the 12th June last, married to Miss Stonhouse, sister of Mrs. George Vansittart's, a very agreeable girl, and above all a young lady of sense.
No news has been received of the Aurora since she left the Cape ten months ago.
I feel greatly for poor Mrs. Van : the loss of a husband and son at once must be a killing stroke to her. Mr. and Mrs. Morse are very deeply afflicted. The Governor and Council are much at variance with General Coote and Sir John Lindsay, and the General is about to sail for Bengal. I laid aside the sword with regret and only in deference to the wishes of my friends.
Tho. Palk
P.S. As I should be very glad to peruse some of the latest of the old news papers and magazines, I hope your goodness will excuse the lib erty I take of requesting you will enclose me a few now and then. My respects to the General and to that good lady Mrs. Bourchier.

Warren Hastings to Robert Palk, Esqr. 1770, October 12th. Fort St. George.

Dear Sir,
I wrote to you two letters by the Anson, and informed you that I had taken the liberty to consign two bulses of diamonds to you, requesting you to sell them and pay the amount of them, of one to Mrs. Hancock and of the other to Mrs. Ironside, for whose use they were sent. Enclosed are duplicate bills of lading mid invoices of both.
I have since received your favors of the 10th November and 23rd March last, with two recommendations, which I will gladly comply with as far as I am able. Mr. Morse has also communicated to me, by your desire,several letters from you to him and Mr. Van, for which I return you my thanks. I wish I could give you any hope of the Aurora, or could form a conjecture that could account for her long absence on the supposition of her safety. I fear it is now impossible.
I presented your letter to the Nabob, who received it with great demon-

strations of friendship both for you and for myself, for which I am bliged to you. I will with great pleasure join Messrs. Morse and Goodlad in the charge of your affairs whenever they shall have any occasion for my assistance. They cannot be in better hands than those they are now in. I am glad to hear that my French bill has been received, and thank you for clearing off so much of my bill due to Sumner. The rest I hope is by this time discharged.

I shall write to you a second letter by this packet, and shall only add in this my desire to be kindly remembered to Mrs. Palk, the General and such of my friends as you shall meet with. I have written a long letter to Mr. Sulivan, which I have desired him to shew you.

I am, dear Sir, your most obedient and obliged humble servant,

Warren Hastings

Warren Hastings

XXXI

The company officials accused of illegal trading, 1770

Sir John Lindsay now accuses company managers of illlegal enrichment - a serious matter for Hastings, Palk and even Clive and one to be taken seriously and resisted at all costs. Famously, in respect of Warren Hastings, such charges were brought to court in England and a four year legal action started. Hastings won, but lost the whole of his fortune in the cost of his defence. John Maxwell Stone adds to the controversy. Warren Hastings has a foretaste of the problems he might face upon his return to England.

Edward Boscawen medal

Warren Hastings to Robert Palk, Esqr. 1770, October 12th. Fort St. George.

Dear Sir,
This letter requires no apology. I have been informed that his Excellency has written a long remonstrance either to the King or to Sir John Lindsay for his Majesty's information, containing the particulars of all the injuries, indignities and losses which he has sustained from the Company and their Governors since his connection with them ; that yourself and Lord Pigot stand among the foremost of these, charged with such high crimes and misdemeanors as, if true, would cost you (to use the expression delivered me) both your heads ; and that whatever had been at any time received by either of you from his Excellency as pledges of his benevolence was extorted from him by violence and conrary to his inclination. This information I received in confidence from Mr. Brooke, by whose permission and desire I repeat it to you, that you may be upon your guard against the effects of such an attack, if it be true that such an one is made upon you. He had it from a friend, who told it to him with authority, having himself received it from some of Sir J. L.'s family who had read the remonstrance. I am told I am also begrimed in the same black list, I am sure without cause.
Stone has already told you that you could not expect any recommendation of young Griffiths in our general letters. It is peremptorily forbid. But I hope you will have interest to obtain his appointment. He is a good, well tempered, decent boy. He has been lately admitted into Stone's office, and is as good a hand as Stone has, willing and improvable. He will do credit to the service, and I heartily wish you may be able to place him in it. He lives with me, is stout and healthy, and advances fast towards six feet.
We are still in peace abroad, but in open war at home. General Coote is returning to England in disgust, because we will not acknowledge his supremacy. Sir J. L. stays, because (as I suppose) his Excellency acknowledges his supremacy. Appeals will be made by both to their respective constituents, and all the powers of the Company and of the Crown called upon to punish us for disobedience, contumacy and rebellion. The history of these contests is too long for a letter. I never was

concerned in any business in which I was so perfectly satisfied of the propriety of my own conduct as in both these instances, yet I doubt the issue of them at home.
The Ministry will certainly support Sir J. Lindsay, and if Coote's friends are in the Direction, they will justify him. Yet I think it impossible to furnish reasons for either. I am very uneasy at the dismal prospects which these contests afford me, and more for other more alarming symptoms which I dare not mention. I have been able to write only to Mr. Sulivan, and, to him I have been very explicit.
I hope I am not unreasonable in desiring your advice and information where you think either may prove of utility to me, as in a thousand instances it would be. I write this in the Council Chamber, and have not time to add more, though I have much that I wish to say to you. I am, with a real regard and esteem, dear Sir, your most obedient servant,

Warren Hastings

John Maxwell Stone to Robert Palk, Esqr. 1770, October 12th. Fort St. George.

Dear Sir,
To increase our perplexity and embarrassments we have lately been engaged in very disagreeable altercations with Sir John Lindsay and Gen- eral Coote. On Sir John Lindsay's arrival the letters and presents from their Majesty s were, agreeable to the Company's orders, delivered to him to be presented to the Nabob. He soon after took an opportunity of acquainting the Governor with the plenipotentiary powers with which he was invested by the King to treat with the Princes of India. His first application to the Board was for them to attend him in the delivery of the letters and presents to the Nabob. This the Board declined, since their acquiescence would have degraded this Government into a mere attendant, and which would not fail lessening its authority in the eyes of the country Powers. Sir John Lindsay then required to be put in possession of our original proceedings, or authenticated copies of them, with respect to the Nabob, the Soubah and other Powers of India since

the conclusion of the Treaty of Paris, to enable him to make a faithfull report to His Majesty of the rise and progress of the war with the Soubah and Hyder Ally. In answer to which he was told that the whole of our pro- ceedings were transmitted to the Company, to whom application might be made in a regular and proper manner; that we had no authority to ex- pose the records of the Company to the inspection of any individual, and which our oaths and covenants to the Company prevented us from doing. He at last, in the course of his correspondence, required the coun- sel and advice of the Board to enable him to treat with the Powers of India ; and offered the sanction of His Majesty's name to give weight to our negotiations. To which it was replied that we had all reason to be- lieve the Company were entirely unacquainted with the powers with which he was invested ; that we understood from the publick papers and pamphlets that the Ministry did apply to the Court of Directors to give the Commander of His Majesty's ships in India a seat and voice in their councils abroad ; that this proposal was laid before a Court of Propri- etors and formally rejected. That we could not therefore agree to what our constituents had refused. This, my dear Sir, is a brief recital of what hath passed with respect to Sir John Lindsay. I shall only add that we begin to feel very sensibly the ill effects of these very extraordinary and unprecedented powers ; and if the Company do not take some measures very speedyly, they may bid farewell to all influence and consequence in India.

I come to General Coote, who arrived here very full of the powers granted him by his commission of Commander-in-Chief, which I must acquaint you is exactly the same as that granted to General Lawrence. He has indeed, by the Company's orders, a power of calling for returns from the several Presidencies, and is authorized to form a general plan of discipline for the whole. The first difficulty which occurred was the manner in which he should be given out in orders. The Board would not consent to his being given out simply as Commander-in-Chief, since the Governor's commission as Commander-in-Chief must thereby be abrogated. It was therefore proposed that the Company's orders of February, 1766, (wherein the powers of the Governor are fully, clearly and positively laid down) should be given out at the same time. To this General Coote objected. It was then proposed that circular letters should be wrote by the Board to the several commanding officers, directing them to make returns to General Coote in the same manner as to the Gover- nor, and for them and all others to obey him as their superior officer. This General Coote approved, and letters were wrote accordingly. Shortly afterwards he put forward a plan for the seniority and promotion of officers and their distribution to commands, which, as it ignored the control and approbation of Government, was rejected. The question as to the superiority of his or the Governor's commission as decided in favour of the latter.

General Coote then withdrew, and declared his resolution of remaining here in a private station untill he could receive the sentiments of the other Presidencies respecting his commission. We have sent a particular account of the above correspondence to Bengali, to which place General Coote purposed proceeding ; but he has since altered his resolution, and embarks toorrow on the Hawke sloop of war, which Sir John Lindsay has lent him, in order to go to Bussorah, and from there over-land to England. His sudden arrival will no doubt have a strange effect in Leaden Hall Street. A short letter is, however, now wrote to the Company to go by the same way, advising them thereof, and desiring them to suspend their judgment till the arrival of the *Lapwing*.

I have thus, my dear Sir, given you as particular an account of our situation as time will admit ; and I believe you will readily allow that, what with Morattas, Hyder, Sir John Lindsay and General Coote, we have had trouble and vexation enough.

J. M. Stone

Robert Palk to William Martin Goodlad 1770, December 7th. Received 11th July, 1771, per *Horsenden*.

My dear Billy,

I have both your letters of the 6th February and 8th April. I have been long a stranger to the politics in Leadenhall Street, but I could never have conceived the giving up of the Circars to be a part of them, and hope they are wiser than to entertain such a notion, since most of the force may be drawn from them upon occasion, and still Masulipatam, Ganjam, &c., be preserved. I am disquieted beyond measure about the safety of the *Aurora*, and begin almost to despair of it.

You do well, my friend, to interest yourself so deeply in the Company's prosperity, and I doubt not in due time your thorough knowledge of their affairs will be amply rewarded.

The Nabob's creditors' agents have hitherto made little stir in their commission, most of them as individuals being inclined to do as you and others have done in India, and expect justice from the Company, who in the end will certainly give their assistance.

You reason very justly on the subject of Colonel Wood's dismission, and I wonder the Governor and Council did not, to silence all clamor, make known their reasons for disagreeing with the Court martial and dismissing the Colonel. I have long entertained the same opinion with you of Call : from the moment the conquest of Misore was projected I foresaw the impracticability of the wild plan and dreaded the event, and was heartily sorry our friend B. had so readily submitted his own judgment to such an extravagant idea. That sore is now in some measure healed, and if you could avoid taking part with Hyder or the Marattas, I think we shall soon arrive at our former prospect of prosperity.

Mr. Bourchier was very well received by the Court of Directors, and having no party to support or enemies to contend with, I think he will very happily enjoy the fruit of his labors among those he loves. His father, after living to see his sons so happily returned, expired in their arms last week.

We are preparing with all our might for war with Spain, whose Ambassador, however, having full powers to settle the dispute, we have some reason to expect an accommodation, more especially as the French are not prepared for war, their finances being undoubtedly in a much worse state than ours, and their country laboring under a prodigious scarcity of grain and a bad vintage.

Little Dick is all ready for imbarking. No contest this year for Directors. Opposition has been crushed with a vengeance, and they make Sulivan the amende honorable by readmitting him to their society in April: indeed it seems necessary that there should be somebody there a little acquainted with India matters.

I am always, my dear Billy, your sincere, affectionate and obliged friend,

RoBT. Palk.
P.S.Thank ye for the bill of £100 12th December. — Alas, my friend, it is but too true that you had no accounts of the *Aurora* the 14th June. Our only small hopes now are on Batavia, or that after attempting the Coast she is gone to the Maldivias or Bengal. Two days since I was surprised with an intended appointment of a Mr. Stewart to be Secretary at Madras. I acquainted Mrs. Goodlad, and we are trying to prevail on our friends that you may at least have it in your option to remain your own time. They say they mean no ill to you, but the contrary, but that this same gentleman, whom I know not, must be provided for.

Robert Palk to Mrs. Goodlad. 1771, January 4th. Haldon House.

Dear Madam,
Finding Mr. Bourchier's letter in my possession, 'tis proper to return itto you, as you may think necessary to send it to Billy.
I have talked to several of the Directors on this subject, and most of them know nothing of the matter, and all seem well inclined to be well pleased and satisfyed with the present Secretary ; but as Mr. Bourchier thinks Billy wants to be relieved from the post, we must rest satisfyed that they will recommend at least his being taken care of. Mr. Bourchier, however, I think must be mistaken that the Governor and Council have requested a perpetual Secretary, for I think Mr. Du Pre and every Governor would chuse to keep the appointment of so material an assistant to himself. However this be, I have no doubt of Billy's deserving the attention of the Directors, and if wrong is done him in this instance they must make amends.
I am come here from Berkshire for a few days all alone. I wish you and all yours most heartily many, many happy new years ; and by the help of pressing, and bad weather, may yet return soon enough to see Mr. Richard before he imbarks. If I should not, pray give him my sincerest wishes.
I am always, dear Madam, your faithful and obliged humble servant,

RoBT. Palk.

XXXII
Ensign John Palk and others are grateful, 1771

John Palk takes 3 weeks to reach Madeira from Portsmouth and finds the merchants there to be most agreeable. He sets off for the Cape of Good Hope though conditions there are far from agreeable.

Ensign John Palk to Robert Palk, Esqr. 1771, February 2nd. Camp near Samulcotah.

Sir,
After the great kindnesses and civilitys I received from you while in London it would be ingrateful in me should I omit any opportunity of letting you hear from me. We sailed from Spithead the 11th of January with a fair wind that carried us clear of the Channel and to the Island Madeira in three weeks. We stopped there 10 days, during which time I found the place very agreable, the English merchants residing there being very hospitable people.
After having sailed from Madeira we had a pleasant passage untill doubling the Cape of Good Hope, where we meet with severe weather and were harassed about for some weeks, in which time we had the misfor- tune to loose several topmasts and to have our rigging damaged much, that it was no small satisfaction to all on board to double that dangerous promontory. We had a very pleasant passage the remaining part of the time we stayed on board ship, and arrived at Johanna the 25th of May. On our landing we found the island very pleasant and agreable. Having stopped there five days, we sailed for Madrass and landed safe on the 30th of June to the great joy of all the passengers. I was much surprised to find the Supervisors had not been seen on the Coast nor heard of, and am sorry to tell you that they are now given over for lost. On my landing I meet with my cousin, who behaved very kind and genteel to me. The letter you was so kind as to give me to Mr. Dupre,

after several applications got me changed from General Coote's regiment at Poonamallee that was formed of this year's recruits, where I was first appointed, into Captain Madge's battallion of seapoys at Samulcotah. I am very much pleased with the situation, and likewise with my command- ing officer, who, I find, is worthy of the great character I have heard given him in England.
I have not seen my brother yet, but expect to see him in a few days, as he is coming down from Condapillee in order to join these six companies that are encamped near Samulcotah, waiting for orders to march against the Totapillee Rajah, who refuses to comply with the Company's demands in paying his tribute. It is thought we shall have a despirate service of it, as we shall be obliged to pursue them over the mountains, which are very unhealthy, and where Europeans never were before. General Coote behaved very kind to me, and I believe would have done anything to serve me ; but his power here was very little on account of the Governor and Council, who took every step in their power to thwart his designs. A story prevails here that he is coming out again. I could wish it were true. At present everything is quiet at the southward. There was a Morattoe war expected this season in the Carnatic, but I beheve at this time it is all hushed up. I am, Sir, with the greatest respect, your much obliged and most humble servant,

J. Palk.

Chocapah to the Honourable Robert Palk, Esqr. 1771, February 5th. Fort St. George.

The Merchants have delivered a great part of the goods for the Company's Investment. In Bengal there has been good rain and grain is fairly cheap, though trade is bad. The news from Manila is that our people have sold the "blue goods" but could not dispose of the "paintings and chey goods" at Pondicherry affairs are stationary through want of money.

Madavarave with his large force came as far as the river Kistna. His intention was to destroy Hyder first, then to trouble us for money if we don't give him assistance ; but in the meantime he had some family disputes, which obliged him to return back to his country. Hyder is at Mysore, and unable to beat off the Marattys that are in his country. I can do nothing with Jangama Chitty. He is very poor, and remains in prison for money due to Mr. Lewen Smith

Chocapah.

Robert Palk to William Martin Goodlad. 1771, April 2nd. London.

My dear Billy,
I have received your letter of the 12th and 13th October, I suppose we shall hear more of the contents of them when Coote arrives: hitherto he has not been heard of. The Court of Directors judged they had given him the same powers with General Lawrence ; but as there is hardly amongst the Directors any who consider these matters attentively or endeavor to make themselves masters of the Company's affairs, such jarring orders and resolutions must always be the consequence. I was amazed when I heard they had appointed Coote to sit as one of the Commissioners. I took an opportunity to remonstrate against the measure, and I thought they had altered it.They are now, I hear, sending up a remonstrance to the King against his intermeddling, and I suppose the commanding officer will be told not to interfere, because the natural consequence must be the destruction of the Company's authority. They talk, I hear, of sending out more Commissioners, but I know not where they are to look for them.
I told you of the intention to send out a Mr. Stewart as secretary. This I was able to prevent, and I said much in your favour. Hastings has been proposed for Bengal, and I supported him, but Mr. Rumbold's interest appears to prevail.
The loss of the *Aurora*, for I now give her entirely up, is a most severe stroke indeed to all this family. Henry VanSittart goes a Writer to Bengal in the Colebrooke. I hope you correspond fully with Mr. Purling, who, I find, is to be the next Chairman. For once there is to be no contest at the

next election. Sulivan comes in singly with the consent of all parties. I should have thought, after all that is passed and in such times as these, he had better have relinquished so troublesome and, to him, so very unprofitable an employ. However, it is to him the summum bonum .

RoBT. Palk

Colonel Gilbert Ironside to Robert Palk, Esqr. 1771, April 7th. Fort William.

Sir,
I cannot let the earliest occasion escape of rendering my sincerest acknowledgements for your polite and friendly offers to Mrs. Ironside, whose happiness, of everything on this side heaven, lies nearest my heart. My request to Mr. Vansittart to furnish her with money was made at a time when I had no opportunity to make the remittances I wished. I have since found means to get home a few thousand pounds ; but still, should any unexpected and pressing necessity require a sudden supply, your favouring her with it will confer an essential obligation on me. That we shall ever see the Supervisors I now totally despond ; but that some tidings of their unhappy fate may still reach us is not, I think, altogether improbable. It has been long believed and currently reported that an outward bound French Indiaman descried the wreck of a vessel off Madagascar, which conjecture led to surmise might be of the Aurora : and on that presumption that some frigates were ordered from Bombay to cruise round that island for further discoverys.
About the 14th of February arrived the *Dolphin*, a King's frigate, at Madras. Captain Dent brought with him, we hear, two red ribbands for General Coote and Sir John Lindsay, with powers and instructions to the Nawab of Arcot to invest them with the Order of the Bath. Also credentials to the Commodore to act as his Majesty's Plenipotentiary to all the European Powers in India. General Coote returned home the latter end of last year by way of Bussorah.
George, who is a sad idle fellow in everything but downright plodding business, asks me to obtain for you the second volume of the Code of

Muhammadan Law. It may be among some oriental manuscripts with Mrs. Ironside, who will submit em to you. Meanwhile I will try to procure the volume in India.
Both George and Palk are at Patna I believe. My latest letters from thence pronounce them all well, and the ladies, as all ladies should be, in a promising way. Permit me to request you will make my best wishes acceptable to Mrs. Palk and my old commander General Caillaud, whom I very affectionately remember .

Gilbert Ironside

Robert Palk to his Excellency the Nawab Walajah. 1771, April 17th.

I have received your letter of the 12th October. I grieve for the loss of Mr. Vansittart on your account as well as my own, for he contemplated the promotion of your interest together with that of the Company. I have often repented not staying longer in India. On many accounts it was necessary, but you know that, seeing my services were not so well received here as I thought they deserved, I determined to make room for Mr. Bourchier, whom I wished to be more fortunate ; but surely no man could take more pains than myself, or was ever better inclined to labor day and night to do my duty both to the Company and yourself. I watched over their expences and yours with the most scrupulous and unceasing attention, and how far I succeeded must be left to the Company and yourself to judge.
A squadron of good ships is now sent to India, commanded by Sir Robert Harland, a gentleman of great experience, and who, I hope, will be able to co-operate in the most effectual preservation of the peace in India. A regiment is also appointed here to raise the best soldiers to be sent out as recruits : all which will shew that neither his Majesty nor the Company are neglectful of proper measures. I only wish that harmony as well as great abilities may be established in the right use of them.
By the eldest son of Mr. Vansittart, who is obliged to seek his fortunes abroad, I send this letter, and also a new Persian grammar for your acceptance. A new dictionary by the same author is soon to be published,

> and shall also be sent to you. General Lawrence and Mrs. Palk add their good wishes to mine for the continuance of your health and the prosperity of the whole family.

Thomas Madge provides a vivid account of the diseases waiting to strike the incomers. Here it is Robert Palk's two cousins who are afflicted and die in a most horrible way.

Captain Thomas Madge to Robert Palk, Esqr. [Endorsed in Palk's hand]. Account of the Death of Thomas and John Palk. 1771, June 15th. Ellore.

> Dear Sir,
>
> My last letter concluded with some accounts of your two cousins, which did honor to their family as well as themselves. It was, however, the last opportunity allowed me to speak of them with satisfaction unalloyed with regret, for very shortly after the despatch of the letter dated from the unwholesome hills which terminate our possessions in the Circars, a pestilential disorder broke out amongst the detachment under my command, which in less than the space of three weeks destroyed two thirds of the Europeans that composed it, and has rendered the condition of those that have survived it little deserving the estimation of existence from the havoc it has made in our constitutions, many of which are irrecoverably ruined !
>
> The end of the expedition into those fatal hills having been accomplished by the successfull effort to surprise the Pollygar by Lieut. Palk, we retired from them the fourth day after his again joining the main body of the detachment, congratulating ourselves on having escaped the disorder so generally experienced in those hills by all strangers who reside any time amongst them. But we had not made one day's march into the open country till it began to shew it had got footing amongst us. Your two cousins and myself were the first officers it affected, and as they appeared to be more so than me, I sent them down to Rajamundry recommended to Mr. Wynch, who at that time resided there on account of settling the revenues of the Circars, and had a surgeon to attend him.
>
> The business of the service would not admit of my availing myself of the assistance of a surgeon, and obliged me to remain so long in the field that

when I got to Rajamundry my condition was pronounced too dangerous by the doctor to admit of my proceeding any further. Your two cousins had almost recovered their health under his management, and were at last thought so far out of danger as to run no risk from proceeding to Ellore, whither they were in consequence sent with some other officers and soldiers under charge of a surgeon. They arrived at Ellore the 18th of March last in a very promising way for recovery ; but the day after their arrival the disorder took an unfavorable turn, and in spite of every possible assistance carried off the eldest almost suddenly: the youngest survived his brother but four days only. The disorder had gained so much ground on me from neglecting it that it was thought impossible for me to survive it many days after my coming to this place, during which time the fate of my two young friends was kept a secret from me. They had, however, all the attendance possible from the surgeons, who never left them for a moment whilst they could be of service to them, but the disorder soon rose superior to medicine and baffled all their skill. After three relapses I have at last some hopes that I have entirely got the better of the disorder, but have suffered so much from its malignant effects in my constitution that I fear I shall never again recover my former state of health. Out of twenty Europeans two only escaped the disorder, and eight only that were infected by it survived it! The concern this unfortunate event must give their mother and every individual of their family may be partly conceived from the universal regret it has occasioned amongst your cousins' slightest acquaintance in India. The gentle manners of the eldest had so much endeared him to me that I cannot refrain from tears whenever I reflect on his untimely fate. I shall endeavor to pay the most essential tribute to their memory and your friendship in my power on the occasion by taking care of their estate, which when collected together will, I hope, amount to nearly 2,000 pags., a sum few subalterns can boast of having honestly acquired in so short a time as the eldest was in the service, and I think does as much honor to his prudence as it will afford satisfaction to his friends.

I have desired our nephew at Madrass to administer to their estate, as there is no will; to whom I shall remit the amount of it as I receive it. And I hope you will have no objection to the money's being paid to your attornies in India, nor to your remitting it to their mother in Cornwall as soon as they advise you of its having been received by them in India. I see no prospect of early promotion, owing partly to supersessions from England and partly to our being saddled with the newly created corps of engineers, who will probably claim a share of off reckonings. My best respects to Mrs. Palk and General Lawrence.

T. Madge

Henry Vansittart, jun., to Robert Palk, Esq. 1771, October 3rd, Cape of Good Hope.

Dear Sir,

After our departure from Madeira the 5th of June we have chiefly met with either contrary winds or calms after the latitude of 8 South. We saw the Canary and Cape de Verd Islands, and crossed the Line the middle of July. About a month afterwards we saw the coast of Brazil at Rio des Ilhos, a little below the Bay de Todos Santos. We spoke with the Britannia the 1st of September, who left England the 23rd of June. We arrived in False Bay the 22nd of September, which is about 20 miles distant overland from the Cape Town. The old Governor died a few weeks ago, and a deputy is appointed till advices are received from Holland. The Lord Holland sailed from hence the 12th, and the Hampshire the 24th. The Britannia goes tomorrow, and the Colebrooke the next day if possible. A French ship bound to Mauritias came in the 25th and sailed yesterday. Sir Robert Fletcher and Captain Parker proceed from hence in the Britannia to Anjango, and from thence overland to Madrass for the sake of expedition. I lodge with Captain Morris at Mr. La Febre's, but proceed tomorrow to False Bay. I have been used very civilly by the captain and the rest of the passengers. Mr. Johnson presents his compliments to you. Pray give my love to Mrs. Palk, and remember me to Nancy and Lawrence. I am your dutiful nephew,

Henry Vansittart.

XXXIII
Goodlad and the Tan j ore affair, 1771

William Martin Goodlad to Robert Palk, Esqr. 1771, October 4th, Fort St. George.

I have not heard from you for some time, and am impatient for a reply to my letter of the 13th October, 1770 by the *Lapwing,* as I think the fate of the Company will depend on the turn of affairs at home after the receipt of the advices by that ship. By the Duke of Portland, which sailed in July last, I gave you a history of the Tan j ore affair.
We were then prepared to call the Rajah to account, and waited only for the concurrence of the Nabob to set an expedition on foot. From his behavior at that time I confess that I little expected he would have been

The Doddington sinks with Clive's gold

brought to act at all, for, baulked in his darling plan of an immediate attack in hopes of introducing the Marattas and thereby obliging us to join them against Hyder, he seemed resolved to pass over the Rajah's conduct rather than call him to account at a time which, however it might promise success, clashed with his favourite project. But matters had gone too far for him to recede, and it was evident to himself as well as his champion that they could not justify inaction. After many objections on his part and repeated urging on ours he at length resolved to commence a negotiation, and we promised to support his demands by a force sufficient to reduce the capital, even should those demands be refused, He would not stir one step till we totally relinquished every idea of becoming mediators in consequence of the guarantee of 1762, and he refused to act unless the negotiation were left wholely and solely to himself. Upon this footing, therefore, was the expedition undertaken. The eldest son proceeded with full powers to negotiate or proceed to hostilities as occasion might require: the second son set forward charged with supplying the army with provisions ; and the English army, the finest I believe that the Company ever had in the field, proceeded as mere auxiliaries, to act hostile or otherwise as the eldest should think eligible. How I feel when I reflect on the situation we are reduced to! The last convoy and the last detachment reached the banks of the Coleroon about the 24th August, but a most untimely swelling of the river prevented their crossing for many days, and it was not till the 12th September that the whole force proceeded from Trichinopoly. Demands on the Rajah had been made and refused previous to their marching from thence.

Hostilities were consequently commenced, and the army proceeded with very little interruption to Vellam (about 6 miles N.W. from Tanjore), where they arrived on the 16th. The place refused to surrender, and it cost four or five days to reduce it, but the acquisition was great indeed, for (Vellour excepted) there is not so strong a fort in the Carnatic. Our army reached Tan j our the 23rd in the morning, and it is expected that batteries must have been opened about the 3rd instant. In that case our accounts give us reason to think it cannot hold out above a fortnight more. Should Tan j ore fall, and fall I think it must, how glorious a stroke for the Company, how fatal a blow to the French! Could there be so dangerous an enemy as one in the heart of the Carnatic ? Could there be so noble an ally for the French ?

Notwithstanding his late defeat, Hyder still keeps the Marathas at bay, so we have little to fear from the latter at present. The Circars are peaceful and the Nizam quiet. We are providing great part of the Investment from the Circars. Sir John Lindsay's recall has, I hope, put an end to disputes with the Ambassador. Sir Robert Harland possesses the same powers, but desires harmony.

I know not what to say to you on the subject of affairs in Bengal. The King resolved many months ago to throw himself into the hands of the Marattas upon their offer to seat him on the throne of Delli. He set forward accordingly, but the rains and the uncertainty of the real intentions of the Marattas detained him on the frontiers of the Corah Province till very lately. He is now again set forward, the Marattas having delivered over the city and fort of Delli to his officers. You will allow that it is hard to judge what may be the event, but troubles I think must ensue should the Marattas assume his name, and make that a cloak for their depredations.

10th October. Since writing the former part of this letter we have news from Tanjore. The enemy made a most vigorous sally on the 1st instant upon the covering party, but were repulsed with great loss after continuing the attack from past 10 in the morning till 3 in the afternoon. Our battery opened on the 2nd, and by the 3rd at night the fire from the fort was reduced. Everything promises fair but they will never lose the fort but by storm, and the issue of such an event is always uncertain. I do not feel satisfied with my own position, though I would not change it for any other outside the Council. Still, I have had over nine years' service, and see little prospect of reaching Council in nine more. " Must I be contented to drudge on in the plain line of preferment ?" I know your answer will be, " Patience and perseverance, Billy"; but can you tell me no method that will push me forward? I have opened a correspondence with Purling : he is certainly my friend. Shall I write to Sulivan? In good truth this fagging and fagging and still fagging on with a prospect almost as distant as the steeple of St. Paul's is not the thing. 14th October. Our latest news of Tan j ore is favourable.

W. M. Goodlad.

Captain James Rennell to Robert Palk, Esqr. 1771, November 12th, Bengali.

> I fear my several letters to you have miscarried, as I have not re- ceived any reply. I asked your interest towards getting me placed on the Invalid List so that I might enjoy a pension.
> I might have saved you the trouble, for by the regulations established I find myself too rich a man to partake of the provision. I have an epithet at my tongue's end which I could with propriety have prefixed to it, but which I suppress out of respect to you. If the makers of those regulations think that a man can subsist genteely on the sum allotted, my only wish is that their fortunes may be stinted to it.
> With respect to my health, I find myself very well during the cold season, but the heats and damps of the other season are too powerful for the present relaxed state of my nerves. I could therefore wish myself at home; but previous to a step of that kind 'tis necessary that I should be provided with means to subsist comfortably. Had the Fund been settled agreeable to the scheme originally proposed, that is, £200, or £180 a year to a Captain, I might at the end of this year have left India and have had sufficient for a decent maintenance at home ; but now I am left to shift for myself.
> I have entirely done my business in the field, and all that remains to be done to compleat the General Survey of Bengali, Bahar, our part of Orixa, and the Provinces of Allahabad and Awd will be compleated within these four months. The sea coast and rivers also have had a regular survey, and a surveyor in a sloop has been all round the Bay of Bengali and described the sea coasts and islands. It will now be my business to compile all these surveys, and for that purpose I am now setting down seriously for at least 13 months. The general and particular surveys are to be drawn in about 45 or 50 large folio maps, and will be a very com- pleat work when finished. Each province is to be drawn in a separate map, and most of these provinces are as big as the County of Norfolk, and some as big as Yorkshire.

I have inclosed this to Mr. Barrington, a very particular friend of mine and a neighbour of yours.

J. Rennell.

Robert Palk to William Martin Goodlad. 1772, February 2nd, Park Place.

Dear Goodlad,
I thank you for your letter of the 21st July which, considering the busy life you lead, is much longer than I had a right to expect. It reached me at my house in Devonshire early in a morning, and I found afterwards that it was dropped by Colonel Campbell, who passed within a mile of me, but was in too great a hurry to call upon me.
I rejoice that the Nabob's creditors are made easy, and hope they are now in a fair way of being paid off. As to the measures of the Directors, they are passed finding out, and every day they are more and more convincing the world that the direction of the Company's affairs by a set of men who have views of their own cannot be managed to advantage. They throw the blame on their servants abroad, and accordingly the King in his speech has strongly recommended regulations to be made; and the situation of affairs at Bengal is soon to be laid before them.
No complaints are made of the management of affairs on the Coast, but the Directors have sent Lord Clive and most of the Bengal Counsellors a long list of informations against them, which have been collected abroad by a Mr. Petre and supported by the Johnstones, proving or attempting to prove many frauds in the salt duties and revenues to the amount of 5 or 600,000*l*. Having never seen these charges, I cannot be more particular, but Lord Clive and the gentlemen themselves make very light of them, and say the Directors will be found much more to blame than their servants. It happens, however, at an unlucky time, mankind in general being willing to suspect that so many great fortunes cannot be fairly acquired. Government, I believe, are far from wishing to take the management out of the Company's hands, but they wish to see their affairs in a better train.
It is now very certain that Choiseu had made preparations for beginning a

war in India, to which is owing the great force collected at the Islands, which Lord North gives us to understand is to be recalled ; but till that happens we are to have a superiority at least in men-of-war, and it is for this reason that two ships of force are soon to sail to join Sir Robert Harland, which, however, are to return when the marine force at the Islands returns.

The approval of the sentence of Wood's court martial was certainly a severe stroke to Government, and till your letter told me so I never conceived any sett of men could have been so wanton in their resentments. I seldom see any of them, and when I do they are too knowing themselves to want any advice, and too secret to be communicative. Nothing, I understand, is yet determined about a successor to Mr. Du Pre, and it is a misfortune to the service that nobody near him in Council is thought proper for the station. Macguire, it seems, applyed, and was very properly refused. Mr. Sulivan wanted to be a Supervisor, and on that account, I hear, they resolve at present to send none for want of being able to find fit men. It is not alledged that the Coast wants supervision.

I am afraid the calling Tan j our to account, which is become so absolutely necessary, will be attended with risk and difficulty. I hope Sir Robert Harland will be a better adviser.

Having long been acquainted with the good heart of Captain Baker, let me bespeak your kindness to him, and likewise to the two Kennaways during their short stay with you. I am satisfyed that you have balanced the account, though I was much more in debt than I expected. May every blessing attend you! I am, my dear friend, most affectionately yours,

Robt. Palk

XXXIV
Trade all over India is bad, 1772

Chocapah Chetti complains about the exchange rate of the Pagoda to the dollar; there has been a huge explosion in the settlement magazine and Thomas Palk is worried not to have heard from his uncle for over a year.

Chocapah to the Honble. Robert Palk, Esqr. 1772, February 28th, Fort St. George

Honourable Sir,
Since I had the honour to write to you under date of the 18th July last the Company's order and appointment of Mr. Hastings [as] Governor of Bengal arrived here, and that gentleman embarked on a brigantine and sailed to that place the 2nd of this month. The ship Carnatic from Manila made an unsatisfactory voyage, selling only part of her cargo, and that at the rate of a dollar per pagoda, "which grieves the merchants' hearts very much." Trade all over India is bad. The Governour and Council appointed Mr. Monkton to go to Quedda with a few soldiers and seapoys and all the necessary servants to settle a trade there for the Company, and also Mr. Desveaux in same manner to Acheen. Mr. Ardley departed this life the 9th of this month, and Mr. Charles Smiths is admitted one of the members in Council.
Our forces was very near of taking Tan j ore, but in the mean time the King made up matters with the Nabob, paying all the expences of the expedition, and the tribute money due from him, and also the plunder and present that he had received from the Maravah of Ramanadapurum. Since my last the French received no ships, money nor anything else from Europe, and they are as poor as rats at present, and if it was not owing to the capacity of Mr. Law, the Settlement of Pondichery would have fallen long before this. The Morattas tryed all they could to see if

our Governour will give them assistance to beat Hyder, but our Governour by his great wisdom made the Nabob settle with the Morattas without sending them any force against Hyder.
A great accident happened at Trichinopoly on the 14th instant. The expence magazine, a large stone choultry, with about 130 barrels of powder and a very large quantity of musket and fixed ammunition, was blown up. Stones of several ton weight were thrown to a considerable distance. By that accident about 200 Europeans and about two thousand black people perished, and several of the houses, stores, etc., damaged, which is a very great loss, and such accident was never heard of in these parts. His Majesty's squadron was at Trincanamally all the winter, and they are now at Madras, which is a great awe to all the country Powers abroad.

Chocapah.

Thomas Palk to Robert Palk, Esqr. 1772, February 28th, Fort St. George.

I received no letter from you during the whole of last year, and feel anxious as to the cause of your silence. By the Colebrooke, whose packet has just reached us, I heard from my father only. Mr. Hastings left in January to succeed Mr. Cartier in Bengal. He promised me, at the request of Mr. Morse, a transfer to Masulipatam under Mr. Brooke, who is to succeed Mr. Wynch as Chief. Of your many friends here none except Mr. Morse has taken the least notice of me. Mr. Morse, however, has been more like a parent than a friend. He has been seriously ill with gout, but is now better. Henry Vansittart, who went on to Bengal in the Britannia is coming here on a visit to Mr. Morse. Mr. Call was expected to succeed Mr. Du Pre as Governor, but now it is said Mr. Cartier will do so.
By letters from my brother, I am sorry to find that the Leaden Hall Street Gentlemen have not forgot the Cozimbazar affair. It is a most cruel thing to refresh his memory with what has already given him so much trouble. He is, he says, called down from Patna, which I should imagine might have been prevented, as Mr. Sulivan is in the Direction, and he consequently must have some friends. He has requested of the

Gentlemen at Bengal to allow him 6 months' longer stay to settle his affairs. He seems to be very happy in his present matrimonial situation. His spouse brought him a son and heir 30th September last.

The country is now very quiet again. The Morattoes have been threatening an invasion in the Carnatic, but are obliged to return to their own country to restore peace to their own dominions ; so that Hyder laughs at them, and is in possession of his country again. The Tan j ore expedition I am almost ashamed to mention ; but let it suffice that after having lost a great many men, and a practicable breach made, our army retreated back to Trichinapoly, notwithstanding I saw under Mr. Dupre's own hand that he was resolved to reduce that Rajah; though it is not surprising, nor unlike every thing else that is done.

The following is an extract from a letter I received from Trichinopoly, dated 16th January, 1772, [from] a gentleman in the family of General Smith :

'I should have set down and given you some account of the calamity that happened here the 14th, but till now I have been employed attending the people at work, at first in endeavouring to save those who had any remains of life, and afterwards getting the dead bodies removed. On the 14th, about 4 in the afternoon, we were surprised with an explosion in the fort, which was so violent that, though we were upwards of a mile distant, the doors and windows of the house, though bolted, were forced open with the shock. On going into the Fort we found the expence magazine, a large stone choultry, with the artillery, part of the infantry barracks and all the buildings adjoining, particularly upwards of 60 feet of a brick wall 4 feet thick and 40 in height, were blown up and laid level with the ground. You know the wall I mean: it is where the gentlemen sometimes play at fives (the Nabob's garden wall), and under which in the day there is a constant thoroughfare of people. About 40 Europeans were killed in the spot and a great number of natives, and had it happened at any other time of the day, God knows what would have been the consequences. The powder that took fire consisted of about 130 barrels, with a very large quantity of musket and fixed ammunition. Stones of several tons weight were thrown at a great distance, many of them into the houses, and after making their way through all, buried themselves in the earth. Ensign McNeal was killed by one on the opposite side of the Rock, though it is of an enormous height. The cavalry that were picketed on the glacis were obliged to fly : part of a six pound fell on the terrace of Warriore Hospital ; in short the poor inhabitants were under, for some time, a most tremendous shower of stones, shells and shot, and the shock so great that they were scarce able to stand. Many thousands fled to the fields, and a more melancholy scene [than] that they left behind cannot possibly be imagined. The unhappy sufferers buried in the ruins, the heads of some appearing above the rubbish, the arms and legs of others, and many torn to pieces. The Tinhappy mothers, who on the first alarm flew to save their children, lying dead with their infants clasped in their arms. Spare me from going farther with this scene ; it is too shocking to bear a recital. The General's house in the Fort is a perfect wreck. Mr. Hay's and many others suffered much, and himself covered with rubbish. Major Braithwate, passing the main guard, was thrown out of his palankeen: his peon, to save him, threw himself on his master, who had just then received a bruise on the side of his head by a six pound shot in its fall. His house is beat in, one of his servants killed and both his horses, which must also have been his own fate had it happened three minutes later and he had time to get home. To mention the particulars of this affecting scene would be endless.

It is not known how the accident happened. There were 13 artillery men and some lascars drying ammunition, who were all killed. It is, however, supposed that one shott falling on another communicated fire to the powder in the linnen bags, and by that means occasioned all that happened'

The above is a very perfect account [of the] melancholy event.

Tho. Palk

P.S. Please do me the favour of having two or three rings made for me in memory of my poor cousin Tom Palk. A newspaper or magazine of recent date will be acceptable.

William Martin Goodlad to Robert Palk, Esqr. 1772, February 28th,- Fort St. George. Received 20th September.

My dearest Friend

To the best of my recollection you have had a clear account of matters to the sailing of the *Stag* in October last. We were then in the height of expectation in respect to Tan j ore. Peace ensued without our accomplishing the reduction of the capital. Various were the conjectures on this occasion, and the motives for such a step are not to this hour ascertained. Six hours more would have rendered the breach practicable, and in all human probability a storm would have ensured us the capture. But curbed by the Nabob ; acting as auxiliaries without a will of our own, and having our operations wholely subservient to Indostan politics, the object of the campaign was in great measure frustrated. Vellum, it is true, was taken and remains in our hands ; a sum of money was paid, and some countries were relinquished by the Rajah ; but our prospects promised more substantial benefits, and we lost the opportunity of compleatly humbling a dangerous rival situated in the very heart of the countries from whence we draw our support. The Nabob, unwilling to discover the real cause of the accommodation, would willingly attribute it to the General, but all unprejudiced minds seem to hold him blameless. For my own part I am willing to believe him so ; and if I could venture to start an opinion of my own, I would declare the loss of Tan j ore to be solely owing to the Nabob's apprehensions of the Marattas. Did I say solely ? I meant it not. A jealousy of the Company, never to be eradicated, had its share in his determination. In short, Tan j ore was within his grasp, but his apprehensions would not suffer him to seize it ; and thus ended our expedition. It has nevertheless certainly been attended with good effects, for the Rajah is evidently humbled, and the possession of Vellum must be a great check upon him ; but there is this to be said, that the Rajah will never regard an accommodation (to which we are not Guarantees) as binding on the Nabob. He will look for fresh troubles when the Nabob has it in his powder, and he will consequently take the first opportunity of throwing off the yoke by adecting [sic] a junction which it was one object of our expedition to prevent. But we must rest

satisfied. The Company are not what they were, and never will recover themselves whilst Ministry interposes ; and this accommodation may justly be regarded as one of the many bad effects of the ministerial plan. The Nabob would never have thought of laying aside the guarantee had he not depended on support from the Crown ; and, had the guarantee been regarded as subsisting, we had never quitted Tan j ore till the Rajah, admitting an English garrison, had put it out of his power to become troublesome in future. And thus ends my history.
Hastings left us the 2nd instant, much regretted, for he is a very valuable man both in his public and private character. Unless my letters from Bengal tell me wrong, he will have much on his hands, for matters there are represented to be in a state which will require the exertion of all his abilities to reform them. Ardley died the 9th instant. Pyne and Charles Smith are in Council. When shall I be there ?

Henry Vansittart, jun., to Robert Palk, Esqr., at Edmund Boehm's, Esqr., Sice Lane, London. 1772, April 2nd, Fort St. George.

Dear Sir,
I landed in good health at Calcutta the 31st of January, and in consequence of several pressing letters I received from Mr. Morse, left it in order to proceed to Madras in the *Lord Holland* in the latter end of February. I had before my departure been introduced to Mr. Hastings, who has invited me to live with him when I return. After a passage of 25 days we arrived in Madras road, and I had a happy meeting with Mr. and Mrs. Morse the next day. The time of my stay here is not yet settled, but, however, I shall find employment in the study of the Persian language and in the instructions of my grand father. The Nabob, having heard from Mr. Du Pre of the letter you have sent by me, has already given me an invitation to come and see him, and when Mr. Morse thinks proper he will carry me there. I have received many civilities here, but I cannot say that I am so fond of this place as Bengal. Mr. Alexander and Mr. Floyer, who are going in the Lord Holland to Europe, have treated me in the most obliging manner during my stay in that ship, and to them I chiefly am indebted for my passage.

Remember me to Mr. Tripe, and give my duty to Mrs. Palk, and love to Nancy and Lawrence. Your dutiful nephew,

Henry Vansittart

Robert Palk to William Martin Goodlad 1772, April 7th, Park Place

My dear Billy
The Directors were well pleased with the last accounts from Madras. The success against Tan j our will not raise the Stock, but if we fail it will have a confounded tumble. Sir Robert Harland possibly may have the same powers with Lindsay, but his instructions must be very different. Whatever they are, the House of Commons will desire to see them, and next Tuesday is appointed for an enquiry into the state of India. On that motion Lord Clive spoke for two hours in vindication of his own conduct. He was followed by Rumbold, Carnac and Coote. The last said that three times the number of troops now employed in India might be paid with the same money, but that the contractors and the canaille spent all the money. All which every officer who ever commanded in India is ready flatly to contradict.
I have done all in my power to bring your merit to notice in Leadenhall Street. Sir George Colebrooke, to whom I showed your last letter, will be pleased to hear from you. I shall also speak to Purling ; but they are all such ignoramus's that they understand little or nothing of the affairs abroad. They are only anxious for appearances and carrying on their own jobbs. Sulivan still is a candidate for the succession at Madras, but there seem to me many difficulties in his way

Robt. Palk

William Martin Goodlad to Robert Palk, Esqr. 1772, April 13th, Madras.

I send this by way of Anjengo in hopes of catching the Bombay ships. The Lapwing arrived here yesterday, but the advices by her give us little information. We shall never be restored to our former footing so long as a

Minister from the Crown is continued in these parts. The little confidence which remained between His Excellency and the Board must be daily lessened as we find his character open more and more. It seems that the Lapwing was freighted with complaints to the Crown, and I suppose the subsequent dispatches have been of the same nature. Is it possible to live on terms with the man who is known to endeavour all in his power to thus stab in the dark ? He makes no ceremony of telling the King that the Company's servants encrease his expences at pleasure. By Jove! I am very angry, for I detest every thing so ungenerous. The Court of Directors are said to be displeased at the tone of recent letters from here. If any changes take place in consequence. Stone will probably become a member of the Board. In that case I shall try for the Military Secretaryship, and slave until I secure preferment. Purling seems to be my friend, and I hope to win over Sulivan. We continue at peace, but an expedition against the Marawars is talked of. On the whole the prospects on the Coast are promising.

W. M. Goodlad.

Colonel Gilbert Ironside to Robert Palk, Esqr. 1772, April 13th, Fort William.

I am very grateful for your civility to Mrs. Ironside and her brother. I have just seen Mr. Palk and his wife. Although he incurred the Company's displeasure some years ago, I think he might have been treated more leniently in consideration of his good service at Patna. From Mr. Hastings, however, I am persuaded he will meet with those instances of esteem and regard he can wish for from the Governour and the friend. George is now next to Council, and I am afraid will soon be called to the Board.
There was a talk not long since of Mr. Hastings' intentions to desire my assistance to promote the public cause, and in consequence to remain at the Presidency with him. Whether he perseveres in his resolution I know not. His accession to the Chair was on the 13th instant. A few days therefore will determine whether I am to continue a devious campaign

life, or to repose under the olive shade 'till my rank entitles me to a brigade. The latter I think most probable, for though experience and disappointments have rendered me rather diffident of cherishing too fond and sanguine expectations from the smiles of power, yet I have the firmest reliance on the obligations of friendship.

From the library of the Nawab Mahmud Riza Chan I had the good fortune to meet with a copy of the digests or pandects of the Arabian Canon and Civil Laws. One volume is entirely transcribed, and my Arabic writers are advanced far in copying the remaining one with the Comment. I thought it preferable to procure both rather than the second volume only that you wrote for, least the first of yours should be imperfect. They will be ready to dispatch by the packet of September.

In political matters here there is nothing very remarkable. The King, in the hands of the Morrattas, gained a considerable victory over the Rohellas in the course of the month of February, and afterwards besieged a strong fortress in the same country called Pattagur, where he took an immense booty. Shujah Dowlah, against whom the Morattas, from former resentments, have long vowed vengeance, is at present with his forces on the Rohellah frontier, and one of our brigades at the Caramnassah in readiness to march to his assistance. But it is now the general opinion that they will not trouble him this season, for they entertain a very formidable idea of our force united to the Vizier's, and with reason. All apprehensions of a French invasion may be laid aside, I think, for this monsoon. Last year, indeed, they might have effected much from the supineness, negligence and weakness of our administration; but neither in present nor in future can they have any great probability of succeeding, for we have now a very large force near Calcutta, and the fortifications on the river and at Fort William are advanced beyond an apprehension of insult. Another year I hope completes them.

Gilbert Ironside

XXXV
Warren Hastings asks for Palk's help, 1772

Warren Hastings expands his view of the situation and hopes that Robert Palk will convey his conclusions to the Directors.

Warren Hastings to Laurence Sulivan, Esqr. 1772, September 7th, Cossimbuzar.

Dear Sir,
I hope you will not expect a long letter from me when you see the name of the place which I write from. I will be more communicative by the Lapwing, which perhaps will arrive as soon as this ship, unless I hear before that you are certainly on your way to Bengal as a Commissioner, or to Fort St. George as a Governor, for report says you must be one.
I have made use of the information and talents of Nund Comar. I have obtained a reward for him equal to his future services, be they ever so important, and far beyond his past deserts. And I have avoided to give him such trust or authority as he could turn to the Company's detriment. This was the proposition laid down for me in the letter of the Secret Committee and enjoined in yours. I beg you will support and confirm your own work. I am happy that you recommended it. It was the only measure which could have effectually broken the power of Mahmud Rizza Cawn.
Munny Begum, the widow of Meer Jaffier, is appointed Superintendant of the Nabob's household, an irreconcileable enemy to Mahmud Rizza Cawn.
Rajah Goordass, the son of Nund Comar is made Dewan of the Nizamut.
The Nabob's stipend is reduced from 32 lacks to 16. This ought to have been done 7 months ago.

The settlement of the revenue of Bengal has been begun and compleated as far as 60 lacks for a term of 5 years upon the plan of which you were informed in a former letter. The remainder will take up some months more. The Company will not lose nor the inhabitants suffer from our arrangements, although the depopulation by the late famine and mortality exceeds all belief. The Collectors still remain, but their power is much reduced. It has been resolved, as the most effectual means of conducting the Dewaunee on the system ordered by the Company, to transfer the collections to Calcutta, which will become the seat of the Dewaunee and the capital of the Province.

Regulations have been framed for the administration of justice, which will do us little credit with the learned in the law, but they will prove of service in a land which to this day exists without any Court or forms of Justice. The principles of all our measures have been to establish the new system which the Directors have adopted ; to break the influence of the former administration ; to avail ourselves of the present minority to establish the line of the Company's power, and habituate the people and the Nabob to their sovereignty, and to make it acceptable to the former by an attention to their ease and by a mild and equal plan of government. I beg of you to read such of the proceedings of this Committee as have been communicated to the Board. You will find them, I suppose, in the Consultations.

Much has been said against Nund-Comar, whose real character I have endeavored to delineate. The reasons assigned for dividing the offices of the Nizamut and giving the chief administration to a woman deserve your attention. The preface to our judicial establishment will also shew the state of the Courts and offices of Justice before in being, and fully evince the necessity as well as the propriety of those which we have adopted.

The examination of Mahmud Rizza Cawn still remains in suspense. I am inclined to leave it to the Supervisors, for I doubt the sufficiency of my own powers to bear me through it.The other enquiries referred to me will only serve to shew the impotency of the authority which constitutionally rests with the President. You empower me to punish, but you give me no means to call the offenders toaccount. But I am going into too wide a field for the time allowed me to finish this letter. This may be the subject of a longer.

We are yet happily at peace, but great pains have been taken by the Vizier to draw us into a war, which I shall use all my efforts to avoid. In this I hope to be heartily supported by my fellow laborers. The Marrattas have retired, as was foreseen, from the Rohella country, and are engaged in a war with the Jauts with little success. They will probably return after the rains. The Vizier has demanded the presence of our forces, which we have promised, with a declaration that they shall be employed only in the defence of his dominions, but not move an inch beyond them unless the Marattas begin hostilities..with us. The King is at Delhi in union, that is, in Subjection to the Marrattas.
I am, with the most sincere regard, dear Sir, your obliged and faithful servant

Warren Hastings.

William Martin Goodlad to Robert Palk, Esqr. 1772, October 3rd, Fort St. George.

In my letter of the 30th September I mentioned the death of Mr. Morse. By this accident and the departure of Mr. Hastings, Wynch and I are left your only attornies here, and he probably will not remain long with us, and it is therefore necessary that you should join someone with me. It will be necessary also that you send particular instructions relative to your affairs in general, for the executors of Mr. Morse tell me that your sentiments are partly conveyed in private letters to him and partly in general letters to your attornies. His affairs are left in so perplexed a state that, though he died in May, I could not obtain the papers till a few days ago.
The amount due to you will be about Pags. 6,500, and to the General Pags. 1,500.
Permit me to recommend Mr. William Petrie to be joined with me in the management of your affairs. I know his worth, or I would not mention him.

W. M. Goodlad

Edward Cotsford to Robert Palk, Esqr. 1772, October 15th, Madrass. Received 12th April, 1773.

Dear Sir,

After so long a silence it is with difficulty I can prevail on myself to address you at all ; not through want of inclination, but from a conviction that it requires more rhetoric than I am master of to set forth sufficient reasons for having so long neglected paying you my respects.About two months after your departure for England I was under the ne- cessity of leaving Ganjam through illness, having been brought to death's door by a violent fever. During my absence Narraindoo Zemein- dar of Khimedy and since dead, took possession of all the northern part of the Cicacole Circar, so that I escaped being made a prisoner, but lost all the effects I had at Ganjam. Some time afterwards, in consequence of the war with Hyder Ally, a very considerable reinforcement of troops were transported to the Coast from Calcutta, and proceeded by the way of Commamett and Worangol towards Hyderabad, which brought the Soubah of the Decan to a peace with us. The Bengal detachment not being wanted in the Carnatic, it was employed in reducing Narraindoo, and in which they so far succeeded as to drive him out of the country and take all his forts and strongholds.

At the time the peace was made with the Soubah I made application to Mr. Bourchier to return again to Ganjam, thinking it a favourable juncture for getting a detachment of sepoys for the service of the Itchapour district, to act under my own orders. The Governour at first did not encourage it, judging there was but a small probability of any advantage ccruing to the Company from the measure, and also a great risque to myself. For my own part, I was an adventurer, and had nothing to lose. So I returned again and carried with me a detachment, and was as expeditious as I possibly could with the Zemeindars that I might not lose the opportunity of the vicinity of the Bengal detachment. At the close of the war with Hyder Ally the Europeans of the Bengal detachment embarked for Calcutta at Vizagapatam, and the three battalions of sepoys proceeded by land, that being an indulgence promised them at their embarkation for the Coast. In their passage through the Itchapour country I made use of their presence as essentially as I could consistent with the time they were to stay and reflections on what my situation would be after their departure. I have since from time to time been reinforced, and we have now stationed in that district fifteen companies of sepoys and the Coffery company.

I have been extreamly fortunate in every measure I have engaged in in that country, and have brought the Zemeindars into some kind of order, though not without a considerable share of trouble and some loss of men, having had killed and wounded in all at different times between 4 and 500 men. However, the Company have not lost a grain of military reputation, and their revenues there are increased. We have not yet began an Investment, the country not being in a state to undertake it without the risking the loss of the money, the weaving villages lying in the Zemeindaries for the most part. At present it yields an annual profit of 150,000 rupees, after paying the charges civil and military, and expence of fortification and buildings.

The Fort is nearly finished with a revetement — I mean the body of the place — and is sufficiently large to contain all the buildings necessary for merchandise and military stores suitable to the degree of importance of the place. As you are the person to whom I am indebted for this post, I have been somewhat more particular than I should otherwise have been. It has answered my expectations in every respect, and I feel the greatest pleasure in informing you that my conduct has always been approved by the Board.

The Zemeindaries dependant on Vizagapatam are for the most part under the immediate management of Sitteram Rauze, which is undoubtedly improper, as it prevents the Chief there from ever gaining such a knowledge of the country as is absolutely necessary to enable him to ascertain the real value of the country, and how far the revenues will bear increasing ; and in all other respects it prevents the authority of the Company from being felt and understood. When that country was first taken possession of, it was, I suppose, absolutely necessary to support Sitteram Rauze in all the power he could possess himself of ; but according to my judgment the reasons for such a conduct do not now subsist. It appears to me that every Zemeindar should be independant of Sitteram Rauze (who himself is no more than a Zemeindar) and of each other, and trans- act all their affairs immediately with the Chief.The only reason which can be offered in favour of it [sic] is that he is more capable, through his authority and knowledge of the country, of keeping in subjection those Zemeindars whose lands lie amongst the hills and in the interior part of the Circar. But this is by no means the case, as I know by experience that 100 our sepoys will go where a thousand of his people dare not shew themselves.

Some months since Hussein Ally Khan died, and the Company, I believe, allow one lack of rupees per annum to his children in lieu of the Jaguire held by the father ; and the lands which formed the Jaguire have been returned to two of the Zemeindars, whose property they originally were, and their tribute in consequence proportionably increased. Since the war with Hyde Ally the Nabob's affairs are, I believe, in a very flourishing state, as he has paid off a very considerable part of his debts both publick and private, besides maintaining a very respectable army. He has been very successful against the Rajah of Tan j ore and the countries of the Great and Little Maravas. In some forts of the last mentioned places he found very considerable riches. An expedition is now talked of against the King of Travancore. Notwithstanding the good state of his affairs, I believe the Nabob was never less at ease than he is at present at any period of his life scarce. The interposition of the Crown in his affairs and the great attention paid to him by Sir John Lindsay caused him to assume an appearance of independence on the Governor and Council he had never before shewn. He has also by the same means acquired a very clear idea of the nature of our Constitution ; but I believe he is loaded with doubts and fears, which the knowledge he has gained seems only to increase. He has discernment enough to perceive that he is in a labyrinth. He knows by experience the power of the Company, and fears the greater power of the Government. A few days since. Sir Robert Harland, with the squadron under his command, left this coast for Bombay. He did not take leave of the Governor,

XXXVI
Nick Morse dies - the end of an era, 1772

Thomas Palk to Robert Palk, Esqr. 1772, November 10th, Calcutta.

I left Madras the beginning of September to come here. I have at last paid my brother the long intended visit. I arrived here the 24th of October, when I found him very well. It is with much concern I tell you of the loss he has lately met with (which gave him much affliction for a long time) by the death of his wife. I cannot help expressing the greatest concern on my side for the loss of that amiable woman.

I am sorry to inform you of the death of Mr. Morse, my most valuable friend, for so he was to the strictest meaning of the word ; and the good old lady has been at death's door herself, but she is now perfectly well again. She has taken her passage with Captain Elphinston of the Triton . I am still under Mr. Secretary Goodlad. Had I been appointed at the time an opportunity happened at Masulipatam, I might in this [have] been money in pocket. I should have been near Captain Madge, whose assistance I should not have found wanting. I had the pleasure of seeing him in my way here at that place, where he commands, who offered me then the loan of a sum of money, which I refused for several reasons. Mr. Bourchier not only talked of his friendship for me, but might have really proved himself a friend, so that I have nothing to thank him for, and very little more - Mr. J. Call. His intentions might be good, but they have proved contrary.

I find from my brother [that] he wrote last year requesting Grace might be sent out to him, and he as well as myself were a little surprised she did not arrive. I should be exceeding glad to see her, as I hear she is grown a fine girl. My brother, notwithstanding his misfortunes, is in a fair way of doing well for himself, though I don't see how he could otherwise, as he has had all the advantages he could wish for.

Thos. Palk.

P.S. Mr. H. Vansittart was at Madras some time with his grandfather. He is now at Patna with his uncle, and no doubt will turn out a clever man, as there is all the appearance at present of it.

Warren Hastings to Robert Palk, Esqr. 1772, November 11th, Fort William. Received 19th April, per *Lapwing*.

Dear Sir,
The last letter I addressed to you, if I am not mistaken, was dated September 7th. This is to acknowledge your favour of the 26th March, 1772. It affords me no inconsiderable concern to observe the people of England, and even our Hon'ble Masters, who should form their opinions with more candour and exactness, thus easily induced to the credit of every calimny put forth by each paltry scribbler of the day. The productions of Bolts and Dowe appears replete, though not in an equal degree, with abominable untruths, base aspersions and absurdities. How cruel to judge the reputation of any one by such criterions !
I have exerted my power to the utmost to destroy even the shadow of Mahomed Riza Cawn's influence. I have placed his enemies in his seat, and have him under a secure confinement. When I shall be able to release him God knows. It is my intention to bring him to his trial : and I flatter myself the issue will prove that if I am not his enemy (as in fact I by no means am) yet I am incapable of being prepossessed either by partiality or bribe to serve him : but I am overwhelmed with present business and cannot look back.
I am sorry the House of Commons should think of establishing laws for this country, ignorant as they are of the laws in being, of the manners and customs of the inhabitants, or of the form of government. I hope the Act will not take place, for should it, everything we have done will be destroyed, and my labour will prove like the toil of Sisyphus.
As before, I enclose my letter to Mr. Sulivan to you. You will read it and then deliver it to him, as I know not where he is and do not admire trusting my correspondence in strange hands.Poor Griffiths is with me. What shall I do with him ? He is a good and a valuable young man, and will do credit to your patronage if you will employ it to get him into the service.
I am, with an unfeigned and most affectionate regard, dear Sir, your most obedient and faithful servant,

Warren Hastings

Thomas Palk to Robert Palk, Esqr. 1773, January 11th, Calcutta.

I am still here with my brother, who contributes everything in his power to my pleasure, as this happens to be the season for all sorts of diversions, of which we have little or none on the Coast.When I hear from Mr. Wynch, who by this time must have succeeded Mr. Du Pre, I shall decide about returning to Madras.
My beloved friend General Smith goes home on the Triton, in consequence of which the command of the troops has devolved on Sir Robert Fletcher, who is universally despised, the court martial business having laid a stain on his principles that will never be forgot or washed out. Consequently I have not the least intimacy with him.
There is a report here, which I do not credit, that Mr. Barwell, of the Bengal Council, is to be Governor of Madras. Should it prove true, I shall take care to ingratiate myself with him.
Mr. George Vansittart is coming down from his Chief ship at Patna to take his seat at the Board. Mrs. V., my brother and myself are going up as far as Cossimbazar to meet him in a week more, a thing not common in this country for a wife to go any small distance to meet her husband. The army here is in motion. They are marched up to the frontiers of Suja ul Dowlah's country to be a check on the Morattoes. They have paid the King of Delhi a visit, and were very ruffly received by him. The King and them have had an engagement, in which the former was worsted, with great loss on both sides Mr. Secretary Goodlad, since I have left Madras, has been in a very dangerous way. He has had a violent attack in his liver, for which he has been cut, and is recovering very fast.

Thos. Palk
P.S. I beg leave to hint to you that it will be doing me in [sic] a great service to prefer me as a tenant to the one in it, as the present one rather makes more use of it as godowns than a dwelling house. Your attorney must also have your directions regarding it. It will be easy to get him out without giving offence by your specifying that you chuse to serve me preferable to one who has less right to expect it. Be so good, Sir, as to take notice of this by the first ship

James Daniell to Robert Palk, Esqr. 1773, January 28th, Cuddalore.

I venture to write to you on behalf of our common friend Sir Robert Fletcher, who has not only felt the effects of Mr. Du Pre's measures since the resignation of General Smith, but has some reason to apprehend his intention Sir Robert is of course obliged to exert all his influ- ence to prevent such an intention ; and as you have been often pleased to serve him at the tribunal of Leadenhall, he hopes you will not forsake him on the present occasion.

I chanced to see the papers relating to recent disputes in Council, which are now transmitted to Europe. They are voluminous, but I can give you an idea of the origin of the trouble in a few words. It began by an application from the Nabob, introduced by the Governor, to be addressed from the Board under the title of Arzdash ; and the impropriety of doing so will appear to you by reading the different dissents. The Governor has, however, succeeded, and though this mode of address is only used throughout Indostan from an inferior to a superior, the Governor and Council have adopted the practise. When a difference of opinion has once appeared between men in power, it seldom ceases on a sudden, but serves only as a prelude to other discords. So it is in the present instance, and as the authority of command is a theme on which Mr. Du Pre has often exercised his abilities, it has been again renewed with all its force. Sir Robert, in consequence, has been voted from the Council and ordered within 2 days to proceed to the command of the fort and garrison of Trinchinopoly, Thus is he placed beyond the reach of opposition and deprived of his seat at the Board, to which the Court of Directors have been pleased to appoint him. On a perusal of the papers you will be able to form a judgment of the propriety of Sir Robert's proceedings, and determine if any part is the effect of private pique, or contrary to the intention of his employers. If not, I presume that you will not only assist his cause, but exert your influence with the Directors to assist the rights of justice and prevent the attempts of a misrepresentation. Sir Robert would have wrote to you on this subject if his time had permitted him to do so. He passed here yesterday on his way to Trinchinopoly, and desired me to communicate the substance of his cause, and hopes you will admit

his apology for not addressing you himself.
You may much better conceive that I can express my feelings by closing this letter with the account of poor Goodlad's death. He had been lately cut for an inflammation in his liver, and a relapse carried him off. He is universally lamented, and the Company have reason to regret the loss of his abilities.

Jas. Daniell.

Chocapah to the Honble. Robert Palk, Esqr. 1773, .January 28th, Fort St. George.

Governour Du Pre takes his passage home on the Nassau and leaves the Government in the hands of Alexander Wynch, Esqr., who is a gentleman that has been a long time in India, and well acquainted with the affairs of this country ; and besides he is civil, good natured, and will undoubtedly make a good Governour. I wish he may keep the Chair for some time, but it is strongly reported here that Mr. Sullivan is coming out for President of this place.
The Morattas will, I hope, give us no trouble this year on account of Madavarave, their Chief, departing this life about two months ago, and his brother Narranrave being appointed Chief in his room, and his uncle Rakobah is appointed General of the Army ; which will take up some time more to settle their family affairs.
The Export Warehousekeeper carrys on the Company's Investment by employing Gomastas in the weaving towns, and the goods he provides now is very good and in proper order. Mr. Samuel Johnson married Miss Law, a lady that came with Mr. Charles Smith from Pondichery lately.

Chocapah.
P.S. Poor Mr. Goodlad departed this life the 24th instant.

XXXVII
Goodlad is no more. 1773

This news must have come as a body blow to Robert Palk who was friend and business partner of Martin Goodlad for all the years in India and again in England through voluminous correspondence. Goodlad was deprived of his retirement in England by his illness - a fate all too common in these times and places.

William Petrie to Robert Palk, Esqr. 1773, January 31st, 3 a.m.. Fort St. George. Received 5th November.

> My much esteemed and invaluable friend Mr. Goodlad, after a long and severe illness, which he supported with the most manly fortitude, bid adieu to this world the 24th instant. So long ago as October last he had adopted a scheme of going to Europe, not so much on the score of health as to promote a favourite plan which he had before communicated to you in his letters. From his masterly abilities and the strongest testimony in his favour from the Board, his friends had conceived the most flattering hopes of his success. Soon after the despatch of the *Nottingham* he was attacked with a violent obstruction and inflammation in his liver, which from the beginning foreboded the most fatal consequences. However, the disease appeared at one time to take a favourable turn, and the operation of opening the side was performed about the beginning of last month with such favourable effects upon his disorder that the surgeons entertained the most flattering hopes. By the advice of Mr. Pasley he determined on a voyage to Europe, and took his passage on the *Nassau* along with Mr. Du Pre. The Board gave him the strongest testimony of their high opinion of his merit and voted him a minute of publick thanks, besides recommending him in the strongest manner to the Court of Directors. But, alas, in the midst of our hopes a general suppuration took place in his liver, attended with a fever and ague, which put a period to his life on the 24th. The service, the Settlement, in short the community, mourn his loss as a servant to the Company, a valuable citizen and an

useful member of society. Had not our friend been involved in joint concerns his affairs would have been distinct and his fortune something considerable, but unfortunately for him and unfortunately for his friends, his affairs are so blended and involved with Mr. James Johnson's that I am much afraid heavy losses may be expected.

For years past he has been vainly urging Mr. Johnson to settle accounts. During our friend's last illness I took every step in my power, and even threatened Mr. Johnson with a Bill of Discovery in the Mayor's Court, but Goodlad thought that legal action would only defeat his object. The executors, Messrs. Macpherson, De Souza and myself will not therefore proceed to extremities. Mr. Johnson is in the capacity of English accountant with the Nabob, and the world supposes him in a fair way of making money, so that there may still be a possibility of receiving at least a considerable part of the debt. You may collect enough from what I have said to perceive that a large part of our friend's fortune is in very indifferent hands.

The will is unfinished. He leaves his fortune, after the payment of his debts and certain legacies, to his sister. Here the will breaks off without relating the legacies. The amount due from Mr. Johnson is believed to be between Pags. 15,000 and Pags. 20,000.

To sum up what I have said in a few words : — if we recover from Mr. Johnson the money he owes the estate of Mr. Goodlad, a considerable balance, I think, will remain in favour of the estate ; but on the other hand, if we cannot recover this debt, I am afraid his estate will fall considerably short.

Shortly before Goodlad's death I handed to Mr. Wynch the papers relating to your affairs and those of General Lawrence, together with Pags. 2,800 in cash. The balance due to you is about Pags. 5,800, and to the General about Pags. 3,800. As suggested by Goodlad, I shall be pleased to manage your affairs in India under a power of attorney.

Upon the resignation of our friend, a young gentleman of the name of Oakely succeeded to the Civil department. He had been in the office of Deputy Secretary for two years, and had recommended himself much by his assiduity and promising abilities. Mr. Stone, who had held his office of Secretary for several months after he had been taken into Council, had continued in it during Mr. Goodlad's illness, as Goodlad intended removing to the Military department ; upon his resignation Mr. Stone quitted his office, and I was appointed Secretary and Judge Advocate General.

The feuds and animosities which have distracted our Council for some months past seemed to collect and unite all their force to overwhelm the President on his departure for Europe. Minutes, dissents and debates of a more violent nature than ever appeared on the records have been entered in the course of this month. The majority of the Board removed Sir Robert Fletcher from his seat by appointing him to the command of Trichinopoly. He pleaded privilege of parliament, and de manded a passage on the first ship for Europe. The Board insisted on obedience to their order : he complied, and proceeded as far as Cuddalore. The Board having inforced their authority, they not only admitted his plea, and exonerated him from all obligation to serve the Company, but also removed him from the command of the Army, and requested General Smith to resume the command and his seat in Council, which he accordingly did. The Board met to take leave of the President and sign the dispatches. But it was decreed that Mr. Du Pre should not depart in peace. An extraordinary circumstance happened : the conclusion was the suspension of Mr. Mackay from the service. The President has been thanked by the Board for his services to the Company, and embarks tomorrow morning with his family on the *Nassau*, and leaves the Government to Mr. Wynch.

These unfortunate animosities have come unseasonably on a young secretary. The business in the Political and Military department has of late years been so extensive from our connections with the country Powers, the frequent wars we have waged as principals and as auxiliaries, and the violent attacks on the Company's rights by the King's Minister, that some months entirely devoted to studying the records would not have been too much to qualify me for the office of Secretary. But I have all at once been hurried into the midst of intricacies and difficulties.

The Carnatick is in profound peace with all her neighbours. The King of Tan j ore, completely humbled by the late siege, makes daily professions of duty and attachment. General Smith, before he resigned the command to Sir Robert Fletcher, subdued the countries of the Great and Little

Marawar. Hyder, yet smarting from his recent losses in the war with the Morattoes, seems to have adopted a defensive plan, but a mere defensive plan is not long to be expected from one of his active genius. The Maharattoes since the death of Mahadevarow seem undetermined as to any plan of action, and are more engaged in the contests of parties at home than in designs against the repose of their neighbours. The squadron is still at Bombay, and is not expected here till March or April.

Wm. Petrie.

Nawab Walajah to General Stringer Lawrence. 1773, February 1st, Chepauk, [Madras].

The Nabob Waulaujah Bahauder, &c., presents his salams to his friend General Lawrence, and sends him the inclosed with his wishes for long life and happiness.

Thomas Palk to Robert Palk, Esqr. 1773, February 30th [sic], Calcutta.

I have never but once asked for anything in the service and that was refused by your most then intimate friend ; and if those professed friends shew themselves backward in serving me, what am I to expect from those who are clear of any such tie? I am not so presuming as to ask any thing : but from Mr. Wynch's readiness in endeavouring to get him appointed to his Chiefship, I did, three months ago, write him a letter requesting he would do something for me, to which I have never yet seen the least reply, which not a little astonishes me. That gentleman is now in the Government, Mr. Du Pre being gone home on the *Nassau*.
General Smith resigned the army command to Sir Robert Fletcher in August last, but owing to a difference between Mr. Du Pre and Sir Robert, he has consented on public grounds to resume it. I learn that General Coote and Mr. Sulivan left England in August, which, was it true, I think we might have seen them on the Coast by this time. I shall be happy if those accounts prove true. I think I may safely depend that he

will do something for me — I mean Mr. S. It is with much concern I inform you of the death of Mr.Goodlad. . . He had been very severely attacked by the liver, and had been cut for it and got pretty well, when he had resolved on going to England for a season or two of cold weather. I have never heard from what cause that he died. I feel for his poor mother. The young brother Dick has also been on the point of death. I saw him last night, and he is recovering fast. I do not imagine Mr. G. died worth much money, as he was a great lover of claret and every thing that was good.

I am about thinking of returning to the Coast. I have, 'tis true, little to do there, and less here. My brother might, if he pleases, assist me greatly, but has not yet shewed any inclination. He might however, I think, make a better use of his money. I suppose he spends not less than 4 or £5,000 a year. He is a lucky fellow.

Thos. Palk

Thomas Palk, to Robert Palk, Esqr. 1773, March 22nd, Calcutta.

Since I last wrote, I have been appointed by Mr. Wynch to Masulipatam in preference to several senior applicants. I am just starting for Madras, so cannot seek a passage direct to Masulipatam.

It was Captain Madge that wrote me of this appointment. He writes to my brother also, proposing a most noble and generous scheme ; that they do in conjunction lend me a sum of Rs. 15,000 ; that my brother contributes 6 or 8,000 of it, and he will do the rest ; that I shall enter into a partnership with Mr. Burton, a gentleman you know at Masulipatam, who has had a deal of experience in the world. What my brother intends to do I know not ; but this I know, that he can well afford it, and that he makes much worse use of his money than he would by setting me out in the world. I shall have the greatest opportunities of making money now, provided this scheme of my friend Madge's takes. I cannot conceive that he can give any justifiable reasons for his not agreeing in it ; but this I shall insist upon, that he gives no reasons to Madge that may in any means whatever prevent him from lending me any money. The amount of this is yet to be determined, and of which I shall not have an opportunity of communicating to you till October next .

Thos. Palk.

Warren Hastings to Robert Palk, Esqr. 1773, April 3rd, Fort William.

Dear Sir,
I request the favor of your care of the accompanying letters. That to Mr. Du Pre I have troubled you with because I am uncertain of his address ; the others, one for Mr. Sulivan and one for Mr. Bolton, I have sent under flying seals for your perusal. I have not time to address you as I could wish, a declaration which I am sure your kindness will admit as a full excuse.
Harry Vansittart has just sent me a history of the Seneassies, which I enclose with this. Perhaps it may amuse you, and you may probably consider it as a curiosity when I acquaint you that it was but yesterday morning (noon) I gave him the original to be translated. The subject is important to us, though to you it may appear trifling, for they are the people who have lately given us so much trouble by their incursions, and have obliged us to employ a considerable force to drive them out of these provinces.
I beg my compliments may be made to Mrs. Palk, the General and all friends. I am, with a most sincere regard, dear Sir, your most obedient and humble servant,

Warren Hastings.
P.S.The letter to Mr. Du Pre and that to Mr. Sulivan, together with the history of the Seneassies are by mistake under another cover to you.

James Daniell to Robert Palk, Esqr. 1773, October 13th, Fort St. George.

In my letter of the 18th January I mentioned Sir Robert Fletcher's contest with the Board. Little did I then imagine I should so soon have occasion to tell you that I likewise have most materially suffered from the exertion of my duty. Mr. Turing and myself have been called from our stations at Cuddalore from a desire of forwarding the Company's Investment at that Factory. From a perusal of the accompanying minutes you will find the truth of my assertion, and though the Governor and Council have been pleased to adopt another pretence for removing us, it cannot alter facts so demonstratively pointed that there remains not a single doubt to oppose them.

We are sending copies of the papers to our friends, so that the Court of Directors may not be prejudiced in their opinion, and I hope for your support against any injurious orders from the Court.

Jas. Daniell.

Anthony Goodlad to Robert Palk, Esqr. 1773, October 20th, Purnea in Bengal.

Your letters of the 9th and 14th April addressed to poor Martin have been delivered to me. I realize your friendship for my family, and trust that you will extend the same favour to his surviving brothers which you always showed to Martin. The disputes between the Government and the Company in England cause disquietude in India. Some definite plan of reform is urgently needed.

Mr. Hastings has been indefatigable in his assiduity and attention to the dutys of his station, but he must have friends to support his measures at home to make them meet with the approbation of the publick ; and the unfortunate event of Mr. Sullivan and his friends being thrown out of the Direction gives me too much reason to apprehend that his plans may meet with disapprobation. I, however, hope for the best, for as I have enjoyed the honor of his confidence, and experienced instances of his friendship, I cannot be otherwise than interested in his success, and ardent in my wishes for his benefit. He has lately been up the country, and settled a new treaty with Soujah Dowlah, but as I cannot acquaint you with the particulars of it so fully and explicitly as Mr. Van, who was on the spot, I shall leave him to relate the matter to you.

After six years of arduous work in the Persian Translator's office I was

transferred last year at my own request to the comparative retirement of the Purnea collectorship, where my brother Dick is my assistant. My prospects, however, are not too favourable.
I thank God I am honoured with the friendship and good opinion of the Governor and Mr. Van, and am sensible that they will assist me whilst they continue in the country ; but, as I look upon Mr. Hastings's situation as precarious, and that there is little dependance to be placed in these times upon a man's holding a station which is so much he envy of half the world, I shall be obliged to you by confirming my connection with Mr. Van (which is already on a proper footing) by urging every thing on your part which you may deem me worthy of.
Mr. Petrie at Madras has succeeded beyond my expectations in the settlement of my brother's affairs. I think there will be enough to pay everybody, though I have little hope that Johnson will meet his debt.
Ay. W. Goodlad.

Reynold Adams to Robert Palk, Esqr. 1773, October 25th, Fort St. George.

My last went by Mr. Ley by the way of China, since which nothing material has happened here but the taking of Tan j ore, which lately fell into our hands and is garrisoned by the Nabob. The captive King is sent to Trichinopoly.
It is with great concern I acquaint you that this last expedition will, I fear, prove fatal to poor Major Madge. He has long been much out of order while he stayed to the northward, and not recovered when he went to the siege of Tan j ore, where, contrary to the advice of his friends, he ventured in the trenches before his health was established. This brought on a relapse and a dangerous illness, so that he was advised to go to Cuddalore. About ten days ago he arrived at my house, where he stayed three or four days, as he allways lives with me when at Madras. But as a cooler apartment was recommended for him, the Governor has given him a room at the Admiralty. Mr. Paissley attends him, but he seems loth as yet to give his opinion about him. It's said, however, that he is not worse than when he first arrived. He is very low spirited, and thinks himself that he cannot live many days.
Reyno. Adams.

XXXVIII
Cotsford and the Dutch threat, 1773

Edward Cotsford to Robert Palk, Esqr. 1773, October 29th, Madras.

About a year ago I gave you some account of my work, in which I believe you are interested, as it was you who conferred on me the management of the Ganjam territory. In all probability it will become a Settlement of importance, it being an establishment in the heart of a country which, from the quantity of grain exported from thence to the Presidency, may be considered as its granary ; and indeed the amazing opulence of Madrass within these three years makes such an one almost absolutely necessary. The money received from Ganjam annually amounts to upwards of 150,000 rupees over and above maintaining near two battalions of seapoys for the protection of the country, and also, if necessary, to keep peace in the southern provinces of the Cicacole Circar.You doubtless will learn from other hands of the success of his Highness the Nabob against Tan j ore. The reduction of that province may, I suppose, in general be considered in a considerable degree as advantageous to our nation. The Nabob is so connected with the English that, if the Government here be prudently administered, it will be very difficult for him to effect any considerable change ; but nevertheless the extraordinary strides he has lately made towards a formidable independency ought to be considered by us as most certainly tending in the end to that degree of subordination we were necessarily obliged to submit to under the government of the Mohammedans in former times. The last siege of Tan j ore has been attended with a circumstance which may by and bye be attended with serious consequences. The deposed Rajah, finding himself in a desperate situation, made over to the Dutch a grant of Nagore (a seaport) and some other districts on the sea coast for a valuable consideration in money. The lands are in value, I think, about four lacks of pagodas. The Nabob considered this act in the King of Tan j ore (according [to] the feudal system of the government) as unwarrantable, and accordingly demanded the assistance of the Company to assist his troops in the recovery of the alienated lands. The Governor and Council determined on assisting him against the Dutch, in which opinion they were strengthened by the concurrence of Sir Robert Harland, the King's Minister. The Dutch are accordingly driven out of their new acquisition, and have made a protest in form to General Smith, which is signed by their whole Council. The recovery of the lands for the Nabob is but a trifle I think, as the Dutch have not withdrawn their claim, and are strengthen- ing their fortress, which, if perfect, would doubtless be held as a strong fortification even in Europe ; and they are collecting all the troops they can draw from Ceylon, and doubtless will have a reinforcement from Batavia as early as the season will permit. I think it is probable the Dutch government at Batavia have taken into consideration the practica- bility of such measures as might lead to their procuring some territorial possessions on the coast of Coromandel ever since the first siege of Tan- j ore. If so, there is no saying at present what revolutions may be brought about by their interfering with the Marattas or any other Powers. I think it is remarked of the Dutch that they are wise in their deliberations and persevering in their conduct.

As the attack of Tan j ore may have serious consequences, I am surprised that the Governor and Council do not garrison the place with Company's troops. The interference of the King's Minister ought not to force the board to any policy detrimental to the Company.

There is still another measure which I shall take leave to say may in the end be of great detriment to the Company — I mean the bargaining with individuals beforehand (a committee of officers) for the services to be rendered by them to take the Fort for a certain sum of money to be payed them in lieu of plunder ; 2,000 pagodas to each captain, and so in proportion to the rest of the army. Officers and men doing their duty under such a condition never consider themselves any other way than as conferring a favour on the Nabob who employs them ; and indeed the impropriety has already appeared, it having been reported here that the officers might probably refuse to act against the Dutch, as that did not appear to come within their agreement with the Nabob. It opens a road for the Nabob to have great influence over our troops, and has many.

I arrived here from Ganjam in the beginning of this month in order to proceed to England, but by the loss of the Lord Mansfield I have been disappointed. However, I hope to make my acknowledgments to you in person about the middle of the next summer .

Edward Cotsford.
P.S. — As I have not time to make a copy, I hope you will excuse all errors and blots.

Robert Palk, jun., to Robert Palk, Esqr. 1773, November 3rd, Calcutta.

Thanks to your influence, the order which removed me from Patna last year has been revoked by the Company, and I am now about to re- turn thither.
Mr. Hastings has been very kind to me on all occasions, and on the present has shown himself particularly so by his readiness to send me back to Patna. Mr. Aldersey has given me many proofs lately of his inclina- tion to promote my interest.
There has been lack of rain, and the price of rice has advanced from 40 to 25 seers per rupee. The export of grain is consequently prohibited. The Renters have lost heavily on their farms. Politically the country is quiet. You will hear of Miss Van from George and others. The early introduction she had into company in England has nearly disqualified her for India. At present we Indians in her eyes are but contemptible beings. However, she is upon the whole a very worthy good young woman, and I hope will be much esteemed and very happy in this country. Harry Van and the Kennaways are well. I enclose two interest bonds from Dr. James Ellis, payable in 1775 ; one on your account for £2,880, being the balance of your money in my hands ; the other for £3,896 on my own account, which sum is to be invested at your discretion. George considers interest bonds a safer mode of remittance than bills.

Robert Palk, jun.

Henry Griffiths to Robert Palk, Esqr. 1773, November 10th, Calcutta.

In my last letter I mentioned the kind proposal of Mr. Hastings that I should accompany him to Bengal. By Mr. Stone's advice I did not immediately accept ; but Mr. Hastings has used his interest in England and now leads me to expect that I shall shortly obtain a nomination to the Bengal estabhshment. My brother William has arrived with Captain Mears, and is about to join his corps. He and I are both grateful to you for your kind exertions on his behalf.
Warren Hastings.

Robert Palk to Thomas Palk N.D. [cir. 1773.]

Dear Tom,
I have this year received from you many letters, and none of them have given me pleasure. I have provided, or endeavoured to provide, for many young men, and you are among those who seem to me least of all to deserve it; for if I can guess from your correspondence, inconsiderate and vacant as it is, you have not only neglected your own improvement and the duty, attention, industry and diligence you owe the Company and your own character, but have given yourself most entirely to idleness, extravagance and folly very unbecoming your situation and circumstances, who have nothing to depend pn but your own merit and he qualifying yourself for those offices which hereafter may fall to your share if your un worthiness does not prevent it. I pass over your hesitating between military and civil, though a young man who, having had some pains taken with his education, might at least have learnt patiently and chearfully to submit to what his parents so much wished and had thought best for him. In short, I cannot observe in your letters or your conduct one generous sentiment which can give me a prospect of your future success and well doing. Character and a virtuous emulation after reputation and a good name seem to make no part of your pursuit, and provided you can support your ill judged extravagance, no matter

from whence it comes. You are descended, if not from very opulent, at least very honest and worthy ancestors. Your father, though distressed beyond measure in his younger years, preferred an honest and virtuous reputation. Your grandfather stayed in the friendship and esteem of all that knew him, and the same have I heard of his father ; and yet they had not those advantages in their youth which (happily we hoped) have fallen to your share. But the dawn of your reason seems not to have been exercised in preserving yourself from ignorance, or accustoming yourself to good habits, or reconciling to yourself the good will and kindness of those with whom you must have an intercourse. You unfortunately have judged that attention and provision is due to you, merit out of the question. It is painful to me to write such a letter, and it ought to be more so [to] you for having made it necessary. I shall mention no particulars of your idle and unthinking conduct : your own memory will serve sufficiently to recollect them. Only imagine to yourself that I am well acquainted with what you would most wish to conceal, and try to retrieve all this by adopting a little more morality into your conduct. Forget not your Creator in the days of your youth, and learn to live on your own allowances without pitifully running in debt with every man you meet or have the least connection with. The allowance I gave you was amply sufficient had you lived in the Fort as you ought to have done, and looked on yourself only as a servant to the Company, from whom only you were to expect the encouragement that was due to diligence and merit.

[Unsigned draft.]

Colonel Gilbert Ironside to Robert Palk, Esq. 1774, January 15th, The Grove, near Fort William.

Some time in October last, soon after her arrival, Mrs. Ironside did herself the pleasure to acquaint Mrs. H. Vansittart of the health and safety of her daughter after a short and not altogether an unpleasant passage. Mrs. Ironside brought with her a greater share of health than she possessed for some years before, and bids fair, thank heaven, to preserve

it.
About two months ago Mr. Palk was restored to his seat at the Board of Revenue at Patna, which is looked upon to be a certain and considerable fortune in the space of a few years.
From Mr. Hastings I never entertained any very ardent expectations of assistance, and it is probable I shall see his entrance and exit with little benefit either to my fortune or preferment.
Dulcis inexpertis (says our friend Horace) cultura potentis amid, expertus metuit ; and as I am of this veteran class, I am not likely to succeed at Court. The unlucky line I am in is a material obstacle besides to my independance, exclusive of the mean talents I have in repetundis, and in the dexterities of political commerce.
For a sketch of our transactions here, please refer to General Caillaud, to whom I have described them. I have paid to Mr. Samuel Beardmore the £100 for which you gave him an order on me in 1772, as he is likely to be long a cadet, and is in need of money.

Robert Clive and his daughters

XIL
Lord Pigot is expected, 1774

Robert Palk, jun., to Robert Palk, Esqr. 1774, January 16th, Patna.

I left Calcutta the 9th November, and arrived at this Factory the 20th; distance about 400 miles. Enclosed I send you a draft on Mr. Kennaway for a further sum advanced his sons. Captain Skottowe undertook the care of a box for you, which I expect you will say contains a monument of my folly. If it should not prove acceptable at Haldon House, I daresay it will be very much so at Yolland Hill. Mrs. Van undertook to forward two or three small parcels for me, directed to you, but containing pieces of muslin, shawls, &c., for my friends at Ashburton; but by whom she has sent them I know not. In addition to the silk stockings I requested you would cause to be sent out annually, I shall be obliged to you if you will add the following : — 2 black and 1 white hat, 6 in. diameter, 1 pair boots and 6 pairs shoes. I shall also be glad of a large alarm watch or small clock of that kind, and a small light royal hunting saddle, red leather and quilted seat, with light furniture for the hind part only.
We have no appearance of any disturbance in the country. Shuja Dowla has paid twenty lacks of the sum he was to give the Company for Corah and Liabad by the Governor's treaty. Mr. Hastings goes on with great spirit reducing the Company's expences, civil and military, but I do not think it possible for the revenues to be increased. The attempt of it has been the error of our Government ever since Lord Clive obtained the Dewanny for the Company. The whole of the provinces have suffered greatly this last season by a heavy fall of water in the month of September, which overflowed the whole country, destroyed not even the grain, but carried away many villages and destroyed the cattle. Since that time we have had a remarkable drought, so much so as to alarm the natives with the fear of another famine. A stop was put to the exportation of grain.
The Collectors are recalled throughout the provinces, and Revenue or

Provincial Councils take their place. I enclose the regulations on the subject, from which you will see that the Company's servants generally are much restricted as to trade.

This Factory is most materially hurt, for in order to grant an allowance of 3,000 Rs. per month to the Member of administration without taking it immediately from the Company, they have claimed in the Company's name all the opium produced in this province, hitherto the particular advantage of the gentlemen at this Factory, which will be about equal to the above allowance. This is a severe loss to all us Patna folks, for there is no one article of trade left us but salt and Europe articles, which barely bring us the full interest of our money. This misfortune make[s] me feel the ill luck I was in by my removal in 1772, for had I staid here to this time, I should in all probability have it in my power to take leave of India, and avoided some misfortunes I have experienced. However, as I am not ambitious, a small matter will satisfy me. I therefore hope it will not be long before I see old England — sometime between this and 1780. We hear Lord Pigot is coming out on the *Eagle* with his new plan of government. Also that Lord Clive has been killed by a young nobleman whose name is not mentioned, nor the cause of their disagreement. I am concerned to mention the loss of my worthy friend Madge. He died at Madras the 8th November last. He estimated his fortune in his will to be about seven thousand pounds, Mr. Baker writes me, which for the most part he has left to his family.

My brother is at Masulipatam, and much pains I have taken to correct his errors and advise him to the best of my judgement ; but whether it will be of service to him or not I can't determine. I have said and done all in my power, and added 4,000 Rs. within these few days to 12,000 which he has already had and, I fear, spent. I have little expectation of seeing my money again. It will, however, be some satisfaction to me if it saves him from ruin. I do not wish you to say anything to him on this subject. I have already said so much as to make him express himself very unguardedly in his replies to my letters of advice. He is yet young enough to reform.

Mr. Petre has been tried for the murder of Mr. Rochford and acquitted, and is already by his countrymen's influence promoted to a good employ, whilst his seniors in the service are out of employ and in want. He renewed his application to George for permission to marry Emelia. George declared he never would agree to it. He then proposed that George should admit of their waiting till such time as he (Petre) could write to Mrs. H. Van on the subject. To this George did not object, and Petre accordingly addressed Emelia on the subject. She mustered up a little resolution, seeing how disagreeable it was to her uncle, and gave her lover a positive refusal ; so I hope that connexion will never be renewed.

The young Kennaways are very well. Dick is with George, and makes himself usefull. Jack was left behind at this place when the brigade marched down to the Presidency, very sick ; for some time dangerously so. I have made a stout man of him again by good nursing, and have just sent him down to join his brigade General Sir Robert Barker is gone home, and the command of the army has in consequence devolved on Colonel Chapman, who is grown old and very unequal to the task. The old gentleman has been remarkably attached to gaming till within these two years, and thereby sunk his estate considerably. His only wish of late has been to accomplish the amount of his loss. It is said a compromise has lately taken place, that the sum of near 80,000 Rs. has been made up to him, that he is to return to Europe with Captain Meers of the Egmont, and Colonel Champion to command the army, a very active officer, and in every respect equal to the station.

Robert Palk.

P.S. I have received your letter of the 15th March, 1773, by Mr. Ives, and will give him every assistance in my power. I've not yet seen him.

Reynold Adams to Robert Palk, Esqr., Park Place, St. James's. 1774, February 2nd, Fort St. George.

I am sending you a pipe of old madeira, which I ask you to accept.

As I have no thoughts at present of leaving this country, and as my employ will be ruined if Mr. Baker should have the watering of the ships, I have thought of a thing which is very advantageous if it can be obtained, and which I think may be done if you will be pleased to favor

me with your assistance. It is to make a tender to the Court of Directors for the Bettle and Tobacco farm and Bang leaves (as they always go together) as soon as the present cowl expires, which will he about two years hence. It was granted to the present renter for Pags. 28,000 per annum, and I mean that my tender for the next term shall be Pags. 30,000, and to give Soucar or other security to the Governor and Council and I will supply the publick in such beatle, tobacco and bang leaves as other renters has done before me.
It has not been customary, it is true, to let the farm to a European, but this is probably because no European has hitherto tendered. I look to you for your kind assistance, and I have written to Mr. Boehm for his.

Reyno. Adams.

John d'Fries to Robert Palk, Esqr. 1774, February 6th, Fort St. George. (Duplicate).

The Tenively business don't go on well. The Renter at first said he had no Star pagodas. When we agreed to take Porto Novos he would not pay, he said, on Captain Cooke's receipt, but must have mine, as the Tanaka runs in my name. I sent Captain Cooke my receipts for the first three payments. When he presented them to the Renter, he said he had no pagodas, but offered to pay in chacram or fanams. These fanams anywhere out of that country is not worth three quarters of the money, and to exchange them there in Porto Novo pagodas or Bombay rupees would take up a very long time. I applied to Buckunjee's House, and offered them to discount five per cent, if they would give me bills. They said they had thirty thousand of those fanams lying there to be exchanged. I considered, however, if I refused taking the fanams it might furnish the Nabob with a pretext to say that I refused, for the sake of a trifle, taking the money when offered ; and the Nabob sending to tell me he would make good the difference, I wrote away to Captain Cooke to receive even the fanams.

I assure you. Sir, I do every thing in my power, but you are too sensible that

it is an affair that requires influence, and I am but a private person.
John d'Fries.

Mudoo Kistna to Robert Palk, Esqr. 1774, February 12th, Fort St. George.

The Nabob resides at Chepauck as usual ; and as he had long design upon Tan j ore, marched his troops jointly with the English forces against it in the beginning of August, and took that Fort and the country on the 19th of September last. The Rajah and his ministers were made prisoners and their effects seized, and they still remain confined in the Fort. The Nabob has placed his own garrison in the said Fort : none of the Company's troops are there. The Company's garrison only remains in the Vellum Fort as usual. The Dutch raised some disputes about certain districts of the Ton j ore country, which at length were settled between them and the Nabob, who has an entire possession and sole management of the Tonjore country and the Fort at present.
Narrain Raw, General of the Maratters, being murdered, his uncle Ragonada Raw succeeded in his room, and took the field with his army, and after having made up the difference which subsisted between him and Nizam Ally Cawn, crossed the river Kishna and is now steering, as it is said, towards Serah in the Balagat ; and it is talked that after he settles with Hyder he will think of marching to the Pain Gaut Carnatick to receive his Chout and to get the Tan j ore country restored to he Rajah if possible. But our Nabob is not unmindful of his own affairs, for he has employed people to negotiate with the said Ragonada Raw, but what success he will meet with none but God can tell. At present the country is very much alarmed of the Marattas.

Kistna.

Robert Palk, jun., to Robert Palk, Esqr., London. 1774, February 23rd,

Patna.

I have unfavourable accounts of our remittance by way of China. Mr. Price could not sell the opium at a profit owing to its poor quality. I shall be lucky if I recover the principal from him. The cost of insurance will fall on me, you and the Adams sisters, unless you think I ought to bear it all. Price ought to pay the insurance, but his affairs are much involved. At the outset I was unwilling to engage with him, but I was overruled by George Vansittart. He and I stand to lose Rs. 36,000. We began a lawsuit, but George has relinquished his claim on Price owing to the latter's misfortunes, and wants me to do likewise. I do not now know of any good method of remitting to England. Unless you can procure money by bills on me, I must send home gold mohurs.
It is reported that the Marrattas have settled all their own disputes, and are now about to take the field ; that a body is to march for Delly and another for Arcot. We are under no apprehension of them this way. Shuja Dowla is fighting with the Jauts, and is now before the fort of Agra, and so is Nudjuff Cawn with the King's troops, but they cannot take it. Shuja has applied for one of our brigades to assist him, and it is now near Banaras marching up. Whether the Governor and Council will permit our troops to march beyond Shuja Dowla's dominions I can't say, but I fancy it's his wish that they shall be employed to reduce all that country.
I believe I have not mentioned some views of Patna and Dinapore cantonments taken by a black man, which I left in Calcutta to be sent you. They are pretty well done. Miss Van was to send them to you by Captain Skottowe

Robert Palk.
P.S. I've just heard that Agra was to be given up to Nudjuff Cawn for the King about the 28th of this month. R.P.

Robert Palk, jun., to Robert Palk, Esqr. 1774, March 11th, Patna.

I enclose for your information copies of correspondence between George Vansittart and myself about the scheme of remittance by way of China. I consider that Mr. Price has not behaved well in the matter. George writes me the Council are going to pay off all the Company's bonds granted before 1769, and that in future no more than 5 per cent, interest will be allowed on borrowed money. Every charge in the Civil department is decreased to the utmost : they are now beginning with the Military. A saving of some lacks is talked of only in the article of lascars stationed with the artillery and at subordinate Factories. A post is to be established all over the country the first of next month, that is to say, from that time all persons are to pay at the rate of 2 annas per hundred miles for a single letter. Hitherto the Dawks have been an annual charge of above 2 lacks of rupees to the Company. It is now expected that the Company will gain by them. At this rate I imagine in 2 or 3 years the whole of the Company's debt in Bengal may be cleared from the savings made during Mr. Hastings's government.

I hear the Marattas have given some alarm at Madras, although they have not entered the Carnatic, nor perhaps intend to. Nothing has been done above since the taking of Agra. Our troops are marching on towards Shuja's frontiers, and it's imagined will be quartered there till the rains. The settlement Mr. H. has made with Shuja Doula for paying the Company's troops when in his country doth not meet with the approbation of people in general. It is called hiring the troops to the country Powers.

Robert Palk

XL
Palk briefs the Nabob, 1774

Robert Palk had always seen the advantage of keeping the Nabob fully briefed about the changing personnel expected to be appointed in Bengal. Also Palk treasures his personal frienship with the Nabob. There follows correspondence initiated by Stephen Sulivan who has no money and hopes to obtain a loan. The circumstances leading up to this unhappy state are recounted in the book *Guardian of the East India Company: The Life of Laurence Sulivan by George K. McGilvary*

Robert Palk to H.H. the Nawab of the Carnatic. N.D. [1774, cir. March.]

To his Highness the Nabob of the Carnateck
Mr. Palk always most fervently wishes an increase of glory and happiness. The gentlemen who are to join Mr. Hastings at Bengal and compose the new Government there now proceed on their voyage, and propose to pay their compliments to your Highness on their way. They come with the best intentions to give their best assistance for preserving peace and prosperity over all India, and from them you will learn the state of affairs in Europe and who is most likely to receive the Government from Mr. Wynch. I hope and believe it will be an appointment to your satisfaction. Colonel Charles Campbel is endeavouring to return to the command of the troops, and as I find he will be very agreeable to you, he shall have all the assistance in my power. General Lawrence joins me to make you his most grateful acknowlegments and, though his memory in other matters begins to fail him, he shall never forget your singular kindness to him. I still endeavor to keep up his spirits and make his life comfortable as formerly, and we often recount the many happy days we have passed with your Highness in the field, in garrison and at the Mount.

Stephen Sulivan to Robert Palk, Esqr., Park Place, St. James's. 1774, April 3rd, 11, Paper Buildings, Temple.

Dear Sir,
Ever since I last troubled you for money my father's circumstances (no secret I dare say to you) barely enable him to supply me with what is necessary. I am sure that I as a son cannot feel more than you as a friend. You have uniformly continued your regard to him, and as for me, you have laid me under the greatest of all obligations. I protest to you, Mr. Palk, that I have no other resource but in your generosity, and therefore I venture to request two or three hundred pounds if you can possibly spare it. The tide is against my poor father in every thing. I see not even a glimmering of chance at the election, and my own prospects here are so gloomy that the East must be my lot, let me go out how I will. I only wish for an opportunity to convince you of my honor and gratitude ; but till that opportunity offers, accept, I entreat, the sincerest sentiments of affection and esteem from, dear Sir, your most faithful and obliged servant,

Stephen Sulivan.
P.S. I earnestly beg an answer from you tomorrow morning.

Stephen Sulivan to Robert Palk, Esqr., Park Place. N.D. [1774, April.]

My dear Sir,
After my last letter it looks importunate to write any more ; but as I have only one guinea, if you could possibly procure me the money and send it me some time this day, you will essentially oblige your ever affectionate

Stephen Sulivan.
P.S. If my servant should happen to be out, your servant can drop the letter, and it will be very safe.

Stephen Sulivan to Robert Palk, Esqr., Park Place. [1774, April.] Wednesday evening. Paper Buildings, Temple.

Dear Sir,
I am infinitely obliged to you for your kind letter, and though I can with truth say I would not have troubled you if a real necessity had not constrained me, I must and ought to wait till it perfectly suits you. When it does, I have not a doubt but you will obligingly keep me in your remembrance. I am happy always to wait on you, and I think myself fortunate in your friendship, which I shall endeavour through life to retain ; but tomorrow I am forced to be out very early to do all that is in my power by solliciting at the door of every Proprietor. The very first leisure moment I can find I will dedicate to you, to thank you for those constant and steady proofs of regard with which you have always distinguished, dear Sir, your most affectionate friend and servant,

Stephen Sulivan

Robert Palk to Laurence Sulivan, Esqr., M.P., Queen Square, Ormond Street. 1774, September 21st, Haldon House.

My dear Sir,
I have your favor of the 15th. Sir George is very good in making me the kind offer of a Grenada security, but as I cannot wait six years for the money, it will not suit me. He has used me very unhandsomely. The Stock which I lent to him and Mr. Motteux,was bought for the purpose and was to have been returned in May 1772. But when Mr. Boehm demanded it, you desired it might remain sometime longer ; so that on the latter I lost 75 per cent., and on Sir George's I find I am in danger of los- ing the whole. At his desire it was transferred the 8th October, 1771, to 4 names, and I was charged with the transfers. It was to have been delivered back the May following ; but antecedent to that, on the 11th April, 1772, it was transferred into one name and sold off, he, who was in the secret, knowing when to sell for his own advantage what did not belong to him ; and to make amends he gives me an Allum security of

£3,000 for what he disposed of to his own advantage at about £4,400. This is the true state of the case. I never asked Sir George but one favour, my nephew's reinstatement, and you know how much I was hurt upon that occasion.

I hope, however, the Allum security is ample and sufficient. Mr. Smith told me it was worth double the sum it stood for, and if Mr. Purling's and Boyd's assignments are discharged from it, I suppose it is still better. Sir George indeed wrote me at that time that this security was given us out of kindness, because our demands would certainly be liquidated in a 12 month ; and I still hope that we shall have a good prospect of receiving our ballances.

I am ever, my dear Sir, yours most affectionately,

Robert Palk

Nawab Walajah to Robert Palk, Esqr. 1774, September 24th, Chepauck House, near Madras.

His Highness Nawab Waulaujah, Ummeer ul Hind, Omdaht ul Mulk, Ausuph ud Dowla, Anwar ul dee[n] Cawn Bahauder, Munsoor Jimg, Sepoy Salaar, Subadar of Arcot and the Carnatick, to Robert Palk, Esqr.

I have already written to you many friendly letters, and have been much rejoiced to hear you are happy, as you are my old friend. I have heretofore made some representations to the Gentlemen in England, but as I have not hitherto learnt that anything has been done to give me satisfaction, I have sent Colonel Macleane and Mr. James Johnson to England. From them all matters may be fully understood. Your friendship for me is of long standing, and I am always thankful for it. I hope the favor of your assistance will not be wanting to settle my affairs, and my obligations will be encreased.

What can I say more ?

XLI
Robert Palk MP, 1774 - 1775

This is a very sad year for Robert Palk. Just as he is settled into his country house with his family about him he loses his lifelong friend Stringer Lawrence on 10 January 1775. Not much correspondence exists about this in Palk's archive. The Laurence Sulivan financial problem continues:

Laurence Sulivan to Robert Palk, Esqr., Haldon House. 1774, September 30th, Queen Square.

My dear Friend,
By the time this reaches you we are no longer Members of Parliament, for I am this moment assured, indeed I know it, that a proclamation for its dissolution comes out to morrow and orders are issued to the Post Office to stop franking on Monday.However convenient it may be to me to have a seat in the next Parliament, I cannot bear the thought of keeping you from Ashburton, and therefore beg that you will instantly secure yourself there. And pray assure our friends the freeholders that I shall ever retain a grateful remembrance of their generous attachment, and that if ever I have power again to oblige individuals, I shall consider my self as much belonging to them as if I was still their Member, and I request Mr. Dunning, senr., the Winsors, Mr. Abraham and Mr. Tripe may in particular know these my sentiments.
I am ever, my dear Sir, your most affectionate and obedient servant

Lau. Sulivan.

James Hodges to Robert Palk, Esqr., St. James's Place, London. 1775, July 4th, Fort St. George.

Since I last wrote to you in 1772, I have been obliged through illness to make a second voyage to China. I returned cured, and my health for the last eighteen months has been better than at any time during the past five years. The interest of my bond shall be duly discharged, but I am not yet able to refund the principal. I have lately been nominated to a seat in the Council at Masulipatam, where I hope to be able to repay to your nephew some of the many kindnesses I have received from you.

James Hodges.

John d'Fries to Robert Palk, Esqr. 1775, July 4th, Madras.

We have now only the amount of the ruby ring and the house to receive from the Nabob, which I make no doubt, if the country continues peaceable, we shall be able to do in the limited time, having obtained Tuncaws for the whole of the amount on the Wongole country, which from its nearness is a convenient assignment
We shall remit through Mr. George Vansittart. The amount due by Mr. George Smith to the estate of Mr. Vansittart is about £400.
Mrs. Vansittart's character is vastly raised by her sufferings. Her misfortune has rendered her mind great. I hope she will hereafter enjoy the satisfaction of seeing her children imitating their virtuous parents. Harry is very promising. Mrs. Parry is happy in her marriage.
Bengal is over run with informers' accusations against each other. Joe Fowke stands foremost in this honorable list. Nuncomar was to be tried for perjury and forgery. The sessions at Calcutta begun the 3rd of last month. Our last advices from there is of the 12th. They continued setting still and were upon Nuncomar's cause. A treaty was concluded.
The Gentlemen of Bombay entered in a war with the Morattas for the conquest of Salsett. They are joined by Ragopah, and have to contend with the Ministerial Party, who, by having the treasure and the army for them, have all the power, and our army has met with a considerable loss in an engagement with the enemy in Cambay.
Here, a great division in Council. The majority in bad terms with the Nabob. It was a great oversight the suffering the Nabob to garrison Tan j ore, and may be productive of disagreeable altercations. Already, I am

told, there have been many warm and many illiberal minutes entered on record. The minority is General Smith, Messrs. Johnson and Stone.

John d'Fries

Colonel Robert Gordon to Robert Palk, Esqr. 1775, September 10th, Bombay.

It gave me much pleasure to receive a letter, dated 7th March, from so valued a friend as yourself.
Mr. Edmund Veale Lane, whom you mention, is a young gentleman that I greatly esteem. He served lately with me as Judge Advocat at the siege and reduction of Tannah in Salsett, on which event that island, contiguous to Bombay, was annexed to the Company's revenues and may be supposed in peaceable times to produce about five lacks of rupees. Mr. Lane is now of the Council at Tannah. By being in the civil department it does not lie in my way to be of much service to him, as you well know ; but if ever it should, I shall be happy to do him every good office in my power. I am happy to hear my old friends Charles Brett and Mac are alive and well. Pray remember me to them and to Colonel John Campbell, whose acquaintance I seem to have entirely lossed, though I do not know how or from what cause, as I do believe our mutual regard and friendship was for many years sincere, and on my side ever has contin- ued the same. Mr. Facey, now a Lieutennant, is at present on duty at Tellicherry, which Settlement, it's said, will soon be reduced from a Chiefship to that of a Residency.

Robert Gordon
P.S. Our Board have lately, and I think contrary to every rule of military service, employed Lieut. Colonel Keating, Chief Engineer and Commanding Officer of Artillery, to command an army as auxiliaries to the side they have taken, vizt. that of Ragaboy, who murdered his nephew, in the present internal disputes among the Maharrattas. This Ragaboy was in possession of the government for sometime after the murder, but it so happened that his nephew's widow was brought to bed

of a posthumous son, whose interest the ministry support, and are possessed of all the country and the revenues. After being four months in the field and nothing done of the smallest importance to the general cause, the ministry very artfully applyed to the Supreme Council and obtained their ex- press orders for a cessation of arms ; and they have sent Lieut. Colonel Upton from Bengali to Poonah as their Ambassador with full powers to accommodat[e] all differences.
From a difference with our Board regarding the meaning of the last instructions of 29th March, 1774, and alluding to a Lieut. Colonel left in the command of Tannah Fort, his not receiving the parole from a Resident, and a very extraordinary letter I received from the Board in consequence, I had then resigned the service when a convenient oppertunity offered for England or by the way of China. Soon after which time the Board took a part in the Maharratta war, and therefore nominated Lieut. Colonel Keating, which I repeatedly opposed, and afterwards offered my service ; but they chose to adhere to their nomination, which I do believe they have since repented, our President and Council having signified their wishes that I should continue in the command till the cause of our differences should be determined by the Court of Directors, to whom they are referred ; which proposal, as an approbation of my passed services, I reddily accepted of.

Chocapah to the Honble Robert Palk, Esqr. 1775, October 10th, Fort St. George.

Since I addressed you by the *Swallow*, man-of-war, on the 2nd July, I have learned with satisfaction that Lord Pigot is coming out on the Greenwille for the Government of Madrass, which gives all the inhabitants, merchants and people in these parts much pleasure and joy, as they lived very happy in his Lordship's Government formerly by his defending Madrass and distressing the French at Pondichery.
We hear that our Government at Bombay and the Marattys are in cessation of arms, and the Gentlemen of the Supreme Council at Bengali sent an English gentleman as Ambasidor to Ponnah to settle the matters with the Marattys, and to settle the difference of their family disputes ; and if

that affair is once settled by our Ambasidor, the Marattys will always be our friends, and we shall have none of their troubles in these parts any more.
Four merchant ships have arrived at Pondicherry from France, bringing goods consigned to MM. Law and Moragin and some warlike stores. Work on the fortifications there goes on.
Mr. Dowsett was obliged to go away from this place to Pondichery about two years ago on account of his creditors, and from thence went to France. Now he came back upon one of these ships arrived lately at Pondichery.
Mr. Monckton's ship has returned from Manila with dollars for the owners and "for the Arminion and Black Merchants of this place," but the goods did not sell well.
Mr. Hastings and the Gentlemen of the Supreme Council, they say, do not agree with one another, and they say both of them are waiting for answers from England about their disputes.
General Smith and Governor Wynch are preparing for their homeward passage.
Mr. Wynch has been very kind and civil to every one in the place. [He] made a good Governour to all the inhabitants and people of these parts.

Chocapah

George Baker to Robert Palk, Esqr. 1775, October 13th, Fort St. George.

In a separate letter I have dealt with the affairs of your deceased kinsmen Thomas and John Palk. Those of Major Madge, I learn, you have committed to his father and family. I congratulate you on the increase to your own family.
I should be glad to give you some account of publick affairs here, but my knowledge in this respect is very confined, though on the whole I think I may say that the Board do not draw well together. The late disputes about the Nabob's sending his second son as Fousdar to Tan j ore gave birth to party and resentment, perhaps to rancour, which has not yet subsided, nor is it like to in the present reign. The expectation of Lord Pigot's speedy

arrival has by no means increased the respect that was paid to the present Governor. He has in general a party of Brooke, Dawson, Palmer and Jourdan, but not always a majority. Mr. Stratton is very lately arrived here from his Chiefship of Vizagapatam, and a few days since resigned it. Dawson and Johnson were the best supported candidates, but the latter carried it for the Chiefship. Brooke sollicited, but had no support. He was told by some that he had had his chance at Masulipatam.
The ramparts of the West front of the town and the faceing thereof are up to the cordong, and bombproof casements all round compleated. The dry dytch and cunette are also in a good degree of forwardness, but the covered way and glacis not far advanced. The ramparts are indeed very substantial, but some cracks in the faceing have already made their appearance, and have very lately been mended without any publick notice taken of it, and plaistered over. The East lire is contracted for by Mr. Binfield, and the foundation to the S.E. was just begun on, but left off again till after the monsoon.
Mr. Stratton has tryed by every means he could to prevail on Mr. Wynch to go on the Nottingham and leave him in possession of the Chair untill Lord Pigot's arrival, but to no purpose. Mr. Wynche's friends prevailed on him to continue, as not knowing what may happen to prevent Lord Pigot's speedy arrival.
Affairs in Bengal you will hear of from your friends there. Our latest news from Bombay was that the Mahrattas and our Gentlemen there had agreed on a cessation of arms; and the Supreme Council at Bengali haveing sent a Colonel Lupton from there over land to Poonah with full powers to treat on a peace, it is supposed that good work will be efected. the General and Colonel Bonjour come home on the *Colebrooke*, which with the *Nottingham*, it is said, will certainly sail on the 15th instant. And on that day also Sir Edward Hughes in the *Salisbury*, together with the *Coventry* and *Sea Horse*, sail for the Mallabar coast. Sir John Clark in the Dolphin sailed in March last from Bengali with a quantity of the Company's opium for Balambungan, since which it has been reported, but without any certain foundation, that settlement is cut off.
Your nephew Mr. Palk at Bengali has been ill of a fever, but is well recovered again. Mr. Thomas Palk at Masulipatam s well a few days since. The Salisbury, man-of-war, was very lately there for some of the

Company's bales, which gave your two nephews, Messrs. T. Palk and R. Welland, an opportunity to see each other. Master Welland is very well, but as he has not been on shore since they came from Masuhpatam, I have not seen him lately. For the Commadore pays close attention to the manner in which all his young gentlemen spend their time, and lets them come on shore when he thinks proper, and then only.

As to myself and my affairs, they remain as they were ; and I confess that I am glad we are to have Lord Pigot or any other new Governor, since, be who it will, he may he less partial — more so than the present he cannot help.

I have in fact been much hampered in my work, and unless matters are placed on a better footing I may have to seek redress in England.

The grand point I have had in view throughout life has been peace and quiet at the eve of it. I will still keep to my own maxim, and procure it if I can at any rate. This I hope you and yours now do, and may long, very long in joy in the most ample degree.

George Baker

George Baker to Robert Palk, Esqr, 1775, December 14th, Fort St. George.

This acknowledges the receipt of your favor of the 12th of April last per Granvil. That ship anchored here about sunset on the 9th instant, Lord Pigot, Messrs. Russel, Dalrymple, Crawfurd, &c., all well. His Lordship, &c., landed the next morning between eight and nine o'clock in the midst of a vast croud of people. Governor Wynch and Council, the Nabob and his family all met him at the seaside and accompanyed him to the Council Room, which was filled with a croud of people. After about a quarter of an hour's stay there, Lord Pigot and the Nabob withdrew to the Admiralty, where they had about half an hour's conversation, when the Nabob retired to Chaupauk and his Lordship returned to the Council Room in the Fort Square. Here his commission was read and the usual compliments paid him. This done, the troops were drawn up on the parade and his commission read again, when he was saluted with three volleys of small arms and nineteen guns from the saluting battery. The late and present Governor, together with the Council, &c., now retired to the Admiralty, where the keys were delivered to Lord Pigot and all the formallityes of his introduction to the Government compleated, and the late and present Governor and Council all dined together both that day and the next, which was a Military Council day and the first of the present Government. But Mr. Wynch never assisted on any publick service after Lord Pigot's landing, though orders have been given to show him the usual publick marks of respect. He lives at the Gardens, where Lord Pigot has hitherto generally breakfasted, though he sleeps in the Fort Square and the young ladyes and the rest of the family live at the Admi- ralty. The day after his Lordship landed he returned the Nabob's visit and passed about an hour and half with him. No extraordinary news of what may be intended to do with respect to the Tan j ore business has yet tran- spired here, though people seem inclined to think that something new may happen.

I have paid my respects to Lord Pigot and Messrs. Russel and Dalrymple. They received me very civilly, but I have not yet had an opportunity to speak to either of them about my business.

I will make further enquiries about poor Goodlad's affairs, but full accounts were sent to England last June. This letter goes by the *Salisbury*, Indiaman, Captain Bromfield, which called here yesterday on her way from Bengal. We hear Sir Edward Hughes arrived at Anjengo on the 18th November.

By letters of the 1st November from Bombay Colonel Lupton,the Envoy from Bengali, was arrived in the neighbourhood of Poonah. Our army was, it is said, advancing from the north nearer to the Maharatah capital, and the Government of Bombay had directed the Chief of Anjengo to advise the trade from Bengali, China, &c., to proceed so high as Tellicherry without fear, but not to run the risk of proceeding further till they sent them convoy. This looks as though all apprehensions of danger from the Maratahs was not yet over.

Our Nabob having desired and obtained the permission of the General Council at Bengali to send Mr. Chambers, a gentleman who has made a great progress in the Persian and other languages, to Poonah as his Embassador, he is to set out on that service in a few days.

Bazzallyzung haveing got together a number of French and other

Europeans, induced our Gentlemen to send Captain Edmonds with about a hundred Europeans to Ongole to be ready to joyn the troops at Ellore if occation should require it, but they have hitherto remained quiet. This chief haveing lately laid siege to the capital of some neighbouring little state, the besieged applyed to Hyderally for assistance. He immediately, and as privately as possible, sent his son Tippa Saib with a large party of horse to the relief of the place, and came upon the besiegers so very unexpectedly and attacked them so vigorously as to cut off a great number of them, and among the rest a great part of Bazzallyzung's Europeans, which has for the present abated our apprehentions of his designs. About ten days since we received certain (though neither publick or particular) accounts that Ballambangan had been taken by the people of Solo. It was a private letter from a Mr. Coles of Council there. He exclaims much against the conduct of Mr. Herbert, both as to his management before and at the attack of the place, for I cannot call it defence. It seems they neither made or endeavored to make any. Looseing gamesters always complain, and Mr. Herbert in his turn may perhaps have as much to say against his colleague in Council. But be this as it may, the Company, it seems, loose two hundred thousand pounds sterling in goods, &c., by it. As they took to their vessels as soon as they could, I don't find that many, or perhaps any, lives were lost on the occation. They are now at a place on the N.W. part of the Island of Borneo which they call Borneo proper, and from whence we expect publick advices from them every day.

Messrs. Stratton, Dawson and Brooke all talk of leaving for England shortly. Mr. Thomas Palk at Masulipatam was well when I last heard from him.

The good old General ! My heart warms as the idea of him comes to my recollection, but I cannot say I lament him. He lived to a fulness of days and glory, and what could vanity itself wish more ?

George Baker.

P.S. Lord Pigot is just returned from a visit to the Nabob in a rich palankin, which he has presented to him.

Major James Rennell to Robert Palk, Esqr., at Haldon House. 1776, January 2nd, Bengali.

Forgive my failure to reply earlier to your letter of March last.
I am aware of the inconveniencies and folly of returning to England without a competency. I thank God Mrs. Rennel and myself look no far ther than for the mere conveniencies of life ; so that what would be a trifling pittance to many will be affluence to us. Mrs. Rennell joins me in best wishes to yourself and Mrs. Palk. We have had the misfortune to lose our little girl, our only child; but I hope God Almighty will in good time give us another.

J. Rennell

Lieut. J. Snelling to Robert Palk, Esqr., Halldon House. 1776, January 4th, Sick Quarters, Vizagapatam.

My ever honoured and esteemed Patron,
Sick as I am at present, gratitude for the numberles[s] favors I have received obliges me to let you hear how I go on and where I am stationed.
I wrote last from Aska, whence I was transferred to Captain Mathews's battalion at Chicacole. This was for me a fortunate event, for Captain Mathews, whome I have the pleasure of informing you is my very generous and sincere friend, is esteemed by everybody to be the most warlike genius in India, and the most enterprizing man that ever drew sword in this part of the country.
Since he took command of the Chicacole battalion he has not only conquered countries before unconquerable, but even with one battalion

exe- cuted greater undertakings than his predecessors durst attempt even with thrice his number of men and some companies of Europeans besides.
What a pleasure and satisfaction it is for a young fellow like myself to be under a man so renowned for every particular of the military art ! Not long ago I was on detachment amongst those hills so famous for their fatality to European constitutions. I got a most severe fever and ague, which had very near ended my life ; and though I have been for six weeks under the doctor's hands, am not as yet perfectly recovered. My friends persuade me to leave northern climes and try those more healthy ones to the southward, but what signifies my going to a place where, with the strictest o[e]conomy I should find it difficult to live on my pay, and probably, from the number of pleasures to be met with there, such as plays, horseracing, cockfighting, in short almost all those expensive amusements you have in England, might be drawn on to live at greater expence than my income can afford ? I can live here very genteelly on my means, and as I shall probably never more visit England, will make every thing as agreable to myself as possible. Nothing but an extraordinary gust of fortune can ever procure a soldier one in these iron days, and to be dependant at home will not agree with my constitution ; consequently I shall never leave India.

Chocapah to the Honble. Robert Palk, Esqr. 1776, February 2nd, Fort St. George.

I hear that the Government of England and the East India Company has given positive orders to Lord Pigot to take Tan j ore and the country belonging thereunto from the Nabob, and to put the same in the King of Ton j ore's possession, where the Company's troops are to be placed, and the King to disburse the charges of the troops. The Nabob at first seemed unwilling, and told the Governour and Council to do herein as they think proper ; but at last his Lordship and the Gentlemen in Council, I hear, are determined, and orders is sent to Trichinopoly for the regiment there to be in readiness to march.
Mr. Macpherson, came here as purser to Captain Macleod in 1767 made

great interest with the Nabob, promising to get some great men in his Majesty's Court in England to his interest, as also that he will come out to India as a covenanted servant to the Company. The said Mr. Macpherson, I hear, when he came out as a Company's Writer, contracted great friendship with the Nabob, and gives him all the intelligence he possibly can of what passes amongst the Gentlemen here. And since the present circumstances commenced between his Lordship, &c., and the Nabob, he was found frequent[ly] going [to] the Nabob in an unseasonable hour, that is, at eleven or twelve at night ; and [a] few days ago he, together with Mr. Stuart that came from Bengali to go from hence, went to the Nabob at about 12 at night. This behavior of Mr. Macpherson coming to the knowledge of the Governour and Council, they thought proper to suspend him the Company's service.
I hear that Mr. Sadleir, Resident at Bandermulunka, behaved very ill to the inhabitants and merchants there, taking their vessels at freight against their will to load them with his goods and merchandise, beating and ill treating several people, taking bribes and extorting money from several people. Some of them, I hear, complained of it to the Governour and Council, upon which the Board was pleased to appoint Mr. Holland, Mr. Perring and Mr. Davidson as [a] committee to examine into this matter. They are now examining this affair at Masulipatam.
Several gentlemen in the place, for want of a way of remitting their fortune to England by bills, sends it in gold and Star pagodas on every ship that goes from hence, which impoverish[es] the place very much.
I hear that the Malays has taken Ballumbungam, and our Gentlemen who were there quitted the place and went to another Malay island. The Company on this occasion, I hear, will sustain a loss of about four hundred thousand pounds on that island. I hear this is all owing to the bad proceeding of our Gentlemen there.

Chocapah

Thomas Palk to Robert Palk, Esqr. 1776, February 8th, Mazulipatam.

Not having received a single letter from you during the past two years, I fear that you must be displeased with me. Were your silence dueto the reports of malicious persons, you would doubtless have given me an opportunity of replying to their charges ; so that I know not to what cause to attribute your displeasure. I owe much to you, and I assure you that my conduct has always been such as you would approve. I have been at this station nearly three years, but my position docs not yet enable me to dispense with the allowance you are pleased to make me. I refer you to Mr. Whitehill, who has resigned the Chiefship and is now going home, for information regarding me. From him I have received many civilities. The Nabob is dispossessed of his newly acquired territory, and our troops are marching to take possession — a severe stroke on the Nabob, and he seems to be sensibly affected. India at present is in a state of tranquility, and likely to continue so if the French do not take it into their heads to disturb us.

Thos. Palk.

Mrs. Mary Turing to Robert Palk, Esqr, 1776, February 10th, Fort St. George. Received 17th Feb., 1777.

I have asked my son to wait on you with this letter. Though I have not received any direct communication from Mrs. Palk, I have had news of her and your family from my friend Mrs. Casamaijor.
My two daughters arrived here in June, 1773, and in August following were both happily married, the eldest to Mr. John Turing, and the youngest to Mr. Saunders. They both made me a grandmother. My eldest son, Taylor, is an officer in the Company's service, so Bob is now my only care. My wish is to get him appointed a Writer in the service at Madras, for which I must solicit and rely upon the interest of my friends. You have upon all occasions shewn a regard for me and my family, which emboldens me to request your assistance towards my son.

Mary Turing

XLII
The Lord Pigot administration, 1776

John d'Fries to Robert Palk, Esqr. 1776, February 12th, Madras.

Mr. George Vansittart is here in his way to Old England on the *Hillsborough*. To him I shall beg leave to refer you for all particulars of India news, confining myself entirely to the subject of our Nabob, who, poor man, has been greatly affected with the Company's orders regarding Tan j ore. Lord Pigot has behaved with a great deal of management and indulgence towards the Nabob in the execution of the orders, and he is himself perswaded of his Lordship's favorable disposition towards him. The English troops were to enter Tan j ore the 9th instant : it is said a part of the Nabob's people are to continue in the Fort. The Nabob agrees Rajah, a proper maintenance to him, a handsome Jaghire for the Company ; I daresay he will give up all the seaports, Nagore, Trimelivashel ; — in short, he will do every thing to save appearances, that the countrey be not wrested out of his hands, which undoubtedly must make him look very little in the eyes of his own people as well as the other countrey powers. His best friends have advised him to submit chearfully to the Company's orders, and then remonstrate to Europe. It has cost him a great deal to bring himself to this way of thinking, which his good sense has at last determined him to. It has certainly been a bitter cup to him, and he has found it out when late that his new friends have been the principal cause of the mortification which he now suffers.
He has great confidence in your friendship and of Mr. Vansittart's family, and tells me he has wrote to you and sent copys of some papers which will inform you of what past in this business. His request is so reasonable now that I dare say you and his other friends will afford him assistance in having him redressed. As it is not sound policy that he should be lifted up too much, I don't think it prudent neither that he should be too much

lowered, as it certainly is the case in this business. The Nabob declares that this business of the conquest of Tan j ore has cost him in the two expeditions three millions of sterling, near three crores of rupees ; and although he has had the revenues of the country for two years, he has been obliged to maintain so considerable a military force that it has, I think, taken off above one third of it ; so that if the country is taken away from him entirely, he must be a great looser by his bargain.
The unlucky turn that the American business has taken has filled us with mtich serious reflection. We anxiously wait to hear from England. God send that matters may have been made up.

John d'Fries

George Baker to Robert Palk, Esqr. 1776, February 23rd, Fort St. George.

The *Hillshorough*, with Mr. and Mrs. Vansittart on board, was dispatched hence for Europe the 16th instant, but on account of light or unfavorable winds she did not get out of sight till the 20th. This letter comes by Captain Pegou, late of the *Huntingdon*. He with Mr. Whitehill and John Sulivan go passengers in the old *Ajax*, now a French Indiaman. A Mrs. Draper of Bombay (who is a niece of Mr. Whitehill's) accompanyes them. They all set out for Pondichery tomorrow.
We have now a garrison in Tan j our. The King is said to be at large ; but what the terms are on which the Nabob made the surrender, or on which the King has been restored, I am utterly ignorant. The transactions of the Board are kept abundantly more secret than they were in the former reign. The Board has struck off all the half batta from the garrisons which had that emolument heretofore, save only that of the commanding officer. You will readyly suppose this will not be considered as a popular act by the army.
Crauford is now in charge at Masulipatam, but the appointment of Chief will probably go ultimately to Russell, though the latter is at present one of the Committee of Circuit.

Robert Palk, jun., to Robert Palk, Esqr. 1776, March 21st, Calcutta.

Received 28th October.

I received your favor of the 9th April. It had been so well ducked in the salt water that it was with great difficulty I could make it out. The packet was dispatched from Madras on a country vessel which was lost near Annoar together with the greatest part of her cargo.
Tom, I believe, can give the best account of himself. He has lately taken me in to pay a debt of 2,000 Rs. for him to Mr. Whynch, money it seems he borrowed of Mr. W. on the footing of an allowance from you, which he was called on to repay ; and rather than plead inability, he chose to draw the money from me by representing that he had incurred several small debts to that amount at Madras for necessarys which he could not do without, &c. I paid the money, but I must confess, had I known the real state of the case, I should have told him that Mr. Whynch was better able to wait his time of payment than myself. I am informed that Mr. Russell is appointed to Masulupatam. In that case I will request he will take Mr. Thomas under his protection and employ his time well. I believe Whitehill and Sulivan were as well please[d] to let him live in idleness.
I am writing with aching bones. Harry and I got overset in a ditch last night returning from town in the midst of a violent storm.

Robert Palk

Sir Edward Hughes to Robert Palk, Esqr. 1776, March 22nd, Bombay.

I received your letter of the 11th April by the ship *Grenville*, which brought Lord Pigot to Madras, and am surprised you had had no letters from me.
Though I sailed from Madras four days before the arrival of the Supreme Council and Judges, I waited in the mouth of the river and never sett my foot on shore till I did so with them at Calcutta. They were well pleased with us, and have continued so ; I wish I could say as much among themselves. Indeed I have had that good fortune at all the Company's Settlements, making their welfare my great object.
The climate agrees perfectly with me. I go early to bed, rise the same,

and very seldom chevaux [sic]. I am told Lord Pigot brings regulations respecting Tan j our, but am afraid not very pleasing to the poor Nabob, who certainly merits every attention from the English, being in my opinion their most sincere friend in this country. Nor has Colonel Upton been able to procure one article for him in his late negociation with the Mharattas. You will hear much said of this Treaty ; that Ragobah has been able to get little security and no share in the government : in short, the Presidency of Bombay made a treaty with him to support his attempt, which that of Fort William disapproved and sent a deputy to make peace, which was concluded and signed at Poonah the 1st of this instant. What they look upon [as] the view and intention of the Court of Directors [is] that, if Salsette and Bassein could not be acquired by treaty, it should not be by force. Yet the presence of the squadron has had its use at this juncture. Docked and refitted, I shall return next month to Madras. Here I must tell you your nephew is perfectly well, a fine lad and will make a very clever man in our profession. He wants for nothing ; has just paid me a week's visit on shore. The demands of so very few ships are so trifling I cannot serve you as you desire, or be assured I would do it. I hear Mr. Vansittart and family are gone home : he was very busy when I was in Bengal.

Edwd. Hughes.

H.H. the Nawab Walajah to Robert Palk, Esqr. 1776, June 20th, Chepauk. His Highness the Nabob Wallaujau, Ummeer ul Hindh, Omdaht ul Mulk, Ausuph ud Doulah, Anweer ud Deen Cawn Bahauder, Zuphur Jung, Sepah Salaur, Subahdar of the Carnatick, to Robert Palk, Esqr.

I have received your friendly letter of the 17th November last. It arrived at a time I was under great uneasiness of mind, and gave me great comfort. I am much obliged to you for your promises to assist Colonel Macleane in my affairs. I have already acquainted you with the arrival of Lord Pigot and his bringing the Company's order in regard to Tan j ore. Though the Fort was provided with all kinds of military stores, I put it into his Lordship's hands without any difficulty, and gave no opposition

to my friends the Company, but submitted to them the state of affairs here. Every gentleman here evidently perceives that it is his Lordship's intention to distress and disgrace me, and he has seized every opportunity of injuring my affairs and of hurting my honor and authority and though I am the firmest ally to his Majesty, the Company and the nation that they have in this country, his Lordship has reduced me to a situation not to be described. The Gentlemen here as well as at Bengal have much disapproved of his Lordship's conduct. I place great dependance upon your assistance, as you are my old friend, and were you here now you would protect my honor from his Lordship's insults; and I now hope that you will explain these matters to your friends, and take measures for giving me redress. As the ship in which this goes sails immediately, I can not now write at length, but I have desired that Colonel Macleane will acquaint you fully with Lord Pigot's behaviour. Mr. Salmon, who will deliver this letter, has been an eye witness to his Lordship's proceedings. Sir Edward Hughes has acquainted me with what you wrote to him about my affairs, and I am much obhged to you for it.
What can I say more ?
P.S. The reason of his Lordship's great displeasure towards me is this : — The order which he brought here in regard to Tan j ore, to answer private views of his own, was prejudicial to the Company and the publick business ; and though I made no opposition to it, and wanted only to explain the true state of my affairs and my rights, and the prejudice that would attend my business, his Lordship endeavoured to shut up my mouth, as he thought that my representations would prevent him from pursueing his private interest ; but I have laid a true state of affairs before his Lordship, and before the Company also. What he now constantly does is with a view of destroying my honor and my rights.

John d'Fries to Robert Palk, Esqr. 1776, June 20th, Madras. Received 5th February, 1777.

I have received your favor of the 15th December, and waited on the Nabob myself with your letter, who seemed very happy at your expressions of friendship, and puts great relyance in your assistance. He has of late been in a very disagreable, nay distressful! situation. The part Lord Pigot had to act of delivering up Tan j ore naturally occasioned a dis- tance between them. Two months after his Lordship's arrival the Nabob consented to deliver up Tan j ore Fort to an English garrison : he could not be prevailed upon to go further. Lord Pigot, after trying in vain for near two months more to perswade the Nabob to surrender the countrey to the Rajah, he went down himself, being vested by the Council with the powers of a deputation for reinstating the Rajah, and he was declared Commander in Chief of all the garrisons he went through. Messrs. Dalrymple and Jourdan accompanyed his Lordship, but they were simple companions, the former doing all his business. The Rajah was accordingly reinstated on the 11th of April. The Nabob had assigned the revenues of Tan j ore proceeding from the February crop of grain to Europeans and others to the amount of, as it is currently reported, fifteen or sixteen lacks of pagodas. Mr. Benfield had the largest Tanakaw ; Mr. Monckton, George Smith, Adams, De Souza and others had also. The grain was a great part cutt and received by the Tanakawholders. However, it did not signifie : the Rajah's people, supported by our troops, possessed themselves of it.Since Lord Pigot's return there has been some division in Council, and the Majority was that the Tanakaws should be paid. The Nabob having applyed to Sir Edward Hughes for his protection, alledging that he apprehended violence from Lord Pigot, has prevented his Lordship from going to him of late. The Supreme Council has also wrote to the Governor and Council here, disapproving Lord Pigot's sending for the Dabir away by a military force from the Nabob's territorys. He was manager for the Rajah, and since for the Nabob, of the Tan j ore country, and he was ordered away to Alianore just before Lord Pigot got to Tan j ore.

These disagreements render the Settlement unhappy, and affects credit very much, and I am afraid the breach between Lord Pigot arid the Nabob is so wide that it will hardly be closed. I apprehend things were pushed rather too far. The Tanakaws was a matter of such general concern to the Settlement that it interests almost every body, and has occasioned much uneasiness. Such is our situation at present, and no doubt very different things will be wrote by the different partys. The Nabob's character will on the one side be made out as a dissipating

intriguing man aiming fast towards independence ; and his own partizans will represent him as ill treated and oppressed grandure. It is very certain that the Nabob is so very different a character now, both in his political as well as personal capacity, to what he was 14 years ago that the method of treating him then can't be any ways proper at present. A vigorous Administration can easily contain the Nabob within the proper bounds, at the same time that he should not be lowered too much in the eyes of the publick, particularly the natives. It is certain that he has not the least notion of order, regularity or economy in his finances, and if our Government could settle the revenues and expences of the Nabob on a proper reasonable footing, it will be the greatest service they could render the publick as well as the Nabob. It will be a[n] arduous as well as a very delicate undertaking : however, in my humble opinion better worth at- tempting than many things else which causes ill blood and no real advantage. Your assisting the Nabob in this time of perturbation to him will be very acceptable.
A peace was concluded with the Morattas the 1st of May.

John d'Fries.

XLIII
Chocopah Chetti tells of unfairness to the Rajah, 1776

Chocapah to the Honble. Robert Palk, Esqr. 1776, June 27th, Fort St. George.

Since mine of the 2nd February last Lord Pigot, Mr. Dalrymple, Mr. Jourdan, Captains Wood and Thomson and one or two officers and doctors, with a battalion of seapoys and fifty European cavalry, and Moodu Kistnah, &c., set out from hence the 28th of March to Tan j ore. And also his Lordship desired Chippermall Chitty, Sunca Rama Chitty and me from this place, and Irshepah Chitty and Sree Salupudy from Cuddalore to accompany him. We did accordingly, and we all, in company with his Lordship, arrived at Tan j ore the 8th April, and the ceremony at the time of the restoration of the Rajah is wrote in a seperate paper and enclosed herein. And by what I heard and saw, the poor Rajah has been treated very ill by the Nabob's people taking every thing from him, and left him in a small place in his palace, and he had only one turband and no coat to put on, or any kind of Jewells or any household furniture. They hardly left the copper potts and things commonly used in their nec- essary affairs, and also took away every kind of Jewells from the Rajah's women, and left them with black beeds on their necks, and with very few clouts and very poor allowance daily given them. He could hardly maintain his family and attendants. Several of his relations and people were kept close prisoners, and they were released after his Lordship's arrival there ; but most of the people thanked the Nabob for keeping the King so long with life. That he would not have done if it were not for his promise, when that plaee was taken by our forces, to the

Governor and Council and General Smith. All which gave much concern to his Lord- ship and the rest of the gentlemen to see the Rajah in such miserable condition as the Nabob's people treated him, and his Lordship was so gracious as to buy a pullenkeen, a horse and a dagger, and presented them to the Rajah, and afterwards remained at Ton j ore about 18 days. Comaroo, who was dubash to Mr. Hay at Trichinopoly, and after Mr. Hay went home he served Mr. Benfield and acted in the saucar business ; and I hear that he played several tricks with the Rajah and hurted the kingdom in several respects before the place was taken. And now he went, with his Lordship's leave, to Tan j ore with us, and as soon as he got there, that very same night he went to the Rajah in the middle of the night and told him: as soon as he get the country to let him have the management, and that he will advance what money he wants. His Lord- ship was informed of it, and sent for the said Comaroo. and ordered him to receive 10 or twelve lashes, and told him to go about his business.

I, in company with Chippermall Chitty and Irshepah Chitty went to see Trichinopoly, Seerangam and Jemboo Kistnah, where I heard by the English gentlemen there that the Maravars of Ramanadapurum and Shivagunga are prisoners there, with very poor allowances given to them by the Nabob's people

The Nawab received private intelligence last September of the Company's intention to restore Tan j ore.

Therefore he collected most of the revenues produced in that country as fast as he could and afterwards gave Tanaca or draft to Mr. Benfield, Mr. Monckton and several other English gentlemen for a considerable sum, upwards of twenty lacks of pagodas.

After the country was put under the Rajah's management these gentlemen that lent the above sums to the Nabob represented their case to the Board and demanded Tanaca from the Rajah, for which the Governor and Council met in council several times, and have not brought it to a conclusion yet. But once seven Gentlemen in Council were of one side, and Lord Pigot, Mr. Dawson, Mr. Russell, Mr. Dalrymple and Mr. Stone on another side, that is seven against five. The Majority gave their opinion that the Ton j ore Rajah must discharge all the Tanaca that was granted by the Nabob, and Lord Pigot and four Gentlemen in Council on the other side gave their opinion that the Rajah or the country of Tonjore had no thing to do with the Nabob's Tanaca, but the Nabob must be accountable for it. The Nabob may discharge the above Tanacas if he pleases, but he will not do it before the Company send out positive orders to him to do so. The Nabob's intention is to ruin the Rajah again, though the country was delivered up to him, but the poor Rajah has no other aid and assistance, but intirely depends on your honour's and the Company's protection.Mr. Dawson resigned the service. Mr. Monckton has married Lord Pigot's eldest daughter March last. Lord Pigot carrys on his government with much civility. There was a peace concluded between our Government of Bombay and the great Marattas, and everything settled in our favour.

Chocapah.

George Baker to Robert Palk, Esqr. 1776, August 30th, Fort St. George.

I heard from Mr. Palk at Bengali under date the third instant Colonel Monson was very ill. The Vizier's troops haveing mutinied for want of pay, and some of our officers haveing been lent him for the discipline of those troops, it is said some five or six of them suffered on the occasion. After some time had elapsed, two battalions of our sepoys had a warm skirmish, or rather a pitched action, with eight or ten battalions of the Vizier's, in which the latter were worsted and suffered a good deal. The commanding officer of our troops has been called down to Calcutta to account either for fighting against orders or without them. This must not alarm Mr. Kennaway for his sons: I have heard from them both since this happened.
The Supreme Council have concluded a Treaty with the Ministerial Party at Poonah, by which Raganout Row is precluded from any share of the government, but allowed a jaghire for his support, though he himself does not accede to the terms. Since this treaty was concluded another chief, who was supposed to be dead, has made his appearance. He is a man banished by a former faction, but now generally acknowledged as the next heir to the Poonah government. Those are the accounts from the

other coast of about the beginning of this month, by which we are also told that Mr. Hornby was then about dispatching a small packet (by the southern passage) to Suez for Europe. By this channel letters of the middle of May last arrived at Bombay on or about the 1st instant from Eng- land for Mr. Hastings, and were immediately forwarded from thence to Bengali, where they are probably ere now arrived.

At our Presidency for the last few months there has been much to do. Lord Pigot arrived here on the ninth of last December to the, in appearance, very great satisfaction of the Settlement, and certainly to the real satisfaction of a very great majority of it. By pacifick though firm and determined measures he got the Nabob to withdraw his garrison from Tan j ore, and to consent to the Company's placeing one there themselves. This was done in last February. The remaining part of that month and all March was spent in prevailing on the Nabob to give the country up to the Rajah. About the end of March or the beginning of April Lord Pigot was deputed by the Board, and set out hence to execute the Company's orders as to the restoration of the Rajah to his throne and kingdom, and which was, I think, done on or about the 9th of April. Dalrymple and Jourdan accompanyied him, but were not of the deputation. The business effected, his Lordship returned here about the end of April or the beginning of May, and made his report to the Board. This was received without any invidious remarks or publick disapprobation, but soon after the cloud began to gather.

A black man of this place, whose name is Comerah, and who was dubash to Mr. Hay while Paymaster at Trichinopoly, had in that capacity been very usefull to that gentleman in the acquisition of a very competent fortune, and in the course of the business (being, though young, very acute) had gained great knowledge and influence in the Tan j ore country. On Mr. Hay's going home, and after the capture of Tan j ore, this man was sought for by many. Mr. Benfield afforded him the largest field of action, and under the auspices of, perhaps in conjunction with, Mr. Wynch, imployed him in negociating money matters in the Tan j ore country to a vast amount ; which, together with the countenance given him by the Nabob, gave him in that country the consequence of a Basha. The Nabob, for prosecuting the siege of Tan j ore and paying the prize money after it was taken, had borrowed of Benfield six lacks and seventy thousand pagodas, for the repayment of which he had assigned the produce of certain districts of that country ; and this Comerah was im- ployed there by Benfield to collect it. When it came under consideration to send a deputation for the restoration of the Rajah, Comerah was (by his master) called down His Lordship desired him to stay till he himself went up. But as this neither suited his, his master's or the Nabob's pur poses, he set off, got before, and, was found there when Lord Pigot arrived at Tan j ore ; which, with some remonstrances made against him by the Rajah, tempted Lord Pigot in an unguarded moment to corporally punish him with twelve lashes in a publick manner. This furnished fuel for a future flame.

The Nabob's manager of the Tanjore country being then at some distance from the capital, Lord Pigot conceived a notion of getting from him the account of the revenues, &c., received ; and in order thereto sent a party of horse to secure either him or the accounts. But the man set off for, and got within the confines of the Carnatick before he was overtaken, notwithstanding which, he or his accounts were seized. This furnished the Nabob with a very specious pretext (perhaps a just one) for complaint, and of which he made the most by addressing the Board here and the Supreme Council at Bengali in terms of strong resentment.

The Nabob's reception of Lord Pigot on his arrival was in appearance the most cordial and affectionate. One day, after Lord Pigot had breakfasted with him at an elegant table, the Nabob sent him the tea service of rich gold and silver plate that he had been entertained with ; which he, after some hesitation, and to preserve as far as might be a good understanding, accepted. By the best account I can get it was worth from three to five thousand pagodas. But the value has been much exaggerated, and Lord Pigot has been threatened by Benfield with a prosecution for venality.

The Nabob very artfully led on Lord Pigot by one finess or other from December to April to delay his departure for Tan j ore till that period, with an intention to collect, or permit his creditors to collect, in discharge of his debt what they could of the crop of grain. As the grain had been cut and stacked, it was marked with Mr. Benfield's chop and claimed as his property. About the time the Rajah was restored this grain was demanded of Lord Pigot by Benfield, but it seems the Rajah applyd it to his own purpose. Benfield calls it a violent seizure of British property by Lord

Pigot, and declares he shall be made by law to account to him for the whole. Lord Pigot says it was a transaction of the Rajah's,and what he has nothing to say to.

Here then is the bone of contention. Benfield and that part of the Council who support his cause say that this grain, assigned to his creditors by the Nabob, should have gone in discharge of his debt, but as it did not, the Rajah ought to be made to pay it. Lord Pigot and his party say ; — Let the Nabob produce his accounts of the Tan j ore country, and if there is any thing remains unpaid we consent that the Rajah of Tanjore be made to pay it ; but if the Nabob will not produce his accounts, let the whole be referred to the Company, and wait their determination. This Benfield and his party will not agree to after much warm debate . Benfield's (or if you please Sir Robert's) party carryed their point of sending Colonel Stuart) to command at Tanjore to assist them there in recovering this money from the Rajah. Next, the scale turned the other way, and Lord Pigot's party got Russell appointed Resident there, he being the man they wished to be with the King. A few days only elapsed when Russell was, in consequence of the Company's orders, directed to go on the circuit. Now things grew serious Sir Robert's party was the Majority (though, as he was ill, he did not always attend Council) and orders were drawn out for Colonel Stilart to proceed to Tan j ore. They lay on the table ready for signing, but the President would not sign them. After much altercation the Secretary has (by Sir Robert's party, who was the Majority) directed to sign them for the President. But the Secretary did not think it safe to do so without a written order. An order for that purpose was accordingly drawn out, and Stratton and Brooke having signed it (as the rest of the Majority were going to do) Lord Pigot desired to see the paper before Brooke had (as he was in the very act of doing) given it to Floyer ; and having thus received it, drew another paper out of his pocket containing a charge against Brooke and Stratton for signing such an order without the President's consent, and immediately moved that they should be suspended the service for it ; which they accordingly were by Lord Pigot's casting voice. Sir Robert, being ill, was not present.

This transaction happened late in the afternoon of the 22nd of this month of August. The Council broke up immediately, and Sir Robert's party met at his house on Choultry Plain that evening, where they stayed till midnight ; then retired, and met at five next morning. Lord Pigot summoned a Council for that forenoon but left Stratton and Brooke out of the summons. Lord Pigot's party met accordingly. The other party did not come, but about noon sent a Notary Publick with a strong protest against the expulsion of Stratton and Brooke, declared the nullity of Lord Pigot's and the Minority's powers, and asserted that the Govern- ment rested in them, the Majority. The party, or Council if you please, broke up with an intention to consider of the matter till Monday the 26th. But while they were at dinner a letter was brought to Lord Pigot by a gentleman who had received it from Sir Robert's party, chargeing him as a Company's servant not to regard any orders of the Minority, as the Government was regularly vested in them the Majority, and that they expected his obedience. This induced Lord Pigot's party to assemble in Council again after dinner. While they were there the officer of the Main Guard brought in another letter to the same purport addressed to him as such. And soon after it was known that similar letters had been circulated to all in office, civil and military. This Lord Pigot, &c., considered as sowing sedition and tending to raise a mutiny in the garrison; and then on that ground (Sir Robert being first put in arrest by Lord Pigot, &c.) they suspended the whole of his party. This last transaction happened on the 23rd in the evening.

On Sir Robert being put under arrest by Lord Pigot, &c., they offered the command of the Army to Colonel Stuart (as I believe the other party did also). Stuart desired a little ime to consider of it. In the evening of the 23rd he accepted of the command from Lord Pigot, &c. and came to breakfast with him at the Gardens, where I happened to be also. After breakfast Lord Pigot and Stuart withdrew and had some conversation together, but they parted soon, and some time after met again in the Council Room. After which they with others dined together, and I think went to Council again after dinner, where they sat till the evening. On breaking up Lord Pigot desired Stuart to sup with him at the Gardens, which the other readyly accepted, but said he was at a loss for a conveyance, as his servants had disappointed him of his carriage. Stone told him his was at Stuart's service, but he declined it and said as his Lordship was going out himself he begged leave to accompany him. Pigot gladly accepted of his company. They set off together about past seven in the evening. In passing over the Island, Captain Lysaght stepped up from the side of the road and stopped the carriage with a pistol in his hand, and told Lord Pigot he was his, Lysaght's, prisoner. At the same instant came up Cap- tain Edington with a party of seapoys to support Lysaght. Then Stuart told Pigot in those words to Get out, get out. Pigot said (speaking to Stu- art), You have deceived me. They then put him into a close chaise, pre- pared and at hand for the purpose, and Lysaght, attended by an orderly, set off full speed with him. He asked where they meant to carry him. They said. To the Mount ; which they accordingly did, and delivered him to Major Horne, then in cantonment there with about 2 or 3 hundred artillery. This happened in the evening of the 24th August.

The principal officers of the garrison had their cue. Stuart returned to them immediately, and his Council, if I may call it such, was into Town and in the Council Room immediately after him. The military were told [that]. Sir Robert being ill, Stuart commanded ; and he with his dependants very luckily preserved such order as to prevent any blood being shed. All the members of the Council slept in the Council Room that night, and the next morning, vizt. the 25th August, a paper was circulated informing the publick that the then Government desired the Company's civil and military servants, as well as the inhabitants in general, to attend at the Council Room at 11 that day ; which being accordingly done by most, a proclamation was read to them and afterwards affixed at the Seagate, setting forth the reasons for the measures which had been taken ; and Mr. Stratton, after haveing been thus proclaimed Governor of Fort St. George and President of the Council and saluted with nineteen guns on the occasion, stood ready to receive the compHments of more than he found disposed to bestow them. The mihtary however (it being a work of their own) together with the principal black and Armenian mer- chants paid their devoirs, but a remarkable backwardness appeared in the bulk of the civil servants. Some few officers, whose approbation of the Revolution was doubtfull, were ordered to the out garrisons.

The Gentlemen now in power being, however, fearfull of some attempt being made to wrest the government out of their hands in favor of Lord Pigot, sent a party privately to the Mount under the command of Captain

Edington, at midnight between the 27th and 28th instant, to remove his Lordship's person elsewhere, but to what place they would not then say (though they have since declared it to be Chingleput). This unreasonable and unexpected measure much surprised Lord Pigot and alarmed his friends, who put the worst construction on it. Edington, by virtue of a written order, peremptoryly demanded his person of Major Home, and Home as peremptoryly insisted for a time on Lord Pigot yielding himself up to Edington ; but he as positively asserted he would not do so, and declared they should not take him away alive.

On this the Artillery (some two or three hundred in number) then in cantonment there were put under arms, and called on to do their duty ; but Pigot harangued them on the occasion, told them that he and he only was their lawful Governor, that his person had been violently seized without a reason, that he was then in secure confinement under them and not possible for him, if he was so disposed, to escape, and on that account there could be' no reason for his removal at such an hour, in such a way, to be carryed he knew not where, and for purposes which he feared could not be good. Home called again on the men to do their duty, told them he was their officer, and asked if they would not obey him. Notwithstanding which they stood stock still under arms and perfectly mute. Home and Edington, haveing thus much reason to apprehend the defection of those troops, dropped the design, and so it ended on September 10th. On the 31st August Lord Pigot applyed by his friends to the Mayor's Court for a writ of Habeas Corpus.

After some deliberation the Court decided it had power to grant the writ, but an adjournment took place on formal grounds and when the Court assembled again on the 2nd September the previous decision was reversed.

And thus that affair ended.

Prior to the subversion of the Government reports of the Board's proceedings and disputes had been sent to the Supreme Council. Sir Robert Fletcher was in correspondence with General Clavering, but no private representations were made on behalf of Lord Pigot 's party. Answers to the whole detail of what was sent previous to the Revolution have been received from the Supreme [Government] condemning in general Lord Pigot's measures, more especially those at Tan j ore, and particularly his seizure of the Nabob's agent within the confines of the Carnatick. No answers are yet received to the accounts sent of the Revolution. They cannot well be expected till towards the end of this month September 21st. The *Swallow*, sloop of war, is to sail the 30th instant with accounts of the Revolution to Suez ; Dalrymple on one part and Colonel Capper) on behalf of the other go on her

George Baker
P.S. October 8th. On the 6th instant the Administration here received publick letters from the Supreme [Council] at Calcutta, acknowledging the receipt of the letter containing the account of the late Revolution here: of which they give their full approbation, and promise to support them in their government. Thus this matter now stands. What measures will be taken on your side the water time will unfold. The *Swallow*'s departure was postponed, but she is now to sail for Suez on the 10th instant.

Richard Welland to Robert Palk, Esqr., Bruton Street, London. 1776, September 6th, Ship *Salisbury*, Madrass Roads.

Honoured Uncle,
We are just come from Bombay and we expect to go to Masulapatam soon. I have done sc[h]ool now, and I do duty on the quarterdeck as Midshipman. Mr. Adams is dead, and I heard he died wo[r]th 80 thousand pounds. Sir Edward Hughes behaves very well to me ; likeways Mr. Baker, for I go ashore very often, and he sends me [plenty] of fruit every Sunday. I am glad brother Robert has made choise of the army. All my cousins in India are well. The governer of Madrass suspen[d]ed some of the Council for private correspondence with the Nabob. The Council tooke him the next morning out of his chariot, and put him in prison at the Mount, and suspen[d]ed him and Mr. Stone and several others, and Mr. Striately [sic] is mad[e] gove[r]ner. All the Company's ships saluted him with 19 guns, and the Fort saluted us with 15 guns, and we returned the same number.
Your affectionate and ever dutiful nephew,

Richard Welland

XLIV
The curious end of Lord Pigot, 1776

Chocapah to the Honble. Robert Palk, Esqr. 1776, September 15th, Fort St. George. Received 21st April, 1777.

Since I wrote to you on the 27th June a revolution has occurred here. The Nawab, forgetting that he owes his position as ruler of the Carnatic to Lord Pigot during the latter 's first administration, has lately supported those who are hostile to the Governor. The Nawab and his sons instigated the Majority in the Council to vote against the appointment of Mr. Russell to Tan j ore, and to require that gentleman to accompany the Circuit Committee to the Northern Circars. On the 22nd August, after Lord Pigot had suspended Messrs. Stratton and Brooke for inciting the Secretary to commit an unlawful act, the Majority, consisting of Mr. Stratton, Sir Robert Fletcher, and Messrs. Brooke, Floyer, Palmer, Jourdan and Mackay, joined (with the exception of Sir Robert, who was ill) Messrs. Benfield and Macpherson and the two sons of the Nawab at night at Mr. Benfield's garden house, where they received communications from the Nawab. Next morning all, except the Nawab's sons, met at Sir Robert Fletcher's garden, where the Majority resolved to assume the Government, and sent out notices to that effect. On receipt of the notice Lord Pigot suspended the Majority members and appointed Colonel Stuart Commander-in-Chief.

Colonel Stuart, after repeatedly enjoying his Lordship's hospitality, drove with the Governor on the evening of the 24th from the Fort towards the Company's Garden, having previously arranged with Benfield, Macpherson and others that the carriage should be stopped by Colonel Edington and Captain Lysaght, supported by an armed party of sepoys and Nawab's troops. The two officers emerged from the shadows of the avenue of trees on the Island, and presenting pistols, halted the chaise.

Colonel Stuart forced Lord Pigot to enter Mr. Benfield's carriage, which was in waiting, and despatched him a prisoner to the Mount, where he was placed in the custody of Major Home. The Majority immediately went to the Fort, and next morning issued orders to all the military and civil servants of the Company and white and black inhabitants of Madrasspatnam to give them their attendance at the Fort Square at 11 o'clock in that morning, and to hear the proclamation they drew out themselves in the names of his Majesty, [the] English nation and the East India Company. On the 26th the Nabob and his two sons with great pomp came to the Fort to give his visit to Mr. Stratton, and [on] the 27th June Mr. Stratton went to the Nabob with great pomp, where he was received very handsomely. On the 28th at midnight Colonel Edington went to the Mount to remove Lord Pigot to Gingee, but through the action of Major Home and Messrs. Russell, Dalrymple and Monckton the intention was not executed.

Mr. Russell came down to Sir Edward Hughes at St. Thome at three in the morning, and got him out of his bed and acquainted him. Sir Edward Hughes immediately came to the Fort, and spoke to Mr. Stratton and the rest of the Gentlemen at 4 o'clock in the morning, and induced them to promise that no further attempt to remove Lord Pigot would be made. Most of the civil servants have refused to recognise any Governor but Lord Pigot, and all the native inhabitants are profoundly grieved and depressed. Many of the military officers have no sympathy with the revolution. We are in hopes that such gentlemen as yourself, Mr. Du Pre and Mr. Call will return to India to put matters right.

I used to get my letters corrected by somebody else before, but I [am] now afraid to shew this letter to any one here, and therefore I wrote it myself as well as I can, and request you will please to excuse me the errors and broken English wrote in this letter

Chocapah

Henry Vansittart, jun., to Robert Palk, Esqr.1776, September 18th, Calcutta.

I have received your favors of the 14th December, 1775, and 7th January, 1776. If I should ever prove an honor to my name, I shall attribute it to my good fortune in meeting with friends who have suggested its importance and animated my pursuit. It gives me uneasiness that I should transmit memorials of myself to my friends in an uncouth form, and hope that my future performances will not be liable to such exception. The friend at whose instance you imparted the counsel being unknown, I can only thank him through you for his kind attention.

H. Vansittart

George Smith to Robert Palk, Esqr. 1776, September 20th, Fort St. George.

How great must be your surprise on receipt of this to know that a revolution has taken place in our Government, that Lord Pigot is a prisoner under a military guard at the Mount, and George Stratton in the chair of Government. To enumerate the circumstances which have led to this change would be to swell this beyond the limits of a letter. I must therefore refer you to the India House and to the public papers for the detail. In order, however, to gratify your curiosity thus raised by me, I will here inform you of a few uncontrovertable facts, which will guide you to the source of this event,

The present Administration accuse Lord Pigot with despotism, arbitrary power, an intention to subvert the constitution of Government, and with the receipt of presents. These are the summary of the accusations against him, which, if true, would scarcely justify the measures which have been adopted ; but, being false, how much more culpable are the men who have seized on his Government and person! If opposition to a venal faction in his Council, and putting a negative on resolves formed on injus- tice and self-interest; if a strict observance of the interest and honour of the Company, and a punctual regard to their instructions and orders can be termed despotic and arbitrary measures tending to the subversion of the Constitution, then is my Lord guilty of the charge against him ; if not, he is innocent. Of these charges I most readily acquit him. Effects but too evidently demonstrate the cause of this revolution ; self interest is the source and spring of it — Tan j ore loans and money from the Nabob to load the Rajah with the payment of these moneys — this the true, the undoubted cause. You know me, and I tell you that I am totally disinterested in my representation ; and to convince you that I am so, I need only tell you that I have a Tanka for pearls, which I last year sold the Nabob, on Tan j ore, unpaid, to the amount of Pags. 31,500, which is a large sum to me, and for which I could now get an order on the Rajah by an application to the present Administration. In regard to the informa- tion of presents, from whom do they [sic] come ? From the declared foes of Lord Pigot Benfield and his man Comaroo. Benfield's enmity against Lord Pigot is incredible: he has said such things to me of him that I could not have believed if he had not told me them himself. Since the revolution the sentiments of the Supreme Council on the conduct of my Lord Pigot towards the Nabob have come to hand. These give great hopes to the present Administration that their measures in regard to him will also be approved. These resolves you will see. Untill you do, and know circumstances, please to suspend your opinion, for I will take upon me to say that they are crude, indigested and malignant.

George Smith
P.S. Bob Munroe considering the present Administration illegal, has had the honesty and fortitude to say so in a letter to them, jointly with 37 other civil servants, and thinking he could no otherways address Mr. Stratton than as ‘stiling himself President and Governor of Fort St. George ', has for this address been suspended the service. The smallness of the crime, the friendship which you had for his father. will, I hope, be incentives with you to aid his other friends in getting him reinstated.In regard to Randall's plot of assassination ; the orders of these gentlemen to Major Horn[e].

That in case a rescue was attempted, as the last resource his Lordship's life must answer for it, and this you are to signify to him ' ; and Colonel Edington's attempt to take him from Horn[e] in the dead of night, are horrible things. The two last bear hard on the new Powers, and resemble much the seven Tyrants of Syracuse. As to the first, every person will judge for himself. I know Omer al Omrah to be a bad man, and I can figure to myself what a bad man is capable of doing.

John d'Fries to Robert Palk, Esqr. 1776, September 21st, Madras.

We have had an instance lately of the dispatch with which advices may be sent from Europe to India by forwarding the letters to Grand Cairo directly, and from thence over the Isthmus of Suez, where vessels may be stationed to fetch them away to India. A private packet for Mr. Hastings of the 20th May from London, with letters from Mr. Graham at Marseilles of 3rd June, was received at Calcutta the 15th August, and we had extracts of it here from Bengal, come overland, the 7th instant. Colonel Monson has been very ailing lately. Lady Monson dyed some months since.
The arrival of the present packet from India will fill you all with much surprize as well as serious concern at the unfortunate lengths to which the animosities and dissentions in Council have been carried, and the violent end it is brought to by the arrest of Lord Pigot, who is now a prisoner at the Mount, and the gentlemen who sided with him in Council, Messrs. Russell, Dalrymple, Stone and Latham being suspended. I enclose you copys of several of the proceedings which were made publick I shall avoid all reflections, but only observe that extremities of this nature must prejudice the Government very much and reduce its dignity and consequence, more so with the Asiatics, whose notion of a Chief Magistrate or the Government of a single person is congenial to them. The Nabob with reason seems to be sorry for what has happened, as I told him that it was out of his power to prevent suspicions being entertained of his having had some hand in all that is come to pass.
You will perceive by the resolutions of the Supreme Council of the 7th August last that they disapproved entirely of most part of Lord Pigot's conduct towards the Nabob, whom they declare they were determined to protect in his just rights. The present Administration waits to hear from Bengal regarding the last act. I may aver for truth to you that if Lord Pigot had been less violent, and more moderate and attentive to the great

interest the Settlement had in the Tan j ore countrey from the Tanakaws and orders for money granted by the Nabob to individuals, much of what has happened may have been prevented, for it was certainly the interest of private individuals that increased the opposition.

It will be strongly urged by those that do not favor the Nabob's cause that he should not be permit[t]ed to reside here, as it gives him a convenient opportunity to form partys in Council, &c. The advantages to this Settlement since his constant residence here for the last ten years are very great and visible, both in the considerable increase of inhabitants, near a third more than before, as well as of the trade and benefits reaped by them by the great consumption of many articles of use and ornament for the Nabob's family and court. But in a political sense also the Nabob should be kept here in preference to any distant place, as we can watch better over his actions. A great deal has been said about the Nabob's aiming at independance, and his great force, &c. The first will never be at- tained by him but by a weak Administration on our part suffering him to do so. He certainly had a numerous rabble, and has still too many useless people that occasions to him a great but unnecessary expence. When our Government is on good terms with the Nabob, he may be easily prevailed upon to regulate many things, but when both sides are in an ill humour it is no time for reforming abuses. It is of the most important consequence to the Company that a sincere harmony and good understanding should subsist between their Government here and the Nabob. During these political contests many things have been said of presents received on both sides. His Lordship was accused also of a large sum received from the Nabob since his arrival.

Mr. Adams dyed lately with a sudden attack of an apoplectick fit. He remained speechless for two days before he expired. He has left upwards of fifty thousand L. The Mayor's Court are going to petition the King for power to grant writ of Habeas Corpus, which will be a great security to the subject, and a very necessary power to the Court here. It is the commonly received opinion here that Sir Edward Hughes has not behaved the most steadily in this business from the rank he holds.

I beg once more you will think of establishing — that is, propose to the Company for doing it — a communication to India through Grand Cairo and Suez, which may be accomplished at very little expence by

appointing an English merchant at Cairo as their agent to forward the letters to Suez, where a small vessell from Bengal or Bombay should be con- stantly kept, relieving each other, to fetch away the packet to India. The Company entertains vessells enough at Bengal and Bombay to be em- ployed in this service without putting them to any additional expence, and by this means we may have intelligence through that channel at least four times a year. If you should have occasion to write us that way, please to recom[m]end your letters to Mr. George Baldwin, merchant at Grand Cairo, who corresponds with us.
The Nabob has lately shewn some kindness to Mrs. Vansittart ; indeed his disposition towards all the family is very friendly. It is much to be regret[t]ed that he will not attend to the regulation of his finances, which are ever anticipated, and thereby it costs him an onerous interest. Ben-field is gone to Tan j ore to endeavor (it is supposed) at the recovery of his property there.

John d'Fries.

H.H. the Nawab Walajah to Robert Palk, Esqr. 1776, September 25th. Chep- auk.

I have received from you, my friend, three letters filled with friendship, and they arrived when my mind was filled with sorrow, and they gave great relief to my heart. I have seen your letter to Commodore Sir Edward Hughes, and am much obliged to you for it, and I hope you will, as usual, give attention to settling my affairs in England. Though I could not but think that the order in regard to Tan j ore was unjust, I would not oppose it, and hoped for redress ; and Lord Pigot not only executed it, but did every thing in his power to destroy my rights and hurt my honor ; and he shewed no consideration to a thirty five years' friendship with the Company and the English nation, but broke the peace of the Carnatick by acting contrary to his Majesty's guaranty. He endeavoured byevery means to disgrace me, thinking to provoke me to some measure that would have given him a pretence to destroy me and my family; but depending on the Company's friendship and justice, I gave him no

opposition.
His Lordship at last, through his own bad conduct, fell from his high station. I had no concern therein, and knew nothing of it 'till after it had happened. You will perceive the concern of my mind by the paper which I wrote to Governor Stratton on this subject the day after the affair happened, a copy of which I enclose you. The Council here, and the Governor General and Supreme Council of Bengal have disapproved of all his Lordship's conduct, as well in what regards my affairs as the Company's. Mr. Hastings, who is your friend and mine, wrote a letter to Sir Edward Hughes (an extract of which Colonel Macleane will show you) by which you will see how nearly your opinion and his agree. People may for their own interest raise what reports they please, but I am an unalterable friend to the Company and the English nation, and nothing will ever change me.
What can I say more ?
P.S. You told me many things which I now recollect, and two of them particularly. The first, that when the news of Lally's beseiging Madrass reached England, the Directors then asked you (as you had then newly arrived from India) would Madrass stand or fall, and you answered that it would not fall whilst General Lawrence commanded there. I hope that you will positively assure them of a similar thing, which is that as long as I and my family exist in the Carnatick, we will never admit of the least diminution of our friendship with the Company and the English.
Secondly, you told me that should the Government of Madrass do me any injury, I should not oppose them, but make my complaint to England. This advice has been of great use to me, and in all the injuries that Lord Pigot has heaped on me I made no opposition.
What can I say more?

XLV
Lord Pigot is deposed, 1776

Charles Floyer to Robert Palk, Esqr. 1776, September 25th, Fort St. George

The news now conveyed to England by His Majesty's *sloop* the Swallow to Suez, and from thence by land, are of so serious a nature as to require the immediate attention of the Court of Directors, the Court of Proprietors and of the Ministry itself. They relate solely to this Presidency, and must be deemed the more important as they contain matters for which no precedent can be traced amongst the Company's records.

In short, my dear Sir, the minion of the public, and the Governor, nominated in so distinguished a manner (Lord Pigot) by a Court of Propri etors, has proved the greatest tyrant you can possibly conceive, not only in his avowed principles of government, but in the most injurious, most oppressive and most illegal measures he has pursued in his attempts to subvert the constitutional rights of our nation and of the East India Company, and in making every thing subservient to his private interests in direct breach of his trust and of the positive orders of the Company. To enumerate a tenth part of the outrageous acts he has committed would require much more time than the present dispatch affords me : permit me therefore to refer you to my brother, whom I have desired to wait upon you with a particular relation of the most important parts of our transactions, by which you will perceive that the Majority of Council has been reduced to the very disagreable necessity of causing the person of Lord Pigot to be arrested, and of suspending Messrs. Russell, Dalrymple and Stone from the service.

His Lordship's grand and favorite object was the restoration of the Rajah of Tan j ore, and the rock on which he and his associates split. That his Lordship came to India at his advanced time of life merely to enforce the orders of the Company on that subject without having in view his private interest also I believe cannot be supposed even by his warmest friends. He had a most extensive field for the gratification of every wish. It was the restoring in his single person a King, dispossessed of his country and reduced to a state of oblivion and obscurity, to a throne. This was the man destined to look up to his restorer as his demi-god, and from whom alone he could expect the future blessings of this life. And in order to effect so favorite a point his Lordship proceeded to Tan j ore to execute singly the orders of the Company. Hence originated all the evils lately experienced, as well from his conduct during and after his public transactions there as from his indecent behavior towards the Nabob, who was doomed to fall a victim to the support his Lordship had determined to give to the Rajah. If we very early conceived suspicions of his Lordship's self-interested motives, the event must prove such suspicions were not groundless, for Mr. Benfield has addressed a letter to the Board wherein he charges Lord Pigot with having received presents in plate, jewels and money to a very considerable amount from Indian Princes; and that having obtained undoubted proofs thereof, he is determined to commence prosecutions against him for a breach of the late Act of Parliament. The charge, I fear, is too true and if public report is to be credited, the sum amounts to between three and four hundred thousand pounds.

In confidence to you, my dear Sir, I shall now inform you of his Lordship's supposed plan, and which has, in my opinion, been so strongly corroborated by his late conduct that I frankly confess I believe it to be true. The greatest part of the above enormous sum was to come from Tan j ore. A Resident therefore. was to be appointed at the Rajah's Court, and that Resident insisted upon by his Lordship to be only his friend Mr. Russell, who was to marry the youngest Miss Pigot (a child of sixteen years of age) ; to have as large a fortune with her as had been given to Mr. Monckton with the eldest daughter (at least £20,000) ; to receive for his Lordship the ballance due to him from the Tan j ore country ; to wait the departure of Messrs. Stratton and Brooke, who had determined to go to Europe, when Mr. Russell becoming second of Council, his Lordship was to embark upon the very next ship for Europe, leaving the Government to his friend and son-in-law. The other son-in-law (Mr. Monckton, who has very handsomely availed himself of his relationship to a Governor) and his lady were to have accompanied the father to Europe. No bad plan, I think, for all the parties concerned. But unfortunately for them it has failed in all its points : — vide the violent efforts of the Minority to send Russell to Tan jore ; the obstacles they threw in the way of the Committee of Circuit of which Committee Messrs. Russell and Dairy mple were nominated members from home ; and the last violent effort attempted by Lord Pigot to suspend Messrs. Stratton and Brooke from the service, who were the only two members between Mr. Russell and the Chair.he Majority having protested against this suspension as illegal, the Minority reassembled, suspended their remaining opponents, and appointed Colonel Stuart Commander-in-Chief. We therefore did assert our rights as a Majority, and causing Lord Pigot to be arrested, we assumed the government of the Company's affairs on the day following (the 24th August), and suspended Lord Pigot from being President of the Council,and Messrs. Russell, Dalrymple, Stone and Lathom from the Company's service. The last named gentleman, although he had been arrived at Madrass twelve days before this happened,in his way to the Committee of Circuit, had never attended a single Council untill the day on which we were all suspended; and finding he concurred in the unanimous resolutions of. the Minority, we included him also in the list of suspended members.

Of the rectitude of the cause I have been under the absolute necessity of espousing . I am under no apprehension. I am well aware that the circumstance of arresting Lord Pigot will be represented in the strongest colours by his friends at home, and that it will at first operate strongly in his favor, because it is an event for which there is no precedent abroad. But when, among the many other reasons assigned in the narrative to my brother, as well as those more fully stated in our address to the Court of Directors, we consider the very violent and uncontroulable disposition of Lord Pigot, who had so deep a stake, and his having a military commission as Commander-in-Chief of the military forces within the garrison of Fort St. George and the Black Town, I am led to hope those reasons will sufficiently evince the absolute necessity of arresting his person as a previous step to the Majority's resuming the Government. Had the Majority contented themselves with merely suspending his

Lordship from the Government, an insurrection must have ensued anthe loss of many lives would certainly have been the consequence, and Lord Pigot's amongst them, for he never would have yielded to any power; whereas by the measures which were taken not a man was seen under arms, and the Government was as peaceable and quiet from the day we resumed it as if nothing had happened, excepting a remonstrance which was signed and sent to us from some of the youngest civil servants of the Company, headed by his Lordship's son-in-law, Mr. Monckton, and two or three Senior Merchants As for his Lordship, it is only the name of an arrest, for he is lodged in the house of Major Home, who commands the artillery at the Mount and who has an order to treat him with all possible respect and attention. The houses at the Mount are filled with his sons-in-law, his daughters and a tribe of his followers; people of all denominations visiting him daily ; and he has the whole Mount for his range of exereise and amusement. He wishes, naturally enough, to return as Governor to his Fort, and has frequently declared to the troops that he would put himself at the head of them and march them into it.This, my dear Sir, is in few words the real matter of fact. If you shall find I have acted upon fair, honest and constitutional grounds in my small attempts to crush tyranny and oppression, I hope I shall meet from the Company, from you and my other friends those tokens of approbation which alone can relieve my mind from the very great uneasiness I labour under.

Charles Floyer.

H.H. the Nawab Walajah to Robert Palk, Esqr. 1776, October 8th, Chepauck.

My letter that goes to you herewith will inform you of the situation of my affairs. You may recollect that at the time the treaty was made by Lord Pigot with the Rajah of Tan j ore in 1762, when you. General Lawrence, Mr. Bourchier and Colonel Call were at Madrass, I com- plained to you and General Lawrence that it was contrary to my inclination that the treaty was made ; that I had told his Lordship so, and had refused to subscribe to it; but that he put a pen in my hand and obliged me to sign it, and also took my Chop and put it with his own hand to the treaty. I hope that you will declare this circumstance to every body, as it will shew how unjust his Lordship's conduct has been. He made a large fortune and went home ; but not content, he has returned to India to pursue his private interests and to make another fortune by repeating his ill treatment to me. What can I say more ?

John deFries to Robert Palk, Esqr. 1776, October 10th, Madras.

This goes by the *Swallow*, which is to put the letters ashore at Suez, to be forwarded from thence to Grand Cairo and Alexandria and so to Europe, and may probably be the first advice that you will receive of the revolution that happened in the Government of this Settlement on the 24th of August last. Mr. Dalrymple goes with Lord Pigot's packet, and Colonel Capper with the Nabob's, by whom I send this.

The measures pursued by Lord Pigot in the surrender of Tan j ore to the Rajah and the total disregard paid to the interest of individuals (English and others) who had a very large amount to receive there by assignment from the Nabob, caused a very great discontent in the Settlement as well as a disgust in the Nabob, and occasioned a strong opposition in Council against his Lordship, who had on his side Messrs. Russell, Dalrymple and Stone ; the Majority consisting of Messrs. Stratton, Sir Robert Fletcher, Brooke, Floyer, Palmer, Jourdan and Mackay. After a contest of three months the grand point of dispute became that Mr. Russell, who had been appointed, by the casting vote of the President only. Resident at Tanjore, was afterwards named on the Committee of Circuit. Colonel Stuart was to be Commandant at Tan j ore. Lord Pigot refused absolutely signing to his instructions, which were drawn out, without Mr. Russell was permit[t]ed to go to Tan j ore for a few days at least. This brought matters to a crisis. Lord Pigot by a finess suspended Messrs. Stratton and Brooke the 22nd, which gave to his party the majority, as he called in the next day Mr. Lathom to Council, who has come down from Cuddalore to proceed on the Circuit.

Mr. Stratton's party would not admit that they were suspended, and on the 23rd met themselves as a Board ; and, as the legal representatives of the Company, signified a protest to Lord Pigot and his party, who thereupon suspended the rest of them and put Sir Robert Fletcher under an arrest. This drove them to the extremity on the next [day], the 24th, of seizing on Lord Pigot, who was carried to the Mount, and is kept there under guard of the Artillery commanded by Major Home. Messrs. Russell, Dalrymple, Stone and Lathom [were] suspended.

We are in daily expectation of hearing from Bengal the opinion of the Supreme Council hereon. In their resolutions of the 7th August they disapproved entirely of Lord Pigot's conduct towards the Nabob and of his proceedings in the surrender of Tan j ore. It will be of the utmost conse- quence that the Company's determination of this important subject be proper, considerate and impartial, as the future well-being of this very considerable Colony and their good correspondence with the Nabob will entirely depend thereon. The most essential thing for the Company as well as the publick is that there be always a good misunderstanding subsisting between their Administration here and the Nabob, who should be used with proper respect, and not slighted and irritated. We have raised him ourselves to what he is, and to think now of treating him as we did twenty years ago will be neither just nor judicious. He is too sensible of his own consequence ; but I do believe that he is a sincere friend of the English. His own good sense will lead him to be so.

The choice of persons to conduct the Company's affairs here should be made with the greatest care and attention to their abilities and characters, as much depends on a vigorous, well conducted Administration. A line should be drawn of the extent of the powers of a Governor and that of a majority of his Council, as different opinions are held thereon by the different partys. In those troubles at Bengal during Mr. Vansittart's government nothing but his incomparable mildness of temper prevented things running into extremities. And it should be clearly pointed out whether the military power should at any time interfere in disputes of the civil overnment, as the not determining it very clearly may leave a door open to dangerous proceedings hereafter. We are quiet in these parts. Although a peace has been made many months ago between the Presidency of Bombay and the Morattas, yet there don't seem to be much cordiality subsisting. Trade is almost ruined all over India. The scarcity of specie is much felt here : the exportation continues as great as ever both to China and Europe.

John d'Fries.
P.S. The Supreme Council have unanimously approved of the act of the Majority, and promise their support, acknowledging them to be the legal representatives of the Company.

George Baker to Robert Palk, Esq 1776, October 14th, Fort St. George

Since I closed my last Lord Pigot has put Sir R. Fletcher into our Mayor's Court for two hundred thousand pounds damages, and required security for that sum ere he leaves the Settlement, which he was about to do for the recovery of his health at the Cape. The Court have accepted bail for ten thousand pounds only, and Sir Robert and Lady Fletcher go on the *Greenwich*. Report says that Miss Pybus is to be marryed to Captain Lysaght.
Mr. R. Adams dyed about six weeks since, worth near two lacks of pagodas. Colonel Monson has been long dangerously ill.
I have made no comment on the narrative sent you. Were I to do so, it would be some thing like what follows : the spirit of liberty within these few years spreading and thriveing throughout the British dominions extended itself even here, and this at the time of a lax and weak government. People, at least some of the Council, dreaded a restraint under Lord Pigot's government which they had not been for a long time used to.
The orders he came to execute as to the restoration of the King of Tan j ore alarmed those who had lent money to the Nabob on his assignment of the produce of parts of that country. The Settlement, it is said, had lent him on such assignments (called Tankas) some fifteen lacks of pagodas, which if they could not recover by virtue thereof, they had no one to look to for it but the Nabob ; and he told them that they haveing accepted of those assignments as their security, they were to look to that and not to him for payment. So that it became their joynt interest either not to restore the country to the King, or restore it only on condition of

its being saddled with the payment of that sum of money. And this, in the opinion of many, was the principal private motive for opposing Lord Pigot's measures, though it was not the avowed one.

This being the case, the Opposition chose the best grounds of argument that offered in a course of long altercation, kept up perhaps for the very purpose of involveing Lord Pigot in inextricable difficultyes, or to compel him to submit to the government of a majority against him, which I suppose his spirit could but ill brook, and which I believe brought things and persons to the state they are now in.

Lord Pigot, moreover, failed to cultivate a good understanding with the Supreme Council, while the members of the Majority corresponded privately with Bengal and ascertained how far they might expect support. The restoration of the Rajah of Tan j ore on terms precluding those from the prospect of recovering it who had lent the Nabob money on that country was to this Settlement a most unpopular measure, and such as rendered the supporters of it odious. Those who opposed it were of course dubbed patriots, though perhaps done for their own sakes.

George Baker

Edmund Veale Lane to Robert Palk, Esq. 1776, December 17th, Salsette. Received 28th July, 1777.

I wrote to you in my last of the peace which the Supremes had concluded with the Ministerial Party of the Morattahs, and that they had compelled the Governor and Council to break their engagements to Ragonath Row (or Ragobah). It was owing entirely to an accident the Treaty was in any shape complied with by the Ministers ; for had not Sudabah, a first cousin of Ragobah's, got released from confinement and very near wrested the government from them. Colonel Upton might have returned to Calcutta without having an article of the Treaty fulfilled. But on Sudabah's success, being apprehensive we should join him, the Ministers made good most of the cessions stipulated for, though they had either refused or evaded to do it for some months before. Notwithstanding this good fortune at first, poor Sudabah was at last betrayed by some of his people, and taken prisoner by Madjee Scindy, one of the Ministerial Generals.

Ragobah, who had resided at Surat ever since our leaving him, finding his relation out of prison, and a promising prospect of success, left that place and made the best of his way towards Basein in order to join Sudabah. But when the misfortune just now mentioned happened, Ragobah was so hard pushed as to be obliged to take shelter on board one of the Company's vessels, and is now safe at Bombay. It is now said the officer who took Sudabah prisoner has declared for him, and means to make him Vizier to the young child, and that Ragobah has in consequence been invited to return to Poonah. However, it is believed by most to be only a finesse of the Ministers to get Ragobah into their hands. Be it as it will, I wish most sincerely there was an end to the dispute. Were the Presidency of Bombay once more permitted to interfere, it would soon terminate to our advantage ; but as that seems to be very uncertain, if not improbable, I fear the present possessors of the Morattah government will continue in power, which if the case, we shall ever have a most inveterate enemy near us, that will lay wait for the first opportunity that offers to injure the Company. As General Carnac is appointed to be our Governor on the resignation of Mr. Hornby, I shall think myself greatly favoured could you procure me a letter of recommendation to him from some of his friends

Edmd Veale Lane.

Thomas Palk to Robert Palk, Esq. 1777, February 6th, Madras.

However unacceptable information of this nature may prove, yet it is, Sir, nevertheless, my indispensable duty to make known to you an event which I dread will meet with your disapprobation, as well as a disappointment to my father, etc. family; but I must say that it would most sensibly grieve me should any one action of my life, though attendingwith the most perfect state of felicity to myself, meet your disapproba- tion I have connected myself to the family of Mr. Thomas Pelling by marrying his fourth daughter, Miss Catharine. With respect to her accompli[sh]ments it would be absurd in me to sound forth, but I must do her that justice to say that they are such as no man would make the least objection to. On the 30th ultimo our nuptials were celebrated

Thos. Palk

George Baker to Robert Palk, Esq. 1778, January 29th, Fort St. George. Received 11th August.

The last letter that I troubled you with was of the 13th of last Octo- ber per *Egmont.*

Russell married Miss Leonora Pigot the day before they imbarked and Stone both went on the Egmont. Messrs. Stratton and Brooke left this early in December for Anjango, where they imbarked on a small vessel the 31st of that month for Suez in their way to Europe. Early in this month the Valantine, in her way hither from Bengali, ran aground on the shoal between this and Pullicat, from which she got off with difficulty after haveing thrown over board the least valuable part of her cargoe, together with most of her guns, and cutting away all her masts. She is now in this road prepareing to sail for and dock at Bombay, from whence she is expected to be here again some four, five or six months hence to load for Europe ; when it is said Jourdan and Benfield will take their passage on her thither. I hear nothing of Floyer or Lathom's proceeding to Europe at present.

Monckton and his family and Colonel Ross, the Chief Engineer, are sailing for England immediately.

Messrs. J. Whitehill, C. Smith, S. Johnson and P. Perring, constituteing our present Board of Government, go on calmly with the administration of public affairs, though the empty state of the Company's treasury has been rather an imbarrassing circumstance. But the Board haveing been successfull in a deputation of Mr. Perring to the Rajah of Tan j ore for anticipateing the payment of the annual four lacks, that circumstance has set them afloat again. We really see the fortifications at the north east and south east angles of the town carrying on briskly.

Parity still subsists in the Settlement. Mackay has prosecuted Monckton for fifty thousand pound damages, as haveing been a principal means of causeing what he calls an illegal inquest being held on the body of Lord Pigot by which he (Mackay, etc.) were charged with a heinous crime and put to much trouble and expence. It is said that the coroner is to be prosecuted apart and the jury joyntly for what they call a conspiracy, the Judges at Bengali haveing declared that the President and Council of Fort St. George have no legal authority to appoint a coroner.

Your nephew is appointed Paymaster of Chingleput, a place equal to his expectations, and in obtaining which he must, I am perswaded, have had Perring's interest. The Nabob has lyquidated his new debt, which is said to amount to some sixty or sixty-five lacks of pagodas, which is now become a new consolidation, for payment of which his creditors have received certain assignments of revenue. It is said there is about five lack of the old debt unpaid.

I have just had a letter from Mr. R. Kennaway at Bengali of the 31st ultimo, by which it appears he has been lately ill, but is now recovered ; though by the advise of his friends he intends to take a trip hither for the reestablishment of his health. I expect him dayly, shall endeavor to accommodate him while here, and make no doubt but (under God) the good Doctor Pasley, with the pure air of Madrass, will soon confirm him in his former state of health. Mr. J. Kennaway was well in December last.

My affair continues still in an unsettled state. As Rumbold is expected soon, I am willing to see if, on his assumeing the Government, it can be fairly and fully adjusted. It is too long and too perplexed a story for me to trouble you with. I have only to say at present that I am very sure that I have in every instance done justly ; and it yet remains to be proved that I have, as my adversarys or enemyes would insinuate, erred in judgement. It is hard, very hard, that my contract should be made a loosing one for no other reasons but because, if I am suffered to compleat it, it may be advantage[ou]s. Mr. Wynch has done me an irreparable injury. I know not whether to blame the defects of his head or those of his heart most for it. I wish not to live for any other thing so much as to confront that man in a Court of Justice or in a General Court of Proprietors. But the chance is against me. I have but too much reason to fear that may never happen ; so that I may dye under a load of reproach and without the possibility of justifying myself. But pardon me ; of this no more.

George Baker

George Baker to Robert Palk, Esq. 1778, March 5th, Fort St. George. Received 5th November.

> Mr. R. Kennaway arrived here the beginning of February last. He is much better, and in a fair way of being restored to his former health soon. He sets out to-morrow on a visit to your nephew Mr. Thomas Palk at Chingleput. The Duke of Kingston (by which ship this comes) arrived here a few days since from Bengali. Mrs. Parry, Mrs. Hessman and a Mrs. Shaw were passengers on her for Europe, but it is said that Mrs. Parry has some thoughts of staying here. Mr. and Mrs. Floyer and Colonel and Mrs. Ross take their passages on her.'The Besborough and Lord North, with Mr. Rumbold, General Monroe, Sir J. Day etc., arrived here the 8th of last month, all well. The Government being again established, we enjoy domestick quiet, and party resentment, it is to be hoped, will in a reasonable time wear away. The new Governor being of course busy, I have not yet had a proper opportunity to speak to him on my af- fair. Some thing must, however, be finally resolved on between this and next October. My state of health and time of life will not allow me to play with time any longer. The French, under the direction of Saint Luban, have hoisted their colours at Choul, a place you know on the sea coast in the Maratah dominions a little to the south of Bombay. The Government of Bombay did some two months since apply to this Presidency for troops. The answer returned was that they could take no step of that kind without the approbation of the Government General, but that they would, as they did, write to Bengali on the subject.
>
> The Company haveing ordered a Court of Enquiry into General Stuart's conduct respecting the late revolution here, he, instead thereof, has requested an immediate court-martial without that previous formality ; but the Board, it is said, have declined a complyance with that request. And it is said that his six months' suspension, which expired on the last day of the last month, is continued. The General has many friends in the army, that corps considering him as theirs. Major Home, Captains

Lysaght and Edington are ordered to repair to the Presidency. While General Stuart's [conduct] remains unimpeached at martial law, theirs (who acted under his orders) may perhaps be unimpeachable. God send a speedy end to this unlucky business.

George Baker
P.S. This letter was wrote but a few hours when I accidentally heard that Mr. Monroe (who was Paymaster of Chinglepat at the time of the revolution in our Government, but who had been dismissed the service by Mr. Stratton) had been restored to that office, and set out to take charge of it yesterday. So that Mr. Kennaway is not only disappointed in his journey, but, what is far worse, Mr. Palk of his place. The former incon- venience we can easyly remedy, but as to the latter it depends on Mr. Palk's friends and good fortune to supply a substitute.

Henry Vansittart, jun., to Robert Palk, Esq. 1778, April 24th, Calcutta.

The eldest Kennaway has been obliged to visit the Coast for the recovery of his health. His brother is present in the scene of emolument, deriving very considerable advantages from his situation in Asoph-ud- Dowlah's country.
We dread a revolution in our Government by the first packet from Europe. I am not very apprehensive of one myself, provided the news of the General's death should have reached England before a new Act of Parliament passed. We think the Minister will be obliged to lay India affairs before Parliament in order to restrain the authority of the Supreme Court.
I think the expedition into the country of the Mahrattoes, though apparently the troops are only to pass through it in their way to Bombay, may raise a clamour at home. However, the Government defends the measure with many plausible arguments, and declares it will produce a good effect even if the troops should be obliged to return. The French had certainly been intriguing with the Mahrattas, and it is a maxim well known to foreigners that the only method of establishing themselves in India is by connecting themselves with the country Powers.
I am obliged to you for interesting yourself in my concerns, and be

assured that I have no friend on whom I can place more reliance, and none whose good offices are more pleasing.

Henry Vansittart.

Thomas Palk to Robert Palk, Esq.. 1778, October 15th, Fort St. George. Received 11th September, 1779.

I am sorry to acquaint you that poor Snelling departed this life the 17th of August in Madras. His station for six years past has been in the Cicacole district (so fatal to many), and had been at death's door several times. Even those who have the shghtest attack of that pernicious disorder, though survive, never get quit of it. He made a will, leaving what little money he was worth to a child and its mother, which I have taken care of for the present, as I hope that Snelling's friends will send for it. I am told it is very white, having not yet seen it. My having no knowledge of Snelling's relations, who they are and where they are, is the reason of my troubling you, Sir, with this information. I learn with much satisfaction from Mr. Baker that Mrs. Palk has recovered from her late indisposition.

Tho. Palk

Mudoo Kistna to Robert Palk, Esq. 1778, October 15th, Fort St. George.

I have received no satisfactory reply from Governor Rumbold to my application for reinstatement — a result which I attribute to the malign influence of the Nawab and his son, who suspect me of being the cause of the rendition of Tan j ore. It is hard that I should suffer when all the Company's servants who were suspended by Mr. Stratton's Government have been restored to the service. My desire for reinstatement is due to a regard for my reputation, as well as for the sake of my son Choliappa, who has been trained in native languages in view to his becoming useful to the Company. I beg that you will use your influence with the Directors on my behalf, and also write to Mr. Rumbold.
Mudoo Kistna

XLVI
Cotsford escapes the French, 1778

Edward Cotsford to Robert Palk, Esq. 1778, October 17th, Madras. Received 17th March, 1779.

> We arrived here safe and sound on the 16th of August last, meeting with our greatest risque when we imagined the cares of the voyage over. Not knowing of our differences with the French, we passed within sight of Pondicherry and their fleet at anchor in the road. When we came off the place in the morning we saw a ship astern crowding after us. At the same time one of those in the road slipped from her anchor and gave us chace. She sailed ill, and the one astern was still too far off to do any thing with us. After a chace of upwards of twenty miles, when the largest began to near us very fast, we saw six sail ahead, and about a quarter of an hour afterwards the two Frenchmen hauled their wind and stood to the eastward. The falling in with Sir Edward Vernon (for they proved to be his squadron) I believe saved us. English ships in the situation of those Frenchmen would certainly have shewn a better conduct. We have had open trenches before Pondichery for some time, where we have met with more opposition than was expected. Considering we were masters of the time for declaring hostilities with the French, it appears to me that the greatest advantage has not been made of so very commanding a privilege. Before discovering our purpose we might have received every kind of information respecting the works of Pondicherry, the strength of the garrison, the quantity of stores and provisions, and numberless other particulars, a knowledge of which might have put it in our power to have carried the place by surprize, or have prepared us for the difficulties we have met with ; for our experience has shewn that we held them too cheap, having either made too light of their strength or given ourselves credit for too much. What I have said is merely my private opinion, and I give it with some diffidence lest I should be mistaken.
>
> We have had a great deal of rain lately, which has impeded our operations, and, considering the season of the year, great vigour and

expedition is necessary. Indeed we expect every hour to hear that the business is decided.
A resolution very detrimental to an increase of reputation and my private interest has been lately adopted here — I mean the calling all the Zemindars up to the Presidency, and in a great measure taking the business of that chiefship out of the hands of the Chief and Council. This, together with other particulars, makes me apprehensive the Otterton estate will not come within my grasp. I have desired Mr. Webster to wait upon you for your opinion. He will shew you my letter to him, and likewise the copy of one which I have writ to Mr. Wombwell by this dispatch, which treats on the affairs of Masulipatam.
Advices are just now received from camp that the Governor of Pondicherry has sent out a flag of truce desiring permission to send out propositions for a capitulation. God grant it may terminate successfully, for much depends upon that event. My situation here is extreamly disagreeable, as all the Zemindars are now here, and when they will return I cannot tell.
If the state of things should put it in your power to serve me towards my promotion in this country, your assistance will always be very gratefully acknowledged by me. My presumption grows in seeing the small abilities of the present Governor and Council.

Edward Cotsford.

Chocapah to the Honble. Robert Palk, Esq. 1778, October 19th, Fort St. George.

I have the pleasure to inform your Honour that Mr. Bellecombe, the French Governour, and his Council were at last obliged to surrender the Fort and town of Pondichery to General Munro by capitulation yesterday under the following terms : that private fortunes of the white and black inhabitants of Pondicherry are to be secured to themselves, and they are to be permitted to carry them where they please ; the fortifications [and] the houses belonging to the Government and the inhabitants both white and black are not to be destroyed untill they further hear from Europe ;

the French troops and the French gentlemen are surrendered themselves prisoners of war to his Britan[n]ick Majesty on condition they are permitted to proceed to Europe under the cost of the English. We the inhabitants under the English protection are very well secured by the present victory, as we shall certainly be under no apprehension from the French, who can do nothing in these part[s] of the world during the present war, as they have no Settlement in the East Indies to send their forces and land them.

Chocapah

Chocapah to the Honble. Robert Palk, Esq. 1778, October 31st, Fort St. George. Received 27th March, 1779.

Since writing to you on the 19th- instant I learn that our Grenadiers marched in at the Villinour Gate and entered into the town of Pondicherry a little before 5 o'clock the 18th in the evening, and [a] little before 6 of the same evening the French troops with their officers marched out, colours flying and drums beating, to the glacis, where they piled their arms and were received prisoners of war by a party of our troops commanded by Captain Lysaght, and marched about a mile beyond our camp, where they remained that night ; and next day they marched down to Madrass, and arrived here the 28th. They were about five hundred prisoners and about forty officers, part of which they keep prisoners in the Black Town, and the rest sent down to Poonamally, where they remain prisoners ; and the officers are set at liberty upon their parole, to live here and at St. Thome. The Company allows them the usual allowance. I hear they have also about two hundred more French prisoners in the hospital at Pondicherry, who are to be brought here by sea. Mr. Bellecombe, Mr. Law, and the rest of the gentlemen of Council and other private merchants and the French inhabitants are still at Pondicherry. M. Bellecombe is expected here early next month. The French frigate that was in the Road of Pondicherry is permitted to go to Mauritius and from thence to France. After the surrender General Munro received the merchants and other native inhabitants with much civility,

and allowed them to reside and carry on business under British protection. The Governor and Council also granted permission to the gentlemen and other residents of French nationality to remain and trade, provided they took an oath of fidelity to the Government.
General Munro returned from Pondicherry this morning. Captain William Rumbold (our Governor's son) is ready to take his passage with all the news on the Cormorant, now under dispatch for England.

Chocapah

Thomas Palk to Robert Palk, Esq. 1779, October 15th, Fort St. George,

I have already informed you of the cause of my removal from the paymastership of Chinglaput. It was a cruel stroke upon me indeed. However, Sir, I flatter myself that you and Mr. Sulivan will endeavor to get me some appointment. I have been out of employ ever since, and see no probability of being otherwise, notwithstanding Mr. Rumbold has so often engaged his word of honor to serve me, and as often forfeited it. Never was a man so universally disliked. He employs people not in the service, and gives away places to the youngest servants which the oldest would grasp at ; takes away places and gives it to others, and such like conduct. There is scarce a foot of land between this and Ganjam but he has sold. The Guntoor Circar the Nabob is to have, or has it. The Jaghire in December last was advertized to be lett, but it did not take place, because of course the Nabob paid handsomely for it. But what could the country otherwise expect from a man of his stamp ? The seeds of corruption have so effectually taken root that I do not think it possible to eradicate [them]. Gaming is arrived to that height that it requires the most vigorous measures to break the spirit of it, and to begin with the Select Committee. I dined with the Governor a few days ago, when he proposed a rubber, which of course was readily assented to. The party consisted of the Governor, Mr. Plumer, Lieutenants Low and Malcolm has scarce begun when dinner came upon table, and kept 60 people waiting for its being finished.
The Circars will soon be in the state of the Nabob's country. The

Zemindars were so very handsomely squeezed when they were called down last year that I hear the zemindaries are in a state of depopulation owing to the oppression of the Zemindars. Thus, Sir, you have but a slight view of our situation, though it may convey a strong idea. Mr. Cotsford will no doubt give you a better view of it than I am able, though not with more truth. The Company are sinking so very gradually step by step into mire as if they really intended it, and I am sure their affairs were never so well conducted as by a Governor and 12 Council, for the less opposition a wicked Governor has to encounter, the more mischief he can do. You are a Proprietor, Sir, so therefore for the Company's sake become a Director. I shall then hope they may still be saved.
You are indebted. Sir, to Mr. Floyer for his kindnesses to me, as I am sure it was on your account I received so much friendship from him.

Tho. Palk

John d'Fries to Robert Palk, Esq. 1780, January 16th, Madras.

Three ships of Sir Edward Hughes's fleet are arrived, the Superb, Eagle and Nymph, which were sent forward with the sick of the squadron, being a great many. The rest of the fleet is expected in a week hence. Mr. Cuthbert is come,so we shall tender money to him on your account for Navy bills. Mr. Stone's affairs here are not as he represented them to his creditors in England, and we shall not trouble ourselves with them unless we find that we can be of use to you and others.
The Maratta war still continues. A few days ago 500 Europeans were sent away from hence to join Colonel Goddard at Surat. This is an improper time to be quarrelling with the country Powers and with so powerful a one as the Marrattas. Hyder seem[s] to be only waiting for an opportunity to break with us. A great fire happened in November last at Bengal in the Company's warehouse, which burnt 18 lacks of rupees of raw silk and piece goods. The treasury at Bengal is very low. Here on the Coast they can hardly make both ends meet, the expences of fortif cation, etc., being very great. We have heard nothing of any French ships in the Indian seas since the taking of the *Osterley*.

It is said that Mr. Rumbold is to leave us in the course of March next, having taken his passage on the *General Barker,*
The Nabob desire[s] his compliments to you and for a continuance of your friendship. His affairs can hardly be worse than they are at present, the drain being continual, and the sources lessening every day. The divided interest in his family continues as great as ever notwithstanding the death of Maphauscawn, which happened some months ago.
John d'Fries

Thomas Palk to Robert Palk, Esq. 1780, January 30th, Fort St. George.

I had, Sir, flattered myself that your displeasure would have in some measure subsided by this time, and that you would have honored me with a renewal of your correspondence ; but I am unhappy enough to find myself still lying under it, and unfortunately at a time that I have more need of your friendship than ever I had.
Being still without employment, I beg you to use your influence to procure me some appointment, such as a paymastership or a seat in the Masulipatam Council.
Mr. Rumbold has put me off ever since I was removed from Chinglaput with the strongest assurances of his serving me. Mr. Sulivan has interposed in my behalf with him in an uncommon friendly manner, but without any other success than promises. In short. Sir, he is blind and deaf to every other consideration but that of establishing a strong interest at home ; and I hope that if he does not do something for me, that he will repent he had not considered it an object to have acquired yours. I do. Sir, assure you that a King of France was never so absolute as he is here. Everything he proposes is carried without the least opposition. He is now on the point of going home, and Mr. Whitehill will of course succeed. I could say a great deal, but at present it would not be prudent. I shall say this much, that the Company is sinking into ruin as fast as possible.
We have accounts that Colonel Goddard has at last taken the field against the Morattoes. A detachment has been sent from hence of 400 Europeans and 2 battalions of sepoys, but they cannot possibly reach Surat till the middle of February. Hyder Ally, seeing how we are entangling ourselves,

is growing very troublesome. A vessel in the month of November coming down the Malabar Coast was taken by one of his, and carried into Callicutt, with six gentlemen and three ladies from Europe by Suez. And 'tis reported that he stopt by the same means Captain Bonnveau and another gentleman with dispatches from the Company so late only as August.

Mr. Grey that was once in the Bengal Council, has been pitched upon, in preference to a Company's servant, to go Ambassador to Hyder. He also had an employ at the siege of Pondicherry and at Mahe, when at least a dozen Company's servants were unemployed. But, Sir, this is nothing to other oppressive acts of Government.

Sir E. Hughes arrived here with his squadron and nine Indiamen the 18th instant. He has this day presented his Majesty's letter to the Nabob. Sir Edward is extremely well and hearty, and Sir E. Vernon goes home in an Indiaman much displeased thereat. Dick Welland is now with me, and is very much esteemed by the Admiral and officers. He seems to think it better he had staid at home, as he would be more in the way of promotion.I send this by his Majesty's ship *Coventry* by way of Suez, though I am very doubtful of his reaching you safe, for the gentlemen that have lately come that way met with a great many difficulties.

I have made a mistake, Sir. Captains Banks and Bonnevaux were coming from Bussora, and [were] taken by the Marattoes and not by Hyder- Ally. I shall esteem it a favor [if] you will send me a line for Mr. Whitehill. My wife is well, and joins me in presenting her respects to you and Mrs. Palk and love to my cousins.

Tho. Palk

Stephen Sulivan to Robert Palk, Esqr. 1780, February 5th, Fort St. George.

I return you my sincere thanks for your obliging enquiries after Mrs. Sulivan's and my health. Mine, you will hear from Queen Square, has been exactly the same as when I partook of red mullets with you in Devonshire. I wish I could speak as favorably of Mrs. Sulivan, who has suffered severely indeed from this relaxing climate so inauspicious to women in general. She is, however, at present considerably recovered, and I trust with suitable care and attention will have no more relapses. On the arrival of Sir Edward Hughes, he scarce waited for an introduction of me to him, but took the first opportunity of mentioning your name and the friendly manner in which you had been pleased to express sollicitude for my prosperity, adding at the same time on his own part he should be happy to forward my wishes in any way I would point out to him from the regard he had for his old friend Mr. Palk.From my father's letters I find you have been equally attentive in desiring Mr. John De Fries to give me his confidence and advice. No man in the Settlement is better calculated for such a task from his local knowledge and long experience in business.

To my father's letters I refer you for particulars of my situation, as I have not a secret upon earth I wish concealed from you. You will there find how mistaken he was when he attributed to the Nabob any other motives of conduct than an artful policy operating from fear, without a single remembrance of past obligations, or a view to present favor but as it may prove a channel for the gratification of his ambition. Mr. Macpherson, who must write because he is hired, may employ volumes to expiscate (in his own elegant new coinage of words) the reverse ; but men who have no restraints of this kind to warp or mislead their judgment are contented with the facts and the evidence before them.

My father will likewise explain to you the reasons for my resigning the Persian Translatorship, which have the sanction of Mr. De Fries' approbation. When I was given to understand that not an iota of confidential communication was to pass through me, but that at best I was to be a mere letter carrier, it was time to recollect I had a commendable pride about me, which will prevent me, I hope always, from being insignificant. The profits of my place of Secretary are so scanty, and the expence of Madras since your time so increased, that it ceases any longer to be an object. In short, my dear Sir, I have laid such stress in my letters to my father on a seat in Council or the Residency of Tanjore as the only two objects on this Coast that can enable me to acquire a competency, that I hope you will use every argument to persuade him to bring either of those points forward, that it may be settled in the new arrangements at home, and not left to be done here.

Stephen Sulivan

XLVII
The death of Robert Palk jnr, 1783

The Company moved to secure a safe trip home for the unwell Robert Palk junior by booking a good cabin and providing a surgeon to oversee his health throughout the voyage. Despite all the precautions Robert had several strokes in succession that were well out of the surgeons capability to treat. The set of letters gives details of the goods Robert thought necessary for his journey and an account of the customs procedure. He was a wealthy man and left £20,000 to his uncle Palk in his will as well as similar sums to his near family.

The Case of Robert Palk, jun., on board the *Surprise*. By Surgeon Adam Burt. 1783, April 3rd, Calcutta.

Agreed to attend as surgeon to Robert Palk, Esq., during his voyage to Europe in the *Surprise* packet. This gentleman appears to be about 38 or 40 years of age. He is of a spare habit of body ; has been at least 20 years in India, and for the most part very healthy during that time. Mr. Campbell, the Surgeon General, informs me that Mr. Palk has had more than one very severe fall within these last two or three years ; particularly once when he was walking on the roof of a house, which in this country is generally flat ; it gave way under his feet, and he fell through from a very considerable height. From this his system in general received a shock, the effects of which confined him several days. However, no remarkable symptoms followed as a consequence immediately after this or any other accident which appened to him.
Mr. Campbell also informed me that, as Mr. Palk was riding on horseback some weeks ago, he suddenly fell to the ground without any apparent cause. The nearest medical assisstants were instantly called : they found him in a state of insensibility, laying as if asleep. It was imagined that some injury had been received from the fall, and phlebotomy was performed. He gradually recovered his senses, but was

affected with spasms, or as he himself expressed it, startings of the muscles of one side of his body. His face was also much distorted. Mr. Stark, Surgeon at Calcutta, took more blood from him, but I do not know what medicines were prescribed. In two or three days after this first attack he was seized with a fit, which Mr. Campbell says was of the apoplectic or epileptic kind. Since then he has had several returns of epileptic fits.

Diary:

16th April. Mr. Palk is in good spirits. The spasms of one side are not so frequent as usual, but his face is considerably distorted. He takes pills of assafoetida as prescribed for him by Mr. Campbell.
17th. He says that ' he had a slight touch of his disorder last night, but he sleeped it away.' Mr. Campbell and Mr. Stark thought it adviseable to put a seton in his neck, which I have performed this day. He is pretty chearful, but his tongue is swelled and he pronounces his words with much difficulty.
18th. This afternoon, as Mr. Palk and I were sitting on the quarter deck, he started up very suddenly from his seat, and without having time to utter a single word he fell down in violent convulsions, which continued near a quarter of an hour. He soon recovered his senses, but continued very languid during the remainder of the day.
I prescribed camphor, antimony wine and assafoetida.
21st. Very free from spasms ; pronounces his words with uncommon ease ; is chearful.
23rd. Mr. Palk had a fit this morning. I prescribed valerian root.
26th. He had a fit this morning at 6 o'clock ; is very, languid ; his tongue s exceedingly swelled. I gave camphor and valerian.
29th. The spasms are abated, and the distortion of his face is scarcely perceptible.
1st May. Mr. Palk is in excellent spirits.
3rd. He is almost entirely free from spasms ; tongue not so much swelled, and he speaks with ease. I continue the camphor and valerian, and also the antimonial wine.

4th. Mr. Palk appears as if in perfect health. Medicines as formerly.
8th. The ease which Mr. Palk has enjoyed for some time is too soon interrupted. He had a fit this morning about four o'clock.
9th. Mr. Palk had another severe attack last night, and was extremely languid this morning.
11th. The spasms of his muscles are very frequent, particularly of the right side of the body.
12th. Mr. Palk had another fit this morning. After the convulsions were over he remained comatose for a considerable time ; is very languid. Medicines given as formerly.
13th. Today he is in extraordinary good spirits ; walked the deck in the evening for a considerable time, and is pretty free from spasms.
14th. Mr. Palk was seized with his disorder this morning about 5 o'clock. The convulsions were uncommonly severe. When these abated he remained without any signs of life for several minutes. At length breathing succeeded, but that more laborious than I ever saw in any other case. By degrees it became more moderate, but he remained comatose, at least for the most part. He is now and then seized with violent convulsions, which gradually terminate in an universal tremor, and leaves him insensible. In the evening the convulsions were very alarming. I accordingly bled him.
15th. We have been becalmed these 2 or 3 days in 2 degrees N. latitude. Mr. Palk remains insensible and in a comatose state, but frequently seized with convulsions.
16th. Mr. Palk does not recover his senses in the least. I applied blisters to his temples.
17th. He gives some signs of returning sensibility, but remains speechless. He is restless, and twists his body into many very awkward postures. 18th. During last night Mr. Palk appeared to be in great agony . His cries were dreadful. The unnatural exertions of his body were so great that it required two men to keep him in the cotte. There is an universal tremor of the muscles. His pulse 80.
19th. He is still comatose ; lies with his eyes open, but now and then he is seized with convulsions, which gradually terminate in tremors. Pulse 100. We are in 28 miles N. lat. and still becalmed.20th. Mr. Palk died about 4 o'clock p.m.

Henry Preston to Sir Robert Palk, Bart. Bruton Street, London. 1783, August 8th, Fort St. George.

As you have always been so sincere a friend to me, I presume to inform you of my safe arrival here after a very prosperous voyage of four months and ten days. We sailed from England on the 11th of March, and touched at St. Jago about 3 weeks after. This was the only place we touched at : we staid there but three days. We met with nothing remarkable till we came in sight of the Coast, July 19th, and we came to an an- chor on the 22nd.
I was greatly surprised to hear of Hyder Alley's death, and also of Sir Eyre Coote's, who died on his passage to Bengal by sea. Hyder's son Tipo Seib carries on the war at present. He is not above 40 miles from hence with all his horse. I hear that there is a cessation of arms for a month to take place, but I am not certain.
There was an engagement the 22 of June between Sir Edward Hughes and Suffrein off Trincoumale. I am not acquainted with the particulars, but I think we had 500 men killed, and the fleet came in here in a very shattered condition.
I began to receive pay as soon as I came ashore. My pay is 18 pagodas per month. I have not had an opportunity to go to Bengal as yet, but I think I shall go in a few days.

Henry Preston
P.S. I return you my most grateful acknowledgements for the genteel station your goodness has placed me in.

Dr. Adam Burt to Messrs. James & David Webster, Leadenhall Street. 1783, September 10th, Limerick, Ireland,

I was ordered by the Governor and Council of Bengal to attend as surgeon to Robert Palk, Esq., during his voyage from thence to Europe. Accordingly I embarked along with him on board the Surprise packet, and we sailed in April. This gentleman had been attacked with an epilepsy, from which, in the opinion of the most experienced medical practitioners in Calcutta, he could not recover in India. I am sincerely sorry to add that his disease defeated my utmost efforts to preserve him. He died about a month after we left Bengal. I proposed to have set off immediately for London, where I might have communicated the intelligence in person to some of Mr. Palk's relations. But I think it is necessary for me to remain here till I shall hear from them. I will be happy if Capt. Asquith of the Surprise has given a satisfying account of matters. I am much afraid, however, that he has not acted with becoming delicacy as a person to whom devolved the charge of effects belonging to a gentleman of very extensive concerns. The captain opened the bureau and escritoire of the deceased, and took into his possession what papers he thought proper. I advised him to call some gentlemen to witness and sign an attestation of the propriety of his proceedings. This he neglected.

Major Macgowane came a passenger in this ship. He will wait on Mr. Palk's relations in England as soon as he can conveniently after his arrival there. I need not now enlarge on the many improprieties of Capt. Asquith's conduct with regard to Mr. Palk. The Major will give them a more particular account of circumstances which render my stay here for a little while adviseable. I write this in a hurry just as the ship is coming to an anchor, lest Mr. Palk's relations should take any measures in consequence of the captain's letters without making further enquiry.

The friends of Mr. Palk may command my services towards procuring all the papers of the deceased, if possible, and to forward the other effects as they shall direct. If, however, it is deemed necessary for me to interfere, a method must be adopted with which the captain cannot elude a ready and implicit compliance. Mr. Palk had a Bengal and a European servant on board. The former was promised a passage out again to India. The latter has not yet received any wages. They both wait here, and will proceed agreeable to directions. Meantime I supply them with what money is necessary for their subsistence.

My stay in England cannot be long. I wish to wait on Mr. Palk's relations, and on many accounts am anxious to get to London. I hope there will be as httle delay as possible, at least after the arrival of Major Macgowane. Now, Gentlemen, as the captain conceals every information he has de- rived from the perusal of Mr. Palk's papers, I do not even know the address of any of his relations. Permit me to request of you to communicate the above as expeditiously as possible.

Adam Burt

Dr. Adam Burt to Major J. McGowan. Memorandum for Major Macgowane from his very obedient servant Adam Burt,1783, circa September 10th.

As you mean to wait on Mr. Palk's relations in England, I trust that you will communicate to them the various improprieties of Capt. Asquith's behaviour. Without doubt his claims on my account will not escape attention. You are no stranger to the unjustifiable manner by which Mr. Palk was compelled to promise to Capt. Asquith the payment of 1,500 rupees for my passage after our embarkation and notwithstanding the sum which Mr. Palk had already given. Besides, the table for Capt. Asquith and his officers has been kept during the voyage entirely at the expence of Mr. Palk, excepting the stores which you brought on board. If Mr. Palk's relations do not dispute the payment of the above 1,500 rupees, they will certainly treat the captain with very undeserved generosity. I shall not be surprised if Capt. Asquith retains in his possession the money he found in Mr. Palk's escritoire, thinking in that way to be sure of payment. If Mr. Palk's relations shall view this claim of the captain in the light in which it appears to me as an unprejudiced person, I will in that case make Capt. Asquith my debtor for attendance on the sick of the ship's company during the passage to Europe, and request of Mr. Palk's friends to delay payment of Capt. Asquith till my bill shall be discharged.

You was present when the captain solicited me to attend the sick people on board. When I complied it was by no means from any pecuniary motives. Afterwards, however, I could understand from Mr. Palk's conversation that he meant to advise me to some measures similar to the above. But if Mr. Palk's relations, after your explanation of the affair, shall on the contrary be of opinion that it is not worth while to elude the payment of 1,500 to Capt. Asquith in addition to the 10,000 which Mr. Palk al- ready paid, then my claim may be laid aside, for I only desire by that means to compel the captain to what Mr. Palk's relations may deem equitable.

Mr. Burt's letter by Major McGowan, and inventory of Mr. Palk's stores.

[Enclosure.] After the death of Mr. Robert Palk on board the Surprise Capt. Asquith opened the bureau and escritoire of the deceased. I observed that the following articles were contained therein, and I instantly made a memorandum of it : — Gold mohurs, 72 ; rupees, 398 ; guineas, 11 ; English silver coin, 13 shillings ; small gold pieces, 8 ; four bags supposed to contain gold chequins, and marked A, B, C, D ; a small box supposed to contain gold, addressed to Messrs. John Gran and Mr Thomas Hinchman in Berners Street, London ; 3 gold watches, chains and a variety of seals ; 1 silver watch ; 1 pair gold sleeve buttons ; a gold stockbuckle ; a diamond breastbuckle ; a silver stock-buckle ;a variety of pocket books and papers contained in them ; a Persian seal ring set in silver ; 2 pairs silver shoe-buckles ; 2 sapphire rings ; one brilliant diamond ring ; 1 hoop ring ; several miniature pictures ; Voltaire's works in English, volumes 39. List of Mr. Palk's stores transcribed from the original in possession of his European servant.

David Asquith to Sir Robert Palk, Bruton Street, London. 1783, September 12th, Surprise packet, Limerick. Received 14th October.

I am sorry to inform you of the death of Mr. Robert Palk, who departed this life May 21st on his passage to Europe. Mr. John Nimmo, who goes up with the packet, will inform you of the particulars. He has left sundry articles on board, consisting of plate, some money in Venetians, and wearing apparel. He has two servants. I shall be glad of your instructions for sending those things round to you, or in what manner you chuse to have them disposed off. Mr. Burt was ordered to attend him home as doctor, for whose passage Mr. Palk agreed to pay 1,500 Rs. He has mentioned it in a small diary he kept while alive, and he likewise mentioned it to the doctor and Major McGowan.

D. Asquith

Dr. Adam Burt to Sir Robert Palk. 1783, September 16th, Limerick. Received 3rd October.

Immediately after my arrival at this place I wrote to Messrs. Websters, enclosing a letter which I hope they will forward without delay. As I did not then know your address, I was obliged to take that method of communicating to his friends the death of Robert Palk, Esq., on board the *Surprise* packet bound from Bengal to Europe. He had been attacked with an epilepsy, and on that account quitted India. I was ordered by the Governor and Council of Bengal to attend a[s] surgeon to that gentleman during his voyage to Europe. You may readily conceive how much the fatal termination of his disease is to me a subject of regret.
In the letter to which I allude I also mentioned that the captain of the ship had conducted himself with great impropriety, in my opinion, with regard to the effects of the deceased, and that I was determined to stay here till I should hear from the relations, and endeavour to procure for them a satisfying account of matters. I am happy to say that I believe the property of Mr. Palk on board the *Surprise* is now in security. The captain is now sensible of what a serious nature the irregularities of his conduct were, and he has adopted measures with which I readily coincided because I thought they tended to the preservation of Mr. Palk's effects. Everything which belonged to that gentleman remaining on board the Surprise packet was locked up and sealed in presence of Captain Asquith, two officers of the ship, Mr. Louch, agent for Colonel Watson in Bengal, the owner of the ship, the late Mr. Palk's servants, and myself. The money, the diamond rings and pearls, also all the kees are deposited with Mr. Lyons, agent for the India Company in this place. I am sorry that I referred for a just account of the business to Major Macgowane, who came a passenger in the *Surprise*. He said that he had business with Mr. Palk's relations, and at any rate intended to wait on them. The Major had a dispute with the captain at sea, but they both behaved with civility to each other afterwards. I relied so far on the Major as to believe that in a matter of such importance to me he would represent things impartially. But I am surprised to find that before he left this place he gave an exaggerated account of the improprieties of Captain Asquith's behaviour to the agent for the Company. The bad conduct of the captain does not require to be magnified. It is therefore necessary for me to say that my memorandums with which I have entrusted Major Macgowane are to be relied on as conveying my sentiment. When Captain Asquith opened the

bureau and escritoire of the deceased, it was in the presence of Major Macgowane and myself, and the watches, rings and other trinkets I saw sealed up. But the captain appeared to me to be most culpable in not taking an inventory of the papers which he took into his possession, though I advised him to it. That neglect first awakened in me suspicions of the captain's intentions, and the imputing it to an impertinent curiosity in him to peruse private papers is perhaps the best construction which it will bear. Several expressions which the captain used encreased my doubts as to his honesty. Mr. Palk's servants are now gone on board to keep an eye over every thing which belonged to their late master. But as they entertained the same ideas as to the captain's intentions that I did, they would not remain in the ship till affairs were more regularly gone about, lest they should be deemed answerable for any thing which might afterwards be missed.
I will willingly proceed agreeable to directions, and will forward or carry along with me every thing belonging to Mr. Palk with the greatest care in case I shall be so authorised.

Adam Burt

Dr. Adam Burt to Sir Robert Palk, 1783, October 3rd, Limerick.

I have just received your letter of the 22nd September in reply to mine of the 10th, but I shall remain here until I get your answer to mine of the 16th. I have no wish to injure Captain Asquith, but there are circumstances which render me suspicious of him. Captain Asquith commanded a small vessell some time ago in India. She was bound from Bengal to Madrass with a cargo of rice, and insured for the voyage at the risque of a society in which Mr, Palk was principally concerned. The captain thought proper to call at Trincomallee with a view, as was said, to get a good price for some commodity of his own. The ship was taken from that circumstance, and the owners lost their property, who certainly had great reason to blame Captain Asquith. This account I had from Mr. Palk himself. I could clearly understand from the captain's conversation that he had perused Mr. Palk's papers about that bussiness, and he hinted

that the claim upon the underwriters would probably be renewed. Since we arrived here I accompanied the captain to see all Mr. Palk's effects on board sealed up, I then insisted that the papers, which the captain brought from his own trunk, should be put up by themselves, and that he should mark them accordingly, with which he complied.
The captain talked of exposing letters for Sir Thomas Rumbold directed to be delivered by Mr. Palk into the hands of Sir T. or his uncle. He threatened to flog Mr. Palk's servant to oblige him to give up a list of Mr. Palk's stores, though a copy would have served every purpose. I hope soon to elucidate more fully the cause of my proceedings when I shall have the honour of a personal interview with you.

Adam Burt

Dr. Adam Burt to Sir Robert Palk, Bart. 1783; October 6th, Limerick.

I shall remain here for a few days longer in the hope of receiving definite instructions from you respecting the effects of your nephew. I fear you have found it difficult to form a just opinion from the captain's communications, the reports of Major McGowan and the 1st mate, and my own letters.
I was afraid that the Major was influenced too much by prejudice against the captain, and might perhaps advise you to measures which would in the end turn out abortive. I understood that before the Major left this place he shewed the memorandums with which I had entrusted him to different gentlemen here, and endeavoured by them to corroborate his own accounts, which were that the captain had certainly embezzled the property of the late Mr. Palk. I readily submit to your decision when you shall have arrived at a thorough knowledge of this business, whether or not the cautions were proper which I gave against the prejudice that influenced the Major.
As regards the captain's claim for 150*l*. for my passage, I suggest your delaying decision until you have examined your nephew's papers.

Adam Burt

Major J. McGowan to [Sir Robert Palk]. 1783, October 10th, London.

I had the honor to receive your letter of the 6th instant. I was present at the opening of Mr. Palk's papers to look for a will, but none, I believe, was found by the captain of the ship. From a knowledge that I had of your nephew's method and attention to his affairs, and that he knew the dangerous tendency of his complaint, I must own I felt greatly disappointed in my expectations in not finding either a will or memorandum which could give the desired information. When you arrive in town I will do myself the honor to wait on you.

M J Mcgowan

Dr. Adam Burt to Sir Robert Palk, Bart. 1783, October 14th, Limerick.

Last night I was favoured with your letter of the 4th October. Captain Asquith at first made objections to delivering any thing over to my charge principally because you sent no order directly to him. Captain Hall, who resides in this town, acquaints me that he is desired by you to assist me. By his advice Captain Asquith consents to deliver to me the money and papers. Mr. Louch, agent for the ship, positively refuses to allow any of the effects of the late Mr. Palk to be carried round to England in the *Surprise*, Limerick being the destined port. I shall therefore provide boats, and will superintend the landing of Mr. Palk's effects. They must be deposited in the Custom House here till some person authorized by you shall demand and forward them in a vessel bound for London. Probably there may be some things which are seizable. I am informed that you can procure an order for the Collector here to deliver the effects to be forwarded to the India House. Captain Hall promises his services.
I really do not know whether or not Mr. Palk left any will. On the 14th May he was seized with violent convulsions, and continued totally insensible till the 20th. Consequently he gave no directions. It was thought that the papers were not safe in any part of the ship : they were accordingly landed, and have remained sealed up in the Custom House. .

I propose to set off for London two days after this.

Adam Burt

Robert Hall to Sir Robert Palk 1783, October 14th, Limerick.

I was favoured last night with your letter of the 4th of this month, and have advised Mr. Burt to get what things are with the captain at Mr. Lions's, and proceed with them to you, as 1 hear they are mostly the papers of your deceased nephew, and may be of much consequence. I find that Mr. Louch, the agent for Colonel Watson, who[m] the ship belongs to, has ordered all the chests, trunks, etc., that are now on board to be sent up to the Custome House here, refusing to let them go round in the ship. I will do all I can to forward them to London by the first convenience after I shall receive your orders. Mr. Burt goes down tomorrow morning to bring them up. Should there be any muslines, etc., which might be me[a]nt by my late worthy friend as presents to his relations, I perhaps may be able to get them out here without much difficulty, or you might get an order from the Tre[a]sury to the Commissioner of the Customes to let them be reship[p]ed here without their being opened.

Robert Hall

James Lyons to Sir Robert Palk1783, October 15th, Limerick.

It having been represented to me by Major McGouan and Mr. Burt that part of the effects of the late Mr. Palk on board was in cash, I gave it as my opinion to have it brought on shore and deposited in the Custom House or in some safe hands, as I could not answer for its safety on board, where the vessell lay 20 miles down our river. Accordingly the purser of the ship, Mr. Louch, the captain and Mr. Burt brought it up, and in Mr. Burt's presence were sealed up ; and agreable to your letter they shall be handed to Mr. Burt.

James Lyons

Certificate by Dr. Adam Burt. 1783, October 16th, Limerick.

At my request Mr. William Douglas, merchant, of Limerick; attended yesterday on board the *Surprise* as a witness to my protest to Captain Asquith and Mr Louch against landing the effects of Mr. Palk. After I had protested a boat was brought alongside and loaded with the goods by the seamen.
Adam Burt

Attested by William Douglas
Certificate by Dr. Adam Burt. 1783, October 17th, Limerick.

Mr. Louch, agent for Colonel Watson, having refused to carry the effects of the late Mr. Palk to London or any part of England, and having insisted on sending them ashore here, I certify that I protested against their being landed.
Adam Burt

Certified to be a true statement. Robert Hall
David Asquith to Sir Robert Palk 1783, October 17th, Limerick.

I am surprised to learn from Mr. Burt that you have received no letter from me. I wrote by Mr. John Nimmo, my chief mate, who carried the Company's dispatches and a bundle of letters addressed to the care of the late Mr. Palk. I instructed Mr. Nimmo to call on you in Bruton Street and give you a detailed account of the effects of Mr. Palk.
Why he has not waited on you or delivered my letter remains a mystery to me. If you please to send to the Swan with Two Neck[s] in Lad Lane, where I find Mr. Nimmo is to be heard of, possibly the above letters may be recovered. Some of them, I believe, contained bills of exchange belonging to the particular friends of Mr. Palk.
Your not receiving any advices from me must no doubt appear very strange to you. I have only to request you will be kind enough to suspend forming any unfavourable opinion of me till I have the honour of seeing you. I have received orders to bring the ship round to London, and now

only wait for a favourable wind to proceed.
D. Asquith

Dr. Adam Burt to Sir Robert Palk, Bart.1783, October 31st, London.

This day I have deposited the effects of your nephew, which I brought from Limerick, in your house in Bruton Street, where I had the honour to receive yours of the 27th instant. You only desired me to bring the articles which were deposited with Mr. Lyons, but Captain Hall concurring with me in opinion that it would give you satisfaction to get the papers as soon as possible, I have also brought all of them that were placed in the Custom House on the 16th ultimo.
I do not wonder that you are surprized at Mr. Louch's behaviour. He and Mr. Lyons, agent for the Company, are joined agents for Colonel Watson in Bengal, the proprietor of the vessel.
I saw 32 packages delivered over to Mr. Sexton Bayllee, Surveyor of the Port of Limerick, among which are a large box for Francis Roberts at Dr. Lawrence's, Essex Street, Strand, and a small box for Mrs. Elizabeth Ironside, at Twickenham, Middlesex, both by favour of Mr. Palk. The effects were delivered to the Surveyor with the seals entire which had been put on on the 16th ultimo. I was not a little astonished to find almost all the seals broken the next day after they were landed. In presence of Mr. Louch and Captain Hall I requested permission again to seal up all the packages, which the Surveyor refused me. He said it was dark when the effects were landed, and the seals might have been broken off by the porters ; but he insisted on immediately inspecting all the packages, and that he himself would open them if no other person would be present to superintend it. I told him that I was not answerable for the consequences of landing the effects, yet I would do all in my power towards their preservation, and had witnessed their being delivered over to him to be deposited in the King's stores merely as a place of security. That I would immediately make an affidavit concerning his proceedings, which, if you pleased, might be laid before the Commissioners. This surely alarmed him, for next day he requested of me to seal up all the packages, to which I consented, at the same time observing that seahng

them up at that time would not supersede my affidavit, which I made accordingly.
Before I left Limerick the Surveyor had set off for Dublin. He gave out that he would lay before the Commissioners information concerning the contents of Mr. Palk's packages, based on statements of Mr. Louch. I represented to the Collector of Limerick that Mr. Louch could not know anything about the contents.
I had so much luggage that I could not possibly bring any of Mr. Palk's servants along with me. Mr. Louch and Captain Asquith had no objection to carry them round in the ship. The European will probably take another mode of conveyance. The Indian proposed officiating as servant to the 2nd mate till their arrival in London, which I encouraged, as I thought it would ensure him protection

Adam Burt
P.S. I am to be heard of at Messrs. Websters.

Henry McMahon to Sir Robert Palk, Bart., Bruton Street, London. 1783, November 2nd, Limerick.

I have been engaged by Dr. Burt to look after the effects of Mr. Palk. Directly after Dr. Burt's departure, Mr. Baillie went to Dublin to see the Commissioners, and on his return made a seizure of the effects. He falsely asserts that Dr. Burt offered him 500/. to give up the goods. I propose to file a claim tomorrow lest the effects should be forthwith condemned, though I am not able to comply with all legal requirements; but I hope you will depute a person who can make a claim in accordance with the Act, of which I enclose an abstract. I have already sent a memorial to the Commissioners praying for a postponement of proceedings pending investigation.
The Speaker of our House of Commons (Mr. Pery) is Baillie's relation and patron, but would by no means countenance him in an act of injustice. I therefore take the liberty to recommend to you either to write yourself, or procure some other gentleman of consequence who may know Mr. Pery, to represent this matter in its true light. If this is done, I

have little doubt that Baillie would instantly be checked in his career, which may save much expence.

Robert Hall to Sir Robert Palk, Bart., Bruton Street, London. 1783, November 3rd, Limerick.

Finding the goods at the Custome House that were sent from the Surprise are to be condemned and sold as a legal seizure, I have directed Mr. Henry McMahon, Attorney at Law, to send a petition and a copy of the affadavit sworn to by Mr. Burt to the Commissioners of the Customs at Dublin, in hopes they will give further time, so that you may have an oppertunity to make such application and send over such instructions as you think proper.

Sober Hall

Henry McMahon to Sir Robert Palk, Bart., Bruton Street, London. 1783, November 4th, Limerick.

I yesterday got at the Custom House a copy of the seizing note lodged for the goods in the stores, and found it dated the 15th of October, being about the day the goods were landed, though I am convinced it was not filed until yesterday morning ; but it was intended so as that the time for claiming may expire before you could possibly have an opportunity of putting in a claim according to the Act, of which I sent you an abstract. I instantly tendered a claim such as the nature of the case would admit of. It was peremptorily refused; not being according to law. I immediately prepared and sent off by Post Office express a memorial to the Commissioners. I refer you for further particulars to copies of the seizing note, memorial and claim herewith sent.

Sober Hall to Sir Robert Palk, Bart., Bruton Street, London. 1783, November 8th, Limerick.

I write for Mr. McMahon to say that the Commissioners have granted time for the submission of a proper claim. You might send Dr. Burt over to make the claim.
Thus far is Mr. Bailie disappointed, who flattered himself with the notion of accelerating matters so as to have the goods condemned and sold before there would be either a claim or tryal.
Henry McMahon
Sober Hall

William Young to Sir Robert Palk, Bart., M.P., Bruton Street, London. 1783, November 9th, Limerick.

Honoured Sir,
I am given to understand your honour is heir to my late master, Robert Palk, Esq. I think it my duty to acquaint you with the particulars which were taken of his stores after his discease. I would have acquainted your honour sooner, but Capt. Asqueth has not sailed for London till last Thursday. I have a particular account of the contents of each of my late master's trunks and effects of every kind, as they were all committed to my charge since they left India till landed and lodged in this Custom House. I request your honour will be pleased to send me directions whether I am to remain with the effects till they proceed to London, or how I am to conduct myself. At present I am at the house of Mr. William Douglas of this town

William Young

William Douglas to Sir Robert Palk, Bart., Bruton Street, London. 1783, November 11th, Limerick.

Inclosed you have a copy of the Board's letter to the Collector. Never the less Mr. Baylie, Port Surveyor, entered the stores yesterday in company with Mr. James Lyons, merchant in this town, broke open every chest and package belonging to Mr. Palk, rummaged and tossed the whole of his effects

William Young, Mr. Palk's servant, is the bearer of this.

William Douglas

Copy of letter from the Board of Customs to George Maunsell, Esq., Collector of Customs, Limerick, dated Dublin, 6th November, 1783.

The Board direct that the tryal be delayed and a proper time given for making a legal claim.
Among the articles expended were — 4 doz. brandy, 7 doz. madeira, 6 doz. waters, 7 doz. shrub, 8 doz. porter, 1 6C-gal. cask of rum broached, 6 tubs sugar candy, 1 bag cheroots, 2 bags walnuts, 15 sheep, 6 goats, 4 kids, 2 hogs, 3 turkeys, 24 geese, and 72 fowls,

Dr. Adam Burt to Sir Robert Palk Bart. 1783, November 30th, London.

I have reason for beheving that Captain David Asquith, of the *Surprise* packet, intends to claim 1,500 rupees on account of my passage, and in addition to the sum which Mr. Palk advanced to him in Bengal. There was not any surgeon belonging to the vessel. At the intreaty of the captain I attended the sick of the ship during the passage. Surely it must be granted that in a ship of so considerable force the assistance of a surgeon in time of war is an adequate recompence for the room he occupies on board. I used no other provisions during the voyage but what had been provided at the particular expence of Mr. Palk. I hope therefore that you will not attend to the above demand of the captain till he shall have consented sufficiently to reward me.

Adam Burt

William Young to Sir Robert Palk. 1783, December 16th. Limerick.

I have the pleasure to inform your honour that the goods are delivered up, and are ready for conveyance to Dublin and thence to the India House. The only cause of delay is Mr. Baylie's bill of expenses, which Captain Hall declines to pay until Mr. McMahon can learn from the Commissioners what amount is just

William Young

Ship *Surprise*, Downs.

Sober Hall to Sir Robert Palk. 1784, January 14th, Limerick.

At last we have been able to get all the chests, etc., out of the Custome House here, and they went off for Dublin under the care of your late nephew's servant (who has behaved with great propriety and attention) and a Custome House officer for Dublin. I enclose you a list of the plate and the other articles [of] that seazable nature for your satisfaction and guide when they arrive at the India House.

Sober Hall

George Maunsell to Sir Robert Palk. 1784, January 15th, Limerick.

I received orders from the Revenue Commissioners to forward your nephew's goods to Dublin as soon as Mr. Baylie's account was paid. The account was settled for 40*l*. by your friend Captain Hall and your attorney, for which I accepted a bill drawn by William Young on Mr. T. Maunsell, as instructed by you. Mr. Hall and I decided that some of the sea stores, which were not worth the cost of carriage, should be sold. They realized over 37*l*. The remaining articles are now on their way to Dublin, and I have asked Mr. Maunsell to forward them thence to London without delay.

Geo, Maunsell

David Asquith to Sir Robert Palk, Bruton Street, London. 1784, January

21st,

I am surprised to learn from your letter of the 17th January that the things have not been delivered. I have written to Mr. Louch on the sub- ject. The delay is by no fault of mine.

D. Asquith

Thomas Palk to Sir Robert Palk 1784, February 2nd, Fort St. George.

This will be delivered to you by Captain Tod with my little boy Tom. The enclosed paper contains a list of the clothes I have sent with him, meant more as a check upon the servant than any thing else, who is a man that never was employed upon such an occasion before. For Tom's passage I have paid 500 pags., which is more than hath of late been paid for such children, so that I hope the captain will make no farther demand on his account.

Tho. Palk.
P.S. The garrison of Palagaut-Cherry, a fort taken during the cessation of hostilities (and after the Embassy) (set out) by Colonel Fullarton, was in its return to join him, having ceded the fort to Tippoo, attacked and sustained a very heavy loss by one of his tributary Polgars. This and other causes of a similar nature will delay the so much desired peace.

Thomas Maunsell to Sir Robert Palk. 1784, February 5th, Dublin.

I had the pleasure to receive your letter of the 22nd in the country, where I have been detained by illness and the severity of the season. I came to town a few days ago, and immediately came to the Custom House about your nephew's effects. In my absence I had a particular friend, Robert Alexander, to attend to this business. We have done all in our power to get the effects lodged with me, and I am really much disappointed it cannot succeed. Mr. Winder wrote to you upon the stores being lodged at the Custom House.and unless you can prevail in England to have them

delivered to me, I shall apply to have them shipped by the first vessel to London.
I was anxious to see William Young, and could not find him out till last Tuesday. I am sorry for the trouble this poor man met with in his journey from Limerick. He was taken up on a suspicion of being a highway man, and Mr. Luke Flood, a magistrate, wrote to me upon the occasion, whose letter I enclose you. He was immediately discharged, but lost his pistols by the villainy of the people. It was fortunate for him that I was in the country about 13 miles from the place where this affair happened.
I shall be impatient to hear what you have done by your application to the Court of Directors and Colonel Barr and have only wrote to you now to let you know what has passed at this side

Thos. Maunsell

Letter from Luke Flood to Thomas Maunsell, dated Corvill, Roundwood, 17th January, 1784

William Young, brought before me this day on suspicion of being a highway man, and who writes to you by the bearer, has mentioned a circumstance of having drawn a draft on you for fourty pound on account of Mr. Palk. I shall be thankful to you for your information if any such transaction happened, and your idea of the matter. Young says he was servant to the deceased Mr. Palk, who was brother to Sir Robert Palk, an English member of Parliament, and is now employed by him in the care of the deceased's property.

Lu. Flood

Thomas Maunsell to Sir Robert Palk. 1784, February 14th, Dublin.

I yesterday received your letter of the 6th to Alexander and me, and went this morning to the Commissioners, from whom I have obtained an order that the effects should be immediately shipped on board the Draper, Capt. Rendell, for London, consigned to you at the India House. I took William

Young with me to the Custom House, and shall have him attended to on board ship, as it is certainly better he should go with the effects.
I am glad to acquaint you that we shall recover the pistols which were taken from William Young.

Thos Maunsell

Lord Rockingham

XLVIII
The Nabob complains. 1784

H.H. the Nawab Walajah to Sir Robert Palk, Bart. 1784, September 15th, Chepauck.

You are my old friend and have been the faithful servant of the Company in an exalted station in this Government. During your government the affairs of the Company were conducted with honour, propriety and advantage ; and you was an eye witness to the friendship and support which I shewed towards the Company, and the sincerity, chearfulness and punctuality with which I paid my current charges with them. But now the misconduct of the Company's servants is the sole cause of the ruin in which their affairs and those of the public and their friends are involved. Lord Macartney has brought utter ruin upon all the affairs of his employers, their friends and the public. In return for the good I have done his Lordship has done every injury to me, my family and country. Large sums of money from the revenues of my country have been dissipated and made away with, and not brought into the Company's treasury to my credit. In short, my friend, a full detail of Lord Macartney's evil conduct towards me and the public would fill volumes. I request therefore to refer you for particulars to Mr. James Macpherson and I flatter myself no exertions on your part will be wanting to the reestablishment of my government and country
It was during my friend's time that the last peace with France was concluded, and you know that Mons Law, who came out as Commissary on the part of the French King, though the villages around Pondichery had been dependant on it from ancient time, yet he did not think it right or proper to hoist the French flag in Pondichery, or to receive the said villages without my concurrence and authority, nor untill he had sent a Vackeel to me and had an interview himself at Sadrass. In that business

you was pleased to show me every token of honour and respect, and you gave me every friendly information and support : we were both one and the same. But now, though the King of Great Britain has engaged in his late treaty with France to procure for that nation the cession of two additional districts of my country, to which the French can claim no right, and as the acquisition will greatly increase their power in this country, they consequently should be bound by stronger restrictions than heretofore with a view to the good of the Carnatic and of the English possessions in this part ; yet Lord Macartney, in his implacable enmity towards me and my family, has endeavoured to deprive me totally of my inherent rights ; and though I chearfully consented to the cession of the districts to the French agreeable to the engagements of his Majesty the King of Great Britain, yet his Lordship denied me the privilege of giving away my own countries, and determined to surrender them to the French without my interference and without making them enter into any Crarnamah. His Lordship accordingly signified to Mons Bussy, through his own private secretary Mr. Staunton, that he possessed the sovreignty of the Carnatic, and that all negotiations must be entered into with him. But Bussy, though an enemy, denied his Lordship's position, as you will understand from the letter to Lord Macartney on this subject. I write this for your information.

My friend will be pleased to recollect that it was himself who delivered to me the letter which was addressed me by the late Earl of Chat[h]am, the father of the present Minister, Mr. Pitt. You have now a happy opportunity of exerting your interest with the Minister and your other friends for the re-establishment of my affairs, and I trust that your exertions will not be wanting. May you long enjoy every earthly blessing.

What can I say more ?

Mrs. Catharine Palk to Sir Robert Palk. 1784, October 8th, Trichinopoly. Received 23rd October, 1785

I have had the pleasure to receive your letter of the 15th of February, and the satisfaction it affords me is more than I can express, particularly for your too kind assurance of taking care of my children in England. My Tom is, I hope, by the blessing of the Almighty safe arrived, of which I am very anxious to hear. We could not possibly hear of him since he left the Cape, when he was well. Catharine is my next, who is four years old. I shall embrace the first good opportunity for sending her to England. My last is Bob, and as every parent is proud of its own, I cannot help saying he is a very fine child, and I flatter myself with hopes that by the time he comes of age to be sent also, that we shall be able to accompany him ourselves.

The loss of our valuable brother was somewhat unexpected, as we flattered ourselves that the voyage would restore him to health. We feel the loss most sensibly.

An end being put to a dreadful war enabled me to return here with Mr. Palk in April last. I hope we shall be allowed to remain here for the future undisturbed.

Your most obliged and most affectionate niece,

C. Palk

Thomas Palk to Sir Robert Palk. 1784, October 10th, Trichinopoly. Received 23rd October, 1785.

Your acceptance of the care of my boy Tom without my having first obtained your approbation impresses me with the deepest sense of gratitude.

Had it pleased the Almighty to have spared my poor brother, he would no doubt have taken those charges upon himself. This unhappy event was first intimated to me by a town report, nor did I see any letter conirming it for many days, so that I was in a painful melancholy suspence during that period. He appears to have possessed a very handsome fortune. Though the peace took place in March last, it is only within the last month that a final exchange of places took place, owing to, I believe, some delay occasioned by the Supreme Council, who, it seems, do not altogether approve of the Treaty, as the Nabob has been totally excluded therefrom. To such a length hath private animosity gone forth ! The

Supreme Council have taken up the matter very warmly, and have threatened our Select Committee with suspension should they not open an immediate negotiation with Tippoo, and insist upon the Nabob's being inserted in the Treaty. The Committee have peremptorily refused doing it, and it is expected that a change in this Government will very soon take place. It appears to me to be at present a very unhappy one, that gives general disapprobation and disgust. It is a very happy circumstance for the Coast that a man of Mr. Hastings's experience and abilities guides the helm. He proves himself a man of inexhaustable resource. The Directors and Company between them have irritated him a great deal, but he has too much honor to leave them in the hour of danger, and hath proven that no ill treatment whatever can swerve him from the publick good. He set out on a tour through the provinces in February last, and returned to Calcutta only in August. You will no doubt, Sir, hear from better authority than mine the good which hath been derived from this excursion to the publick.
Mrs. Palk wishes to have sent her a picture of her son Tom. Should you think of it. Sir, you will oblige us by getting one taken.

Tho. Palk

George Baker to Sir Robert Palk, Bart. 1784, October 10th, Fort St. George.

I know of no publick news worth your notice except the mutinous disposition of the Army, which has shewn itself a second time very lately. The 36th Regiment took to their arms, and were with difficulty prevailed on to lay them down after one of the most active had been blown from a gun. Their complaint was the want of their arrears, aggravated perhaps by the knowledge of all Batta but in a few particular places being to be taken off about the end of the year. This, it seems, has been resolved on in Committee, and may perhaps have been published in General Orders. It may be difficult wholly to suppress the spirrit of dissatisfaction for a long time, and perhaps equally so to pay up their arrears in a short one. The different Powers of Hindostan are at peace, but the rumour of an approaching rupture between the Nizam and Maratahs as allyes and

Tippoo is very prevalent. Some think that in such a case we shall keep aloof.
Sir Edward Hughes sailed early this morning with his squadron for the other coast. A dispute having arisen in our Select Committee between the Gove[r]nor and Mr. Sadleir (our friend) about the time of the Juno's departure, the former gave the latter at the Council Board the lye direct. This terminated in a duel between them after the Juno sailed. The Governor was wounded, but not dangerously, in the left side. The partyes are said to be reconciled — in appearance only I should suppose. I had got thus far in my letter, and was about to tell you that the *Cornwallis* arrived here on the 7th instant, when Mr. Abraham came into my room with your most kind and acceptable favor of the nineth of March last. I offered him and indeed pressed him to accept of a room with me dureing his short stay here, but he being as he said well accommodated with Captain Abercrombie in the Fort, and being to depart in very few days for Bengali, declined the acceptance of it. It appears that the *Cornwallis* has been remarkably healthy, haveing not buryed a man since she left England. My residence is at St. Thome : Mr. Abraham might perhaps think the situation inconvenient.
We are indeed in quiet possession of the Carnatick, but it is desolated to the extent of any representation that I have seen of it; depopulated, uncultivated and deprived of its manufactures of course. And, what I conceive to be no inconsiderable thing, its stock of cattle of every species exhausted by the destruction or pillage of the late enemy, or the consumption of the Army, Settlement and Squadron for draught, carry age and food. A country in such a state surely requires time to recover itself before it can either furnish the sinews of war, the means of commerce or a sourse for revenue. Pardon, I pray you, the obtrusion of these reveries.

George Baker

Thomas Palk to Sir Robert Palk. 1784, October 12th, Trichinopoly. Received 22nd April, 1786.

I did myself the pleasure to address you by the *Pigot* ; and this is chiefly to introduce to you Major Geils, who is lately arrived from England, but owing to the neglect of the Court of Directors is obliged to re- turn thither for ascertaining what corps he is to serve in, which after 19 years' zealous and faithful service is a hard case. He is a very brave and excellent officer in various departments of the service. Upon those grounds may I presume, Sir, to hope that you will promote his views so far as to hasten his return to this country ?

Tho. Palk

Henry Vansittart, jun., to Sir Robert Palk. 1784, December 4th, Calcutta.

I am exceedingly obliged to you for your congratulations to me on my marriage, for the kind notice which you. Lady Palk and my cousins have taken of your new relation [s]. It is a circumstance esteemed extremely fortunate by them, and brings to mind the friendly attentions which Mrs. Powney experienced from you at Madras. They hope to enjoy the continuance of your regard, and do not doubt of making you every return of gratitude which it is in the power of sincerity to inspire. Kennaway, in a joint letter with me, has informed you fully of the state of your nephew's affairs. We hope that, immediately after your knowledge of the contents of his will, you will send us explicit instructions regarding the legacies and the disposal of the property remaining in this country. It is now almost confined to the house in Calcutta and the Company's bonds. The house, I think, should not be sold for much less than 50,000 S.Rs. Mr. Hastings has rejoined us in Calcutta, but before his return had the misfortune to lose his only friend in Council, Mr. Wheler. The other members have not yet commenced an active opposition, but the Settlement is now trembling and confounded with the expectation of a change of Government. Mr. Hastings has declared himself on the point of departure, and desired that the Burrington, Indiaman, may be detained for him.

Our situation at present is very disagreable. There is talk of a reform and retrenchment of expences. The latter is to be effected by a reduction of the avowed allowances of the Company's servants, of which a complete statement has been made out. The amount of my commission is very considerable, and in case such a plan should be carried into execution, more liable to reduction than any other. The secret and illicit emoluments will be untouched, so that persons whose advantages are of this description will have a great superiority over those to whom the Council have thought proper to allot a fair and legal recompence for their services. I speak only of reports, and am by no means certain that such an event will happen. On the contrary, I think the measure will not be pursued in the tottering state of the present Council on the eve of a change.

In July last Mrs. Vansittart presented me with a son, who has been named Henry. Mr. Abraham is living with me, but he will shortly move into Writers' Buildings. Kennaway, Stables and I agree in advising him to enter the Commercial branch, where he may have an initial salary of Rs. 400 to Rs. 500, rather than the Political or Revenue

Henry Vansittart

Henry Vansittart & Richard Kennaway to Sir Robert Palk, Bart. 1784, December 28th, Calcutta.

You were informed in our letter by the *Surprise* of the application from Captain Asquith for payment for the passage to England of Mr. Burt the surgeon, and of the refusal we gave to it. Lest this matter should be litigated in England we think it necessary to inform you of the following circumstances, the knowledge of which may be serviceable in resisting the claim. Colonel Watson demanded passage money upon this plea, that no surgeon was necessary for the care of the ship's company, whereas it happened on the passage that many of the seamen had absolute occasion for his assistance, which Mr. Burt gave them at the formal requisition of Captain Asquith. After this he became to all intents and purposes surgeon of the ship, and has recovered allowances in that capacity from Colonel Watson by the decision of referees or arbitrators. The claim to passage money of course, if any previously existed, was done away with by this act, which rendered him an officer of the ship. We observe that in the will Mr. Palk bequeathes 2,000/. to his brother Mr. Thomas Palk on the Coast, from whom is due by his books Current Rupees 20,359 12as., in part of which his bond for Current Rupees 19,290 10 is in our possession. This bond we recommend to be delivered up to him, the debt being about cancelled by the legacy.

Henry Vansittart, R. Kennaway.

Henty Vansittart

IL
Warren Hastings, 1785

George Baker to Sir Robert Palk, Bart. 1785, January 25th, Fort St. George.

My last letter, dated 10th October, was sent by the Pigot, which was due to sail for England on the 15th idem. For want of cargo, however, and to save demurrage, she was diverted to the eastward, but she has now returned here, and will leave for Europe early in February.
Colonel Pearse's detachment is, I suppose, arrived in Bengali by about this time. The last letter that I had from Captain J. Kennaway was on his leaving Ganjam, in which he told me he hoped to be in Calcutta about the end of the year.
Mr. Hastings came down to Calcutta about the beginning of November, and it was then said that he intended to go home by the ships of this season ; but as a copy of Mr. Pit[t]'s amended Bill has been received here with a few letters from England dated the 6th of August last, and as the purport of the whole has been received in Bengali, it is now confidently reported here that the Governor General has declared it to be his intention to continue in India some time longer.
It is said that Lord Macartney keeps the *Greyhound* packet, which [is] now in this road, till the new Bill shall have passed and be received here, together with the Court's of Controul and Directors' Orders in conseuence thereof, that he may be sure of a passage home immediately if he shall then be either desireous or in want of it.
The bulk of the troops are in cantonment at Arcot. The King's officers there have complained loudly of the impropriety of the commanding officer's (Brigadier General Horn[e]) privilege of selling arrack to the troops ; in consequence of which our Government have by public advertizement signified their desire to receive proposals for furnishing the troops with that article by contract. Horn[e] is called down, but is

appointed to command all the troops to the southward of the Colleroon, and General Campbell is sent up to Arcot to command there in his stead. The Batta, which was to have been taken off on the 31st of the last month, the Board have now declared to be their intention to continue till further notice. Indeed they could not do otherwise, the clamours of the Army haveing been so loud on that score that I believe nothing less than a general mutiny would have been the consequence of their persisting in their former resolution.

It is proposed to send a Committee, comprising the Commander-in-Chief and Chief Engineer, to examine the forts throughout the Carnatic with the object of determining which shall be preserved and which demolished. A Committee of Accounts has lately been appointed to examine all financial claims on the Company. Mr. William Jackson, one of the members, who has been deputed to the country south of the oleroon, finds huge war claims put forward there.

A small American ship (the first belonging to the United States) from Phyladelphia arrived at Pondichery on the 26th of last month. The captain and supracargoe have been here, and are just gone back to that place, and talk of returning to America soon.

The 52nd Regiment now at Poonamaly are at this moment in mutiny.I have not yet heard their pretext or complaint, though I understand that it is rather specious than well grounded ; for however much the Company's troops are in arrear, it appears that the King's are so regularly paid as to leave little reason of complaint on that score.

Mr. Bussy dyed in the begin[n]ing of this month at Pondichery. Orders have been received by our Government from the Governor General and Council to receive from and restore to the French and Dutch the several places agreeable to the terms of the respective treatys. Mr. Floyer is gone to the southward as Commissary for that purpose.

Mr. Daniel, who has for the last three or four years been Chief of Masulipatam, came up here with his family this month on the Pigot, and means to send them home on that ship.

Dureing his Chiefship in that Circar he has used extraordinary exertions with great moderation and good effect in collecting a very great part of the arrears of the revenue, amounting, I think, in the whole to some thirty lack of pagodes, and thereby rendered himself a good and faithfull servant to the Company, and a friend to this Settlement, with the character of an able, worthy, honest man.

George Baker

Chocapah to the Honble. Sir Robert Palk, Baronet. 1785, February 2nd, Madrass.

Nothing extraordinary has happened since I last wrote except that Lord Macartney and Mr. Sadleir challanced with pistoles on the 23rd of September last near Egmore Fort, when his Lordship was wounded on his right side, and soon after he is recovered. Orders have been sent to this Presidency from Bengal forbidding the drawing of bills. As this part of the country has been ruined by the enemy, there is difficulty in finding money to pay the troops, who are giving trouble.
General Bussey is dead at Pondichery the 5th of last month, and since [then] we have taken charge of Cuddalore, and the French have taken charge of Pondichery.

Chocapah

William Wynch to Sir Robert Palk 1785, February 3rd, Madras.

I enclose a letter from Mr. Pybus relating to Goodlad's estate. Lord Macartney's new system is disliked by tho Company's servants, and the economy he talks of has injured credit.
It's now with the greatest difficulty even a trifling loan can be obtained from a black man. Those of the Company's servants who have applied for their arrears of pay have been paid in Bengal bills, which bills were discounted at 50 per cent., while Lord Macartney himself regularly every 3 months pocketed his own pay of 10,000 pagodas, and his Council receiving theirs at a discount in Bengal bills. Nothing but the most disagreable circumstances have attended us lately, duels, dissensions in Council and mutiny among the King's troops. After being eighteen months without employment I have been appointed a Commissioner of

the Board of Accounts, thanks to the exertions of my friend Mr. Barclay, one of the Council. I beg that you will interest yourself on his behalf. He is desirous of succeeding Mr. Sulivan as Resident of Tanjore when the latter leaves for Europe.

W Wynch

Abraham Welland to Sir Robert Palk, Bart. 1785, March 21st, Calcutta.

I am still serving as Assistant in the Import Warehouse. I was lately recommended as Deputy, but that post has been otherwise filled. I hope to repay shortly the sum which Mr. Kennaway advanced from the estate of the late Mr. Palk on account of my brother Richard.
Your dutiful nephew,

A. Welland

Ozias Humphry to Sir Robert Palk, Bart., M.P., Bruton Street. 1785, May 15th, Cape of Good Hope.

I have just heard of the death of Mr. Wheler, the resignation of Mr. Hastings and the return of Sir John D'Oyley, to each of whom I carry recommendations.
You had the goodness to promise me your kind favor with Mr. Vansittart if he should be appointed Governor.
I take the liberty to write to you from hence to entreat it, as I shall sensible how slight a claim I have to your favor, but any service you have the kindness to do me with Mr. Vansittart, or the present Governor, or who- ever is appointed to succeed him will be received with thankfulness, and remembered with the warmest gratitude.

Ozias Humphry

Ensign William Preston to Sir Robert Palk1785, May 16th, Madras.

As a supernumerary officer of Captain Edmonds battalion I am not eligible for the allowance in lieu of half batta ; but General Lang has been good enough to transfer me to a regiment at Trichinopoly where I can draw it.

We are informed [that] General Sloper is to command in India, and General Dalling on the Coast. I shall be very thankfull if you will please to recommend me to these gentlemen or to Mr. Holland, who [it] is expected will govern.

I find this service to be very good, particularly for a single man, but the pay of an ensign is not sufficient to support a family. Several subalterns who have their familys with them were immediately provided for. A fort adjutant's appointment is very good, I am informed. They are frequently appointed by the Court of Directors, or strongly recommended by them to the Governor or Commander-in-Chief for the succession of a place. I trust. Sir, your goodness will assist me with your interest, so that I may have it in my power to get my family out.

Wm. Preston

Thomas Palk to Sir Robert Palk. 1785, May 20th, Trichinapoly.

Though it is now a year since the restoration of peace, I do not find that in population or cultivation any material increase has occurred : so effectually has the sword and famine swept away its inhabitants and destroyed agriculture. I did think that the Poligar countries would have been conducive to the saving of thousands of lives, and that at the conclusion of peace they would be flocking back to their former residencies ; but in this hope I have been cruelly disappointed. From the Colleroon to Arcott the country is almost laid waste from the want of inhabitants to cultivate, and other countries which have not been so destitute have failed in their crops from a scarcity of rain ; and from those causes are we still labouring under a heavy debt and large arrears, which the con- tinuance of the Assignment and peace can only relieve us from. God grant them both is my constant prayer, but sorry I am to say that I fear neither will be of long duration.

I am anxious to have some account of Tom, which I am now in daily

expectation of.
Tho. Palk

Messrs. Felling & de Fries to Sir Robert Palk, Bart. 1785, June 12th, Fort St. George. Received 30th March, 1786.

We thank you for your information regarding the disposal in Eng- land of the business of the Nawab's creditors. Mr. Call's diligence and assiduity on this occasion deserves the particular acknowledgement of the creditors, who are now put on a public and solid footing. The Nabob will no doubt for some time find much difficulty to fulfil his engagement of paying annually sixteen lacks of pagodas, 12 on account of his debt to the Company and creditors and 4 for the expences of the army, from the ruined state of some part of the country, which has been almost entirely unpeopled ; but it is possible with good management and strict economy, should we continue in peace and tolerable plentiful seasons.
Lord Macartney left us the 4th instant on the *Greyhound* packet for Bengal. He is to call at Vizagapatam, from whence it is said he means to send his resignation. Our Administration at present consist of Mr. Davidson, General Sir John Darling, Mr. Danniell and General Sloper, who as Commander-in-Chief of India has a seat and vote in Council.
The Company's letter to the Nabob has been delivered, and security demanded for the payments he is to make. We are told the Nabob is to give Souckar securities, such as they are, on which the countries will be delivered up to him. Much will depend on the person presiding over the Company's affairs keeping always a strict hand in exacting a due compliance with the different parts of the agreement. Lord Macartney would have been an excellent person for this purpose, but he was absolutely against having any thing to do with the Amier, who has still the manage- ment of his father's affairs, which made him quit his station sooner than otherwise he would have done ; and he has declared that he would not accept of the Government of Bengal should he be appointed to it.
We are in peace with all the Powers of India, and likely to continue so, in which will depend our salvation, for the arrears and bond debt of the

Company in India at present amounts to upwards of seven millions sterling, to clear which will require at least fifteen years of a continuance of peace. The discount of bonds here is 40 per cent., at Bengal 25 and Bombay 70. At this last Settlement no interest has been paid for four years.
The French seem to turn their views in India entirely to commerce. They have a small garrison at Pondicherry and has done nothing to the fortification of that place. Trincomali has been delivered up to the Dutch, who has not yet taken possession of their Factories on this coast. They have been at war with the Mallays, and in the whole their power in India seems] to be very much on the decline.

Pelling & DE Fries

Thomas Palk to Sir Robert Palk 1785, July 12th, Trichinopoly. Received 10th April, 1786.

This goes by a French ship. I am glad to learn that my little boy was safe arrived at Haldon House. Your intentions of putting him to the school at St. Mary Ottery has given us much pleasure, and I doubt not from the tendency of his disposition but he will give Lady Palk and you, my very much esteemed Sir, satisfaction. Mrs. P. is very desirous of embracing the opportunity of General Lang's return to Europe to send Kitty and Bob with her sister Mrs. Lang, but I think Bob too young to be parted with. By the late orders from home the Nabob is upon the point of being again put in possession of the Carnatick. This day or tomorrow it will, I believe, take place, his Highness having engaged to pay to the Company 4 lacks of pagodas more than the Presidency had authority to stipulate for.
Should the old gentleman perform, we shall have no occasion to repent the change, though our situation cannot well be worse than at present. Besides the old arrears to the troops we are incurring new ones from 1st February last, going on 6 months. Having told you this, you will be naturally led to conclude that there are defects somewhere. It is a melancholy truth, as is that of the troops having suffered a loss of 8 per

cent, in all payments since Mr. Irwin received the management of this district, arising from his introduction of the debased coin of Tinnevelly, and stopping the coinage of this. Complaints have been made, but the transaction has been so plausibly coloured over that Lord M. approved of it. Such injustice to troops meriting the most kind treatment, who have to my knowledge for the last 4 years laboured under the most uncommon hardships, is most sensibly felt, and if not redressed by this Government, which I hope is a more moderate one than the last, meaning Lord M.'s, a very unpleasant detail of grievances will be laid before the Company. Believe me, Sir, I have seen the native troops perishing in the streets, selling their children for a rupee, and it is not a month ago that they were begging about the cantonments almost in the same condition.
These, Sir, are truths that happen under my own eye. The native troops are so sensible of the ill-treatment they have received from Government that it is the general opinion they never will suffer themselves to feel the like distress again. The reasons are many and obvious for my communicating these facts to you, for it is my opinion that the existence of the British Empire in India depends upon their being redressed or not. Mr. Davidson is at present in the Chair, and I cannot say that our honourable masters have shewn their wisdom in providing a successor to Lord M., but we are in daily expectation of Mr. Holland's arrival.

Tho. Palk

Chocapah to the Honble. Sir Robert Palk, Baronet. 1785, September 17th, Madrass.

In May last orders arrived from the Company to restore the As- signed Districts to the Nawab, and to receive from him yearly 12 lakhs of pagodas on account of his debt to the Company and private creditors, and 4 lakhs for current charges. Lord Macartney, disapproving of these instructions, resigned and proceeded to Bengal on his way home. The Company's packet delivered here on the 16th July nominated him Governor General of Bengal. The orders were at once forwarded to Calcutta, but Lord Macartney declined the appointment and sailed for

England in the Swallow on the 10th August. The Government here is in the hands of Mr. Davidson, with Sir John Bailing and Mr. Daniell as Councillors. They arranged to deliver the territories to the Nawab, but the latter could not find sowcar security for the payment he was bound to make. He promised, however, to pay three lakhs this month, six in January and seven in June.

The Marattys sent their Vackeel here to request for our assistance to beat Tippoo. By what I hear our Government does not chuse to do it. I hope they will do, and destroy Tippoo entirely, as he is always [an] enemy to us.

It is reported that General Campbell is to succeed Lord Macartney. As the latter has refused Bengal, it seems likely that the General will go there, in which case another appointment will be made to Madras.

Chocapah

L
Educating the next generation, 1785

Futwood Smerdon to Walter Palk, jun., Ashburton. 1785, November 8th, Ottery.

As it is usual with me to send my bills half yearly, I have taken the liberty of writing out Master Palk's, which you will, I trust, find perfectly right. He is in good health and spirits, and has no suspicion that the Christmas vacation is drawing on. The dancing master, Monsr. Faye, having succeeded Tolver in his schools, demanded no entrance for your nephew. Master Tom begs me to present his affectionate duty to his Uncle and Aunt, who will have the goodness to accept of mine and Mrs. Smerdon's respectful compliments.

Futwood Smerdon
Master T. Palk to Michaelmas, 1785 {half-year).
Board and tuition, £15 15s. ; washing, £l Is. ; mending, 5s ; servants, 5s. ; shoe-cleaning, 2s. 6d. ; in weekly threepences, 5s. 9d. ; spelling book, Reading made easy. Watts' hymns and a smaller book, 2s. 6d. ; April 11, a pair of gloves and garters, 1s. 6d. ; June 17, paid driver for conveying Master P. to Exeter, 2s. ; gave Master P. at same time, 6d. ; to cutting hair at different times, 1s. ; a hymn book and prayer. Is. 4d. ; Total £18 3s. Id. Dancing master to Michaelmas, £1 11s. 6d. ; entrance, nil ; writing master, 12s. ; shoemaker's bill, 1s. 3d. ; two pair of worsted stockings, 3s. Total, £2 17s. 9d.
[Endorsement.] Mr. Smerdon's bill, £21 0. l0d. ; to a pair shoes, 2s. 9d. ; to breeches and waistcoat, 14s. 7d. ; to a hat, 4s. 3d. ; to entrance at Mr.Smerdon's School, £4 4s. ;to Mrs. Cooksley for schooling, £3 Is. 6d. ; to Mr. Davis for cloath, £l 6s. ; to Mr. Stone for shoes, 7s. ; to a hat, 10s. Total, £31 10s. lid.

9 Nov., 1785. Received the above. Walter Palk, Junr

Lawrence Palk to Sir Robert Palk, Bart., Haldon House, Exeter. 1785, December 3rd, Neuchatel.

I enclose a letter for Sir Bourchier Wrey. I am happy to find that my sister has made so good a choice, and it is the most anxious wish of my heart that she may meet with that happiness she most justly merits. I am but just risen from my bed, to which I have been confined this week past by an operation which has given me the greatest pain, but the good effects of which I already begin to feel. Having been recommended to a dentist, the excellency of whose talents has gained him a decided superiority over the other masters in his profession, I determined to follow the advice of my friends, and summoned up sufficient resolution to have one of those great tusks entirely pulled out, and the rest of my teeth put in order. The operation, I can assure you, has succeeded, and though the pain has not entirely left me, I have every reason to be satisfied, and my mouth is no longer ashamed to be seen.I am now quite settled, and find my residence very agreable. The language comes apace, and I am now able to join pretty well in the conversation. At present the French and fencing masters only give me employment, but I intend taking a drawing master, as I find there is one of ability here, and every day convinces me of the utility and pleasure which is to be derived from a knowledge of that art.

Lawrence Palk

Abraham Well and to Sir Robert Palk. 1785, December 13th, Guttaul.

By the arrival of the last ships from England we find that the Court of Directors have thought proper to reduce our salaries more than one half, and also to add that this is but a trifle to what we may expect. Small as they may conceive it to be, I am apprehensive it will cause a very great change, for how can it be supposed that when we are not allowed a sufficiency to live on we shall scruple at peculation of any thing else to procure a competency ? Should they also, as we hear it is intended, cut off the batta from the allowances of the officers, this country, I fear, will not remain much longer in their hands. A number of gentlemen have already resigned their offices, and are gone to live at Serampore, Chinsurah and Chandernagore on account of every thing being much cheaper at those places than in Calcutta. Many others have given up the Company's service altogether, and are going home on the ships that are now about to sail. A captain of one of the Indiamen has received a lack and [a] half of rupees for passengers only. Five and twenty families, besides a number of other gentlemen of the first rank in the service intend to reurn this year to Europe.

Mr. Larkins, the Accountant General, has had fifty thousand rupees cut off from his salary. Mr. Kennaway is reduced from two thousand to five hundred rupees per mensem, and the rest in proportion. Small as my allowances were, they have, however, thought fit to deduct four hundred rupees from it monthly. In short, there is not a Company's servant from a Senior Merchant to a Writer but who has in some degree suffered ; so that the misfortune, being general, is not so severely felt as it otherwise would be. The saving altogether to the Company amounts to about fifty lacks of rupees. The Governor and Council had, before the arrival of these orders, reduced our establishment as low as was thought possible, but this was so very small in comparison to the Court of Directors' [instructions] that they will gain neither credit nor honor by it.

On the 6th instant the Montague, Capt. Brittel, was burnt at her moorings at Diamond Point. Fifty of her people perished, among whom [was] her chief officer. The Dublin was much hurt by the explosion. It was occasioned by the carelessness of the arourer, who in carrying some fire from the galley to the forge let drop a few coals on the salt petre, which instantly took fire, and notwithstanding all the exertions of the crew communicated itself to the whole ship. This is the fifth Indiaman the Company have lost by fire within these two years past. Our petition to the House of Commons (against certain clauses of Mr. Pitt's Act of Parliaments) will be ready to be sent home by the last ship of the season. A committee of fifteen gentlemen have been sitting for these six months past, among whom is Mr. Vansittart. The petition has been framed, and signed by most of the people here. Old Price, (the person who wrote so

> virulently against Mr. Macintosh) and Mr. Francis, has, under the feigned name of An Inhabitant of Calcutta, given every support in his power to the Bill. No person on its first arrival could say more against it than he did, and I am very certain that he was one of the party who at a drinking bout burnt it.
> Accompanying I have the pleasure of sending you all the news papers for the last year, and also Mr. Dallas's speech at a meeting of the inhabitants of Calcutta, with many other publications, which I hope will afford you some amusement.
> Your very dutiful nephew,
>
> A. Welland

Now we meet F. d'Ivernois who is appointed by Robert Palk to undertake the education of his son. Evidently a man of letters and with accomplishments in languages, he is given the task of conducting the young Palk through the *Grand Tour* of Europe. This means managing the young man's expenses and reporting the spend to father Palk. It also entails planning the journeys and obtaining the letters of introduction that were essential if the doors of the rich and famous were to be opened. Regular reports were required and a careful wathc on the company kept by the young Palk is revealed.

F. D'Ivernois to Sir Robert Palk, Bart., Haldon House, Exeter. 1785, December 24th, Neuchatel.

> I notice the hint you have given your son regarding an early move to Germany and Italy. I was about to make a similar suggestion. The fact is, your son is too much at home at Neuchatel. His familiarity with the society we meet tends to make him relax that effort to please which he would be compelled to exert with fresh acquaintances of superior rank. The notion which Mr. Beeke has imparted to you of your son's spending the coming summer in Germany is well adapted to this end, provided that his halts are limited in duration, that he obtains recommendations to the Courts of Dresden, Berlin and Vienna, and that he associates with people of the country rather than with young English travellers. Here he is too

intimate with Mr. Spencer, who resides in this house. The latter is of good family and possesses many excellent qualities, but he has more to gain by association with Palk than your son with him. Spencer is apt to be idle, and he deprives your son of time which would otherwise be devoted to literature. Your son will certainly be reluctant to quit Neuchatel, but there is no object in his remaining save the improvement of his French, in which he makes steady progress. I suggest that you might urge him, as if of your own motion, to spend March in the south of France in order to perfect himself in the language, which is spoken more rapidly there than in Switzerland.

F. d'Ivernois

Abraham Welland to[Sir Robert Palk. 1785, December 25th, Calcutta.

I am sorry to hear that my friends consider me backward in writing to them. I would willingly compound with their employing one hour to my two in our correspondence. I have not received more than twelve letters from them since my residence in this country, which is now almost four years. I do not, however, include you in this number.
I shaJl certainly follow your advice with regard to my cousin Abraham. He at present lives with me in the Writers' Buildings, to which I have, since the late reductions, been entitled to a room. I must indeed own that my utmost exertions have lately been used to rid him of a little of his country rust, and by dint of perseverance my efforts in some respects have not been rendered ineffectual. I shall now, however, change my conduct, and from being master submit myself to be a scholar. He undoubtedly deserves great credit for his attention to business, and in lead- ing so regular a life. If one may judge of his future fortune by his present manners, I will venture to say that he will not discredit your opinion of him. I always have and shall continue to apply to Mr. Kennaway for his advice or assistance, whenever necessary. The late reduction in his salary has given him much discontent, and I should not wonder if he was, in the space of one or two years, to return to Europe. Captain Kennaway is at present at Benares, but will come to Calcutta

soon. Since his arrival from the Coast he has laboured under a severe fit of sickness, and we were at one time in some anxiety for fear that his ill state of health should oblige him to quit the country.

The *Surprise* packet has, we hear, brought great news, but the particulars have not yet transpired. We are all much surprised at Mr. Macpherson's being continued in the Government. His abilities are no ways suited to it, nor indeed are any of his coadjutors, particularly Mr. Stables, whose head is too thick ever to cut a very conspicuous figure. I think the character Mr. Hastings gave of them in his last letter to the Court of Directors was a very just one. Six lacks of rupees were dispatched the other day to Bombay, and they have also incumbered themselves with the whole debt incurred there by the Maratta War. Twelve lacks more are ordered on board the *Rodney* for Madrass, while our most capital merchants here are distressed beyond measure for cash, and have almost stopped business for want of money.

General Sloper has lost a good deal of his popularity here by appointing King's officers to the command of the out stations, greatly to the detriment of the Company's military, who have held several meetings to consult about it.

Your dutiful nephew,

A. Welland

P.S. Major Cloud's regiment of seapoys have confined their officers, and will not march till their whole arrears of pay are given to them

Thomas Palk to Sir Robert Palk. 1785, December 25th, Trichinopoly.

I have just heard that the *Rodney* Indiaman is to be at Madras about the end of the month, and to wait there but twenty-four hours. By her I have the pleasure to send you duplicate of a sett of bills for £2,000, and the first of another sett for £4,400, both made payable to you. The first remittance of £800 through the same channel is, I hope, paid.

Mrs. Palk and the three young ones are very well. We were disappointed in not having a single line by the Surprise, but suppose her dispatch to be delayed

F. D'lvernois to Sir Robert Palk, Bruton Street. 1786, January 17th, Neufchatel. Received 28th January.

I hasten to give the information you ask for about your son's teeth. Two of the upper ones were irregular, a circumstance which not only affected what may be called la decoration de sa bouche, but interfered with its hygiene. A lady who is a friend of your son advised him to avail himself of the skill of a dentist of repute who visits Neufchatel twice a year. The dentist was at first inclined simply to remove both teeth, but he afterwards judged that the interval left by one of them would allow of his replacing the tooth after he had extracted it and reduced its size. This was the operation which he skilfully performed on a courageous patient. The space left by the tooth which was entirely removed has already diminished. Our only fear now is that the other tooth, which was taken out and replaced may not become as firm as the rest.
I thank you. Sir, for your interest in what concerns myself. I am entirely at your service if you wish me to continue the tour as your son's companion. His friend I shall ever remain. He is prepared to leave Neufchatel in March if the roads are then practicable. In travelling through Germany I propose that we hurry over the smaller Courts and make a prolonged stay only in the. three or four principal cities. Dresden would be the first place for such a stay on our way to Berlin, unless the Court Palatine should be at Mannheim. Letters of recommendation we shall of course need.

F. d'Ivernois
P.S. In the account which I sent you last October there was a slight error, although the total was correct. The personal expenses for three travellers should have been L5,057, and the common expenses L8,676 16. Total Ll3,733 16.9. Of the personal expenses I owe L626. The balance relates to Messrs Palk and Beeke. Our further expenses from the 27th Sept. to the 31st Dec. have been L6,863 15 6., of which Ll,689 10 5. is due from me. Grand total, L20,597 lis. Should you wish it I will furnish a more detailed statement.

Thomas Abraham to Sir Robert Palk, Bart. 1786, January 23rd, Calcutta.

I now hold two appointments in the Commercial Department, one in the office of Secretary to the Board of Trade on 100 sicca rupees a month, the other in the Export Warehouse on 150. In the Revenue Department I receive 100, so that with my Writer's allowance I draw about 450 sicca rupees in all. Although the greater part is paid in paper, on which there is a heavy discount, I esteem myself fortunate.
Every person here, I think, seems tired of the present Government, and I believe it is the general wish that Mr. Hastings may come out again ; but nobody supposes he will, unless possessed of greater powers than the Board of Controul will be willing to give him. There has been some talk lately of a French war, and that the Council here were going to send a vessel to the Mauritius to make enquiry relative to some troops that are there ; but I hope it is without foundation, as if a war was to break out now, they would probably take many of our homeward bound Indiamen, which would be a very great loss to the Company, especially those from China of this year, as they have so much tea on board.

Thos. Abraham

Lawrence Palk to Sir Robert Palk. 1786, February 4th, Besancon.

My dear Father,
You will no doubt be surprised at receiving a letter from me at this place. Thus far I have accompanied my friend Spencer on his return to England, and shall leave him tomorrow to proceed on his journey. He has promised me to be the bearer of this letter himself. From your last letter to M. D'lvernois I judge that you wish us to leave Neufchatel in March. I fear, however, the weather will not permit us to start so soon, for there is every reason to expect snow. I hear with pleasure that Lord Macartney is returned from Madras, and has refused the Governor Generalship with pleasure, because in that case my Uncle George may be sure of gaining the election if he has the least idea to attempt it
I now begin to talk French fluently, but never expect to arrive at the same

point of perfection as my friend Spencer, whose accent cannot be distinguished from that of a Frenchman. You may perhaps have an opportunity of hearing him and judging yourself. For the German, it goes on very slowly, but when the first difficulties are surmounted, I flatter myself I shall make sufficient progress to be able to make my way through Germany, that is to say at the inns, etc., for as for talking it fluently, I give up all hopes.

Lawrence Palk

F. D'Ivernois to Sir Robert Palk, Bart., Bruton Street. 1786, February 6th, Neuchatel.

Your son has just returned after accompanying Mr. Spencer on part of his journey. M. de Traytorrens went with them. You seem to be unfavourable to the intimacy with Mr. Spencer, but as the latter lived in the same house, ordinary courtesy compelled some association, and it is impossible not to like him. The disadvantage of the tendency of the two young men to converse in English is now removed by Mr. Spencer's departure. You are desirous that we should leave Neuchatel as soon as possible, but I suppose not before March. Your son would like to stay longer, and many here will certainly regret his departure. I beg you to intimate to him, as of your own motion, the beginning or middle of March as the time for leaving Switzerland.

F d'Ivernois

The Revd. Samuel Badcock to Sir Robert Palk, Bart. 1786, February 11th, South Molton.

I received the box of MSS. last week perfectly secure. I shall soon be at leisure to examine them with the care which they deserve, and will ...endeavour to reduce this disordered mass to some degree of consistency. I am more and more convinced of their utility to any one who may have health, abilities and spirit to undertake a History of the

County ; and when arranged on the plan I have projected, they will be a most curious repository of materials both to amuse and to inform the antiquary. I may at some future period engage in an undertaking of which indeed I had formed no conception a short time since. I would not indeed have it publicly known that I entertain even the most distant prospect of writing a regular History of the County of Devon, nor would I have it supposed that I shall proceed beyond an arrangement of the papers which you have done me the honour of entrusting to my charge. After I have classed the MSS., and written a catalogue of them and such an index to their several contents as may facilitate the researches and inquiries of any person who may have the curiosity to inspect them, I will return them to you with care and fidelity.

Samuel Badcock
P.S. I hope I have not taken too great freedom by enclosing a letter to a friend who hath the superintendence of the Monthly Review.

Lawrence Palk to Sir Robert Palk. 1786, February 13th, Neufchatel.

My dear Father,
At my return from Besancon last Monday I found a letter from you. With regard to quitting Neuchatel, we shall be ready whenever you think proper. For my own part I must own I shall be rather sorry to leave it so soon, as I am convinced it is almost impossible, at least very difficult, to find another little town, the society of which is so excellent and the manners so polished. By the departure of Spencer there is no Englishman but myself in Mrs. Borel's house, and in the town but two, so that I shall undoubtedly acquire the French much quicker than I did heretofore.
I am happy to hear that things are so nearly settled relative to my sister's marriage. That she may derive from it every happiness and blessing is the only desire of my heart.
Mr. D'lvernois tells me he has satisfied you with regard to the sums we have expended since your last letter of credit. I shall wait till I receive another letter from you before I consult Mr. D'lvernois upon our tour for the spring. He seems, however, to prefer Germany to the South of

France, and wishes our first course to be to Berlin.
I suppose Haldon will be so entirely altered when I return that it will almost be impossible for me to recognize it. I hear the winter has been remarkably severe in England, and has done considerable damage. I hope your plantations have not come in for their share. My best duty attend my mother, with love to Nancy and Emelia.

Thomas Palk to Sir Robert Palk. 1786, February 15th, Trichinopoly.

By this conveyance (a Dane) I transmit you a third sett of bills on Copenhagen for 2,400/., which sum will, I hope, bring my remittances to near 10,000/., to which Walter will, I imagine, add the legacies.
The funding of the Company's debts incurred in India was very much to be wished by us all, but we have not been guilty of peculation to that extent as to induce us to accept of it upon the terms it offers for doing it. However wanting its constituents may be to do their servants justice, I never despaired of receiving it from the hands of our employers, but the proposed exchange of Is. 6d. the rupee manifests them to be no better ; though I cannot think but some error has been committed somewhere, which the arrival of General Campbell must clear up. Were it not for the general good character given of him, we should have little more to hope for than what we experience from the present Administration. Lord M. is certainly very culpable in leaving the Chair to so weak and indolent a man as fills it at present, that never was capable of conducting even his own domestick affairs. Mr. Daniell, appointed Governor C.'s successor, sailed the very day before this news arrived, and though it is evident the Company never meant that Mr. Floyer should hold a seat at the Board, he was sworn in the 14th day after Mr. D.'s departure, though his appointment to Cud- dalore was known before it took place, and of Mr. Cas[a]major's to succeed Mr. Daniell.

Messrs. Ayton, Brassey & Co., to Sir Robert Palk, Bart., Bruton Street. 1786, February 17th, Lombard Street.

Messrs. Agassiz, Rougemont & Co., to whom we gave a guarantee to pay bills up to 500/. drawn by your son, inform us that this sum is exhausted. Please state whether you wish us to give a further guarantee.

Ayton Brassey & Co
[Endorsed in Sir. R. Palk's hand]. — Desired Lawrence may have a credit for a 3rd 500/. more.

Messrs. Henry Vansittart & R[ichard] Kennaway to Sir Robert Palk 1786, February 22nd, Calcutta.

A bond from Mr. Droz to Mr. Palk for Current Rupees 9,000 at 1 per cent, was found among the latter's papers. It was payable on the 31st January, 1784, when we claimed the amount, but Mr. Droz denied having received any consideration for the bond. We enclose his affidavit. He states that the intended consideration was a Filature or building for winding silk, in the neighbourhood of Cossimbuzar, of which he should have received possession to render the obligation of the bond complete, but which was never yielded to him : on the contrary, that Mr. Palk, holding a contract for raw silk under another name with the Board of Trade, continued to employ this Filature in the provision of his silk.The latter part of this statement is confirmed by the inquiries we have made. As to whether the Filature was the consideration for the bond, we cannot speak positively, but we are inclined to think that Mr. Droz's assertion is correct. The Filature was sold by Mr. Palk before his departure for Rs. 8,000. Mr. Droz says that Mr. Palk promised to return the bond, but the matter was delayed partly by the latter's illness, and partly by his own absence from Calcutta. We have no power ourselves to grant release, but refer the case to you for disposal

Henry Vansittart, R. Kennaway."

Thomas Abraham to Sir Robert Palk. 1786, February 25th, Calcutta.

Since my last we have had agreeable news from England for those who are in the possession of Company's bonds, and much in arrears, vizt. that the Government General have permission to draw on them to the amount of 6 crores of rupees — about 6 million sterling. The only objection to this mode of payment is that it is rather a bad remittance, as the Current Rupee is to be drawn only at 1s. 8d., and the payment in England will be so very long and doubtful. There is also a new plan adopted here in the payment of the Company's servants with a view of stopping the present very high discount on the Company's treasury orders, and making the late reductions as light as possible, which at best must be bad. This is a plan of Mr. Larkins's, the Accountant General. How far it will succeed time only will discover. The mode is by certificates bearing interest.

I had, a few weeks ago, some prospect of going up as an assistant to the Collector of Chittagong from the promises Mr. Macpherson made me, and of his wishes to serve me in consequence of my letter to him from Lord North. Indeed I cannot blame him for it, as another gentleman was applied for by the Collector, and it is a compliment generally paid the Chiefs and Collectors of appointing the assistants they apply for. I have still some hopes of getting up the country some where.

Mr. Macpherson has always been very friendly to me whenever I have gone to speak to him, and expressed his wishes to serve me, which gives me the greater hopes of success in my application, as I see everything still goes by interest notwithstanding the late Act of Parliament. I can convince you of this no better than by telling you that the greatest part of the many appointments that have been given away lately have been given to Scotchmen.

Mr. Williams from Exeter has got a very good appointment lately, but it was, I believe, owing to his being appointed by the Court of Directors to succeed upon the first vacancy. We are in very great hopes of getting a new Governor in a little time. Every person seems to be tired of the present one already.

My best respects to Lady [and] Miss Palk, Emelia, and Lawrence when you write him, as I suppose he is in France.

Thos. Abraham

Lawrence Palk to [Sir Robert Palk]. 1786, March 2nd, Neufchatel.

My dear Father,
I am happy to hear that Mr. Spencer has given you the letter with which I charged him, but am sorry that he has given you so bad an account of my progress in French.
I shall be ready to leave Neuchatel directly I receive letters of recommendation and credit. I fear there is no prospect of meeting Lord Wycombe, as we cannot reach Vienna under three weeks, by which time he will have left. I am distressed to hear of Emelia's serious illness, but hope soon to have better news.
I shall be extremely happy to hear that my sister is united to Sir Bourchier. I willingly promise that I never will propose to any lady to whom either you or my mother object, and your goodness to me upon every occasion makes me flatter myself you would not wish to oblige me to make choice of one that I do not approve. Your fortune is certainly of your own acquiring, and I would not wish to have the least share of it if you have the least reason to imagine I do not deserve it. Hitherto I have done every thing in my power to show you how grateful I am for all the kindnesses bestowed upon me — kindnesses which I never shall forget, and in return for which I shall ever make it my study to oblige you.
Adieu, my dear Father ; I earnestly join in every wish that it may be possible for me to render myself such a character as you desire, and to deserve which will always be the endeavour of
Your ever dutiful and affectionate son,

Lawrence Palk

Lawrence Palk to Sir Robert Palk, Bart., Bruton Street. 1786, March 5th,

Neufchatel.

My dear Father,
I received this morning your letter of the 13th last month. As it seems to be your desire that I should quit Neuchatel immediately I should do it with the greatest pleasure, did not the want of letters of recommendation hinder me, and more so as it is impossible to arrive at Vienna before the departure of Lord Wycombe.The character I have heard of Sir Bourchier from every quarter, and especially so from our common friend Mr. Becher, makes me exceedingly happy in the thoughts of his alliance to our family.
Mr. D'lvernois has accompanied his sisters on their return to Geneva. They have been here for a few days to assist at a ball I have lately given to my friends at Neuchatel selon Vusage. I can assure you he justly merits my confidence. I esteem myself superiorly happy in having joined so good and amiable a friend.
Your account of Lord Cornwallis's success with regard to the Governor Generalship gives me rather more pain than pleasure, as I expected my Uncle George would have been appointed, knowing he rather desired it.

Lawrence Palk

F. d'Ivernois to Sir Robert Palk, Bart., Bruton Street. 1786, March 9th, Neuchatel.

I enclose an account of the money we have drawn since we left England, so that you may judge what fresh credit will be needed. There is still a balance of 200 louis with Messrs. Pourtales. Your son gave a very pleasant entertainment a week ago to his acquaintances, for it is the custom with the English on leaving to acknowledge thus the various attentions received during their stay. What pleased me most was the general praise accorded to Mr. Palk for the ease, gaiety and air of distinction with which he did the honours. He was kind enough to invite my sisters, so I had to be absent four days to escort them homeward until we could meet my mother half way from Geneva. On my return your son told me that you had again urged his departure. He wished to wait for letters of recommendation to Germany, but I conclude that we shall find these at Vienna. The cold, however, is so severe just now that I think we cannot start before the beginning of April. It would gratify you and Lady Palk could you both witness the signs of regret which all who know your son show at his impending departure, and could you realize how greatly he is esteemed. His progress in French has been marked since Mr. Spencer left ; and I can promise that before he returns to England he will be able to speak, if not like Mr. Spencer without accent, at any rate sufficiently well for an ambassador, the standard generally aimed at by young Englishmen. As you direct our journey towards Vienna, I suppose you have given up the idea of including Italy in our tour. I should like to know what you propose, so that I may be able to refresh my knowledge of Italian. Please intimate to Lady Palk the pleasure I feel at hearing of your younger daughter's convalescence.

F. d'Ivernois.
P.S. Since our departure from London to the 9th March we have received the following : From Mr. Beeke, London, for expenses in England, 66L 5s. 6d. sterling 1,590 6 Mr. Beeke, on our arrival at Calais, 75 guineas 1,904 Sir J. Lambert, 21st July, 200L sterling in notes 4,966 Mr. Beeke at Neuchatel . . . . . .
72 Messrs. Pourtales, in August, 98 louis for lOOl. sterling 2,352 Mr. Beeke at St. Gall and Constance. . . .
600 Mr. Beeke at Berne, a note for 1,000 livres, which realized only 972 Messrs. Pourtales, 26th September, 150 louis 3,600 Carried over 16,056L s. Brought over 16,056 6 From Messrs. Pourtales, 8th Oct. to 31st Jan., seven payments of 50 louis each 8,400 ,, Messrs. Pourtales, 28th February, 100 louis 2,400 L26,856 0s.

George Baker to Sir Robert Palk, Bart. 1786, March 12th, Fort St. George. Received 26th August.

It is now about two months since that a report of Tippoo Sultan's death was first reported and generally credited here. It continued in this state for about a fortnight, then became doubtfull or disputed, and continues so to the present hour. It would gratifye my curiosity if I could but know what our Government say on that subject to the Company by this dispatch, for hitherto they appear to have been as ignorant of the truth as I am. But whether Tippoo be dead or alive, we are, thank God, in peace. Report[s] of the Marahtas' and Nizam's joynt hostile intentions against Tippoo's co[u]ntry are very prevalent.

Harvest in the Carnatick, now gathering in, is, compared to the few cultivators of the land, very plentifull, and the great quantityes of various kinds of grain brought by sea from the northward has brought the respective prices thereof down as low as I have at any time heretofore known it.

You undoubtedly know that a cantonment was (before the Assignment of the Carnatick was yielded up) fixed on, and barracks prepareing for about twelve thousand men at or near Sheveram, a small village in the road from Canjeveram to Chingleput, and at about the distance of eight or ten miles from the former place. The site of this cantonment is, for by far the greater part, within the boundary but on the very verge, of the Companye's Jaghire ; and in order to compleat the plan thereof to its necessary extent and in the precise situation that was deemed most eligible, it has been made to extend in one or more particular parts for a very little space and distance into the Nabob's country — a circumstance that either gave his Highness umbrage, or that he did not at least approve of. This then became a subject of conference or discussion between his Highness and our Government, which terminated about a week since in the following manner, vizt. : The Nabob, his son the Ameer, Mr. Davison our present Governor, and General Balling went to the spot, where and when the former party formally yielded up to the Company that part of its domain which fell within the limits of the cantonment on their receiving from the Company as a compensation for the same such a portion of the Jaghire as was deemed equivalent thereto. This done, his Highness the Nabob, either at the desire or with the approbation of our Governor and General, gave the place his name of Wahlahjah, which when announced to the publick by a salute of twenty-one guns, all party s returned to their respective places of residence.

Thus far was wrote on the 12th. I had more to say, but was through indisposition obliged to stop, and thus conclude on the 16th.

Thomas Palk to Sir Robert Palk. 1786, March 15th, Trichinopoly. Received 26th August.

The Nizam and Marattoes have actually taken the field with a view of attacking Tippoo, who is not dead, as was the general belief for two months, and is very busy disciplining his troops and bringing them together. From hence you may infer that we keep ourselves exceeding ignorant of what passes beyond even the walls of Madras, which is truly the case, so indolent and inactive we are. I cannot penetrate Tippoo's real design by feigning himself dead and keeping the gates of Seringapatani shut for so long a time, which we know beyond a doubt to have happened, at a time that his brother and chief officers are so disaffected to him, and his country threatened with invasion, unless the report of the intentions of those powers be not true, and so draw us into a scrape by supposing we would put in our claims in the participation of his country, which (fortunately perhaps) our situation has forbid, were the present a more enterprizing Government than it is. Every one is dissatisfied, and looking out with the most painful anxiety [for] the speedy arrival of Governor Campbell.

Tho. Palk

Messrs. Pelling & de Fries to Sir Robert Palk, Bart. 1786, March 18th, Fort St.George. Received 26th August.

General Campbell is not arrived yet. We want much an able Governor : our present Administration is but a feeble one. Mr. Floyer was taken in to fill the place of Mr. Daniell, who is returned to Europe. Storms brewing around us. A formidable army of the Marattas, aided by most of their principal chiefs, together with the Nizam's army have crossed the Kistna and invaded Tippoo's country. It is the general opinion that they will not be satisfied with money only, but intend recovering.the countries taken by Hyder from the Marattas, Nizam and the Patau Nabobs. Tippoo has a very considerable force, but from his tyrannical disposition don't stand so well in the affection of his subjects as old Hyder did, whose political abilities were infinitely superior. The frontiers and confines of the Carnatick will be filled with armed troops, and although we have nothing to apprehend directly with the present quarrel with these Indian Powers, yet in their consequences may affect us if proper care is not taken by wise and skilful negociation to preserve our neutrality and our rights unaffected. There was no truth in the reports of Tippoo's death.

The Nabob has paid regularly his first and second kists, amounting to nine lacks of pagodas, and yet no dividend made to his private creditors. A notice from the Government came forth on the 14th instant that a dividend of one lack and [a] half of pagodas will be made on the 1st April, and we are told that the Company is to have a share of this trifling sum, the Government licre construing that the dividend is to be made only annually at the end of every year after the 12 lacks of pagodas are received. This is a great hardship on the creditors, and we don't know how to help ourselves but by a reference to Europe.

The Bengal Government has afforded great assistance to this Presidency in money, etc., and have taken upon them entirely to pay the King's troops on this coast ; but we apprehend these great aids have not been made properly use of. The arrears of the army still unadjusted. Mr. Sadleir and Hodges) are removed from Masuhpatam.

The Court of Directors have sent out orders under date 15th September last for liquidating their bond debts in India with bills of exchange to begranted on them. The exchange for Madras and Bombay is left to the Bengal Government to fix upon, which is not done yet. Unfavourable as this remittance will be, for it will take up near fifteen years before the bills can all be cleared on the footing they are granted, yet it will be of great service, as numbers may avail of this mode of realising in preference to keeping their bonds in India without any prospect of payment, the Company's credit in India being very low indeed. Bills granted by this Presidency on that of Bengal are discounted at 30 per cent., and Company's bonds 35 to 40.

Pelling & DE Fries

Thomas Abraham to Sir Robert Palk, Bart. 1786, March 24th, Calcutta. Received 8th October.

I should imagine this Government will incur the displeasure of the Board of Controul when they find out what little attention has been paid to the late Act of Parliament in general, but particularly those parts of it relative to giving away all appointments according to seniority in the service, which has scarce been attended to in any one instance, as the number of memorials that are gone home to the Court of Directors on the subject will evince.
It is a Scotch Government, and very few but Scotchmen get anything. Amongst the number of expedients lately thought of to alleviate in some measure the present public distress for want of money there has been one lately suggested, and I think seems to be approved, which is to establish a bank under the denomination of ' the General Bank of India ' (a small one we had before) to consist of 100 subscribers, and also meant to extend to the other Presidencies in the following proportion : — Bengal, 75 subscribers, Madras, 15, Bombay, 10, at 20,000 rupees each, making a capital of Rupees 20,00,000, equal to about 200,000/. sterling. If the subscription is filled up, it is likely to turn out a very advantageous institution, not only to the proprietors of it, but the public in general, by lowering the present enormous discount on Company's paper, etc., and of course making money more current in Calcutta.

Thomas Abraham

Lawrence Palk to Sir Robert Palk, Bart., Bruton Street. 1786, April 10th, Constance.

My dear Father,
We quitted last Thursday with great regret our abode at Neuchatel. For my own part I resembled very much the knight of the sorrowful countenance. Among the different people to whom I am most particularly obliged for their kindnesses and attentions there is no one who more deserves my thanks than Mr. Beaufoy and his amiable wife.Their house was the resort of the best company ; and by being often admitted to their

society I have in great part got rid of that shyness which you have so often and so justly found fault with. I trust in time I shall intirely shake off this failing.

Our route has been retarded by the breaking down of our carriage twice. Mr. D'lvernois having expressed a desire to remain here one day to see his brothers in exile, whom the Emperor has permitted to establish their manifactories in this town, gives me this opportunity of writing to you. The Colony succeeds even beyond their expectations, and it is to be expected that this once flourishing city will soon regain its ancient opulence and splendour. Their manifactories consist of watches and enamels which the Emperor admits into his territories subject to very small dutyes. The number of Genevans who have voluntarily expatriated them- selves amounts at present to nearly 200.

The tyranny of the aristocrats ever since the late revolution, and the means they employ to oppress the natives have rendered Geneva disgusting to its inhabitants.The Emperor does every thing in his power to favour this rising colony : to many particulars he has given places of abode for themselves and their families, and to all a free exercise of their religion and the permission of forming their own laws.

Tomorrow we set out for Vienna through Munich, where perhaps we may find a boat which will conduct us and our equipage, by descending the Danube, to that capital of Austria.

I do not yet give up all hopes of meeting with my friend Lord Wycombe at Vienna. Perhaps he stays there to accompany the Emperor to Chinon, where the Emperess of Russia means shortly to hold her Coronation.

Your account of my sister's marriage gives me real pleasure. Every person speaks well of Sir Bourchier and thinks that he will make one of the best of husbands.

You give me but a very midling account of my poor Emelia.

I forgot to send you in my last letter a copy of the will of a Mr. DesPlans, late Lieutenant Colonel in the service of the East India Company. His sister, who has been particularly kind to me, desired me to recommend her case to your notice, that if you had any acquaintance at Bengal, you would be kind enough to endeavour to procure her that justice which has been so often denied her. You are no doubt acquainted with the parties concerned. One of them, Mr. Bonjour enquired very kindly after your health, and said that if I mentioned his name to you, he was certain you would recollect him.

F. d'Ivernois to Sir Robert Palk. 1786, April 22nd, Vienna.

Now that we are 200 leagues from Neuchatel I can, without alarming you, give the true reason for my long-standing wish to see your son away from that place.
Soon after his arrival there he was attracted by a young lady of irreproachable character. Within a month the budding preference became so marked as to cause me some disquiet. I heard that the young lady's parents were building hopes for the future on the attachment, although Palk had spoken plainly of the impossibility of his marrying outside his own country. This disturbed me, and I begged you. Sir, to prepare him for departure. Now, Sir, you have the key to all Palk's delays. Perhaps you may blame me for not keeping you informed, but I was unwilling to alarm you needlessly. It is unnecessary to say that the young lady was as much in love as he was. I could not save Palk from final heart-rending interviews ; but he made no promise except that he would pay another visit to Neuchatel when he could. He was rather depressed during the first few days of our journey, but soon brightened up. He assured me yesterday that he had never been so happy as during the last six months — and he might have added nor so prudent, for his whole behaviour shows that he can unite the sensibility of a young man with the reserve of a man of experience who knows the value of honour too well to offer anything which can be construed as a promise.
We left Neuchatel on the 5th instant after settling our bills and drawing the amount of your last credit on Messrs. Pourtales. When we started there remained only L5,076 6s., which we took with us in cash and letters of credit. Our expenses were certainly high, considering the habits of the people among whom we lived. I several times discussed this point with your son. Though it would be unfair to charge him with extravagance, he is certainly inclined to be careless in business matters.

Lawrence Palk to Sir Robert Palk, Bart., M.P., Bruton Street. 1786, May 21st, Vienna. Received 2nd June.

My dear Father,
The Court having accompanied the Emperor to Luxembourg, Vienna is become quite empty and consequently dull ; therefore I think the sooner I quit it the better. Mr. D'lvernois seems to be of the same opinion with me, and only waits to hear your intentions upon the subject, and the re- ceit of that letter relating to our tour which you informed me Lord Lans- down was about to send him. The only houses into which I am now admitted are those of Prince Kaunitz and the Russian Ambassador's. The former is opened every evening, and I must own that I have taken so great a liking to its owner, who is reckoned the Oracle of Vienna, that I scarcely ever miss. The only thing however to be gained by this constant attendance is the ton and manners of a man of the world : as for politics, you never hear talk of them, and I believe the Emperor has enjoined si- lence upon every one of his Ministers. Your letter to Madame la Comtesse de Thun was of particular use to me, as she is the only lady who admits the English constantly into her house. She was made choice of by the Emperor to accompany him to Luxembourg I am very disturbed about Emelia's health and anxiously await news.

[Signature removed.]
P.S. Monsr. D'lvernois desires you will be kind enough to beg Mr. Du- mont, who is at present at Lord Lansdown's, to send us without delay at Berlin the letter of introduction for the Count de Goertz which he had the goodness to promise us.

Lawrence Palk to Sir Robert Palk, Bart., M.P., Bruton Street. 1786, June 3rd, Vienna.

My dear Father,
Your observations are very just, and I really remained in Switzerland longer than I ought to have done. I informed you of the loss of Mr.

Cleveland's. introductory letter to Madame de Prangin. This is the sole reason that deprived me of the pleasure of paying my compliments to her during my residence at Neuchatel. Vienna has been for the last week remarkably dull owing to the departure of most of the nobility for their country seats, and particularly those who kept open house for strangers ; during which time we have visited every thing that is curious, which consist only in some very fine edifices, the Treasury and the Arsenal. The Treasury is remarkably rich, and contains the jewels, etc., which have been collected from every part of the dominions belonging to the house of Austria.

The Arsenal is a very large pile of buildings, and contains arms for upwards [of] 350,000 men. They show you the jacket which Gustavus Adolphus wore when he was treacherously murdered at the battle of Lutzen, which was afterwards gained by the Imperialists, and the chains which the Turcs had brought with them to lead the then Emperour in captivity to Constantinople.

[Signature removed.]

F. d'Ivernois to Sir Robert Palk, Bart., M.P., Bruton Street. 1786, June 10th, Feslau, near Vienna.

About a week ago we told you of a little expedition we were about to make into Hungary. Our three-day visit enabled us to form an idea of the inexhaustible fertility of that kingdom. We are now staying with the Countess de Friez, four leagues from Vienna. Your son would like to prolong the visit, but an engagement to dine with Prince Kaunitz obliges us to leave to-morrow. Our departure from Vienna is fixed for the 16th. We should have started even earlier but for the festival of Corpus Christi and the installation of the Bishop of Liege. Palk is as ready to leave Vienna as he was reluctant to say good-bye to Neuchatel. Our business will end with Paris now that he is familiar with its language. Though I have no reason to be partial to Frenchmen, the more I travel among continental people the more convinced I am that the French are the most interesting for a young foreigner to cultivate. The advantages and dangers of the capital depend on the society with which he mixes, and it would be well for you to provide us with some good letters of introduction. I hope that Madame de Friez will give us a letter to the Austrian Ambassador at Berlin. This, with the one I expect from my friend Dumont to Count de Goertz, will suffice us for that capital. We expect to be there by the end of the month, halting only at Dresden and Prague. Through the Cheva- lier Keith your son has just drawn on you for £250 sterling in bills of exchange.

[Signature removed].

Lawrence Palk to Sir Robert Palk. 1786, June 26th, Dresden. Received 19th July.

My dear Father,
My last letter made you acquainted with my intended tour through a small but interesting part of Hungary in company with a very agreable party of my English friends. After having travelled for the space of about ten German miles through a beautiful and well cultivated country we arrived at Esterhazi, the seat of the Prince of that name. The flattering accounts I had heard of it from every quarter made me anxious to be myself a spectator of its beauties. I am sorry to say, however, my expectations were very much disappointed. The Palais, though large, contains nothing which deserves the title of real magnificence, and out of nearly two hundred rooms there are only two that are above the usual size. The gardens, on the contrary, are in general very prettily laid out and pleasantly interspersed with grottos, hermitages, temples, etc., etc. One building in particular (which is called the Belvidere) attracted our notice not only for its elegance and simplicity but also for its novelty, being entirely different from the German taste, who admires nothing but what is entirely covered with gilding and awkward ornaments. The present Prince has continually about his person a guard of two hundred men collected from amongst his tenants, dressed in magnificent uniforms, and as many more inhabit the other country seats. Two companies of players, the one Italian, the other German, perform

alternately in a new and very beautiful theatre. Every stranger has the permission to enter, even without having been presented to the Prince, who very seldom shows himself and lives here quite a retired life.
From Esterhazi we proceeded as far as Presburg, the capital of Hungary, a very ugly, ill-built town situated upon the Danube, over which you pass by a flying bridge. The town, since the Duke of Saxe Teschen has removed his residence to Brussels, has fallen into decay. The castle is a very large and rather beautiful building inhabited by nearly six hundred young men, all of the country, who are there bred up for the church. They received us very politely and showed us every curiosity they possessed. We saw the window from which the late Empress Queen addressed the people in a most pathetic speech, holding in her arms the present Emperour, then a child of scarcely a year old, imploring their assistance to extricate her from those calamities which her numerous enemies heaped upon her. Her faithful Hungarians, softened by this spectacle, swore to sacrifize the last drop of their blood in her and her son's defence; but little did they think at that time that the child would one day prove their greatest oppressor, and make slaves of those. people, to whom he not only owed his life but his crown, by overthrowing their rights and liberties, which he had religiously promised to maintain.
We talk of setting off tomorrow or the day after for Berlin through Leipsig. You are now thinking, I suppose, of going into Devonshire, the Parliament being nearly at an end.

Lawrence Palk

Thomas Palk to Sir Robert Palk. 1786, July 2nd, Trichinopoly.

I send you a first Bill of Exchange payable six months after sight. My remittances to you to this date have aggregated 13,724/. 10. This sum I hope to increase to 20,000L through the supercargoes of Canton. As soon as the whole is realized, I propose to follow it home.
Mrs. Palk is exceedingly desirous of seeing her unknown relations, and so am I of her seeing England before it be too late for her to benefit any thing by the change.

Sir A. Campbell arrived in good time, and promises to make a very good Governor ; so the general voice says. Boards of Commerce and Revenue are established, and the Army encreased and brigaded. The Morattoes are still at war with Tippoo, but not carried on with that vigour which it is our interest to wish should be. The former show some degree of determination to carry their point by keeping south of the Kistnah, and Tippoo by negotiation is trying to gain his. The French, as well as ourselves, are lookers on. Pondicherry is still an open town, except a barrier which has been thrown up around it, and seems calculated for a defence against cavalry only.

Tho. Palk

The Rev. J. Bradford to Sir Robert Palk. 1786, July 4th, Ideford.

My second son, just turned of sixteen, has been educated chiefly at Mr. Crawford's Academy at Newington. He understands French and all sorts of accounts, writes an exceeding good hand, and is, I flatter myself, perfectly free from vice, and of a compilable, steady, sober disposition . I had at first thoughts of putting him into trade, but find upon enquiry that the premiums they expect in any reputable shop are not less than four or five hundred pounds. This is so far beyond my finances that I must decline all thoughts of it, and am sorry to be under the necessity of being trouble some to my friends. If, my dear Sir, you would oblige me so far as to put me in a method of getting the lad a clerkship in any public office or reputable banking house, I would willingly advance 200. if required, and think myself under the greatest obligation to you.
I beg leave to congratulate you and Lady Palk on the marriage of your daughter. I had lately the pleasure of meeting Sir Bourchier Wrey at Star Cross, when he told me Miss Palk was much recovered, which we are most sincerely glad to hear.

J. Bradford

Lawrence Palk to Sir Robert Palk, Bart., M.P., Bruton Street. 1786, July 6th, Berlin.

Had your last letters to Vienna been addressed to Leipzig, we could have profited of Lord Lansdown['s] kindness, and have been introduced to the Prince Anhalt Dessau, whose place we have visited and admired. It is really the best copy of an English park and garden I ever beheld. There are few seats in England more beautiful than Dessau. Nothing, I can assure you, made me regret Vienna more than the Prince Kaunitz. He ever treated me with particular attention and affability, and at the same time that I admire him as being one of the greatest politicians and the best of men, his politeness and kindnesses to me have gained him my esteem. Sir Robert Keith too merits the esteem of every Englishman, nor is there a minister upon the continent who takes more pains to introduce his countrymen into the best society.
Tomorrow we intend to deliver our letters of recommendation to Lord Dalrymple and the Prince de Reuss, the Imperial Ambassador.
The King of Prussia still continues in a very alarming situation, and it is the general opinion that he will not live out the winter. Our stay at this place will be about a month, but as we are informed the King will not permit any strangers to pay their court to him, and as most of the fash[i]on able world have quitted the capital, perhaps we shall remain here but half that time.
Your accounts of my dear mother as well as of Emelia have given me the greatest pleasure, and I trust her new physician will soon operate a complete cure.
Lawrence Palk

Lawrence Palk to Sir Robert Palk, Bart., M.P., Bruton Street. 1786, July 10th, Berlin.

Our stay at this place, I apprehend, will be rather shorter than we originally intended, as Lord Dalrymple informs us that most of the beaumonde have retired from this city, some to Potsdam, but most of them to their country houses. Tomorrow we are to be presented to the

Queen and some of the Princes. The King, not being entirely recovered from his late indisposition, does not as yet show himself at Court, and remains at Potsdam with a chosen party of his Generals. People say here that he is pretty well, as he gallops on horseback for two German miles ; but this circumstance in my opinion proves better the strength and health of his steed than of his own.

I hope Emelia's speedy recovery will soon permit you to visit Haldon. The late acquisition you have made will certainly render it, if possible, more beautiful and more compact than ever. The most earnest of my wishes is that you may long live to admire its beauties.

Lawrence Palk

Lawrence Palk to Sir Robert Palk, Bart., M.P., Bruton Street. 1786, July 21st, Berhn. Received 2nd August.

At our return from Potsdam last Wednesday, where we had been invited to dine with the Prince of Prussia, we received your last favour of the 4th instant, inclosing a letter of credit, for which we return you our most sincere thanks, particularly so as the money we took up at Vienna is now entirely expended.

You say in your last kind letter, ' My inducement to send my son abroad was to supply the want of study at home, to teach him to be a good citizen, and that *qui mores homimim multorum vidit et urbes* might make his own remarks, adopt the good and avoid what was otherwise.' During my travels on the Continent my time has been principally employed in reading the histories of the several States I have passed through, in acquainting myself with the different objects of commerce, and of their different manner of government. These have been my principal studies, and if I have not succeeded in my attempts, the fault ought rather to be imputed to the badness of my memory than to my want of application .

Berlin is at present remarkably dull, most of its inhabitants having retired to their country seats, or to Potsdam, where the alarming indisposition of the King calls for their almost constant attendance. It is generally feared that he will not survive the winter. His legs are swelled in such a manner

as to prevent his walking without the assistance of his servants even from one chamber to another. He has not, however, lost his accustomed chearfulness, but dines every day in company with a chosen party of his generals. Great expectations are formed of the abilities of his successour, the Prince of Prussia, and the generallity of people imagine that the kingdom will be in the same flourishing condition during his administration as it has been during that of his uncle. Be this as it may, the death of the present king cannot but cause great disturbance and be sin- cerely felt in every part of the kingdom. The Emperour has his eyes con- tinually fixed on Silesia, keeps his troups in readiness, and waits only for that event to attempt the conquest of that province, which has been so unjustly ravished from him. The Prussian army, is however, on a very good footing, commanded by excellent and very expert generals. But if the Prince of Prussia does not, upon his coming to the throne, augment the pay of his soldiers, and relax in some measure the severity of their discipline, it is feared that nearly half his army will desert upon the first breaking out of a war. The soldiers complain very much, and honestly confess, even to their own officers, that they only wait for a good oppor- tunity to quit their present masters.
We intend setting off the day after tomorrow for Brunswick and Hanover. After having been presented to the Duke of York we shall proceed to Dusseldorf, from whence we shall descend the Rhine to Wesel, where I hope to have the pleasure of hearing from you. We expect to be there in about six weeks. If you do not think your letters can arrive there by that time, I shall be obliged to you to direct them to Amsterdam.

Lawrence Palk

F. d'Ivernois to Sir Robert Palk. 1786, July 30th, Brunswick. Received 17th August.

We arrived here yesterday, and have already been received by the Duchess, sister of the King of England, with the greatest affability.
Your son felt that he deserved your little lecture on economy, and was anxious to reduce his expenditure, which, though considerable, could not

be called extravagant. Part of it was due to beneficence : in other cases he was duped by the false prejudices which most young Englishmen bring to the Continent. But he is rapidly curing himself of them, and our expenses are certainly less than at Neuchatel, where no display was called for. Moreover, rapid travelling and brief halts, such as we have had in Germany, involve increased cost. At Vienna we spent nearly 250/. in two months, but it was less than Mr. Spencer's expenditure, and much below that of Mr. Duntz, who got through £100 in one month all by himself. Still, I am glad that you have read your son a homily, and I shall be happy if you will say a further word on the subject when we reach Paris, where opportunities of spending will be both numerous and tempting. I shall send you a detailed statement of account from Cassel, where we are to attend the ceremony, with which Lord Dalrymple is charged, of investing the Landgrave of Hesse with the Garter.

F. d'Ivernois

The Rev. Samuel Badcock to Sir Robert Palk 1786, August 1st, West Sandford.

I have taken the liberty of transmitting to you a paper, which, if it meets with your approbation, I should be glad to see published in the Gentleman's Magazine. I flatter myself that I have expressed myself at the conclusion in a manner sufficiently delicate not to give you offence. I wished to have given wider scope to my gratitude, but was restrained by the sense of that very liberality to which I found myself under such great obligations. If you approve of this paper and will permit it, I will communicate to the Editor some farther account of the MSS. which you have entrusted with me. But I will not move a step without your permission.

I had drawn up a catalogue, with some general account of the contents of the several papers, before I had the honour of writing to you an account of the progress I had made. Since that I have heard of a very curious MS. in Mr. Coffin's library, entitled Hooker's Survey. I believe it is the only one now existing, and I wish to procure a sight of it, that I may extract from it whatever is curious to be added to your collection. I doubt not but Mr. Coffin would very readily permit it if the favour were asked him either by yourself or Sir John Chichester.

Samuel Badcock

F. D'lvernois to Sir Robert Palk. 1786, August 9th, Pyrmont, near Hanover. Received 23rd August.

Since I wrote from Brunswick we have visited Hanover. We were there presented to the Duke of York, who honoured us with an invitation. Leaving Hanover for Cassel, we made a circuit by Pyrmont, where the German society of the vicinity had assembled to take advantage of the mineral springs. We expected to meet here the ruling Duke of Courland and his Duchess, whose acquaintance we had made at the residence of the Crown Prince of Prussia. This is the second day of our stay, and as we have no need of the cure, thank heaven, we shall make for Cassel very shortly. That place is not likely to offer attractions, as the Court is in retreat. We shall go a little out of our way to visit Gottingen, get a glimpse of its celebrated university, and be presented to the young Princes, as General Grenville has been good enough to give us a letter to their Goverror. From Cassel there are two routes to Holland open to us ; one to Wesel through Westphalia, which is direct but devoid of interest ; the other, double the distance but much more attractive, by Frankfort and the Rhine. We shall probably adopt the latter, as it will enable us to see Coblentz, Cologne, Dusseldorf, etc. This route will take us a fortnight or more. Allowing from two to three weeks to reach Wesel and two more for passing through Holland, we ought to be at the end of our travels by the middle of September. This is rather earlier than you expected, and is the result of our having visited the capitals at a period when the nobles were out of town. As I believe that the cultivation of good society rather than topographical knowledge is your chief aim for your son, there would have been no advantage in prolonging our halts in Germany. The question now is whether you wish us to establish ourselves at once in Paris until next February, or whether we should travel a little in France before settling down. As you are aware. Sir, there is one essential difference between the capitals of France and England. The English people can be studied adequately in London; but to know the French nation it is not enough to reside in Paris. One must penetrate the country. Meanwhile I suggest that you should procure for us as many letters of recommendation as possible, for it is chiefly on them that your son must rely for the connections he will form in the capital. A letter to the Ambassador is of little service by itself.

F. d'Ivernois
P.S. August 11th, Gottingen. We arrived here yesterday, and have already been presented to the three young Princes, who have asked us to supper this evening. We also met Sir Isaac Heard, who told us the Cassel ceremony was over. Apparently we have not lost much by our absence from it. What we regret much more is that the letter which you entrusted to him for us has not been delivered. Sir Isaac handed it to Lord Barnard, who is taking it to Berhn, where he expects to find us. Palk, though disappointed, is cheered by the good account of your health which Sir Isaac gives. Your son has had the pleasure of meeting several of his Oxford friends, who all agree that he never looked better. By Sir Isaac Heard I am sending you a copy of our accounts from the time we left London. The balance of cash remaining on this date is Crowns 311-23-6, besides 100/. of the letter of credit of Sir R. Herries and Co.

Henry Vansittart & Richard Kennaway to Sir Robert Palk. 1786, August 13th, Calcutta.

We are very glad your brother and nephew have taken on them the debt of Lieut. Welland to his brother. Our payment of it was a serious object to young Welland's convenience. We believe Welland has a proper sense of errors, and disposition to reform, which regulates his present conduct ; but his embarrassments from the past we believe are not small, and such as time and economy only in the present situation of this service can entirely remedy.
Tom Palk's legacy being set off against his debt to the estate ; as it is not

only for the convenience of the estate but agreeable to his wishes to receive the sum still intended him in England, whither our attention is engaged in remitting the property, we recommend his being indulged with the payment of it there. We hope you duly received bills for a lakh of rupees, and also those for our remittance of 8,859/. We shall shortly send the accounts of the estate.

Henry Vansittart

Simeon Droz to General John Caillaud. 1786, August 19th, Arlington Street.

I arrived in England the 6th instant, and landed at Weymouth. from thence I proceeded with my family to Bath, where I left Mrs. Droz very poorly indeed, her nerves being much shook by the fatigues of the voyage, and they were in a very indifferent state before. I had the pleasure of seeing our sister, being well at Bath. I arrived in town last Thursday night, and am comfortably lodged for the present in the same house with John Boileau. My chief object in writing is to ask you to use your influence with Sir Robert Palk, with whom I am not acquainted. The case is this: when I succeeded my late friend Mr. Palk in the chiefship of Cossimbuzar, he proposed that I should take off his hands some concerns in small Filatures or places for making silk, which he possessed in the neighbourhood of the Factory ; and in consequence I gave him at his request a bond for 9,000 Rs., bearing interest at 1 per cent, per annum, and payable in 3 years ; but I never received the said Filatures or any small advantage from them whatever. Mr. Palk promised to return the bond, but forgot to do so, fell ill, and died on his way home. Messrs. Vansittart & Kennaway afterwards presented the bond for payment. I explained the matter and, in return for the original bond, gave a bond of indemnity to cover them in case Sir Robert Palk and the other executors should insist on payment. I now beg you to interest yourself with Sir Robert on my behalf and secure the return of the bond of indemnity

Simeon Droz

Lawrence Palk to Sir Robert Palk, Bart., M.P., Bruton Street. 1786, August 21st, Wesel. Received 5th September.

We arrived here yesterday evening some moments after the express which brought the account of the King of Prussia's death on the 17th instant, and of the heri[di]tary Prince's accession to the throne by the name of Frederick William the 2nd. This morning we were at the parade when the troups comprising this garrison took the oath of fidelity and obedeance to their new souverain. Notwithstanding the trouble and confu- sion this event cannot fail of producing in every part of the Prussian territories, it seems here to be the general opinion that the Emperour, actually in Transilvania and far removed from the frontiers of Silesia, will not strike a blow in attempting to regain this part of the possessions anciently belonging to his family.
I this moment receive your kind letter of the 11th inst. Your accounts of my dear mother's health have given me the greatest uneasiness, and make me accept with the sincerest acknowledgements your permission to return to England as soon as possible. Had you not desired me to continue my tour through Holland, I might perhaps have been the *avant coureur* of this letter. The alarming state of my poor Emelia's health, joined to th[at] of my dear mother, makes me uncom[mon] anxious to join my endeavours to yours in searching a means to render them every consolation in my power.
Mr. D'lvcrnois, whom I have consulted with regard to our proposed tour through Holland, is of opinion it will not take up more than three weeks, at the end of which time I hope to add to the pleasure of embracing that of assuring my dear father by word of mouth how truly and sincerely I am his most dutiful and affectionate son,

Lawrence Palk

Henry Vansittart jnr., to Sir Robert Palk. 1786, August 26th, Calcutta. Received March, 1787.

I am very much obliged to you for an intimation contained in one of your

letters to Kennaway and myself that you would get us recommended to Lord Cornwallis. This I believe will be the last instance of assistance which I shall require from you after the many which I have received, both in fixing me upon this establishment and in promoting my successful progress through this service. Every consideration inclines me to go home next year. I gain very little more than a subsistence, and my situation is rendered every year more disagreable by the interference of the Government here, the Court of Directors and Parliament.
We expect Lord Cornwallis in a fortnight, and the business of Government is in suspence untill his arrival. His appointment may be productive of much good or much harm, and it will not be in the power of the best intentions to prevent the latter, either if his Lordship acts without device or if he is influenced by bad.
I think we shall be able completely to close our administration of your nephew's estate this year.

Henry Vansittart

Messrs. Pelling & de Fries to Sir Robert Palk, Bart. 1786, August 29th, Fort St. George.

The Nabob has regularly compleated, even by anticipation, the payment of his annual subsidy of sixteen lacks. The Government has not been quite so regular in making the dividends to his creditors, some part being still unpaid. We shall remit you whatever dividends we may receive on account of the Nabob's bond to General Lawrence, and for your concern under the late Mr. Morse. The executors of Goodlad have not made any further payment. We do not fail to remind them from time to time, but until money becomes more plenty in the Settlement punctuality will not be observed in dealings.
Lord Cornwallis arrived here on the 22nd instant after a very short passage, and is to leave this for Bengal the 1st of next month. People's mind[s] are made easy for the repeal of the obnoxious part of Mr. Pitt's India Bill. We are peaceable throughout all our possessions in India. Tippoo, the Marattas and Nizam [are] fighting out their own battles. This

last has lost the whole of the Adoni country to Tippoo. The rains at present on that side prevent operations in the field, but it is likely to take place with more vigour the next spring.

Pelling & de Fries

Thomas Palk to Sir Robert Palk. 1786, September 7th, Trichinopoly.

I am happy that so handsome an addition has been made to my poor brother's legacies to my sisters, and thankful for the cancelling of my debt to him, which in that event has been, I hope, carried to my credit in England. When all the bills which I have transmitted to you are paid, with the legacy, their amount will be 18,976/.
You may, my dear Sir, very naturally conclude that I am most anxious to see those dear friends at home once more, and that 1 am straining every nerve to effect it, but alas fortunes are not to be made so rapidly now asbefore the war. People in my situation have never made them by their employs, but by loans of money to the country at, as you know, an high interest ; but it is no longer safe to do it on any terms ; and the Nabob, since the restitution of the Assignment, has not practised that good old custom. A most cordial understanding exists at present between me and his Highness, and it shall not be my fault should it not continue.
My brother I see, is purchasing away. I hope you will be able to do something of the same sort for me soon. I forgot to tell you, after enumerating the sums I had remitted, that I have Company's paper for Pagodas 60,000, for which I have the bond of the Bengal Government ; so that, all things considered, my having been 12 years without any employ, and finding myself much in debt on my coming here, you will not think I have been idle. I hope, however, that by the end of '87 I shall find myself in very comfortable circumstances, and that the January following will enable me to leave India.
I am happy to find Tom is well and improving. When you think him of age to be put to a school at or near London, I shall be much pleased. In January next we intend to send Kitty and Bob by Mrs. Lang, Mrs. Palk's sister ; the former in particular to be presented to Lady Palk. She is a

sweet child, and will I doubt not be a great favorite. Neither of them as yet have had the smallpox. They will go on the *Manship*, Capt. Gregory.

Tho. Palk

Lawrence Palk to Sir Robert Palk. 1786, September 8th, La Haye.

We arrived here yesterday in company with the Count de ourghaus and his family, who were kind enough to offer us a place in their boat from Amsterdam. At my arrival I had the pleasure of receiving the letters you had entrusted to the care of Sir Isaac Heard, amongst.which I found a recommendatory one to Sir James Harris. I do not suppose it will be of any great use to me, being informed our Ambassador is at present entirely occupied with the Prince of Orange's affairs, which seem to grow every day worse and worse, insomuch that a civil war appears now to be almost inevitable. The States of Holland, who assembled this morning, have come to a resolution almost unanimous, not only to divest him of all his employments, but also of his Statholderat. The King of Prussia has sent one of his principal Ministers, the Count de Gortz (late envoy to the Court of Petersbourg) to endeavour to accomplish a reconciliation between the Prince of Orange and the States ; but they seem to be so easperated against [him] that it is feared this negotiation will turn out unsuccessful.
I cannot conceive how the Stadholder, united solely with the province of Gueldre, can resist the united efforts of the remaining six, whose troups are at least five [times] as numerous as those at present under his command, unless his brother in law the King of Prussia makes a diversion in his favour, which in the present position of affairs appears to be very improbable.
In addition to this piece of news we have received advice of the declaration of war between Russia and the Turks, and that we have sold Gibraltar to the Empress for the sum of 2,000,000 pounds sterling. I am to[o] good an Englishman not to wish this piece of news to be authentic, as it has been sufficiently proved that this fortress is of no real use to us, but on the contrary puts us to a much greater expence than we can at

present afford.
We have been thus far very much delighted with our tour through Holland. At our entrance into this country everything announced to us the riches and general ease of its inhabitants, and this spectacle was greatly heigthened by the idea of the marks of misery and oppression we had left behind us in the deserts of Westphalia. But what particularly attracted our attention was the astonishing neatness and cleanliness of all the houses both great and small.
I cannot give any idea of the societies, as, not having any letters of recommendation for Amsterdam or any other town through which I have passed, I was not admitted amongst them. The Dutch seem to me to be in general a very good kind of people in their own way, who understand speculation as well, if not much better than their neighbours.
Your letter to Mr. D'lvernois, which we yesterday received, gives me no account of Emelia, though it makes me happy in the receit of [news of] the better health of my dear mother. We intend setting off in three or four ays for Brussels, and on our way we shall pass through Rotterdam and Breda. We expect to arrive at Brussels in about a fortnight, when I flatter myself I shall have the pleasure of hearing from you.

Lawrence Palk

Thomas Abraham to Sir Robert Palk. 1786, September 18th, Calcutta.

It is reported that Mr. Stables intends going home this season on one of the Indiamen. Mr. Macpherson will also go probably, in consequence of having lost his appointment, and having such little influence from this being only a Member of Council. The Governor, I suppose, will do anything now even without the Council. It is rather dangerous now, I believe, to say much about public affairs in consequence of the late orders from home, which I shall accordingly take care to pay attention to; indeed there is very little to say if one wished it.
General Lang intends embarking for Europe this season in an Indiaman from hence that is to call at Madras. Mr. Jackson, son of the musician at Exeter I believe, is gone from Madras to China and thence to England.

I have not yet met Ensign Preston. He called on me once in Calcutta, but I missed him, and he left directly afterwards with Colonel Pearse's detachment. Ensign Preston of the Coast establishment was here some time ago. He proposed, after returning to Trichinopoly, to proceed to England to bring out his wife and children. I thank you for recommending me to Lord Cornwallis and Mr. Shore, and congratulate you on Miss Palk's marriage.

Thomas Abraham

Chocapah to the Honble. Sir Robert Palk, Baronet. 1786, September 30th, Madras.

Sir Archibald Campbell is arrived here the 6th April last. According to the Company's order a Board of Revenue and a Board of Trade were appointed, the former consisting of Mr. Davidson as President, and Messrs. Oakeley, Moubray and Halburton members ; the latter consisting of Mr. Casamaijor as President, and Messrs. Hollond, Hamilton and John Balfour members ; and the Governor is to take his seat in both these Departments whenever he pleases.

Earl of Cornwallis arrived here with a commission for the Government of Bengali, and with a new one for Sir Archibald Campbell as Commander-in-Chief of the Coast army. Lord Cornwallis sailed for Bengal on the 31st August.

Hyder's son Tippoo directed his war in another part of the world. He declared against the Nizam and Marattas, and has marched with a large army against Adoni, the capital of the late Basalat Jing. He invaded the fort, but was repulsed with great loss by Bassalat Jing's son, who was in the fort with his family. The Nizam, hearing of Tippoo's great army, dispatched a large force under the command of his brother Mokar Ally, assisted with a body of the Marattas horse, who were safely arrived into the fort of Adoni. But unfortunately for the Nizam the conductor of this large army came in such haste that he had not taken the usual precaution to bring provision sufficient for his army as well as [to] supply those in the fort, and exhausted the little provision that was in the fort in a few days after their arrival. When they found it difficult to get provision into the fort on account of Tippoo's being on the frontiers of it, they thought it proper to evacuate the fort of Adoni, and marched with all their forces to the fort of Royachoor ; and Tippoo immediately entered into the fort of Adoni. Tippoo, after this success, intends to march against Conoul, which if not timely succoured by the Nizam will, it is thought, fall into his hands.

Sir John Dalling will, I think, sail for England soon according to the orders of the Court of Directors. He is very sorry at the death of his son Lieut. Dalling, who died here the middle of this month. The Committee of Circuit, having examined the Circars under Vizagapatam, are now in the Masulipatam district.

Chocapah

Messrs. Pelling & de Fries to Sir Robert Palk, Bart. 1786, October 14th, Fort St. George.

Although the Nabob paid very punctually his stipulated sum of sixteen lacks for last year, this Government has not compleated the pay- ment due for the creditors' share. We are promised a dividend soon.

The Nabob was lately very ill, but he is now in a fair way of recovery, and continues his payments regularly. He sent us word by his Braminy to present his compliments to you his old friend.

Lord Cornwallis took possession of his Government on the 12th September. Mr. Shore was unwell : the damp climate of Bengal will be unfavourable to his asthmatick complaint

Tippoo and the Marattas are gone into winter quarters, to recommence their operations after the rains.

The rate of bills granted by the Presidencies in India on the Company in liquidation of their debt is so low — 7 shillings per pagoda for this place — that we don't imagine much of their debt will be transferred to Europe

Pelling & de Fries

The Rev. Samuel Badcock to Sir Robert Palk, Bart., Bruton Street. 1786, October 19th, South Molton.

I have frequently made enquiries after the health of Lady Palk, but the accounts I received were so very unfavourable that I was fearful of writing to you lest I should intrude on you.

I most sincerely sympathize with you in the affliction you have lately gone through.

Since my last I have received Hooker's Account of Devon from Mr. Coffin's library. What is valuable shall be transcribed. I expect Westcote's Description that a copy of it may [be] procured for your collection. A very large folio of arms and genealogies is the only remaining MS. in Portlege's library that respects the County.

In Fuller's Worthies, under the article of Devonshire, mention is made of a manuscript relating to the County written by Northcote, Baronet. Fuller refers to it several times, and even gives some extracts from it. Bishop Nicholson, however, in his Historical Library supposes that Fuller had confounded Northcote with Westcote, and then says in a punning way that 'the author was often at a greater distance from truth than North and West.' Yet Mr. Gough seems positive that Fuller made no mistake, and says that the late Sir Henry Northcote (who practised physic and lived in the parish of Tawstock) had the manuscript in his possession that Fuller quotes, and intended to have published it with considerable enlargements. He further says that the MS. was afterwards in the possession of Mr. Hesket, I have desired Mr. Chichester of Hall to ask his relation Sir Stafford Northcote if he possesses any MSS. that may be worth transcribing relating to the County. The Mr. Heskett mentioned by Gough is supposed to have been the same gentleman who some years since possessed Aldiscot near Torrington, now Mr. Rowe's estate. What became of his papers I could never learn.

I will take care to have the MSS. belonging to your collection bound in the way you have mentioned, and will superintend the business that no mistakes may be made.

I have lately spent a fortnight at Colonel Simcoe's and at other places in the neighbourhood of Exeter ; and then took the opportunity of writing to my uncle to inform him that I had at last come to a resolution to quit my office among the Dissenters. I explained my reasons, and then left him to judge whether I had not taken a right step. It was the step that my inclination, my judgment and my conscience equally concurred to dictate. The risque I ran with my uncle I was well aware of, but I was resolved to hazard it .

The Bishop hath offered me ordination, and was so obliging as to say that he considered me as a great acquisition. I told the Bishop that ordination was too serious a business to be determined on in haste but it was probable that I should avail myself of his Lordship's offer next summer. I have no ambition of preferment. A very moderate competency is all I wish, and my prospects do not exceed a hundred a year. If I could secure that, I shall be perfectly resigned to the loss of my uncle's favour and fortune.

S. Badcock

P.S. I am much with Sir John Chichester, who often, very often, speaks of you and Lady Palk with great friendship and esteem. I went to call on Sir Bourchier Wrey this week, but he and Lady Wrey were gone to Barley. We wished much to know how Lady Palk was ; and Sir John (whom I shall see this afternoon) will rejoyce to hear that any favourable circumstance appears in her Ladyship's complaint.

Thomas Abraham to Sir Robert Palk 1786, November 12th, Calcutta.

It is with extreme concern that I communicate to you the melancholy event since my last of the death of my poor friend Mr. Vansittart, universally beloved, lamented and regretted, of which, as you will have no doubt very particular information, I shall quit the painful and disagreeable further relation by only observing the bad effects of too long a stay in this country, both in this and another recent instance. The bill I drew on my father for 150/. I hope has been honoured. I shall use my utmost endeavours to prevent any necessity for drawing again. I can live upon my present salary without running into any debt, which I shall always studiously take care to avoid : it hangs like a millstone about the neck of a young man. Now certainly when there is so bad a prospect of ever being able to repay it. My salary has been reduced so much lately that I should imagine it will be cut no more, or that I may be able to get some little encrease to it

.Thos. Abraham

Thomas Palk to Sir Robert Palk. [17]86, November 14th, Trichinapoly.
These few lines will be conveyed by the *Swallow* packet. By the Mailship, which will sail from Madras about the 15th of next month, I shall have the. pleasure to write you again. General Lang and family will go on this ship, and will have my children Kitty and Bob under their care. We are about setting off for Madras for that purpose. I shall write to Ashburton by that conveyance, though I have not heard from thence this year.

Adrian de Fries to Sir Robert Palk, Bart. 1786, November 20th, Fort St. George.

On the 16th instant I sent you a First Bill of Exchange for 2,000. on account of Mr. Thomas Palk of Trichinopoly. I now enclose a First of Exchange drawn by the Governor and Council of Tranquebar on the Royal College of Economy and Commerce at Copenhagen for 1,856/. 5s., payable to your order for credit to Mr. Palk.

Adrian de Fries

The Rev. Samuel Badcock to Sir Robert Palk, Bart. 1787, March 1st, South Molton.

I was sorely disappointed in missing the opportunity of seeing you on Tuesday, as I proposed and most earnestly wished, at Sir John Chichester's, but a violent attack of the headach (my old and unconquerable enemy !) confined me all day to my bed at Hall.
I beg that when you return to London you will be so obliging as to second my application to Sir George Yonge for any little thing that he may

have it in his power to procure for me, as the time approaches when I wish to get orders, and I have no prospect from any other quarter. I have stated to Sir George my situation; and as I have the History of the County greatly at heart, and will exert myself to complete it to the best of my power so as to make it a monument for futurity, I only want a present support to sit down without care ; and a little, a very little, will suffice. I shall then have leisure to prosecute my engagement with you in this great and arduous undertaking.
And as to yourself — my recompense hath exceeded not only my expectation but my desert.

Sam. Badcock
P.S. I will beg the favour of you to direct the enclosed to Mr. Beeke at Oxford.

So ends the correspondence carefully preserved by Robert Palk at his home on the Haldon Hills. It represents several periods during which he was successively a greatly admired administrator, a polititian, as governor of Madras, as a confidant and friend to many of his colleagues and then, in a new life as an MP at Westminster. He returned to England with great wealth that showing that he was a businessman capable of amassing a huge fortune. All of these periods of his life are illustrated by letters he received.

Palk Family Crest

LI
Postscript, 1786

Robert Palk was a naval chaplain with Admiral Boscawen's fleet in 1749 and transferred to the Company's service when the quarrelsome, abusive and aggressive Rev. Francis Fordyce was dismissed from service after coming to blows with Robert Clive in Cuddalore.

Palk served nine years as chaplain in Fort St. David, Cuddalore, and at St. Mary's in Fort St. George. During this period, he was on numerous occasions sent to conduct political negotiations with the French and the Rajah of Tan j ore. For successfully negotiating with the latter, his inseparable friend Major Stringer Lawrence, founder of the Madras Regiment and "Father of the Indian Army", recommended that he be presented a diamond ring of value 1000 pagodas.

Though he later renounced his vows, Robert Palk was the first man of the cloth to become not only a civil servant but also a Governor in India in Medieval and Modern History. He was appointed Governor of Madras in 1763 and his period of office passed off peacefully. One of his significant contributions was his appointment, in 1765, of Lt. William Stevens of the Engineers to survey Adam's Bridge. in the Carnatic. Stevens' extensive survey was enthusiastically encouraged by Palk and, as a result, the Strait between India and Sri Lanka, the bay and the hills beyond were named Palk and Palkonda Hills in his honour.

The political role he had played in the Carnatic led to Robert Palk being asked to join the Company's civil service. As Third in Madras he returned in 1761 after two years in England. The Governorship followed, during which his second significant contribution to the history of the times was to negotiate a treaty with the Moghuls and obtain for the Company the Northern Circars, today known as Northern Andhra Pradesh and Southern Orissa.

He retired to England in 1767 and bought the Haldon House and estate in his native Devonshire. There he lived with his permanent guest Major General Stringer Lawrence. When he died, in 1775 Palk raised a tower on the summit of Haldon Hill in memory of his friend.

Palk served in Parliament for 14 years.

Stringer Lawrence (6 March 1697 – 10 January 1775) was an English soldier, the first Commander in Chief in India and celebrated as the "Father of the Indian Army".

Lawrence was born at Hereford. He entered the army in 1719 and served in Gibraltar and Flanders, subsequently taking part in the battle of Culloden. In 1748, with the rank of major and the reputation of an experienced and successful soldier with a safe pair of hands, he went out to India to command the East India Company's troops. Dupleix's schemes for the French conquest of southern India were on the point of taking effect, and not long after his arrival at Fort St David, Stringer Lawrence was actively engaged. He successfully foiled an attempted French surprise at Cuddalore, but subsequently was captured by a French cavalry patrol at Ariancopang while leading forces in support of Admiral Boscawen to Pondicherry. He was kept prisoner until the Peace of Aix-la-Chapelle.

In 1749 he was in command at the capture of Devicota. On this occasion Robert Clive served under him and an unusual friendship, based upon mutual respect, began. Clive was not an easy man to know and made very few friends but Lawrence was certainly one of these. On one occasion, after Robert Clive had become famous, he honoured the creator of the Indian army by refusing to accept a sword of honour unless one was also voted to Lawrence.

In 1750 Lawrence returned to England but in 1752 he was back in India. Here he found Clive in command of a force intended for the relief of Trinchinopoly. As senior officer Lawrence took over the command, but was careful to allow Clive every credit for his share in the subsequent operations, which included the relief of Trichinopoly and the surrender of the entire French force. In 1752 with an inferior force he defeated the French at Bahoor and in 1753 again relieved Trichinopoly. For the next seventeen months he fought a series of actions in defence of the place, finally arranging a three months' armistice, which was afterwards converted into a conditional treaty. He had been Commander in chief up to the arrival of the first detachment of regular forces of the crown.

In 1757 he served in the operations against Wandiwash, and in 1758-1759 was in command of Fort St George during the siege by the French under Lally. In 1759 failing health compelled him to return to England but, again, he resumed command in 1761 as major general and commander-in-chief. Clive supplemented his old friend's inconsiderable income by settling on him an annuity of £500 a year. In 1765 he presided over the board charged with arranging the reorganization of the Madras army and he finally retired the following year.

The East India Company erected a monument to his memory in Westminster Abbey. A marble statue of him, dressed in classical Roman Army uniform, stands in the Foreign and Commonwealth Office and a codestone version in the Haldon Belvedere (Lawrence Castle) built to his memory by Robert Palk. There is also a me- morial to him in nearby Dunchideock church.

When, in England, the East India Company was experiencing trading difficulties in India, at the Company's London Headquarters during discussions concerning who might be able to help with the problem, one of the members declared: 'Gentlemen, you forget, we have Palk at home.' With one voice the members replied 'The very man!' So Robert Palk returned to India in October 1761. He was invited to serve on the Council of the Company, and was appointed to membership of the Treasury Committee. He also served as the Export Warehouse Keeper.

When George Pigot resigned in November 1763, it made way for Palk to take up the post of Governor of Madras. With his new-found authority Palk dived deeper into the world of trade, all the time enlarging his personal wealth.

Palk eventually left India in January 1767 at the age of 50, and was well received by both the King and the Court of Directors on his return. However, returning to England was not the end of his involvement with India. He introduced and was patron to many, who, like him, went with the intention of making themselves a fortune from India. He now had a fortune and could indulge whatever new interest came his way.

His nephew Jonathan Palk said this of his Uncle Robert:

'Rectitude of mind and benignity of heart formed the outline of his character. Uncorrupted by the luxury of the East, he was an encourager of bodily and mental exertion, furnishing his friends with the means not of idleness, but of being active for their own good and the good of society. My father was a little farmer with a large family; for him my uncle bought an estate, which enabled him to live a credit to his mother, and respected by his neighbours.'

Robert Palk became MP for Ashburton in 1767, again between 1774 and 1787 and during the intervening years, MP for Wareham. This was due to the influence of Calcraft, at the time Secretary for War. His brother Walter Palk also became an MP for Ashburton. Palk was a Tory by sentiment.

Despite living in Torquay and then at Haldon House near Exeter, he remained involved with Ashburton for many years. His interest lay in acquiring land and properties mostly between Dunchideock and Torquay. He also owned land around Kenn and Ashburton and even supplied the church there with a new organ. Many famous people came to stay at Haldon including Hannah More the poet and Victorian feminist and reformer who arrived almost every summer to enjoy the fresh Devonshire air. Even King George III, who was on his way to Plymouth, stopped to enjoy Palk's hospitality, The progress and advancement of Robert Palk's son, Lawrence, who had been named as a tribute to Stringer Lawrence, was another of his great interests. Lawrence followed Palk as MP and also had property interests including the development of his own seaside village called Torquay. For over 30 years Palk was a key figure in local affairs in Exeter and the surrounding area where, for example, he supported the opening of the Exeter Racecourse on the Haldon Hills and became a regular visitor with the family.

All his life he had been a busy man, able to turn his hand to a great variety of task and now he added to his property and local affairs involvement an abiding interest in political matters, mainly supporting the government, but taking an active interest in any matters concerning India. His archive of letters received shows this. Though a few of his own letter appear in the archive, when he thought it advisable to keep a copy, there is a considerable collection of his own correspondence in the British Museum covering the period 1767 - 1782 in the Warren Hastings archive. Palk particularly resented Lord North's Act, passed in 1773, for the regulation of the East India Company.

Robert Palk was made a baronet on 19 June 1782 during the reign of King George III. This was in recognition of his efforts in securing India for Britain. His coat of arms portrayed an eagle displayed and the crest had a semi-terrestrial globe of the northern hemisphere with an eagle rising from it, supported by two Asian Indians in loincloths and turbans. The family motto was *Deo Ducente* - ‘God is my Guide’. This was followed by the Mayor of Exeter adding him to the centuries-old roll of the City of Exeter Freemen, a privilege that his son and successive heirs retained until 1883.

A flavour of the busy life led by Robert Palk in Westminster is provided through his close relationship with Laurence Sulivan. Sulivan’s early life is obscure, and the first record of his activities occurs in March 1740 when his appointment as assistant to the governor of Bengal was confirmed and antedated to 1st Jan. Appointed factor in February 1741, he did useful work but rose slowly through lack of interest at home. In 1751 he became chief of Mahim and took his seat on the Bombay council. He returned to England in 1753 with a moderate fortune, engaged in agency business, and in 1761 purchased for £13,500 the estate of Ponsbourne. About the same time he was able to give up or greatly reduce his business activities. He said later of his resources, though I was independent, not anxious for more, I never was rich.

In 1755, when the cry was being raised for men with local knowledge on the direction of the East India Company, he was elected a director, and thus began what was to be the absorbing interest of his career and a close relationship with Palk developed.

Sulivan's parliamentary ambitions arose directly out of his activities in the Company, since relations between state and Company were close and of growing importance. At first received somewhat coldly by ministers accustomed to deal with those whom he had superseded, he benefited from the changes following the accession of George III and attached himself to Bute and in particular to Shelburne, with whom he soon became on intimate terms. At the general election of 1761 he contested Ashburton, a borough over which Lord Orford was accustomed to exercise control. He was probably introduced there by John Dunning, a friend of Shelburne, and encouraged by Shelburne to make the attempt. Sulivan was defeated but expressed his determination to petition. He wrote to Shelburne on 7 Sept. 1761:

I have the high opinion of Lord Bute as sincerely to believe he will not suffer me and the rights of a free people to be sacrificed by a minister [Newcastle] who avows his boasted influence shall operate against me.'

But Henry Fox asked to be excused from presenting the petition,and Bute persuaded him to abandon it. On 2 Mar. 1762 Sulivan wrote to Newcastle:

I owe that respect to your Grace as to acknowledge your intended kindness ... but as my future expectations are from Lord Bute alone, at whose desire I gave up the contest, I can only offer your Grace my thanks.

On 24 March Sulivan was returned for Taunton on Lord Egremont's interest. In 1768 he transferred to Ashburton as a result of an arrangement made with Robert Palk.

In the House Sulivan was a frequent and successful speaker on East India affairs and until 1769 a personal follower of Shelburne. The Company's growing responsibilities led to dissensions within its general court which were intensified by the violent personal enmity between Sulivan and Clive. In the 1763 election of directors Clive, at the head of a number of dissatisfied Company servants, created a large number of fictitious votes in an attempt to drive Sulivan from power. Sulivan defended himself by similar measures, and triumphed with the aid of funds and influence put at his disposal by the Administration. On the fall of the Bute Administration, however, Clive gained the support of the new ministry and Sulivan lost control of the Company's affairs. Maintaining his close relations with the Shelburne group, Sulivan, assisted by Henry Vansittart (Palk's wife's father), embarked on a struggle to recover his authority in the Company, and when Shelburne returned to office in 1766 suc- ceeded in influencing materially the settlement between the state and the Com- pany over their claims on the territorial revenues of Bengal. But the Chatham Administration was too divided to give him the help which would restore his control over the Company. The intimacy which developed between Lauchlin Maclean and Shelburne, and the part Macleane began to play in the specula- tion which sprang up in East India stock at this time, brought Sulivan into even closer relations with Shelburne. It was with the aid of the Shelburne group and a related group of speculators headed by Macleane and including a number of M.P.s (e.g. William Burke and Lord Verney) that Sulivan, Robert Palk and Henry Vansittart planned, in 1769, an expensive campaign to get back into power, a campaign in which they at last succeeded. It was during the administration of Shelburne in 1766 that Robert Palk became involved leading up to the 1773 Act of Lord North. Palk much disagreed with the act and his parliamentary life devolved around this. Palk maintained a London House as did Stringer Lawrence and, though there is no direct evidence to be found in the literature of the time, there is little doubt but that General Lawrence joined Palk with enthusiasm in his opinions about the East India Company's development.

Sulivan's and Vansittart's success proved a disaster, for a sudden fall in the value of East India stock plunged all the participators into acute financial difficulties; Sulivan and Vansittart were left liable for a 'sum not less than £60,000', and the loss of Vansittart at sea, (earlier described), on his way back to India to retrieve his fortunes, made Sulivan's position still more serious. By 1772 he estimated his debts uncovered by securities at some £17,800, and his estate was mortgaged to Dunning. Though he was owed large sums by Macleane, and though Macleane was sent to India in the hopes that he would be able to repay his creditors, little in fact was obtained from this source, and the failure of Sir George Colebrooke depressed Sulivan further, since Colebrooke also was his debtor. He managed by desperate efforts to keep his head above water, and succeeded in 1778 in getting his son Stephen out to India, where Warren Hastings befriended him, but he never regained his former prosperity. As late as 1779 Hastings, hearing of his straitened means, offered him a gift of £10,000, which he was prepared to accept if the transaction could be carried out secretly.

The financial disaster of 1769 also ended his relations with William Petty, 2nd Earl of Shelburne (himself a sufferer). In September he complained that 'to me all are ill-disposed' and in October went over to Administration in the hope of obtaining their support in the Company. The support of Administration did not at once benefit him, as a combination of his enemies ousted him from the direction in 1770, but at the election of 1771 the personal intervention of North effected his restoration and, once there, his knowledge and ability began again to make their mark. By the end of 1771 it was noted that 'if he remains united as at present with Sir George he will very shortly lead the India House'.

When the Company had been rescued from its straits by North's East India legislation of 1773 and the Treasury began to exercise a continuous indirect control over the Company's affairs, it was made plain to Sulivan that it was intended to exclude him henceforth from the direction. Complaining of 'the cruel unmerited conduct of Lord North', he persisted in standing for the direction in 1773, but was defeated, and despite the unwilling support, on occasion, of the Rockingham group he did not succeed in again becoming a director until 1778.

The general election of 1774 came when his affairs were at their lowest ebb. In view of his alienation from Shelburne (though he still maintained some re- lations with Dunning) he could hardly have hoped to retain his seat at Ashburton, but the news that his friend Palk intended to resume his seat seems nevertheless to have been a blow to him. He wrote to Palk, 23 Aug. 1774

From public motives alone I sought Parliament, but so little satisfaction have I experienced within these walls that, had I now my then independence, no temptation upon earth should have carried me thither again. But the melancholy change makes it (if possible) necessary to the future prospects of my family that either I or my son should be in the Senate.

Yet in the end he withdrew all claims on the seat, and appears never to have tried to enter Parliament again. His ambition in the Company remained, however, unabated, and he was at the centre of the activities in which state and Company were concerned in the following years. In 1778 confusion among the supporters of Administration enabled him to slip back on to the direction, and John Robinson was soon complaining that he was 'forming a cabal and party in the direction and is nearly getting a majority'. In 1780 the Administration accepted the new situation and formed an alliance with him in the Com- pany which subsisted until North fell in 1782. While this return to power enabled him to carry out some of his projects in the Company, his alliance with Administration and his support of Warren Hastings called down upon him the enmity of the Opposition; and after North's resignation he was attacked in the seventh report of the select committee, and by Burke and others in the House of Commons in the debate of 1 Apr. 1783 on the printing of the report. Lord Rockingham died from influenza in 1782.

Sulivan and Palk played an active part in the struggle against Fox's East India bill in 1783, and in ensuring the Company's support for the Pitt Administration. Though now old and somewhat infirm, Sulivan hoped to enjoy his old supremacy in the Company; but the new ministers refused to support him as a candidate for either of the chairs. He remained a prominent director, but his in- fluence was in decline. By now Robert Palk was in his 66th year and ready for a genteel retirement though he continued an MP for Ashburton until 1787. Stringer Lawrence had died in 1775 leaving his property mostly to the Palk family and it was time to enjoy rural Devon living. He remained in politics until 1787 but with less energy for the fight. The plain truth was that by now the success of the company's trading in India was much too important to the nation to be left to commercial chance and with the death of Shelburne and Rock- ingham and the demise of Sulivan much of the organised opposition disappeared.

It was the Palk family future and his property dealings that now were more important than Indian business as the content of his archive shows. In addition to Lawrence Palk, he had three daughters, Anne, Catherine and Emelia. Both Catherine and Emelia died young, while Anne who had married Sir Bourchier Wrey in 1786, died at the age of 24. Lawrence was engaged in property transactions and developments in and around Torquay and as MP for Ashburton from 1787 to 1796.

Sir Robert Palk died at Haldon House on 29 April 1798, ten years after his wife Lady Anne. They were both buried in Dunchideock.

Notes on sources

The inspiration for writing this book about two eighteenth century adventurers came from the work of restoring the the Devon Historic Trust's property "The Haldon Belvedere" or "Lawrence Castle" as it has been called. The building is a remnant of an estate that bubbled with activity during the second half of the century following the return to England of Stringer Lawrence and Robert Palk. People often ask about the history of the building and the reason for its construction and they almost always wish to know more than is available from current easily accessible literature.

An excellent guide to the Palk family is available from its author Iain Fraser entitled *The Palk Family of Haldon House & Torquay* and there is a short monograph produced by the Rev'd Christopher Pidsley titled *The Tower on the Hill.* Interesting though architectural and genealogical descriptions are it seemed to me that there is so much more to the story of the General and the Clergyman that should be collated in an accessible form.

Having said that, there is a bibliography, dealing with separate parts of the story, dating to 1820 and before, that is exceptionally detailed. It is a period of history that has attracted many authors. Any study of the two gentlemen and their life and times must draw heavily on such sources and in this case those most consulted are Col. J. Biddulph's *Stringer Lawrence, The Father Of The Indian Army*, 1901, *The Pirates Of Malabar*, *An Englishwoman in India,* 1907 and *Dupleix*, 1910. Most important of all is the report that Col. Dove was commissioned to write in 1922 that reviews the letters preserved by Robert Palk during the years after he returned from India until approximately1786. This archive consisted of over 600 letters and documents collected by Mrs Bannatyne (made available by her for research purposes in 1920) that give an unique insight into the formation of the British Empire in India at its most critical period.

François Pierre Guillaume Guizot 1787–1874) was a French historian, orator, and statesman who was a dominant figure in French politics prior to the Revolution of 1848, who produced *Mémoires pour servir à l'histoire de mon temps* (8 vols., 1858–1861). This work has an interesting section about Dupleix and his colleagues with lithographs, some of which are reproduced in this book. Guizot provides a French perspective on the times when it could well have been France and not England who built an empire in the sub-continent.

In the following notes on sources and in the bibliography the value of Stringer Lawrence's and Palk's interacting contributions are evaluated in a way, I believe, not previously attempted in a single book.

I have chosen to present the material in the form of a description of the battles fought by Stringer Lawrence that surely establish a reputation as brilliant as Robert Clive's, followed by extracts from Palk's archive with commentary and more detailed notes about his correspondents drawn from a wide variety of sources listed below in a select bibliography.

An important source is Orme for details of the Indian campaigns and Polwhele's *History of Devonshire*. Orme does not make for easy reading because of his bewildering use of Indian place names. Many of the "potted biographies" in these notes are borrowed from the Wikipedia websites with amendments as necessary.

No attempt is made in this book to follow the fate of the family after Robert Palk died because the subject is centred on the story of Palk and Lawrence working and living together in India, London and Devon.

I A Friendship Formed

Lieutenant-General Sir Eyre Coote KB (1726 – 28 April 1783) was a member of the Coote family headed by the Earl of Mountrath. He was born near Limerick, Ireland, the son of the Reverend Chidley Coote and Jane Evans, daughter of George Evans and sister of George Evans, 1st Baron Carbery. He entered the 27th Regiment of Foot. He first saw active service in the Jacobite rising of 1745, and later obtained a captaincy in the 39th Regiment, the first regular British regiment sent to India.

1. The Honourable Edward Boscawen was born in Tregothnan, Cornwall, England on 19 August 1711, the third son of Hugh Boscawen, 1st Viscount Falmouth (1680–1734) by his wife Charlotte Godfrey (d.1754) elder daughter and co-heiress of Colonel Charles Godfrey, master of the jewel office by his wife Arabella Churchill, the King's mistress. He was promoted rear-admiral of the blue on 15 July 1747 and appointed to command a joint operation being sent to the East Indies.

2. The *Compagnie Française pour le Commerce des Indes Orientales* resulted from the fusion of three earlier companies, the *1660 Compagnie de Chine, the Compagnie d'Orient and Compagnie de Madagascar.*

3. The peace of Aix-la-Chapelle, sometimes called the Treaty of Aachen, ended the War of the Austrian Succession following a congress assembled on 24 April 1748 at the Free Imperial City of Aachen—called Aix-la-Chapelle in French and then also in English—in the west of the Holy Roman Empire. The resulting treaty was signed on 18 October 1748 whcih was when Major Lawrence was released.

4. Robert Clive, then Colonel Clive, was the instigator of the pension awarded to Stringer Lawrence which he personally increased by a private annuity of £500.

II India before the English, 1482

1. The Register of Letters &c. of the Governor and Company of Merchants of London trading into the East Indies, 1600–1619. On page 3, a letter written by Elizabeth I on 23 January 1601 ("Witnes or selfe at Westminster the xxiiith of Ianuarie in the xliith yeare of or Reigne.") states, "Haue been pleased to giue lysence vnto or said Subjects to proceed in the said voiadgs, & for the better inabling them to establish a trade into & from the said East Indies Haue by or tres Pattents under or great seale of England beareing date at Westminster the last daie of december last past incorporated or said Subjecte by the name of the Gournor & Companie of the merchaunts of London trading into the East Indies, & in the same tres Pattents have geven them the sole trade of theast Indies for the terme of XVteen yeares.

2. Captain Henry Every, also Evory or Avery, (23 August 1659 – after 1696), sometimes erroneously given as John Avery was an English pirate who operated in the Atlantic and Indian Oceans in the mid-1690s. He likely used

several aliases throughout his career, including Henry Bridgeman, and was known as Long Ben to his crewmen and associates.

3. Sir John Gayer (died 1711) was an English governor of Bombay for the East India Company. He assumed the office on 17 May 1694; he officially left office on November 1704. Gayer's tenure as Governor was dominated by difficulties with the English Company Trading to the East Indies (New Company), set up in 1698; and he was kept imprisoned for much of it.

4. Robert Clive was born at Styche, near Market Drayton in Shropshire, on 25 September 1725 to Richard Clive and Rebecca Gaskell Clive. The family had a lengthy history of public service: members of the family included an Irish chancellor of the exchequer under Henry VIII, and a member of the Long Parliament. Robert's father served in Parliament for many years, representing Montgomeryshire. Robert was their eldest son of thirteen children; he had seven sisters and five brothers, six of whom died in infancy.

III Fort St George, 1639

IV Competition between England and France, 1742

V The French in India

1. Joseph-François, Marquis Dupleix (1 January 1697 – 10 November 1763) whose father was François Dupleix, a wealthy farmer, was governor general of the French establishment in India

2. Bertrand François Mahé de La Bourdonnais was born in Saint-Malo, Brittany. He went to sea when he was at the age of 10, and in 1718 entered the service of the French East India Company as a lieutenant.Joseph-François,

Sources: Guizot and Orme

1. Charles Robert Godeheu de Zaimont was Acting Governor General of Pondicherry and the Commissioner of the French army during Dupleix's reign.In 1754, Charles Robert Godeheu gave the English the Indian territories, especially Madras which was conquered in 1746 by Dupleix.

Sources: Guizot and Biddulph

VI Seven Years' War 1754 - 1763

A curious feature about the treaty was that it did not fully provide for the restoration of prisoners of war. It provided only for a mutual exchange, man for man. No less than 670 French prisoners were in Trichinopoly at the time. Of these some died and some Swiss and Germans entered the English service : but when war broke out again in April, 1757, there were still 500 French prisoners in Trichinopoly. These prisoners were not exchanged till May, 1759. No sooner had they rejoined the French army, under Lally, than they raised a mutiny, and some sixty of them marched off in a body to join the English

1. Marc Antoine René de Voyer, marquis de Paulmy and 3rd marquis d'Argenson (1757) (22 November 1722, Valenciennes – 13 August 1787), was the only son of René-Louis de Voyer de Paulmy, marquis d' Argenson. He should not be confused with his grandfather, Marc-René, or his great-grandfather, also Marc-René, or in particular with his cousin Marc-René (1722-1782). In 1750 he was appointed to head the stables of King Louis XV and appointed governor of the Château de Vincennes in 1754. He was forced to retire through the influence of Madame de Pompadour in 1758.

2. Anne Antoine, Comte d'Aché (23 January 1701, Marbeuf – 11 February 1780) was a French naval officer who rose to the rank of Vice Admiral. He is best known for losing the Battle of Cuddalore and Battle of Pondicherry. He also failed to provide adequate naval support to French troops attempting to capture Madras in 1759.[1] After he received rumours of a British attack on the major Indian Ocean naval base Mauritius he did not go to the aid of the French forces in Pondicherry which was being besieged by the British. Pondicherry, the French capital in India, subsequently surrendered leaving Britain dominant in the continent. After the war he retired to Brest where he died in 1780.

3.Charles Joseph Patissier, Marquis de Bussy-Castelnau (1718 – 7 January 1785) was the Governor General of the French colony of Pondicherry from 1783 to 1785. He servied with distinction under Joseph François Dupleix in the East Indies, receiving the Order of Saint Louis.

VII Stringer Lawrence in India.

The story of Clive refusing to receive the sword voted to him by the East India Company, unless one was also given to Lawrence, rests on the authority of Clive's biographer. It is indirectly supported by the few accurate records now in existence. Lawrence's sword was not voted to him until three months after a testimonial to Clive had been determined, and then in such a manner as to show that it was an afterthought. It is remarkable also that, in repairing the oversight, the Directors voted a sword worth £750 to Lawrence, after granting one worth £500 to Clive, as if they had at last become aware of Lawrence's claims. Clive was in London at the time, Lawrence being still in India

1. Nazir Jung: Mir Ahmed Ali Khan Siddiqi was the son of Nizam-ul-Mulk by his wife Saeed-un-nisa Begum. He was born February 26, 1712. He succeeded his father as the Nizam of Hyderabad State in 1748. He had taken up a very pompous title of Humayun Jah, Nizam ud-Daula, Nawab Mir Ahmad Ali Khan Siddiqi Bahadur, Nasir Jung, Nawab Subadar of the Deccan.However, he is most famously known as Nasir Jung.

VIII Stringer Lawrence arrives in India

IX Lawrence and Clive foil the French, 1754

John Caillaud arrived in India with a British detachment in 1753, and was commissioned Captain in the Madras Army. He served under Lawrence in Trichinopoly, and from 1755 to 1759 commanded in the Southern districts. During that period he operated against Mahfuz Khan in Tinnevelly andMadura and reheved Trichinopoly, which was besieged by d'Auteuil. At the siege of Madras by Lally, Caillaud commanded the field force at Chingleput, and fought a vigorous action at St. Thomas's Mount in February, 1759. Appointed to command the troops in Bengal, he saw active service in Bihar in 1760 and 1761. Returning to Madras, Colonel Caillaud reduced Nellore in 1762 and laid siege to Arnee. In the following year he became Brigadier General, and in 1766 took possession of the Circars, which had been ceded to the British by the Mogul. To placate the Nizam, Caillaud was deputed to Hyderabad, where he concluded a treaty under which the Company agreed to pay a tribute for the new territory. On retirement he settled in Oxfordshire, where he died in 1810.

X The siege of Trichinopoly, 1753

XI Renewed French Assault on Trichinopoly, 1753

1. Admiral Samuel Cornish reinforced Steevens at the siege of Pondicherry

in 1761, and in the following year, in conjunction with General Draper, conducted the expedition against Manila.

2. Colonel the Hon. George Monson entered the army in 1750, came to India with Draper's Regiment and served at Wandewash and Pondicherry in 1760, Manila in 1762 and Madura in 1763. Eleven years later he came again to India as a member of the Supreme Council of Bengal, and united with Olavering and Francis against Hastings until his death in 1776.

XII The English Army arrives in India, 1756

The expedient of senior officers volunteering to join a campaign was occasionally used because it neatly avoided difficulties posed by rank and seniority without ruffling miliary feathers. Stringer Lawrence, of lesser rank than Aldercron could now exercise command without being challenged.

In March, 1759, the Directors sent orders uniting the command of the King's and Company's troops in Bengal under Coote. At the same time, it was

provided that, in the event of Coote's death, the nomination of his provisional successor wasto be made by Lawrence, and was " on no pretence whatever "to be set aside by the civil authorities.

1.After the siege, d'Estaing was released on parole. He broke his word and assisted in destroying the Company's factory at Gombroon a few months later, much to the annoyance of the Directors. He was again taken prisoner at sea, and brought to England.

XIII Return of Lawrence to India, 1761

XIV The Palks of Ashburton, 1717

XV The Robert Palk archive

Col Dove, in 1922, prepared a report to the India Office with an acknowledgement to the then owner of the collection, Mrs. Bannatyne, for placing her collection at his disposal and affording facilities for their examination and study. He thanks Sir Murray Hammick, K.C.S.L, CLE., and Mr. Wilham Foster, CLE. The original collection is now preserved in the Manuscripts Department of the British Museum. In addition Mr. John S. Amery for particulars of the Palk family and Mr. Demetrius C Boulger for notes on the Marathas, to Mr. Stephen Wheeler for information concerning sundry Anglo-Indian notables, to Mr. Hugh R. Vibart for research in the British Museum, and to the Rev. Frank Penny's History of the Church in Madras for details of the ecclesiastical portion of Sir Robert Palk's career.

1. Lieut. Colonel Stringer Lawrence to Charles Watson, Esqr., Rear Admiral of the Red, and Commander in Chief of all His Majesty's Ships employed in the Indes. Lawrence's narrative was perhaps handed to the Admiral by Lawrence to relieve the tedium of the voyage. Other MS. copies of the account exist, one in the King's Library of the British Museum, and one in the Orme collection at the India Office. The narrative was edited and published by R. O. Cambridge in his Account of the War in India.

Covent Garden. 1760, November 10th.

1. East Indies. 1755, October 8th. Fort St. George:

2. Mr Pye to Robert Palk 1758, February 5th. Bombay.

3. William Fergusson to Robert Palk, Esqr., at Mrs. Ray's in Tavistock Row,

XVI letter from the King, 1762

1. Lord Egremont (a Secretary in Bute's ministry of 1762).

2. Brother Salvator a Sanctis D'fonseca to Governor Palk, Madras. 1765, Sept. 27th. San Thome.

3. Nawab Walajah :Honble. Robert Palk, Esqr., Governor. per Pacific, 3rd April, 1766.

4. Henry Moore to the Honorable Robert Palk, Esqr. 766, December 18th, Ship Osterley, near Anjengo:

XVII Company Friends, 1767

Hyder Ali 1721 – 7 December 1782, was the sultan and de facto ruler of the Kingdom of Mysore in southern India. Born Hyder Naik, he distinguished himself militarily, eventually drawing the attention of Mysore's rulers.

Tipu Sultan 20 November 1750 – 4 May 1799, was the eldest son of Sultan Hyder Ali by his wife Fatima Fakhr-un-Nisa and known as the Tiger of Mysore and ruler of Mysore from 1782 to 1799, and as a scholar, soldier and poet.

1.Robert Palk to Martin Goodlad 1767, January 25th. On board the Lord

Camden, Madras Road

2.Ensign J. Carpenter to Robert Palk. 1767, January 25th. Tritchinopoly.

3.George Vansittart to Robert Palk, Esqr. Duplicate. 1767, February 15th. Madras.

4.Robert Palk jun. to Robert Palk, Esqr. 1767, February 19th. Fort St. George.

XVIII Indian Traders and officials, 1767

1.Chocapah Chetti to the Honourable Robert Palk, Esqr. 1767, March 3rd. Fort St. George.

2. Mrs. Mary Powney to Robert Palk, Esqr. 1767, March 12th. Fort St. George.

3.George Vansittart to Robert Palk, Esqr. 1767, March 16th. Calcutta.

4. Mrs. Rebecca Casamajor to Robert Palk, Esqr. 1767, March 16th. Fort St. George.

XIX Colonel John Call reports, 1767

1. Colonel John Call to Robert Palk, Esqr. Duplicate. 1767, March, 19th.

XX Transferring profits to England, 1767

John Call, member of a Cornish family, began his Indian career in 1751 as an assistant to Benjamin Robins, F.R.S., Engineer General, and was graded as a civil servant. Working first on the St. David fortifications, he succeeded Captain John Brohier in 1757 as Engineer at Fort St. George. He developed and extended the latter fort, and was largely responsible for its successful defence during Lally's siege of 1758-59. He was then given military rank as Captain, and laid out the western extension of the White Town. In 1761 he conducted the siege ofPondicherry, and became Engineer in Chief in India. In 1762 he was in the Madras Council, and two years later was present at the siege of Madura. In 1768 he was one of the Field Deputies with the army. He retired to England as Colonel in 1770, became a member of parliament in 1784, was elected a Fellow of the Royal Society, and in 1791 was created a baronet.

1. Colonel John Call to Robert Palk, Esqr. 1767, March 21st, Madrass

2.Gocull Tarwaddy to Messrs. John Call and William Cotsford, General Post

Office, London. 1767, March 21st, Madrass.

3. Charles Bourchier to Robert Palk, Esqr. 1767, March 22nd, Fort St. George

XXI Updates from William Goodlad, 1767

1. William Martin Goodlad to Robert Palk, Esq.1767, March 22nd, Fort St. George
2. Chocapah to the Honourable Robert Palk, Esqr. 1767, April 3rd, Fort St. George
3. Colonel John Call to Robert Palk, Esqr. 1767, April 6th, Madrass.

XXII The Nabob's debt is settled, 1767

Ali Muhammed Ali Khan Wallajah (1717 – 16 October 1795) was the Nawab of Arcot in India and an ally of the British East India Company. Muhammed Ali Khan Wallajah was born to Anwaruddin Muhammed Khan, by his second wife, Fakhr un-nisa Begum Sahiba, was a niece of Sayyid Ali Khan Safavi ul-Mosawi of Persia, sometime Naib suba of Trichonopoly on 7 July 1723 at Delhi. Muhammed Ali Khan Wallajah the Nawab of Arcot often referred to himself as the Subedar of the Carnatic in his letters and correspondence with the then Mughal Emperor Shah Alam II.

John Pybus arrived in India as a Writer in 1743. After the capture of Madras by de la Bourdonnais he went to Fort St. David, and in 1751 was one of the eight volunteer officers who joined Clive in the attack and subsequent defence of Arcot. Pybus was Supervisor at Fort Marlborough, Bencoolen, in 1754, and four years later, when in charge of the Fort St. George Mint, was taken into Council. In 1762 he was sent on a political mission to the King of Kandy, and wrote an interest- ing journal of his proceedings. He was a Trustee for the Nawab's consolidated debt of 1767. Pybus married Martha Small in 1753.

1 .James Johnson to Robert Palk, Esqr. 1767, April 11th, Fort St. George. 2. John Maxwell Stone to Robert Palk, Esq. 1767, April 15th, Fort St. George 3. John Pybus to Robert Palk, Esqr. 1767, April 15th

XXIII The China Trade, 1754

1. George Smith to Robert Palk, Esqr. 1767, October 30th, Fort St. George

2. John Calland to Robert Palk, Esqr.1767, November .3rd, Fort St. George
3. Mooperala Kistnia and Rama Kisna to Robert Palk, Esqr. 1767, November 4th, Fort St. George. 22nd April, 1768
4. Nawab Walajah to General Lawrence, Behauder, Hous Bur Jung. 1767, November 5th, Fort St. George.
5. Copy letter: Robert Palk to William Martin Goodlad. 1767, November 15th, Spring Gardens.
6. To the Editor "For the Morning Chronicle." 1767

XXIV Perils at sea, 1750

Sources: Chatterton Kent, Orme, Biddulph,

XXV John Calland's problem, 1768

John Wood was commissioned Ensign in the Company's Europeans in 1753, and held the rank of Captain five years later. He served as Major at the second siege of Madura in 1764 under Colonel Charles Campbell. In 1767 Lieut. Colonel Wood moved from Trichinopoly to join Colonel Joseph Smith against Haidar Ali, and was present at the battle of Trinomalai. In 1768 he commanded an independent division in the Baramahal, where he met with remarkable success. On the summons to Madras of Colonel Smith, Wood assumed chief command, but displayed incapacity and sustained such serious reverses that he was recalled. He was tried by court martial in 1769 on charges of misappropriation of stores and misconduct in the field, and though acquitted by the Court was dismissed the service by government. The Directors subsequently upheld the acquittal. He married Elizabeth Owen in 1762, and died at Madras in 1774.

1. John Calland to Robert Palk, Esqr. 1768, April 25th, Fort St. George. 2. James Bourchier to Robert Palk, Esqr. 1768, May 2nd, Madrass.

3. George Smith to Robert Palk, Esqr. 1768, May 7th, Fort St. George. 4. Thomas Palk to Robert Palk, Esqr. 1768, May 7th at Sea.

XXVI Poor Griffiths dies, 1768

1. The Rev. John Thomas to Robert Palk, Esq. 1768, Sunday May 7th, Fort

St. George.

2. William Martin Goodlad to Robert Palk, Esqr. 1768, May 12th, Fort St. George.

3. Laurence Sulivan to Robert Palk, Esqr 1768, May 19th, Great Ormond Street.

4. George Vansittart to Robert Palk, Esqr. endorsed 'Received 2nd May 1769, per Valentine. 1768, September 6th, Midnapore.

5. Thomas Palk to Robert Palk, Esq. 1768, September 30th, Camp near Colar to the southward of Madras.

6. Lieut. Thomas Palk to [Robert Palk, Esqr.] 1768, October 24th, Samalcotah. XXVIII Contact with Company in London, 1768

1. Robert Palk to William Martin Goodlad. 1768, November 1st, London. Received 18th May, 1769, per Lioness.

2. George Vansittart to Robert Palk, Esqr. 1769, January 5th. On my way from Calcutta to Midnapore.

3. Robert Palk to William Martin Goodlad. 1769, March 17th. London. Received 3rd September.

XXVIII Warren Hastings is expected, 1769

Warren Hastings was born at Churchill, Oxfordshire in 1732 to a poor father and a mother who died soon after he was born. He attended Westminster School where he was a contemporary of the future Prime Ministers Lord Shelburne and the Duke of Portland as well as the poet William Cowper. He joined the British East India Company in 1750 as a clerk and sailed out to India reaching Calcutta in August 1750. Hastings built up a reputation for hard work and diligence, and spent his free time learning about India and mastering Urdu and Farsi. He was rewarded for his work in 1752 when he was promoted and sent to Kasimbazar, an important British trading post in Bengal where he worked for William Watts. While there he received further lessons about the nature of East Indian politics.

He was impeached for crimes and misdemeanors during his time in India in the House of Commons upon his return to England. At first deemed unlikely to succeed, the prosecution was managed by MPs including Edmund Burke, Charles James Fox and Richard Brinsley Sheridan. When the charges of his indictment were read, the twenty counts took Edmund Burke two full days to read.

The house sat for a total of 148 days over a period of seven years during the investigation. The investigation was pursued at great cost to Hastings personally, and he complained constantly that the cost of defending himself from the prosecution was bankrupting him. He is rumoured to have once stated that the punishment given him would have been less extreme had he pleaded guilty. The House of Lords finally made its decision on April 1795 acquitting him on all charges

Charles Bourchier, son of Richard Bourchier, Governor of Bombay, arrived at Madras in 1741 as a Writer. Ten years later he was Secretary, and in 1754, when Military Storekeeper, Rental General and Scavenger, was taken into Council. He succeeded Palk as Governor in 1767. His period of office was marked by the occurrence of the first Mysore war, and by the execution of a permanent rampart around the Black Town of Madras. Bourchier resigned and retired to England

1. Josias Du Pre to Robert Palk, Esq. 1769, June 15th. Fort St. George.

2. Nicholas Morse to Robert Palk, Esq. 1769, June 26th. Fort St. George 3. Charles Bourchier to Robert Palk, Esq. 1769, June 29th. Fort St. George.

XXIX Palk is concerned about trade, 1769

1. Robert Palk to William Martin Goodlad 1769, November 5th. London. Received 1st May, 1770.

2. Lieutenant Thomas Palk to Robert Palk, Esq. 1770, January 12th. Condapillee.

3. Thomas Palk to Robert Palk, Esq. 1770, January 31st. Fort St. George. 4. Thomas Palk to Robert Palk. Esq.1770, February 5th. Fort St. George 5. William Martin Goodlad to Robert Palk, Esq. 1770, February 6th. Fort St. George.

6. Robert Palk to William Martin Goodlad. 1770, March 15th. London. 7. Warren Hastings to Robert Palk, Esq 1770, April 3rd. Fort St. George. 8. Warren Hastings to Robert Palk, Esq. 1770, April 7th. Fort St. George.

9. William Martin Goodlad to Robert Palk, Esq. 1770, April 8th. Fort St. George. Received 15th October.

10. Robert Palk to William Martin Goodlad. 1770, June 16th, per Dolphin frigate. Received 20th February, 1771.

XXX The loss of the Aurora, 1770

1. George Vansittart to Robert Palk, Esq. 1770, September 5th. Calcutta
2. Robert Palk jun. to Robert Palk, Esq. 1770, September 8th. Calcutta.
3. Thomas Palk to Robert Palk, Esqr. 1770, October 9th. Fort St. George. 4. Warren Hastings to Robert Palk, Esqr. 1770, October 12th. Fort St.

XXXI Sir John Lindsay accuses company servants of illegal trading, 1770

1. Warren Hastings to Robert Palk, Esqr. 1770, October 12th. Fort St. George.

XXXII Ensign John Palk and others are grateful, 1771

1. Ensign John Palk to Robert Palk, Esqr. 1771, February 2nd. Camp near Samulcotah.
2. Chocapah to the Honourable Robert Palk, Esqr. 1771, February 5th. Fort St. George.
3. Robert Palk to William Martin Goodlad. 1771, April 2nd. London.
4. Colonel Gilbert Ironside to Robert Palk, Esqr. 1771, April 7th. Fort William.
5. Robert Palk to his Excellency the Nawab Walajah. 1771, April 17th.
6. Captain Thomas Madge to Robert Palk, Esqr. 1771, June 15th. Ellore. 7. Henry Vansittart, jun., to Robert Palk, Esq. 1771, October 3rd, Cape of Good Hope.

XXXIII Goodlad and the Tan j ore affair, 1771

1. William Martin Goodlad to Robert Palk, Esqr. 1771, October 4th, Fort St. George.
2. Captain James Rennell to Robert Palk, Esqr. 1771, November 12th, Bengali.
3. Robert Palk to William Martin Goodlad. 1772, February 2nd, Park Place.

XXXIV Trade all over India is bad, 1772

Gilbert Ironside, descended from two Bishops of Bristol of that name, was a son of Edward Ironside, banker, of London, who died when Lord Mayor in 1753. Born in 1737, Gilbert was educated at Winchester, and went to India in 1756 as Ensign of an independent company. Returning to England by way of China, he re-embarked in 1759 as Ensign in the Bengal Army. He accompanied Hastings to Patna in 1762, was employed on the Staff by both Clive and Vansittart, became Lieut. Colonel in 1768, and served as Hastings's Military Secretary in 1772. As Colonel he commanded a brigade in 1774, retired in 1786, and died in England in 1801. Ironside married in 1763 Letitia, daughter of the Rev. Robert Roberts. He left unpublished works on logic, tactics and Persian grammar and the inexperience of the men of the Navy in these seas.

1. Chocapah to the Honble. Robert Palk, Esqr. 1772, February 28th, Fort St. George
2. Thomas Palk to Robert Palk, Esqr. 1772, February 28th, Fort St. George.
3. William Martin Goodlad to Robert Palk, Esqr. 1772, February 28th,- Fort St. George. Received 20th September.
4. Henry Vansittart, jun., to Robert Palk, Esqr., at Edmund Boehm's, Esqr., Sice Lane, London. 1772, April 2nd, Fort St. George.
5. Robert Palk to William Martin Goodlad 1772, April 7th, Park Place
6. William Martin Goodlad to Robert Palk, Esqr. 1772, April 13th, Madras.
7. Colonel Gilbert Ironside to Robert Palk, Esqr. 1772, April 13th, Fort William.

XXXV Warren Hastings asks for Palk's help, 1772

1. Warren Hastings to Laurence Sulivan, Esqr. 1772, September 7th, Cossimbuzar.
2. William Martin Goodlad to Robert Palk, Esqr. 1772, October 3rd, Fort St. George.
3. Edward Cotsford to Robert Palk, Esqr. 1772, October 15th, Madrass.

XXXVI Nick Morse dies - the end of an era, 1772

Nicholas Morse (died 28 May 1772) the great-grandson of the British statesman and revolutionary Oliver Cromwell and served as the last Presi- dent of Madras before the Battle of Madras and the French occupation of Fort St George and its surroundings in 1746. Morse's Presidency was short and was characterised by hostilities be- tween the British and the French. This hostilities culminated in 1746 by the occupation of Madras by the French under Bertrand François Mahé de La Bourdonnais ending Morse's short tenure. Morse's daughter Emilia was married to Henry Vansittart, Governor of Bengal from 1759 to 1764. Nicholas Morse is buried in St Mary's Church in Madras. A website on slave trade has named Nicholas Morse along with another Governor of Fort St George William Gyfford as a prominent slave-trader.

1. Thomas Palk to Robert Palk, Esqr. 1772, November 10th, Calcutta
2. Warren Hastings to Robert Palk, Esqr. 1772, November 11th, Fort William. Received 19th April, per Lapwing.
3. Thomas Palk to Robert Palk, Esqr. 1773, January 11th, Calcutta
4. James Daniell to Robert Palk, Esqr. 1773, January 28th, Cuddalore. 5. Chocapah to the Honble. Robert Palk, Esqr. 1773, .January 28th, Fort St. George.

XXXVII Goodlad is no more. 1773

1. William Petrie to Robert Palk, Esqr. 1773, January 31st, 3 a.m.. Fort St. George. Received 5th November.
2. Nawab Walajah to General Stringer Lawrence. 1773, February 1st, Chep-auk, [Madras].
3. The Nabob Waulaujah Bahauder, &c., presents his salams to his friend General Lawrence, and sends him the inclosed with his wishes for long life and happiness.
4. Thomas Palk to Robert Palk, Esqr. 1773, February 30th [sic], Calcutta.
5. Thomas Palk, to Robert Palk, Esqr. 1773, March 22nd, Calcutta.
6. Warren Hastings to Robert Palk, Esqr. 1773, April 3rd, Fort William.
7. James Daniell to Robert Palk, Esqr. 1773, October 13th, Fort St. George
8. Anthony Goodlad to Robert Palk, Esqr. 1773, October 20th, Purnea in Bengal.
9. Reynold Adams to Robert Palk, Esqr. 1773, October 25th, Fort St. George.

XXXVIII Cotsford and the Dutch threat, 1773

1. Edward Cotsford to Robert Palk, Esqr. 1773, October 29th, Madrass.

2. Robert Palk, jun., to Robert Palk, Esqr. 1773, November 3rd, Calcutta. 3. Henry Griffiths to Robert Palk, Esqr. 1773, November 10th, Calcutta.

4. Robert Palk to Thomas Palk N.D. [cir. 1773.]

5. Colonel Gilbert Ironside to Robert Palk, Esq. 1774, January 15th, The Grove, near Fort William.

XIL Lord Pigot is expected, 1774

Alexander Dalrymple, a Madras civil servant of 1753, was in 1755 appointed Assistant to the Assaymaster at Fort St. George " to be instructed in the art of assaying." During the siege of Madras he was Sub-Secretary. In 1769 he was sent on a commercial mission to the Eastern Islands, where he spent two and a half years, and concluded a treaty with the Sultan of Sulu. In 1762 he was given the command of the ship *London*, in which he passed a further period of two years among the islands, establishing a settlement at Balambangan, off the coast of Borneo, and constructing a series of charts. In 1765 he returned to England and published works on geography and hydrography. In 1775 Dalrymple sailed for Madras with Lord Pigot, as a member of Council. He sided with the Governor during the revolution, and was suspended by the Majority. Recalled to England in 1777, he was appointed Hydrographer to the Company in 1779 and to the Admiralty in 1795.

1. Robert Palk, jun., to Robert Palk, Esqr. 1774, January 16th, Patna.

2. Reynold Adams to Robert Palk, Esqr., Park Place, St. James's. 1774, February 2nd, Fort St. George.

3. John d'Fries to Robert Palk, Esqr. 1774, February 6th, Fort St. George. (Duplicate).

4. Mudoo Kistna to Robert Palk, Esqr. 1774, February 12th, Fort St. George.

5. Robert Palk, jun., to Robert Palk, Esqr., London. 1774, February 23rd, Patna.

6. Robert Palk, jun., to Robert Palk, Esqr. 1774, March 11th, Patna.11, Paper Buildings, Temple.

7. Stephen Sulivan to Robert Palk, Esqr., Park Place. N.D. [1774, April.]

8. Stephen Sulivan to Robert Palk, Esqr., Park Place. [1774, April.]

Wednesday evening. Paper Buildings, Temple.

9. Robert Palk to Laurence Sulivan, Esqr., M.P., Queen Square, Ormond Street. 1774, September 21st, Haldon House.

10. Nawab Walajah to Robert Palk, Esqr. 1774, September 24th, Chepauck House, near Madras.

XL Palk briefs the Nabob

1. Robert Palk to H.H. the Nawab of the Carnatic. N.D. [1774, cir. March.]
2. Stephen Sulivan to Robert Palk, Esqr., Park Place, St. James's. 1774, April 3rd, 11, Paper Buildings, Temple.
3. Stephen Sulivan to Robert Palk, Esqr., Park Place. N.D. [1774, April.]
4. Stephen Sulivan to Robert Palk, Esqr., Park Place. [1774, April.] Wednesday evening. Paper Buildings, Temple.
5. Robert Palk to Laurence Sulivan, Esqr., M.P., Queen Square, Ormond Street. 1774, September 21st, Haldon House.
6. Nawab Walajah to Robert Palk, Esqr. 1774, September 24th, Chepauck House, near Madras

XLI Robert Palk MP, 1774 - 1775

1. Laurence Sulivan to Robert Palk, Esqr., Haldon House. 1774, September 30th, Queen Square.
2. James Hodges to Robert Palk, Esqr., St. James's Place, London. 1775, July 4th, Fort St. George
3. John d'Fries to Robert Palk, Esqr. 1775, July 4th, Madras.
4. Colonel Robert Gordon to Robert Palk, Esqr. 1775, September 10th, Bombay.
5. Chocapah to the Honble Robert Palk, Esqr. 1775, October 10th, Fort St. George.
6. George Baker to Robert Palk, Esqr. 1775, October 13th, Fort St. George.
7. George Baker to Robert Palk, Esqr, 1775, December 14th, Fort St. George.
8. Chocapah to the Honble. Robert Palk, Esqr. 1776, February 2nd, Fort St. George.
9. Thomas Palk to Robert Palk, Esqr. 1776, February 8th, Mazulipatam.
10. Mrs. Mary Turing to Robert Palk, Esqr, 1776, February 10th, Fort St.

George. Received 17th Feb., 1777.

XLII The Lord Pigot administration, 1776

1. John D'Fries to Robert Palk, Esqr. 1776, February 12th, Madras.
2. George Baker to Robert Palk, Esqr. 1776, February 23rd, Fort St. George
3. Robert Palk, jun., to Robert Palk, Esqr. 1776, March 21st, Calcutta. Received 28th October.
4. Sir Edward Hughes to Robert Palk, Esqr. 1776, March 22nd, Bombay.
5. H.H. the Nawab Walajah to Robert Palk, Esqr. 1776, June 20th, Chepauk
6. His Highness the Nabob Wallaujau, Ummeer ul Hindh, Omdaht ul Mulk, Ausuph ud Doulah, Anweer ud Deen Cawn Bahauder, Zuphur Jung, Sepah Salaur, Subahdar of the Carnatick, to Robert Palk, Esqr.

XLIII Chocopah Chetti tells of unfairness to the Rajah, 1776

1. Chocapah to the Honble. Robert Palk, Esqr. 1776, June 27th, Fort St. George.
2. George Baker to Robert Palk, Esqr. 1776, August 30th, Fort St. George.
3. Richard Welland to Robert Palk, Esqr., Bruton Street, London. 1776, September 6th, Ship Salisbury, Madrass Roads.

XLIV The curious end of Lord Pigot, 1776

1. Chocapah to the Honble. Robert Palk, Esqr. 1776, September 15th, Fort St. George. Received 21st April, 1777.
2. Henry Vansittart, jun., to Robert Palk, Esqr.1776, September 18th, Calcutta.
3. George Smith to Robert Palk, Esqr. 1776, September 20th, Fort St. George
4. John d'Fries to Robert Palk, Esqr. 1776, September 21st, Madras.
5. H.H. the Nawab Walajah to Robert Palk, Esqr. 1776, September 25th. Chepauk.

XLV Lord Pigot is deposed, 1776

Robert Fletcher was engaged locally as a monthly Writer in Madras in May,

1757, but was shortly afterwards commissioned as Ensign. In 1760 he was dismissed for insubordination, but was reinstated at the instance of Eyre Coote. Captain Fletcher served as Brigade Major in the Manila expedition of 1762, and in the following year was transferred to Bengal as Major. In 1766 Lieut.-Colonel Sir Robert Fletcher, who was then commanding one of the three brigades of the Army; supported the junior officers who combined to protest against the withdrawal of Mir Jafar's special grant of batta. He was tried by court-martial and cashiered. Returning to England, he obtained reinstatement on the recommendation of Lawrence and Caillaud, and he was posted to Madras as Colonel. Succeeding General Joseph Smith in the command of Army in 1772, he proved so obstructive in Council that he was ordered to Trichinopoly by Du Pre's Government. He claimed to resume his seat in Parliament and returned to England. In 1775 Sir Robert Fletcher again arrived in Madras as Brigadier General, took command of the Army, and supported the Majority of Council against Lord Pigot, in whose deposition he assisted. In 1776 he sailed for the Cape on sick leave, and died on the way at Mauritius.

1. Charles Floyer to Robert Palk, Esqr. 1776, September 25th, Fort St. George

2. H.H. the Nawab Walajah to Robert Palk, Esqr. 1776, October 8th, Chepauck.

3. John deFries to Robert Palk, Esqr. 1776, October 10th, Madras.

4. George Baker to Robert Palk, Esq 1776, October 14th, Fort St. George 5. Edmund Veale Lane to Robert Palk, Esq. 1776, December 17th, Salsette.

Received 28th July, 1777.

6. Thomas Palk to Robert Palk, Esq. 1777, February 6th, Madras.

7. George Baker to Robert Palk, Esq. 1778, January 29th, Fort St. George. Received 11th August.

8. George Baker to Robert Palk, Esq. 1778, March 5th, Fort St. George. Received 5th November.

9. Henry Vansittart, jun., to Robert Palk, Esq. 1778, April 24th, Calcutta.

10. Thomas Palk to Robert Palk, Esq.. 1778, October 15th, Fort St. George. Received 11th September, 1779.

11. Mudoo Kistna to Robert Palk, Esq. 1778, October 15th, Fort St. George.

XLVI Cotsford escapes the French, 1778

Captain Edward Cotsford entered the military service in Dec, 1758, as Practitioner Engineer and Ensign, but his name was also borne on the civil list from 1759. He served in the Manila expedition of 1762 and in the two sieges of Madura. After a visit to England he was appointed by Palk in 1766 to be Resident in Ganjam, a post he occupied for several years. He was independent of the Chief at Vizagapatam and was responsible directly to Madras. In 1776 he prepared for Orme a monograph on the development of the Fort St. George defences from 1743 to the time of the siege of 1758-59.

1. Edward Cotsford to Robert Palk, Esq. 1778, October 17th, Madrass. Received 17th March, 1779.

2. Chocapah to the Honble. Robert Palk, Esq. 1778, October 19th, Fort St. George.

3. Chocapah to the Honble. Robert Palk, Esq. 1778, October 31st, Fort St. George. Received 27th March, 1779.

4. Thomas Palk to Robert Palk, Esq. 1779, October 15th, Fort St. George.

5. John d'Fries to Robert Palk, Esq. 1780, January 16th, Madras.

6. Thomas Palk to Robert Palk, Esq. 1780, January 30th, Fort St. George.

7. Stephen Sulivan to[Robert Palk, Esq.. 1780, February 5th, Fort St. George.

XLVII The death of Robert Palk jnr, 1783

1. Henry Preston to Sir Robert Palk, Bart. Bruton Street, London. 1783, August 8th, Fort St. George.

2. Dr. Adam Burt to Messrs. James & David Webster, Leadenhall Street. 1783, September 10th, Limerick, Ireland,

3. Dr. Adam Burt to Major J. McGowan. Adam Burt,1783, circa September 10th.

4. David Asquith to Sir Robert Palk, Bruton Street, London. 1783, September 12th, Surprise packet, Limerick. Received 14th October.

5. Dr. Adam Burt to Sir Robert Palk. 1783, September 16th, Limerick. Received 3rd October

6. Dr. Adam Burt to Sir Robert Palk, 1783, October 3rd, Limerick.

7. Dr. Adam Burt to Sir Robert Palk, Bart. 1783; October 6th, Limerick.

8. Major J. McGowan to [Sir Robert Palk]. 1783, October 10th, London.
9. Dr. Adam Burt to Sir Robert Palk, Bart. 1783, October 14th, Limerick.
10. Robert Hall to Sir Robert Palk 1783, October 14th, Limerick.
11. James Lyons to Sir Robert Palk1783, October 15th, Limerick.
12. Certificate by Dr. Adam Burt. 1783, October 16th, Limerick.
13. Certificate by Dr. Adam Burt. 1783, October 17th, Limerick.
14. Dr. Adam Burt to Sir Robert Palk, Bart.1783, October 31st, London.
15. Henry McMahon to Sir Robert Palk, Bart., Bruton Street, London. 1783, November 2nd, Limerick.
16. Robert Hall to Sir Robert Palk, Bart., Bruton Street, London. 1783, November 3rd, Limerick.
17. Henry McMahon to Sir Robert Palk, Bart., Bruton Street, London. 1783, November 4th, Limerick.
18. Sober Hall to Sir Robert Palk, Bart., Bruton Street, London. 1783, November 8th, Limerick.
19. William Young to Sir Robert Palk, Bart., M.P., Bruton Street, London. 1783.
20. November 9th, Limerick
21. William Douglas to Sir Robert Palk, Bart., Bruton Street, London. 1783, November 11th, Limerick.
22. Dr. Adam Burt to Sir Robert Palk Bart. 1783, November 30th, London.
23. William Young to Sir Robert Palk. 1783, December 16th. Limerick.
24. Sober Hall to Sir Robert Palk. 1784, January 14th, Limerick
25. George Maunsell to[Sir Robert Palk. 1784, January 15th, Limerick. 26. David Asquith to Sir Robert Palk, Bruton Street, London. 1784, January 21st, Ship Surprise, Downs.
27. Thomas Palk to Sir Robert Palk 1784, February 2nd, Fort St. George.
28. Thomas Maunsell to Sir Robert Palk. 1784, February 5th, Dublin.
29. Luke Flood to Thomas Maunsell, dated Corvill, Roundwood, 17th January, 1784
30. Thomas Maunsell to Sir Robert Palk. 1784, February 14th, Dublin.

XLIX The Nabob complains. 1784

1. H.H. the Nawab Walajah to Sir Robert Palk, Bart. 1784, September 15th, Chepauck

2. Mrs. Catharine Palk to Sir Robert Palk. 1784, October 8th, Trichinapoly. Received 23rd October, 1785

3. Thomas Palk to Sir Robert Palk. 1784, October 10th, Trichinapoly. Received 23rd October, 1785.

4. George Baker to Sir Robert Palk, Bart. 1784, October 10th, Fort St. George.

IL Warren Hastings, 1785

George Baker, of Tor Mohun (now called Torre, near Torquay) a seafaring man, made his first voyage to India in 1743. In 1747 he was with Boscawen at Pondichery, and ten years later, as master of the Cuddalore, did good service during the siege of Fort St. George. In 1762, when commanding the London, he was appointed first Master Attendant of the port of Madras. On resigning this post he went to England, and in 1771, when residing at Kenton near Haldon, made a contract with the Directors to deliver water to the Madras Fort and shipping from a source north of Black Town, himself re- ceiving fees for 21 years. He returned toIndia in 1772 and duly executed the work. Baker died at Madras on the 4th July, 1799. A monument to his memory was erected in Torre Church by his nephew William Baker.

Ozias Humphry, portrait painter and associate of Romney and Blake, painted portraits in India from 1785 to 1788. He was elected R.A. in 1791, and died in 1810.

1. George Baker to Sir Robert Palk, Bart. 1785, January 25th, Fort St. George.

2. Chocapah to the Honble. Sir Robert Palk, Baronet. 1785, February 2nd, Madrass.

3. William Wynch to Sir Robert Palk 1785, February 3rd, Madras.

4. Abraham Welland to Sir Robert Palk, Bart. 1785, March 21st, Calcutta.

5. Ozias Humphry to Sir Robert Palk, Bart., M.P., Bruton Street. 1785, May 15th, Cape of Good Hope.

6. Ensign William Preston to Sir Robert Palk1785, May 16th, Madras.

7. Thomas Palk to Sir Robert Palk. 1785, May 20th, Trichinapoly.

8. Messrs. Felling & de Fries to Sir Robert Palk, Bart. 1785, June 12th, Fort St. George. Received 30th March, 1786.

9. Thomas Palk to Sir Robert Palk 1785, July 12th, Trichinapoly. Received

10th April, 1786.
10. Chocapah to the Honble. Sir Robert Palk, Baronet. 1785, September 17th, Madrass.

L Educating the next generation, 1785

Samuel Badcock was a Nonconformist minister of South Molton, Devon, who contributed to literary magazines, especially the Monthly Review. He entered the Established Church in 1786, and died two years latey at tbe age of 41

1. Futwood Smerdon to Walter Palk, jun., Ashburton. 1785, November 8th, Ottery. Walter Palk, Junr

2. Lawrence Palk to Sir Robert Palk, Bart., Haldon House, Exeter. 1785, December 3rd, Neuchatel.

3. Abraham Well and to Sir Robert Palk. 1785, December 13th, Guttaul.

4. F. D'Ivernois to Sir Robert Palk, Bart., Haldon House, Exeter. 1785, December 24th, Neuchatel.

5. Abraham Welland to[Sir Robert Palk. 1785, December 25th, Calcutta.

6. F. D'lvernois to Sir Robert Palk, Bruton Street. 1786, January 17th, Neufchatel. Received 28th January.

7. Thomas Abraham to Sir Robert Palk, Bart. 1786, January 23rd, Calcutta.

8. Lawrence Palk to Sir Robert Palk. 1786, February 4th, Besancon.

9. F. D'Ivernois to Sir Robert Palk, Bart., Bruton Street. 1786, February 6th, Neuchatel.

10. The Rev. Samuel Badcock to Sir Robert Palk, Bart. 1786, February 11th, South Molton.

11. Lawrence Palk to Sir Robert Palk. 1786, February 13th, Neuchatel.

12. Thomas Palk to Sir Robert Palk. 1786, February 15th, Trichinapoly. 13. Messrs. Ayton, Brassey & Co., to Sir Robert Palk, Bart., Bruton Street.
1786, February 17th, Lombard Street.

14. Messrs. Henry Vansittart & R[ichard] Kennaway to Sir Robert Palk1786, February 22nd, Calcutta.

15. Henry Vansittart, R. Kennaway." Thomas Abraham to Sir Robert Palk. 1786, February 25th, Calcutta.

16. Lawrence Palk to Sir Robert Palk, Bart., Bruton Street. 1786, March 5th, Neuchatel.

17. F. d'Ivernois to Sir Robert Palk, Bart., Bruton Street. 1786, March 9th, Neuchatel.
18. George Baker to Sir Robert Palk, Bart. 1786, March 12th, Fort St. George. Received 26th August.
19. Thomas Palk to Sir Robert Palk. 1786, March 15th, Trichinapoly. Received 26th August.
20. Messrs. Pelling & de Fries to Sir Robert Palk, Bart. 1786, March 18th, Fort St. George. Received 26th August.
21. Thomas Abraham to Sir Robert Palk, Bart. 1786, March 24th, Calcutta. Received 8th October.
22. Lawrence Palk to Sir Robert Palk, Bart., Bruton Street. 1786, April 10th, Constance.
23. F. d'Ivernois to Sir Robert Palk. 1786, April 22nd, Vienna.
24. Lawrence Palk to Sir Robert Palk, Bart., M.P., Bruton Street. 1786, May 21st, Vienna. Received 2nd June.
25. Lawrence Palk to Sir Robert Palk, Bart., M.P., Bruton Street. 1786, June 3rd, Vienna.
26. F. d'Ivernois to Sir Robert Palk, Bart., M.P., Bruton Street. 1786, June 10th, Feslau, near Vienna
27. Lawrence Palk to Sir Robert Palk. 1786, June 26th, Dresden. Received 19th July
28. Thomas Palk to Sir Robert Palk. 1786, July 2nd, Trichinopoly.
29. The Rev. J. Bradford to Sir Robert Palk. 1786, July 4th, Ideford
30. Lawrence Palk to Sir Robert Palk, Bart., M.P., Bruton Street. 1786, July 6th, Berlin.
31. Lawrence Palk to Sir Robert Palk, Bart., M.P., Bruton Street. 1786, July 10th, Berlin.
32. Lawrence Palk to Sir Robert Palk, Bart., M.P., Bruton Street. 1786, July 21st, Berhn. Received 2nd August.
33. F. d'Ivernois to Sir Robert Palk. 1786, July 30th, Brunswick. Received 17th August. F. d'Ivernois
34. The Rev. Samuel Badcock to Sir Robert Palk 1786, August 1st, West Sandford.
35. F. D'lvernois to Sir Robert Palk. 1786, August 9th, Pyrmont, near Hanover. Received 23rd August.
36. Henry Vansittart & Richard Kennaway to Sir Robert Palk. 1786, August

13th, Calcutta.
37. Simeon Droz to General John Caillaud. 1786, August 19th, Arlington Street.
38, Lawrence Palk to Sir Robert Palk, Bart., M.P., Bruton Street. 1786, August 21st, Wesel. Received 5th September.
39. Henry Vansittart jnr., to Sir Robert Palk. 1786, August 26th, Calcutta. Received March, 1787.
40. Messrs. Pelling & de Fries to Sir Robert Palk, Bart. 1786, August 29th, Fort St. George.
41. Thomas Palk to Sir Robert Palk. 1786, September 7th, Triehinopol]y. 42. Lawrence Palk to Sir Robert Palk. 1786, September 8th, La Haye.
43. Thomas Abraham to Sir Robert Palk. 1786, September 18th, Calcutta. 44. Chocapah to the Honble. Sir Robert Palk, Baronet. 1786, September 30th, Madrass.
45. Messrs. Pelling & de Fries to Sir Robert Palk, Bart. 1786, October 14th, Fort St. George.
46. The Rev. Samuel Badcock to Sir Robert Palk, Bart., Bruton Street. 1786, October 19th, South Molton.
47. Thomas Abraham to Sir Robert Palk 1786, November 12th, Calcutta.
48. Thomas Palk to Sir Robert Palk. [17]86, November 14th, Trichinapoly.
49. Adrian de Fries to Sir Robert Palk, Bart. 1786, November 20th, Fort St. George.
50. The Rev. Samuel Badcock to Sir Robert Palk, Bart. 1787, March 1st, South Molton.

LI Postscript, 1786

Sources for Laurence Sulivan are the DNB and the British Museum Warren Hastings archive. Letter to Robert Palk from Sulivan and his son Stephen are included above.

Hannah More: The First Victorian by Anne Stott contains descriptions of Halden House visits.

Hannah More: The First Victorian by Anne Stott

Select Bibliography

Love, Colonel H. D. (1922) Report on the Palk Manuscripts, in the possession of Mrs. Bannatyne of Haldon, Devon. Historical Manuscripts Commission. London.

Worthy, Charles – Devon Parishes, 1889 Memoirs of Captain Dalton, John Dalton

Cambridge's Hist, of the War in India (2nd edit. 1761) ; Orme's Military Trans, in Indoostan (London, 1803)

Colonel Mark Wilks; Hist. Sketches S. India (London, 1869); Mills Hist, of India, vol. iii. ;

Wilson's Hist. Madras Army (Madras, 1881-3), vol. i. ; Hist, of the Madras Fusiliers (London,

1843; Philippart's East India Mil. Calendar (London, 1823), vol. ii. : Malcolm and Wilson's Biographies of Clive

Macaulay's Essay on Clive;

Malleson's Dupleix, a biography (London, 1890).

The Brit. Mus. Addit. MSS. contain a few letters of Lawrence between 1754 and 1759

Fraser, Iain – Hennock: A Village History, 2004.

Fraser, Iain – Haldon House & Torquay, 2008

Polwhele, Richard – History of Devonshire, 1793.

Love, Colonel H. D. (1922) Report on the Palk Manuscripts, in the possession of Mrs. Bannatyne of Haldon, Devon. Historical Manuscripts Commission. London.

Worthy, Charles – Devon Parishes, 1889 Haldon Belvedere DHBT archive

Donkin, Robin A. (August 2003). Between East and West: The Moluccas and the Traffic in Spices Up to the Arrival of Europeans. Diane Publishing Company. ISBN 0-87169-248-1.

Time. 20 August 2001

Olson, James (1996). Historical Dictionary of the British Empire. Greenwood Publishing Group. ISBN 0-313-29366-X.

Gardner, Brian (1972). The East India Company: a History. McCall Publishing Company. ISBN 0-8415-0124-6.

Tyacke, Sarah (2008). "Gabriel Tatton's Maritime Atlas of the East Indies, 1620–1621:

Portsmouth Royal Naval Museum, Admiralty Library Manuscript, MSS 352". Imago Mundi 60 (1): 39–62.

Bernstein, William J.,A Splendid Exchange: How Trade Shaped the World, Atlantic Monthly Press, 2008, p. 238.

Fox, E. T. (2008). King of the Pirates: The Swashbuckling Life of Henry Every. London: Tempus Publishing. ISBN 978-0-7524-4718-6.

The British East India Company—the Company that Owned a Nation. George P. Landow

Oxford Dictionary of National Biography, Oxford University Press, online edn.

Holmes, Richard (2005). Sahib: the British soldier in India, 1750–1914. London: HarperCollins. ISBN 0-00-713753-2.

East India Company Factory Records

Anthony, Frank. Britain's Betrayal in India: The Story of the Anglo Indian Community. Second Edition. London: The Simon Wallenberg Press, 2007

"The Company that ruled the waves", in The Economist, December 17–30, 2011

The Striped Flag Of The East India Company, And Its Connexion With The American "Stars And Stripes"

Sutton, Jean (1981) Lords of the East: The East India Company and Its Ships. London: Conway Maritime

Farrington (ed.), Anthony (1976). The Records of the East India College, Haileybury, & other institutions. London: H.M.S.O.

Bowen, H. V. (1991). Revenue and Reform: The Indian Problem in British Politics, 1757–1773. Cambridge, U.K.: Cambridge University Press. ISBN 0-

Bowen, H. V.; Margarette Lincoln, and Nigel Rigby, eds. (2003). The Worlds of the East India Company. Rochester, NY: Brewer. ISBN 0-85115-877-3.

Brenner, Robert (1993). Merchants and Revolution: Commercial Change, Political Conflict, and London's Overseas Traders, 1550–1653. Princeton, NJ: Princeton University Press. ISBN 0-691-05594-7.

Carruthers, Bruce G. (1996). City of Capital: Politics and Markets in the English Financial Revolution. Princeton, NJ: Princeton University Press. ISBN 978-0-691-04455-2.

Chaudhuri, K. N. (1965). The English East India Company: The Study of an Early Joint-Stock Company, 1600–1640. London: Cass.

Chaudhuri, K. N. (1978). The Trading World of Asia and the English East India Company, 1660–1760. Cambridge, U.K.: Cambridge University Press. ISBN 0-521-21716-4.

Chaudhury, S. (1999). Merchants, Companies, and Trade: Europe and Asia in the Early Modern Era. London: Cambridge University Press.

Farrington, Anthony (2002). Trading Places: The East India Company and Asia, 1600–1834. London: British Library. ISBN 0-7123-4756-9.

Furber, Holden (1976). Rival Empires of Trade in the Orient, 1600–1800. Minneapolis: University of Minnesota Press. ISBN 0-8166-0787-7.

Harrington, Jack (2010), Sir John Malcolm and the Creation of British India, New York: Palgrave Macmillan., ISBN 978-0-230-10885-1

Keay, John (2010). The Honourable Company: A History of the English East India Company. HarperCollins UK. ISBN 978-0-00-739554-5.

Lawson, Philip (1993). The East India Company: A History. London: Longman. ISBN 0-582-07386-3.

O'Connor, Daniel (2012). The Chaplains of the East India Company, 1601–1858. London: ISBN 978-1-4411-7534-2.

Imperial Gazetteer of India, 2, Oxford: Clarendon Press, under the authority of H.M. Secretary of State for India

Risley (ed.), Sir Herbert H. et al. (1908), The Indian Empire: Administrative, Imperial Gazetteer of India, 4, Oxford: Clarendon Press, under the authority of H.M Secretary of State for India

Sen, Sudipta (1998). Empire of Free Trade: The East India Company and the Making of the Colonial Marketplace. Philadelphia: University of Pennsylvania Press. ISBN 978-0-8122-3426-8.

Sutherland, Lucy S. (1952). The East India Company in Eighteenth-Century Politics. Oxford: Clarendon Press.

Ames, Glenn J. (1996). Colbert, Mercantilism, and the French Quest for Asian Trade. DeKalb, IL: Northern Illinois University Press. ISBN 0-87580-207-9.

Boucher, P. (1985). The Shaping of the French Colonial Empire: A Bio-

Bibliography of the Careers of Richelieu, Fouquet and Colbert. New York: Garland.

Doyle, William (1990). The Oxford History of the French Revolution (2 ed.). Oxford; New York: Oxford University Press. ISBN 978-0-19-925298-5.

Malleson, G. B. (1893). History of the French in India. London: W.H. Allen & Co.

Subramanian, Lakshmi, ed. (1999). French East India Company and the Trade of the Indian Ocean: A Collection of Essays by Indrani Chatterjee. Delhi: Munshiram Publishers.

McAbe, Ina Baghdiantz (2008). Orientalism in early Modern France. Berg. ISBN 978-1-84520-374-0.

The Curate and the General

Index